PROPHETS AND PROPHECIES

ALSO BY ALBERTUS PRETORIUS:

THE END OF CHRISTIANITY
JESUS OF NAZARETH, A DELUDED MESSIAH
WHO, WHERE, AND WHAT IS GOD?
THE GOSPELS EXPLAINED
TO HELL WITH THE DEVIL
HEAVEN AND HELL

Mosaic of Moses at the Burning Bush, from St. Catherine's Monastery, Sinai
(eighth century AD)

ALBERTUS PRETORIUS

PROPHETS AND PROPHECIES

A HISTORICAL AND NEUROPSYCHOLOGICAL ANALYSIS OF ANCIENT SCRIPTURAL PROPHECIES

WIPF & STOCK · Eugene, Oregon

PROPHETS AND PROPHECIES
A Historical and Neuropsychological Analysis of Ancient Scriptural Prophecies

Copyright © 2025 Albertus Pretorius. All rights reserved. Except for brief quotations in critical publications or reviews, no part of this book may be reproduced in any manner without prior written permission from the publisher. Write: Permissions, Wipf and Stock Publishers, 199 W. 8th Ave., Suite 3, Eugene, OR 97401.

Wipf & Stock
An Imprint of Wipf and Stock Publishers
199 W. 8th Ave., Suite 3
Eugene, OR 97401

www.wipfandstock.com

PAPERBACK ISBN: 979-8-3852-7038-5
HARDCOVER ISBN: 979-8-3852-7039-2
EBOOK ISBN: 979-8-3852-7040-8

CONTENTS

PREFACE		xii
1.	INTRODUCTION	1
2.	SCRIPTURAL PROPHETS AND THEIR CALLING	31
3.	OLD TESTAMENT PROPHECIES REGARDING CURRENT AFFAIRS	88
4.	NEW TESTAMENT PROPHECIES REGARDING CURRENT AFFAIRS	197
5.	OLD TESTAMENT PROPHECIES REGARDING THE MESSIAH	285
6.	PROPHECIES REGARDING THE MESSIAH IN THE NEW TESTAMENT	343
7.	OLD TESTAMENT PROPHECIES REGARDING JUDGMENT DAY AND THE AFTERLIFE	399
8.	NEW TESTAMENT PROPHECIES REGARDING JUDGMENT DAY AND THE AFTERLIFE	446
9.	MUHAMMAD AND THE HOLY QUR'AN	498
10.	FINAL THOUGHTS	533
BIBLIOGRAPHY		575
LIST OF ILLUSTRATIONS		596
INDEX OF SCRIPTURAL TEXTS		604

ABBREVIATIONS USED:

APA	American Psychiatric Association
Enc Brit	Encyclopaedia Brittanica
Hist Eccl	Historia Ecclesiastica
Jewish Enc	Jewish Encyclopedia

PREFACE

Both my parents were devoted Christians and loyal members of their church, the Dutch Reformed Church in South Africa. My father served many years as an elder and my mother was an enthusiastic Sunday School teacher. Every evening, after our family's supper, my father read to us a passage from the Bible and did a prayer. As a young child, I heard many Bible stories from my mother. I was taught to read a part of the Bible and do a prayer on my knees every night before I went to bed.

When I went to university, I studied ancient languages, philosophy, psychology, history, and theology. After my admittance to the ministry, I continued my studies and eventually acquired two doctorates, as well as some other qualifications. These studies helped me to prepare sound and persuasive sermons to the congregations I served.

All this meant that I have had a life-long relationship with the Christian Bible. After my retirement from the ministry, I continued to study the Bible and that led to the production of a few books dealing with theological and biblical subjects.

My naïve, unsophisticated, and conventional religious beliefs changed over the years, though. As a youngster, as a student, and as a young minister of religion, I accepted the going belief that every word in the Bible is divinely-inspired and, therefore, absolutely true. However, this belief changed as the years went by. It slowly, but surely, dawned upon me that the Bible contains many mistakes, contradictory notions, as well as erroneous, absurd, irrational, improbable, incredible, and outdated beliefs. But, despite this, the Bible does contain much of value.

Although many Christians have also noticed these flaws in the Bible with its primitive world-view, they are still convinced that they hear the voice of God when reading the Bible. To them, it is still the Word of God, despite all the defects. Contemporary educated Christians have rejected the ancient biblical cosmology and supplanted that with a more scientific view of the cosmos.

This all meant that I had to learn how to study the Bible without any dogmatic prejudices and with an open mind – just as any other piece of literature from antiquity ought to be studied, analyzed, and interpreted.

The present book is the result of a life-long encounter with the Bible. It deals mainly with the many types of prophecy we find in the Scriptures. To be able to interpret a certain prophetic utterance, one must know the background of that particular prophet. For that reason, the prophecies in the Scriptures will be dealt with in this book in a chronological sequence – from the earliest to the latest – while attention will have to be given to the circumstances during which those prophecies were spoken or written and recorded.

Readers of this book must beware: the views expressed here contradict many conventional Christian beliefs and dogmas. I am, though, convinced that I have presented a water-tight case with alternative and credible interpretations of various scriptural passages, based on rational and scientific methods for analyzing ancient documents, as taught to me during my studies in Europe.

During my years in the ministry, I also took note of the contents of the holy book of Islam, the Qur'an. This holy book can only be understood with a knowledge of the Christian Bible, since it often refers to events and characters appearing in the Bible. The present book will also deal with the prophecies found in the Qur'an.

Albertus Pretorius, Cape Town, South Africa, November 2025

CHAPTER 1
INTRODUCTION

THEME OF THIS BOOK

The foundational texts of the three monotheistic religions, Judaism, Christianity, and Islam, namely the Hebrew Scriptures, the New Testament, and the Qur'an, contain many types of literature. There are historical narratives, poetry, practical wisdom, legislation, ethical and moral guidelines, stories and parables, letters, dialogues and debates, philosophical discourses, sermons, and lectures – and also prophetic pronouncements. This book is mainly concerned with the last-mentioned type of literature, namely prophecies, as well as the descriptions of the actions of some prophets.

This book is, therefore, an endeavor to find answers to the following questions:

- What is the nature or essence of the phenomenon of prophecy?
- Who were the prophets who pronounced these prophecies?
- When and where did these prophets live and work?
- What prompted them to become prophets?
- What is the quality of the prophecies in die Sacred Scriptures and how credible and reliable are these prophecies?
- What were the sources and inspiration, if any, for these prophecies?
- How, when, and where were these prophecies recorded and by whom?
- What are the functions of these prophecies inside the parts of Scripture where they appear?

- What role did these prophecies play in subsequent events?
- How, when, and where were these prophecies accepted as authoritative or divinely inspired?
- Which methods and criteria were used to discriminate between genuine and false or spurious prophecies and predictions by later preachers and theologians?
- How and when were these prophecies ever fulfilled?

Answers to these questions will be sought by employing the tested-and-tried methods of rational and scientific biblical interpretation and historical research, together with explanations from the insights of the science of neuropsychology when investigating the mental processes displayed by these prophets.

Special attention will be given to prophetic utterances regarding the ultimate Messiah of Israel. Answers to the following questions must be sought:

- What did the Israelites and Jews expect of their Messiah(s)?
- Were these prophecies in the Hebrew Scriptures realized and fulfilled in the person of Jesus of Nazareth, as the authors of the New Testament claim?
- Did the authors of the various books of the New Testament quote and interpret the messianic prophecies of the Hebrew Scriptures correctly and accurately?

THE PRINCIPLES OF RATIONALITY AND NATURALISM

When analyzing and discussing the various prophecies found in the Scriptures, it is necessary to do so with an open mind, without any dogmatic or ideological prejudices.

There is more than one possible way of dealing with this subject:

- One may take it for granted that the various prophets received clear and genuine revelations and visions, given to them by God, and that their prophecies ought to be regarded as authoritative and should be treated with the necessary respect (this is the traditional approach);
- It is also possible to decide *a priori* that nobody is able to predict the future and that all these prophecies are nothing but wishful thinking or intelligent guesses (this is the approach of liberal or modernistic theologians and investigators); or
- Each prophecy ought to be investigated on its own, against its historical background, to determine whether that forecast had any validity and whether it was perhaps fulfilled at a later date.

This book chooses the third possibility as its starting point.

It is also necessary that this investigation must adhere to scientific principles with the goal of reaching credible and acceptable conclusions.

Some thoughts about the methods and assumptions of most practitioners of various sciences must be explained here. Almost all scientist, of whatever discipline, regard it as axiomatic that the scientific principles of rationality and logical consistency are the most important principles to be kept in mind whenever any aspect of reality is being analyzed, investigated, described, or explained.

This principle also applies to the topic of this book – an investigation into the words and activities of prophets of whom we read in the Holy Scriptures. This principle or test must be applied, even if this topic is approached with an open mind.

Rationality

The term *rationality* may be regarded as the principle that statements and conclusions must be consistent with and derived from the laws and rules of logical thought and reasoning. The discipline of logics investigates and describes the rules of rational thought, which constitute the formal framework of the truth and acceptability of accurate and verifiable ideas, thoughts, or statements.

The concept *truth* must be defined as the principle that all thoughts, statements, and descriptions of certain aspects of reality must be consistent with the information embedded in objects, events, and processes that are being investigated. It is always possible to describe these objects, events, and processes by means of words in any human language or by means of other symbols. The results of any observation, analysis, or experiment regarding any aspect of reality must, therefore, tally with the qualities and characteristics of any object, event, or process to be accepted as true.

Furthermore: any description, analysis, or observation in any human language or by means of mathematical symbols must be rational and logical to be accepted as an established fact. If any description, analysis, or observation proves to be irrational or illogical, it cannot be true and must be discarded.

Aristotle

Logics

The Greek philosopher Aristotle of the fourth century BC was the first thinker to formulate a set of logical rules, which may be regarded as axioms, unprovable, yet universally accepted truths.[1] The discipline of logics was further developed through the ensuing centuries.

---

[1] Stanford Encyclopedia of Philosophy, "Aristotle's Logics".

The most basic rule of logics is the rule of consistency, namely that two conflicting or contradictory statements cannot both be true; at least one of them must be untrue.

Another important rule of logics is that any statement, declaration, or explanation in whatever language must be backed by established facts and sufficient proof to be acceptable and useful.

Mathematics and the Laws of Nature

During the Renaissance of the sixteenth and seventeenth centuries, scientists such as Galileo Galilei and Isaac Newton found that certain regularities in nature can be reduced to mathematical formulae.

The ancient Greek mathematician, Euclid, already found that the discipline of geometry rests upon a set of axioms, unprovable, yet universally accepted, theorems. Euclid's geometry is still being taught in schools all over the world. Newton found that the movements of planets around the sun can be explained by certain mathematical formulae and principles, using Euclid's geometry.

Practitioners of the exact sciences such as astronomy, physics, geography, and geology express the laws of nature they discover by means of mathematical formulae. Humanitarian and life sciences, such as economics, psychology, sociology, and biology all make use of the branch of mathematics known as statistics to unearth certain tendencies or risks.

Jurisprudence and Natural Law

The disciple of jurisprudence and the application of legislation makes use of the rules of logics to test the testimony of witnesses in court. If any logical rules are broken by a witness, it is a sign that that person's testimony cannot be true in all respects. The rules of logics are applied to decide whether an accused person in a criminal trial is guilty or innocent or where the respondent or defendant in a civil case is liable to pay a certain sum of money or must be compelled to perform certain actions.

The discipline of jurisprudence makes use of certain laws of natural justice, which may be regarded as axioms, unprovable truths. These rules include the stipulations that the presiding officer in any dispute must be impartial and may not be a party in the dispute, that an accused must be deemed to be innocent until proven guilty, and that both sides in a dispute must have the right to present evidence and state their cases (see: Lev 19: 15; Deut 1: 17; Prov 18: 5).

Naturalism
All the sciences taught at universities – except for theology – take the philosophy of naturalism as another starting point in all their investigations, observations, experiments, and explanations. Naturalism takes it for granted that nothing exists outside of nature or physical reality and that supernatural causes and explanations for observed events or phenomena must be ruled out.

This way of thinking may also be labelled as secularism and humanism. Secularism is the philosophy that propagates the division of state and religion, but it may also mean that religious concepts and supernatural explanations for earthly phenomena ought not to play a role in human affairs. Humanism teaches that human affairs ought not to be determined by religious or supernatural considerations and that human life is worthy of preservation and development.[2]

Psychiatry and Clinical Psychology
The principle of rationality and the philosophy of naturalism play an important role in psychiatry and clinical psychology. According to

---

[2] Enc Brit, "Secularism" and "Humanism".

the Diagnostic and Statistical Manual of Mental Disorders of the American Psychiatric Association, 5th Edition, Text Revision (2022) – also known as the DSM-5-TR (2022) – good mental health is, amongst others, characterized by rational thought processes and actions.

Certain mental health problems, especially psychotic conditions, mood disorders, phobias, and personality disorders, are accompanied by irrational thoughts, absurd convictions, spurious fears, and destructtive behaviors, often accompanied by magical thinking. The whole DSM-5-TR, with its classification and descriptions of a whole range of mental disorders, is based upon rigorous empirical investigations and a rational classification system.[3]

The approach of the DSM-5-TR can certainly be described as naturalistic. A natural cause for all mental disorders is being sought and no consideration is given to purported supernatural causes for these disorders, such as demonic possession, sorcery, or magic spells or curses.[4]

This approach will be followed in this book whenever the Scriptures describe cases of abnormal or strange behavior where prophets are concerned.

---

[3] APA, *DSM-5,* 10, 92, 101, 128, 241, 283, 650, 652, 655–60, 668, 784, 786.
[4] APA, *DSM-5,* 293, 824, 836.

THE SCIENTIFIC QUALITY OF THEOLOGY

The Academic Discipline of Theology

The theme of this book deals with the phenomenon of prophecy as found in the Sacred Scriptures. That means that the academic discipline known as theology is involved.

Practitioners of the art of astrology are convinced that they are gathering good scientific knowledge. According to them, it is necessary that someone's precise moment of birth be known to work out what kind of person he or she is or will become and what fate awaits him or her.

It is necessary to know the exact time of birth so that the position of the heavenly bodies at that stage – the sun, moon, and planets – can be plotted against the background of the so-called fixed stars. These fixed stars are grouped into constellations. The annual path of the sun through twelve of these constellations constitutes the so-called Zodiac. The character and fate of that person is then calculated by taking the position of the heavenly bodies, the constellations of the Zodiac, and their distance from the horizon into account.

Astronomers and other scientists insist that astrology is a pseudoscience. According to them, it is an ancient Babylonian superstition and there is no known scientific explanation for the purported results of a so-called horoscope, the astrological "map" used to predict a person's character and fate.[5]

This controversy regarding astrology causes one to wonder: is theology a real science or a pseudoscience, such as astrology? After all, theology is the only subject taught at universities where attention is given to a supernatural entity, called God, who is deemed to be the Creator and Ruler of the universe.

---

[5] Eysenck, *Astrology,* passim.

The sciences of astronomy and physics claim to have found natural causes for all observed physical natural phenomena – except for the origin of the universe. Some of them are confident that a natural and rational explanation for the existence of the universe will be found, but that confidence has not yet been vindicated.[6]

Theologians counter that they can explain the existence of the universe, namely that it was created out of nothing by an eternal and almighty God. That means that the possibility exists that the discipline of theology may be regarded as a true science and not as a pseudoscience, such as astrology.

However, there is no unanimity among theologians about what the field of study of this discipline is or should be. Theologians have mentioned basically four possible fields of study:

- The study of God and his actions;
- The study of the Scriptures as the written Word of God as revealed by him to the scriptural authors;
- The study of the religious convictions of people, including the contents of the Christian faith; and
- The study of God's revelation in Scripture and nature; in other words: the Scriptures, as well as the whole of reality, must be investigated.[7]

These descriptions pose some difficulties.

The trouble with the first description is that God cannot be studied directly and no experiments can be performed with him as participant because he is not part of nature or physical reality.

The second description doesn't satisfy because theologians study much more than just the contents of the Scriptures. Secular

---

[6] Hawking & Mlodinow, *The Grand Design*, 11–20; Joubert, *Die Groot Gedagte*, 235 – 50.
[7] Schulze (1995: 8; König 1978: 31; Oden 1982: x; Heyns en Jonker (1974: 62

subjects such text criticism, the archaeology of Palestine, the history of religious dogmata, the history of Christianity, and the study of non-Christian religions usually form part of the curriculum at any theological school.

When the phenomenon of the Christian faith and its role in society is studied, it is done as part of cultural anthropology or sociology and cannot be regarded as theology *per se.*

The fourth possibility seems to be the most satisfactory because it does describe what is, in fact, being taught at most theological schools. When theologians study the whole of reality from the perspective of God's revelation, it means that they must take note of all the other sciences taught at universities – which is a rather tall order

Something that casts a serious shadow over the scientific value of the study of theology, is the fact that there are so many schools, movements, sects, and directions in the theological world. One may study theology from any one of the following paradigms or frameworks: a Roman Catholic, Orthodox, Reformed, Lutheran, Pentecostal, Charismatic, Liberal, Marxist, Liberation Theological, or Unitarian perspectives.

This plethora of theological directions is the result of the fact that the Scriptures have been interpreted and understood in various conflicting ways, especially the more ambiguous and unclear parts.

Historical Method

This book will approach its subject matter with an open mind, as already stated. That means that it won't identify itself with any of these theological schools. It will merely investigate the phenomenon of prophecy from the point of view of a disinterested historian and psychologist who is eager to find the most rational and plausible explanation for every event or though encountered. Since all the prophets and the authors of the different parts of the Scriptures were human beings, their thought processes and experiences may also be investigated from the perspective of neuropsychology.

Answers must be found to the following questions to follow established methods in the discipline of historical research:

- Are there any written or documentary sources that can be consulted to reconstruct or describe certain events from the past – inscriptions on monuments, reports by eye-witnesses, and participants, correspondence, and notices?
- How and when were these written historical sources compiled?
- Are there any available written documents drafted by direct participants or contemporary observers and commentators?
- Is there more than just a single source to attest to the historical reality of a certain event?[8]
- Who exactly were the authors of these sources?
- How much time elapsed between the events and the description thereof in the extant written reports?
- Did these authors rely on other sources – written and/or oral – or did they report their own experiences or observations?
- How reliable were the written and oral sources consulted by the authors of the extant and available sources?
- What were the religious and political convictions, nationalities, and social positions of these authors and how did these factors influence their descriptions of the events they reported on?
- What was the general social, political, economic, and military situation during the time of the described events, as well as at the time of the compilation of these written sources and reports?

---

[8] This axiomatic requirement is also a biblical principle: the truth about an event must be established by at least two witnesses whose testimonies must agree (Numb 35: 30, Deut 17: 6, 19: 15, Matt 18:16, John 18: 17, and 2 Cor 13:1).

- Were the beliefs, experiences, and actions of the role players influenced by their medical and psychological conditions?
- Which objectives did the authors of the available written sources wish to achieve with their letters, documents, and reports?
- The application of the razor of Occam: the most simple and least complicated explanation of a phenomenon, an event, or a text is usually the correct or most likely explanation.

These principles are like those used in a court of law to determine the credibility of evidence placed before it.

All this means that a distinction must be made between primary and secondary sources. Secondary sources are usually reports that quote or make use of primary sources.

The primary sources that must be consulted are the original writings of the prophets as they are preserved in the Sacred Scriptures. The historical narratives to be found in the Old Testament about the history of Israel and in the gospels and Acts about the lives of Jesus and the apostles must be regarded as secondary sources, since they present information gathered from eye-witnesses or other people who have preserved memories and traditions of certain events.

It is also necessary to remember that the interpretation of historical sources always happens against the religious or ideological position of the researcher. For instance, Christian and Muslim historians may create different narratives and draw different pictures about the Christian crusades during the Middle Ages. Church historians who write about the Reformation of the sixteenth century will, inevitably, present their publications from a Roman Catholic, Protestant, or Anabaptist perspective.

Because of all the preceding considerations, it must be evident that historical research cannot be an exact science, such as physics, astronomy, chemistry, geology, or any of the other natural sciences. Very often, the historian must be honest and declare that he can only reconstruct certain aspects of the past with variable degrees of certainty or probability.

Prescientific Worldview

It must be kept in mind that the scriptural authors lived many centuries ago when a primitive worldview was shared by all. It was believed that the earth was the center of the universe and consisted of a flat disk with edges. This disk rested upon pillars that stood in waters, the primeval flood. The netherworld, the abode of the dead, was below the surface of the earth. Heaven consisted of three layers – the heaven filled with clouds, the heaven filled with stars, and the top heaven where God or the deities resided. The stars were seen as spirits or angels or even deities, who influenced events on earth.[9]

This primitive worldview appears, for instance, in the Ten Commandments:

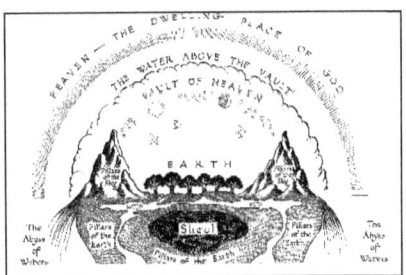

Simplified primitive biblical worldview

"You shall not make for yourselves an idol, nor any image of anything that is in the heavens above, or that is in the earth beneath, or that is in the water under the earth" (Ex 20: 4).

The Apostle Paul held a similar view in Phil 2: 9–10:

---

[9] Pretorius, *To Hell with the Devil,* 32–83.

> "Therefore, God also highly exalted him [Christ], and gave to him the name which is above every name; that at the name of Jesus every knee would bow, of those in heaven, those on earth, and those under the earth."

It goes without saying that no educated person in the twenty-first century still adheres to this primitive cosmology. It is common knowledge that the earth is a globe that rotates around its own axis and circles around the sun, the center of the solar system. The stars are not deities or angels, but other suns.

One may safely say many educated people of our time can be regarded as deists. The philosophy of deism teaches that there is a Supreme Being or God who may be seen as the Creator of the universe. He is, though, not involved with his creation anymore and the universe runs totally according to its inherent natural laws. This philosophy may be seen as a variety of naturalism or rationalism.[10]

PROPHECY AND FORTUNE-TELLING

Antique Pagan Examples

The Israelites and the early Christians were not the only groups in Antiquity that knew prophets and seers. All the nations with which the Israelites and early Christians came into contact had oracles, prophets, soothsayers, necromancers, and astrologers.

The ancient Egyptians practiced incubation. A priest or a seeker for advice from the gods would sleep in the temple of a certain deity with the hope that the relevant deity would appear to him during a dream.[11] The biblical book of Exodus (ch 41) tells the story of the Egyptian Pharaoh's dream that had to be interpreted and explained by Joseph, the Hebrew slave.

---

[10] Manuel, "Deism.
[11] Enc Brit, "Divination".

Archaeologists have found the residues of hallucinogenic drugs in an ancient Egyptian drinking vessel – probably used to induce hallucinations, visions, and revelations from the gods.[12]

Priests in Mesopotamia – Sumer, Akadia, and Babylonia – were also astrologers, since watching the night sky with its stars, thought to be their gods, was regarded as a religious activity. They kept careful records of their observations of celestial phenomena and used these to predict the outcome of battles and the fates of kingdoms, kings, and other important people.[13] These priests also interpreted dreams.

The Persian religion of Zoroastrianism was based on the visions and insights of the prophet, Zoroaster (also known as Zarathustra), who preached a form of monotheism.[14]

The Greek Oracle at Delphi was the most famous oracle in Antiquity. Less famous Greek oracles also existed at Thebes, Tegyra, Ptoon in Boeotia, Abae in Phocis, Corope in Thessaly, Delos, Patara, Branchidae, Claros, and Grynium. The oracle of Zeus at Dodona in northwestern Greece was regarded as the oldest. People visited these oracles for advice regarding the future. They usually didn't communicate directly with the pythia or sybil, the seer, but through intermediaries. Messages from the deities were usually brief and ambiguous.[15]

Tartarus was a system of tunnels at Baia, a few kilometers north of Naples in Italy, where the so-called Oracle of the Dead was situated. People who wished to consult their deceased relatives were led in a drugged state through this system of tunnels simulating the underworld or Tartarus where the souls of dead people were thought

---

[12] Cassella, "Ancient Egyptian Hallucinogens".
[13] Scholtz, *Revelation*, 302.
[14] Pretorius, *Heaven and Hell*, 29–32.
[15] Enc Brit, "Oracle".

to exist, until they reached the sybil, the prophetess, who purportedly brought them into contact with the souls of the dead – actually associates of the prophetess, playing the parts.[16]

The entrance to the Oracle of the Dead (Tartarus) at Baia near Naples, Italy.

A Roman priest, called a "haruspex", read omens, and sought the wishes of the gods by investigating the entrails of sacrificed animals. Priests also interpreted the flight of birds.[17]

A German priestess and prophetess, Veleda, daughter of the chieftain of the tribe of the Bucteri in the lower Rhineland and who lived a secluded life in a tower on the banks of the Lippe River, inspired the members of her tribe and the Batavians of the present Netherlands to attack the Roman legions occupying their country – precisely at the time when the Roman Army was waging war against the Jewish rebels in Judea during AD 66–70. After many initial

---

[16] Scholtz, *Revelation,* 302.
[17] Merriam Webster Dictionary, "Haruspex".

successful battles, the German rebellion was eventually subdued. Veleda was captured and taken to Rome where Emperor Vespasian sought her advice and honored her as a divine person.[18]

Biblical Prophets and Oracles
This book deals with scriptural prophets, their actions, and their pronouncements, called prophecies. It is, therefore, necessary to get clarity about the question: what do the Scriptures mean when prophets are being mentioned?

The word used in the Hebrew Scriptures is נָבִיא (*nabiy*) and it may be translated as "spokesman, speaker, prophet". It is usually applied to prophets who served or spoke on behalf of YHWH, the God of Israel, but it was also applied to so-called false prophets and even pagan prophets. It occurs in 316 cases in these Scriptures.

According to Isa 15: 16, God said to the prophet Isaiah: "I have put my words in your mouth..." That made him God's messenger or spokesperson.

The Hebrew word for "oracle" (דְּבִיר – *debir*) occurs 21 times in the Old Testament – of which 1 Kgs 6–8 contain eleven examples. It is usually translated as "inner chamber" or "holiest of holies" when used in conjunction with the temple of Solomon. In other words, the innermost chamber of the temple, which was only visited once a year by the high priest, was seen as an oracular space.

There can be little doubt that various prophets of the Old Testament saw themselves as oracles. The last prophet of the Old Testament, Malachi, explicitly called his message an "oracle of the Lord" (מַשָּׂא דְבַר־יְהוָה – *massa' debar YHWH*) (Mal 1: 1).

The Christian Scriptures use the Greek word προφήτης (*prophetes*). This word was borrowed from other Greek writings

---

[18] Fisher, "Veleda".

where it was used for the interpreter of oracles, somebody skilled in divination, or a person who could explain the will of the gods regarding the future. In the New Testament, it is – according to a biblical lexicon – used of "one who, moved by the Spirit of God and hence his organ or spokesman, solemnly declares to men what he has received by inspiration, especially concerning future events, and in particular such as relate to the cause and kingdom of God and to human salvation."

This word was applied to prophets of the Old Testament, personages such as John the Baptist or Jesus of Nazareth, or "men filled with the Spirit of God, who by God's authority and command in words of weight pleads the cause of God and urges salvation of men," as well as persons who "appeared in the apostolic age among Christians." This word is used in 149 cases in the New Testament.

The Greek word for "oracle" (λόγιον – *logion*) is used in four instances in the New Testament. It may also mean a "brief utterance" – doubtless because divine oracles were generally brief. In 1 Pet 4: 11 we read: "If any man speaks, *let him speak* as the oracles of God..." The other three examples refer to prophecies in the Old Testament.

By means of a summary, it may be stated that a prophet is somebody who receives visions and revelations from God, a person who speaks on behalf of God, and acts as God's messenger.

Inspired by God

The prophets of the Old Testament were convinced that God spoke through them. One often gets the formula in the prophetic writings that "the word of God came to..." [the name of some or other prophet] (for instance: Jer 1: 2, 4; Ezek 1: 3; Hos 1: 1; Joel 1: 1; Jonah 1: 1; Zech 1: 1; *etcetera*).

Jesus was also of the opinion that God spoke through the

prophets of the Hebrew Scriptures (for instance: Matt 5: 18; 24: 35; 26: 53 –56; 27:35; John 10: 35; 12: 38, 39; 19:28, 36, 37).

In 2 Tim 3: 16, Paul declared:

> "Every Scripture inspired by God is also profitable for teaching, for reproof, for correction, for instruction which is in righteousness."

2 Pet 1: 19–21 adds:

> "We have the more sure word of prophecy; whereunto you do well that you take heed, as to a lamp shining in a dark place, until the day dawns, and the day star arises in your hearts: knowing this first, that no prophecy of Scripture is of private interpretation. For no prophecy ever came by the will of man: but holy men of God spoke, being moved by the Holy Spirit."

The apostle Paul, who is called a prophet in Acts 13: 1 and Rom 12: 6, claimed that his insights came from the visions and revelations he had received:

> "But I make known to you, brothers, concerning the gospel which was preached by me, that it is not according to man. For neither did I receive it from man, nor was I taught it, but it came to me through revelation of Jesus Christ" (Gal 1: 11–12; see also Rom 15: 18; Gal 1: 16–19; 1 Cor 2:10; 11: 23; 12: 10; 15: 1–9; Eph 3: 3; Col 1: 26–27).

According to *1 Pet 1: 10–12*, the prophets of the Old Testament predicted the suffering and resurrection of Christ:

10.	Concerning this salvation, the prophets sought and searched diligently, who prophesied of the grace that would come to

> you,
>
> 11. searching for what or what kind of time the Spirit of Christ, which was in them, pointed to, when he testified beforehand the sufferings of Christ, and the glories that should follow them.
>
> 12. To whom it was revealed, that not to themselves, but to you, did they minister these things, which now have been announced to you through those who preached the gospel to you by the Holy Spirit sent forth from heaven; which things angels desire to look into.

It is the purpose of this book to test this point of view. Did the prophets in the Hebrew Scriptures really foresaw how Jesus would be killed and resurrected and thereby gain the salvation of sinners?

Divination, Sorcery, Necromancy, Astrology, and Soothsaying

The Old Testament and the New Testament forbade very clearly and definitely any form of soothsaying, necromancy, astrology, divination, or sorcery (Ex 22: 18; Lev 19: 26, 31; 20: 26, 27 Deut 4: 19; 18: 10–12; 1 Sam 15: 23; 28: 3, 7, 9; 1 Chron 10: 13; 2 Chron 33: 6; Isa 8: 19, 20; 47: 13–14; Acts 19: 19; Gal 5: 20).

We read in Numb 22: 7–41 of the diviner Balaam who was consulted by the enemies of the Israelites, with the request that he curse the Israelites and for that purpose they brought him some gifts. However, an angel sabotaged his efforts and he was compelled to bless the children of Israel instead.

Likewise, the young man Saul sought the help of Samuel, the prophet, about the whereabouts of his father's stray asses. He also brought Samuel some gifts, as was the custom when seeking the advice of a seer (1 Sam 9).

The question now arises: how does the work of a biblical

prophet differ from fortune-telling and the activities of a pagan prophet, astrologer, sorcerer, diviner, and soothsayer? An answer will be endeavored in the last chapter of this book.

In the discussion of the various biblical prophecies, it will become clear that the topics or themes of these prophecies can be divided into the following categories:

- Prophecies and promises regarding important current events;
- Direct orders from God;
- Prophecies regarding Israel's Messiah, and
- Prophecies regarding Judgment Day and the afterlife.

DATING SCRIPTURAL ELEMENTS AND EVENTS

It is always useful to compile a chronology of events to make sense of a complicated sequence of episodes. The following chronology of scriptural incidents and the authorship of the different parts of the Sacred Scriptures is based on the work of Boshoff *et al.*, Loubser, Rylaarsdam *et al.*, and the present author, unless otherwise indicated in a footnote.[19]

To understand any part of Scripture, it is always necessary to place it against the background of the date and place or origin – hence the following chronology. The category "Scripture" is used here in a somewhat loose and broad manner. Deuterocanonical and apocryphal books that originated in Israel are included because they often influenced the authors of the books of the New Testament.

The holy book of Islam, the Qur'an, must also receive attention since it claims to contain the revelations and communications received by the prophet Muhammad.

---

[19] Boshoff, *Geskiedenis,* passim; Loubser, *Dating Adam,* 436; Pretorius, *The Gospels Explained,* passim; Rylaarsdam *et al.,* "Biblical Literature".

The Composition of the Hebrew Scriptures

We know much more about the origin, historical background, and composition of the Bible than earlier generations. Dedicated linguists were able to tease the various layers, elements, additions, and components of the various biblical books from each other. This enables one to understand the contents of the various biblical documents so much better.

In the past, it was assumed that Moses was the author of the first five books of the Bible, called the Pentateuch. For instance, in his parable of the rich man and Lazarus, Jesus referred to the writings of "Moses and the prophets" (Luke 16: 29), indicating his belief that Moses wrote the first five biblical books. Scholarship has shown, though, that Moses could not have written these books and that they are a merger of four earlier independent sources, namely:

- The J- Document, which uses the name *YHWH* (יהוה) for the God of Israel
- The E Document, which mostly uses the name of *Elohim* (אֱלֹהִים) for the God of Israel;
- The D Document, which comprises most of the book of Deuteronomy; and
- The P Document (or Priestly Document), containing most of the purity and ceremonial laws of the Israelites.

These documents originated at different times at different places and were only finally amalgamated and accepted as authoritative during the fifth century BC, after the Babylonian Exile. There are various indications that these documents also combined older sources and oral traditions, such as the patriarchal tradition, the Exodus tradition, and the Sinai tradition. It is possible and even probable that a core of these books does originate from Moses. Moses is also the main character in the stories in the books of Exodus to Deuteronomy.[20]

The two books of Samuel, written during the Babylonian Exile, clearly combined more than one source regarding the founding of the Israelite monarchy. More than one event is described by two conflicting and contradictory reports.[21]

The book of Isaiah consists of three parts that date from different periods, namely Isa 1–39, 40–55, and 56–66.[22]

The books of Zechariah and Daniel are, likewise, each composed of two separate parts from different authors.

Apocryphal books such as the books of the Maccabees, Jesus Sirach, Enoch, and the Book of Jubilees were written during the third and second centuries BC.

The Composition of New Testament Writings

The Gospels of Matthew, Luke, and John are also composite works. Matthew and Luke are both combinations of three sources:

- Large parts were copied from the earlier Gospel of Mark;
- The Q Documents – the parts that Matthew and Luke share and that do not appear in Mark; and
- Material unique to Matthew or Luke.

The Q document consists mainly of sayings and stories of Jesus and is silent about his birth, crucifixion, and resurrection. It seems to have been compiled a decade or a little more after the time of Jesus when memories about his sayings were still relatively fresh.

The Gospel of Mark was only written after the destruction of Jerusalem by the Romans in AD 70. Matthew and Luke, containing

---

[20] Boshoff *et al.*, *Geskiedenis en Geskrifte*, 212–13; Hagedorn, "Taking the Pentateuch", 53–58.
[21] Enc Brit, "Samuel, Books of".
[22] Enc Brit, "Isaiah, Book of."

large parts of Mark, were compiled afterwards, during the eighties.

The Gospel of John can easily be divided into two parts: an earlier narrative part in a sober and straightforward style, and some later philosophical and theological elements containing dialogues, debates, and sermons of Jesus. The earliest parts were probably written during the fifties or early sixties AD, before the destruction of Jerusalem in AD 70, and containing the recollections of the Apostle John, while the rest was added much later, probably during the nineties by John's pupils.

The apostle Paul lost his life in Rome, according to extra-biblical sources, during the time of Emperor Nero, during AD 64 or 65. His letters to various churches date from the fifties and early sixties of the first century, although some letters written under his name may have been written by some of his helpers or pupils on his behalf.

The oldest part of the New Testament seems to be the Epistle of James, written by the brother of Jesus who succeeded him as leader of the Jesus Movement. It may have been composed during the forties of the first century, more or less during the same time as the Q Document, with which it shares some similarities.[23]

The Revelation of John of Patmos can be dated to AD 96.[24]

Chronology

It is not always possible to date certain events and documents in the Bible precisely. It is, though, sometimes possible to coordinate certain biblical episodes with extra-biblical incidents with known dates. It is also possible to calculate the date of a certain occasion or document that coincided with a reported solar eclipse or another

---

[23] Pretorius, *The Gospels Explained,* passim.
[24] Scholtz, *The Prophecies of Revelation,* passim.

astronomical occurrence, whose date can be calculated accurately.

2753 BC	Birth of Adam, the ancestor of Abraham[25]
2205 BC	Flood in Noah's time
±1560 BC	Abraham leaves Ur to settle in the Promised Land
±1500 BC	Volcano on Greek island of Thera, causing famine in Egypt and Canaan in the time of Joseph[26]
1279–13 BC	Ramses II reigns in Egypt (Pharao of the Exodus?)
13th cent BC	Exodus of Israelites from Egypt[27]
±1208 BC	Stele of Merneptah, son of Ramses II; earliest extra-biblical mention of Israel
02.08.1133 BC	Total solar eclipse; defeat of Sisera, commander of the Canaanite army, by Israelites under Barak and Deborah (Judg 5: 20)[28] [Alternative date: 30.09.1130 BC]
1050 BC	Saul anointed king of Israel by Samuel
1000–960 BC	David king of Israel
980–930 BC	Compilation of the J Document during the time of King David – parts of Genesis, Exodus, and Numbers
960 BC	Solomon king of Israel

---

[25] Michael Loubser, a mathematician, wrote a book, *Dating Adam,* in which he analysed the numbers in the genealogy of Abraham in Genesis 5, going back to Adam (not to be confused with the first human being in Genesis 1–3) and came to the conclusion when the clay tablets with Abraham's genealogy were translated into Hebrew, the translators misunderstood the Sumerian number system and allotted incredibly long lifetimes to the men mentioned in the genealogy. Loubser deciphered the original numbers and calculated that Adam was born in 2753 BC in Sumeria.

[26] Enc Brit, "Thera"; Ben-Menahem, "Cross-Dating", 186–87.

[27] Biblical Archaeoological Society, "The Exodus: Fact or Fiction?"

[28] Ben-Menahem, "Cross-Dating", 182; NASA, "Five Millennium Catalog of Solar Eclipses".

967 BC	Start of building of the temple in Jerusalem[29]
922 BC	Rehoboam king of Israel
931 BC	Israelite kingdom divided
931 BC	Jeroboam king of Israel
914 BC	Abiyah king of Judah
912 BC	Asa king of Judah
909 BC	Nadab king of Israel
908 BC	Baasha king of Israel
885 BC	Elah king of Israel
884 BC	Zimri king of Israel
884 BC	Omri king of Israel
880–830 BC	E Document compiled – parts of Genesis, Exodus, and Numbers
873 BC	Ahab king of Israel
871 BC	Jehosaphat king of Judah
870 BC	Elijah starts career as a prophet
852 BC	Ahaziah king of Israel
851 BC	Joram king of Israel
848 BC	Jeroham king of Judah
848 BC	Elisha starts career as prophet
843 BC	Ahaziah king of Judah
842 BC	Atalia queen of Israel
842 BC	Joash king of Israel
842 BC	Jehu king of Israel
819 BC	Jehoahaz king of Israel
805 BC	Amaziah king of Judah
805 BC	Joash king of Israel
790 BC	Jeroboam II king of Israel
788–742 BC	Uzziah king of Judah

---

[29] Eames, "Who was the Pharaoh of the Exodus?"

INTRODUCTION

±762 BC   Amos starts career as prophet
15.06.762 BC   Solar eclipse mentioned by Isaiah 13: 10, 24: 23 and Amos 5: 8 and 8: 9
750 BC   Zachariah king of Israel
758 BC   Jotham king of Judah
749 BC   Shallum king of Israel
749 BC   Menahem king of Israel
742 BC   Agash king of Judah
742 BC   Start of prophetic career of Isaiah
738 BC   Pekahiah king of Israel
735 BC   Peka king of Israel
732 BC   Hoshea king of Israel
721 BC   Northern kingdom conquered by the Assyrians – J Document and E Document combined
715–±686 BC   Hezekiah king of Judah
14.03.711 BC   Solar eclipse in Isaiah's time
697 BC   Manasseh king of Judah
642 BC   Amon king of Judah
640 BC   Joshiah king of Judah
635–612 BC   Habakuk's career as prophet
±630 BC   Zephaniah operates as a prophet
627 BC   Start of Jeremiah's career as a prophet
621 BC   Discovery of D Document in temple – reforms by king Josiah
609 BC   Battle of Megiddo; King Josiah killed; Jehoash king of Judah
620–600 BC   Parts of D Document compiled – parts of Exodus and Deuteronomy
598 BC   Jehoiachin king of Judah
597 BC   Zedekiah king of Judah
±600 BC   Nahum active in Judah

7rh Cent BC	Zephaniah active in Judah
600–590 BC	Joshua compiled by D historians
597 BC	Ezekiel banished to Babylon after the surrender of Jerusalem to the Babylonians[30]
590–580 BC	Judges compiled by D historians
586 BC	Destruction of Jerusalem; Start of second Babylonian Exile
After 586 BC	Obadiah active in Jerusalem
21.09.581 BC	Total solar eclipse described by Ezekiel (ch 30: 8)[31]
580–560 BC	Compilation of 1 & 2 Samuel and 1 & 2 Kings by D historians
560 BC	Traditions about Elijah and Elisha recorded
560–540 BC	Compilation of P Document; editorial work on JED Document
538 BC	Conquest of Babylon by Cyrus the Great; Jewish exiles allowed to return to Judea
540 BC	Final edition of the Torah by the P writer
523 BC	Second return of exiles; Zerubbabel appointed as governor; Joshua, the high priest, takes the final edition of the Torah to Jerusalem
520 BC	Zechariah (first part)[32]
520 BC	Haggai
28.03.516 BC	Solar eclipse observed by Zechariah (ch 14: 6–7)[33]
515 BC	Second Temple completed
±500 BC	Torah accepted as Scripture

---

[30] Ben-Menahem, "Cross-Dating", 177.
[31] Ben-Menahem, "Cross-Dating", 180; NASA, Five Millenium Catalog of Solar Eclipses.
[32] Ben-Menahem, "Cross-Dating", 177.
[33] Ben-Menahem, "Cross-Dating", 177; NASA, Five Millenium Catalog of Solar Eclipses.

INTRODUCTION

25.11.492	Solar eclipse observed by Zechariah (ch 14: 6–7 alternative date)
458 BC	Third return of exiles under Ezra who was appointed by Artaxerxes as special religious envoy
5th Cent BC	Malachi
29.02.356 BC	Total solar eclipse observed by Joel 2: 30–31[34]
04.07.335 BC	Total solar eclipse, mentioned by Zech 14: 6–7
332 BC	Alexander the Great conquered Palestine
310–300 BC	Compilation of 1 & 2 Chronicles, Ezra, and Nehemiah
3rd cent BC	I Enoch
2nd cent BC	Jubilees
167 BC	Start of revolt under Judas Maccabeus against King Antiochus IV of Syria
164 BC	The book of Daniel
110 BC	Judea gains independence
104 BC	Aristobulus I king of Judea
103 BC	Alexander Jannaeus king of Judea
76 BC	Salome Alexandra queen of Judea
67 BC	Aristobulus II king of Judea
63 BC	Pompey invaded Palestine; Judea a Roman province Hyrcanus king of Judea
47 BC	Herod the Great governor of Galilee
40 BC	Antigonus II Mattathias king of Judea
40 BC	Herod the Great appointed by the Roman Senate as king of Judea
4–1 BC	Birth of Jesus of Nazareth before the death of Herod
23.03.04 BC	Total lunar eclipse shortly before the death of Herod

---

[34] Ben-Menahem, "Cross-Dating", 177; NASA, "Five Millenium Catalog of Solar Eclipses".

	the Great[35]
10.01.AD 00	Total lunar eclipse shortly before the death of Herod the Great (alternative possibility)
29.11.AD 29	Total solar eclipse over Galilee; baptism of Jesus?
03.04.AD 33	Crucifixion of Jesus; lunar eclipse after sunset
± AD 45	Q Document
± AD 50	Letter of James
AD 50–63	Letters of Paul
AD 50–66	Proto-Gospel of John
AD 66–70	Jewish War against Rome
30.08.AD 70	Destruction of Jerusalem and the temple
20.03. AD 71	Total solar eclipse over Greece – probably mentioned in Mark (ch 13: 24)
± AD 75	Gospel of Mark
± AD 85	Gospels of Matthew and Luke
AD 90–95	Additions to John's Gospel
AD 96–97	Revelation[36]
AD 570	Muhammad born
AD 610	Muhammad's first vision
AD 632	Death of Muhammad

---

[35] Josephus, *Antiquities* 17.6.2–4 & 17.149–67.
[36] Scholtz, *The Prophecies of Revelation,* passim.

CHAPTER 2
SCRIPTURAL PROPHETS AND THEIR CALLING

Before the various prophecies, promises, prescriptions, and predictions in the Sacred Scriptures can be described, scrutinized, analyzed, and evaluated, it is necessary to introduce the most prominent prophets, highlighting the times when they were active, as well as how they were called to become the messengers of God.

JOSEPH

The story of Joseph, the beloved son of the patriarch Jacob, is told in Genesis 37–50. These chapters form a coherent story or novella dealing with the life and family of the first major prophet and seer in the Old Testament.

His jealous brothers sold him as a slave and he eventually attained the position of prime minister and minister of economic affairs in the court of the Egyptian king, the Pharaoh.

There is a clear dependence of this story on the Egyptian story, the "Tale of Two Brothers", which casts a shadow over the historical accuracy of the biblical story. It may well contain legendary and fictitious elements. It is unclear where the author(s) of the story of Joseph gathered all the information used. More than one episode happened without any witnesses who could have reported on what they have seen and heard. We have, at most, only the memories of Joseph, which he could have passed on to others. If that was the case, it means that we have only Joseph's version of events without any corroboration or verification by others.

The famine that prompted the family of Jacob to move to Egypt, according to the biblical story, could have been caused by the outbreak of the volcano on the Greek island of Thera, around 1 500 BC. The smoke and ash spewed into the atmosphere could have blocked the rays of the sun and caused crop failures.

Joseph is noted as a dreamer, but also as the interpreter of the dreams of others, including those of the king.[37]

MOSES

A Controversial Figure

There can be no doubt that Moses must be regarded as the most influential prophet of the Old Testament. The books of Exodus, Numbers, Leviticus, and Deuteronomy contain his story and he is often mentioned in the New Testament and even in the Qur'an.

He is, though, a controversial figure in our time and various scholars even doubt that he had ever lived and they maintain that his story is based on mythological beliefs and legends. Various diverging interpretations of his story were published over the years.

For instance: the well-known Austrian psychiatrist and founder of psychoanalysis, Sigmund Freud – a Jew by birth, but an atheist – wrote a book about Moses in 1939, "Der Mann Moses und die Monotheistische Religion". It was translated into English with the title "Moses and Monotheism" and was reprinted more than once. According to Freud, Moses was an Egyptian in the time of Akhenaten, the Pharaoh who introduced monotheism in his country by declaring the Aten, the sun disk, to be the only deity. Moses was

---

[37] Enc Brit. "Joseph"; Hood & Vermeule, "Aegean Civilizations"; Rylaarsdam *et al.* "Biblical Literature".

supposed to have been influenced by Akhenaten's ideas. He led a revolt against the Egyptians and succeeded in escaping from the country with some followers, but was later murdered by them.

This interpretation of the story of Moses does not find any supporters today.

The Biblical Story

The story of Moses, as related in the Bible, is well-known. His parents were Hebrew slaves in Egypt, known as the "Habiru" in Egyptian texts. To save his life when the Pharaoh decided to have all Hebrew male infants killed to prevent the Hebrews from outbreeding the Egyptians, he was placed in a basket and allowed to drift on the Nile, while his sister, Miriam, watched over him.

Fresco from a synagogue in Dura Europos, depicting the discovery of baby Moses by the Egyptian princess Thermouthis. Ca 244–355 CE.

An Egyptian princess found the baby and adopted him with the result that he became an Egyptian prince. He fled, however, to the country of Midian when the danger arose that he could be arrested after killing an Egyptian who had maltreated a Hebrew slave. The Midianites were related to the Israelites as descendants of Abraham (Gen 25: 1–4).

He married a Midianite girl and while tending the sheep of his father-in-law, he heard a voice calling to him from a burning bush that was not consumed by the flames. It was God who ordered him to return to Egypt and to demand the freedom of the Hebrew slaves from the Pharaoh. It is likely that Moses, a former Egyptian prince familiar with the Egyptian pantheon, learned about YHWH, the God of his ancestors, from his father-in-law, Jethro, who was a priest of YHWH (Ex 3: 1; 18: 8–12).

Of course, the Pharaoh was not impressed by Moses' demand, but after the Egyptians suffered ten natural disasters sent by God, Moses and the Hebrews managed to escape to the desert.

Moses received the Ten Commandments from God in the wilderness of Sinai on a mountain. This document amounts to a covenant between God and his people, the Israelites.

The Israelites wandered through the desert for forty years and after Moses had died at the age of 120, they settled in Canaan, the country previously promised by God to their ancestor, Abraham.

Flavius Josephus
In addition to the biblical story, the Jewish historian of the first century AD, Flavius Josephus, wrote that the daughter of the Pharaoh who adopted Moses was named Thermuthis. When Moses was a grown man, he was promoted to the rank of general in the Egyptian Army during a war with the Ethiopians. He attacked the Ethiopian army through the desert and not along the Nile and caught the enemy by surprise, which led to his victory. He fled to Midian when he was suspected of plotting the overthrow of the Pharaoh.[38]

---

[38] Josephus, *Antiquities* II, IX & X.

Dating Moses

Most scholars of the Old Testament are of the opinion that Moses was a real historical figure, although much of what we read in the Bible about him must be regarded as legendary. It is, however, difficult to pinpoint the time when he lived. Some scholars use I Kgs 6: 1 as a starting point:

> "It happened in the four hundred and eightieth year after the children of Israel were come out of the land of Egypt, in the fourth year of Solomon's reign over Israel, in the month Ziv, which is the second month, that he began to build the house of YHWH."

Salomon started the building of the temple more or less during 960 BC and, therefore, the Exodus must have happened 480 years previously, during 1440 BC.

This date, however, is not supported by known historical and archaeological evidence. For instance, the cities of Pithom and Raamses, erected by the Hebrew slaves (Ex 1: 11), were only built much later. The story implies that the Pharaoh's capital city with his palace was in the vicinity of these cities, which was not the case at that time. The kingdoms of Edom and Moab, which the migrating Israelites had to avoid, only came into being long after 1440 BC.

It may be argued that the period of 480 years must be regarded as a symbolic number denoting twelve generations of 40 years each – 40 being a symbolic number connected to the time the Israelites spent in the desert and connected to the three periods of 40 years each in Moses' life. He was supposed to be 40 when he fled to Midian, 80 when he returned to Egypt, and 120 when he passed away. It is also reported that Moses spent 40 days on the mountain where he received the Ten Commandments (Ex 24: 18). If a generation is taken to be something like 25 years, then the actual date of the Exodus must have been 300 years before the building of the temple – more or less during 1260 BC.

Most scholars believe that the Pharaoh during the Exodus was none other than Ramses II, also known as Ramses the Great, who reigned during *c* 1304–*c* 1237 BC.[39]

Historical Reliability of the Story of Moses and the Exodus
Although it may be assumed that a man named Moses really lived and played an important part during the Exodus, there are various aspects of his story that cannot be accepted as historical facts.

He was supposed to be the leader of the Hebrew slaves or Israelites between the ages of 80 and 120. These advanced ages seem to be improbable and must be regarded as multiples of the symbolic number of 40.

The report of the burning bush with the voice of God in Ex 3 & 4 cannot be accepted at face value. The only source for this story – if it happened at all – must have been Moses himself since no witnesses observed what had happened. Therefore, we only have Moses' word, without any independent sources to back him up.[40] He could have told his family and friends of this private and personal encounter with God, but the repetition of the story through the decades could have distorted the details.

This story seems to be part of the J Document of the 10th century BC from the time of David and Salomon – three centuries later. Exaggerations and twists of the original tale are quite likely.

---

[39] Biblical Archaeoological Society, "The Exodus: Fact or Fiction?"; Enc Brit. "Moses".

[40] Deuteronomy 19: 15 stipulates clearly: "One witness shall not rise up against a man for any iniquity, or for any sin, in any sin that he sins: at the mouth of two witnesses, or at the mouth of three witnesses, shall a matter be established" (see also Numb 35: 30, Deut 17: 6, Matr 18:16, John 18: 17, and 2 Cor 13:1 for the requirement that the truth must be established by more than one witness).

Moses with the Ten Commandments, painting by Rembrandt, 1659

When Moses was on Sinai to receive the stone tablets with the Ten Commandments from God, he was again on his own and there was nobody to confirm or verify his story. We have, again, only his word about what had happened, which places a question mark over the accuracy of the description of this incident.

Exodus seems to suggest that there was a volcanic outburst on Mount Sinai when Moses received the Ten Commandments (Ex 19: 16–18, 20: 18; 24: 17).

If Mount Sinai was in the present Sinai Peninsula, then a volcano can be ruled out since there are no signs of any volcanoes there. There are, though, extinct volcanoes in northern Arabia, where the Midianites were living. It is possible that Moses, who had married a woman from those parts, led the Hebrew fugitives thither.

It may, therefore, have been possible that "the thunderings, the lightnings, the sound of the trumpet, and the mountain smoking" (Ex 20: 18) could have occurred. It is even possible that some of the Midianites joined the Israelites because this group seems to have disappeared after the Exodus.

The Ten Commandments are to be found in Ex 20 and Deut 5. In both cases, we are told that Moses received the stone tablets with the commandments directly from God while the wandering Israelites were camping at the foot of Mount Sinai. When one reads these commandments carefully it appears that the two versions, which are supposed to contain the same text, differ from each other in a few respects. One must, therefore, ask: which one of the two versions is the original?

It is also apparent that the Ten Commandments could not have been proclaimed in the desert during the Exodus; they rather reflect a sedentary existence with agricultural activities that partly depended upon slave labor, which only became possible much later in the Promised Land of Canaan. The Israelites were, after all, warned not to be jealous of their neighbors' houses, slaves, or animals and they were supposed to rest on the Sabbath from all their agricultural work, together with their farm animals and slaves.

The Israelites who escaped from Egypt were supposed to be former slaves and during the Exodus they certainly did not possess any slaves themselves. Therefore, the Ten Commandments could only have been formulated long after the Israelites got settled in in the Promised Land of Canaan where landowners acquired farms, slaves, and animals – certainly not during the Exodus.

The first chapter of the book of Numbers contains a list of the adult men of military age of the twelve tribes of Israel who supposedly left Egypt en route to the Promised Land. A total of 603 550 men was counted. The tribe of Levi was not included because they were not supposed to do military service. If one assumes that the Levites made up one-twelfth of the total, then the number of adult men amounts to 653 846. If one assumes that there were an equal number of women, then the total number of adults was 1 307 692. If one, in addition, assumes that there were on average two children per household, then the total number of Israelites who supposedly left Egypt was 2 615 384. That number is comparable with the number of inhabitants of the City of Tswana (Pretoria) in South Africa where 2 921 488 people resided according to the census of 2011. The provision of clean water and sanitation to the people of Pretoria is a major and sophisticated undertaking. How would Moses and the other leaders of the Israelites have been able to provide these services to 2,6 million people for more for 40 years in the Sinai Desert? That must have been a totally impossible task. Such a large migration of Israelites just could not have happened.

Only one conclusion is possible: the Exodus did not happen as described in the Bible. It is quite possible that a relatively small group of slaves under the leadership of Moses slipped out of Egypt, that other people later joined them and identified themselves with the tradition of the Exodus.[41]

SAMUEL

The prophet Samuel (Hebrew: שְׁמוּאֵל – *Shemuel*, meaning "God has heard") was more than just a prophet. According to his story in 1 Samuel 1–25, he was also a military commander, a judge, an oracle, and a king-maker during a time when the Israelites were not yet a political unit but a loose confederation of tribes. He is also briefly mentioned in 1 Chron 6 as a descendant of Jacob's son, Levi.

It is told that Samuel's childless mother prayed that she may become pregnant. When her prayer was answered, she dedicated her son to the service of God at the tabernacle, the Israelite sanctuary and place of worship, under the guidance of the high priest, Eli.

Samuel was called to become a prophet as a boy when he heard a voice at night, telling him to inform Eli of the downfall of his family – which happened at a later stage when both his sons fell during a battle and Eli broke his neck when falling from his seat.

Samuel anointed the first two kings of Israel, Saul and David, in an effort to unite the tribes under a central authority, although he also had doubts about the wisdom of such a step.

---

[41] Boshoff *et al. Geskiedenis en Geskrifte,* 73–75.

The story of Samuel was written by the D historians during the Babylonian Exile, utilizing different traditions, probably oral traditions. If Saul was anointed king by Samuel more or less during 1050 BC, then five centuries must have elapsed since his time and the recording of the event. That explains the conflicting and contradictory repetitions of certain episodes in Samuel's story.

There can be little doubt that a prophet named Samuel played a role in the history of Israel, but many details about his life in the Bible must be regarded as tainted by later exaggerations.[42]

SOLOMON

Shortly after he had succeeded his father David as king of Israel, he went to Gibeon – a prominent place of worship in those days – to have a meeting with YHWH.

YHWH did appear to him during a dream and asked him to wish anything. Solomon answered: "Give your servant therefore an understanding heart to judge your people, that I may discern between good and evil; for who is able to judge this your great people?" (1 Kgs 3: 9).

God liked his request and promised to fulfil his wish and grant him riches, honor, and longevity in addition (1 Kgs 3: 10–14).

This was a case of incubation, as also exercised in Egypt, where somebody slept in the sanctuary of a certain deity in the hope of receiving a message from that deity.

ELIJAH

Background

The wild prophet, Elijah, appeared during the time of king Ahab of

---

[42] Garsiel, "The Book of Samuel"; McKenzie, "Samual"; Enc Brit., "Samuel, Books of"; Encyclopedia.Com, "Samuel".

Israel. We know nothing about his background, except that he hailed from Tishbe in Gilead, on the eastern side of the river Jordan. The Bible is silent about his calling by God to become a prophet. His name in Hebrew is אֵלִיָּה or אֵלִיָּהוּ (*Eliyyahu* – "YHWH is my God"(.

Ahab became king of the northern Israelite kingdom, around 873 BC. The king of the southern kingdom of Judah, Jehosaphat, ascended the throne two years later. Elijah must have made his appearance shortly thereafter in the northern kingdom. His story is told in 1 Kings 17–19 and 2 Kings 1–2.

Activities

Elijah first act was to warn King Ahab that there would be a drought, which would only end when he decreed that it would rain again. The drought indeed happened and Elijah fled for his life to stay out of the clutches an angry Ahab. He initially hid in the wilderness and afterwards stayed with a widow whose stocks of flour and oil miraculously never ran out. He also revived her dead son.

A contest with the 450 prophets of the Canaanite deity Baal followed. These prophets were sponsored by Ahab's wife, Jezebel, a Phoenician princess. Elijah managed to prove that YHWH was the only God by drawing fire from heaven onto a sacrifice, which was followed by a heavy rainstorm. His followers slaughtered the Baal prophets. Jezebel sought Elijah's blood and he fled to Horeb, the mountain where Moses had a meeting with God.

God also appeared to him there – although not in various spectacular natural phenomena as in Moses' time, but in silence.

Elijah denounced Ahab for having a certain Naboth killed because he refused to sell his vineyard to the king.

He healed Ahab's son and successor, Azariah, after he had unsuccessfully sought the help of Baal. Then Elijah vanished from earth on a chariot of fire, appointing Elisha as his successor.[43]

Historical Reliability

The tales about Elijah were recorded in the book of Kings during the Babylonian Exile, about three centuries later, when memories about him preserved by some of the exiles were gathered. The exiles in Babylonia were mostly from the former kingdom of Judah, while Elijah operated in the northern kingdom, which had vanished many decades earlier. There must have very few informants who had heard stories about Elijah from their parents and others.

There were certainly enough eye-witnesses when Elijah had his meetings with Ahab and Azariah and his contest with the prophets of Baal. It is, therefore, quite possible that a core of these stories is based on real events.

His sojourn in the desert and with the widow, as well as his meeting with God on Mount Horeb, could not have been observed by others. His ascension into heaven on a flaming chariot was only witnessed by Elisha. There is no way to confirm the accuracy of these stories and one may well doubt their factual accuracy.

AMOS

Amos is the first biblical prophet of whom we have his *verba ipsissima*, his precise prophecies against the northern Israelite kingdom, but also against Israel's neighboring nations. His prophecies seem to have been published or distributed by an editor who added the following introduction:

Introduction to Amos
Amos 1: 1–2

---

[43] Smyth, "Elijah"; Encyclopedia of the Bible, "Elijah".

> 1. The words of Amos, who was among the herdsmen of Tekoa, which he saw concerning Israel in the days of Uzziah king of Judah, and in the days of Jeroboam the son of Joash king of Israel, two years before the earthquake.
>
> 2. He said, YHWH will roar from Zion, and utter his voice from Jerusalem…

The word used for "among the herdsmen" is בַּנֹּקְדִים (*bannoqdim*). This word has more than one meaning: "sheep-raiser, sheep-dealer, sheep-tender". It seems that Amos could have been a stock-farmer with his own farm at Tekoa, south of Bethlehem in Judah.

He was active during the eighth century BC, during the reigns of King Uzziah of Judah (*c* 783–742 BC) and King Jeroboam of Israel II (*c* 786–746 BC). It is not known how he had received his calling to become a prophet.

Amos made much of the value or principle of social justice. He condemned the rich land-owners who exploited the poor.

Archaeologists are convinced that they have uncovered evidence of the earthquake mentioned by Amos 1: 1 that occurred around 760 BC. The epicenter of the earthquake, with a magnitude of 8.2, seems to have been in southern Lebanon.[44]

ISAIAH

The book of Isaiah is one of the three major prophetic books of the Old Testament, together with Jeremiah and Ezekiel. The name Isaiah (Hebrew: יְשַׁעְיָהוּ – *Yeshayahu*) means "YHWH is salvation" or "YHWH has saved".

The book consists of three parts, written at different times:

---

[44] Eames, "Amos's Earthquake".

- Isa 1–39, written during the reigns of Uzziah, Jotham, Ahaz, and Hezekiah, kings of Judah, which makes him a contemporary of Amos (Isa 1: 1);
- Isa 40–55, written during the Babylonian Exile and usually called Deutero-Isaiah or Second Isaiah; and
- Isa 56–66, written during the time after the Exile and usually called Trito-Isaiah or Third Isaiah.

It is unknown when and by whom these three components were combined into a single book. The second and third parts were most probably written by followers or pupils of Isaiah, who wished to supplement his initial prophecies.[45]

The book is described as a "vision" in Isa 1: 1 (Hebrew: חזון – *chazown*, which means "vision, oracle, or prophecy"). The first verse of the book was evidently added by an editor because Isaiah is mentioned in the third-person singular ("he"), while the words of Isaiah, where he refers to himself in the first-person singular ("I"), follow that.

It seems that the order of the chapters got scrambled because the calling of Isaiah, which should have appeared at the beginning of the book, only occurs in chapter 6. The calling of Isaiah to become a prophet of YHWH is described in *Isa 6: 1–8* –

1.	In the year that king Uzziah died I saw the Lord sitting on a throne, high and lifted up; and his train filled the temple.
2.	Above him stood the seraphim: each one had six wings; with two he covered his face, and with two he covered his feet, and with two he did fly.

---

[45] Boshoff *et al.*, *Geskiedenis*, 135 – 37; Rylaarsdam *et al.*, "Biblical Literature"; Blank, "Isaiah".

> 3. One cried to another, and said, Holy, holy, holy, is YHWH of Hosts: the whole earth is full of his glory.
> 4. The foundations of the thresholds shook at the voice of him who cried, and the house was filled with smoke.
> 5. Then said I, woe is me! for I am undone; because I am a man of unclean lips, and I dwell in the midst of a people of unclean lips: for my eyes have seen the King, YHWH of Hosts.
> 6. Then flew one of the seraphim to me, having a live coal in his hand, which he had taken with the tongs from off the altar:
> 7. and he touched my mouth with it, and said, Behold, this has touched your lips; and your iniquity is taken away, and your sin forgiven.
> 8. I heard the voice of the Lord, saying, whom shall I send, and who will go for us? Then I said, here am I; send me.

This passage is usually interpreted as an extra-sensory vision in which God appeared to the prophet in the year when King Uzziah of Judah died (742 BC).

There is, however, also the likelihood that Isaiah described the starry heavens and this possibility must be explored, especially because he twice referred to "YHWH of hosts" (Hebrew: יְהוָה צְבָאוֹת – *YHWH Tsebaoth*) on his throne in this passage. The god of the heavens of the ancient Sumerians, Anu, had his throne at the northern astronomical pole. This identification of the divine throne with the northern celestial pole makes sense from the viewpoint of the ancient cosmology, since everything in the sky, as well as the earth, revolved around that central point.

Similar ideas are to be found in the Hebrew Scriptures. The king of Babylon, for instance, is addressed in *Is 14: 13* –

> "You said in your heart, I will ascend into heaven, I will exalt my throne above the stars of God; and I will sit on the mountain of congregation, in the uttermost parts of the north ..."

In *Job 37: 22* it is written:

> "Out of the north comes golden splendour; with God is awesome majesty."

We read in *1 Kgs 22: 19* –

> "I saw YHWH sitting on his throne, and all the host of heaven standing by him on his right hand and on his left."

In other words: the throne of God was thought of as being situated between the stars – the host of heaven. According to the extrabiblical book of I Enoch (third century BC), the throne of God was also to be found among the stars (I Enoch 14: 18).

This idea was also applied in the case of the visions of John of Patmos in the book of Revelation,[46] and something like that must have been the case with Isaiah's initial vision.

The description of Isaiah's calling dates from the time before the Babylonian Exile, at a time before the Judeans were profoundly influenced by the Babylonian civilization with its highly developed astrology. The Babylonians named the various starry constellations and we still use their names, albeit in their Greek and Latin translations. That the Jews knew of the Babylonian constellations even before the Babylonian Exile is evident from Amos 5: 8 where "the Pleiades and Orion" are named. These constellations, together with the Great Bear (Ursa Major) are also specified in the post-exilic book of Job (ch 9: 9 and 38: 31). Isaiah 13: 10 alludes to "the stars

---

[46] Scholtz, *Revelation*, 64–66.

of the sky and the constellations", which demonstrates his familiarity with the astrology of the Babylonians.

It is, therefore, highly probable that Isaiah's vision of God on his throne and the "seraphim" was a description of the starry skies at some or other time during 742 BC. The expression "YHWH of hosts" refers to the thousands of stars, which were thought to be angels in the Old Testament – instead of deities as the pagans believed in those days. In Deut 4: 19, the stars and constellations are explicitly called the "host of heaven" (see also Ps 103: 20–21, Ps 148: 2–3, and Neh 9: 6 for the same idea). In other words: the throne of God, called "YHWH of hosts", was perceived to be placed between the stars and the constellations – also in this vision of Isaiah.

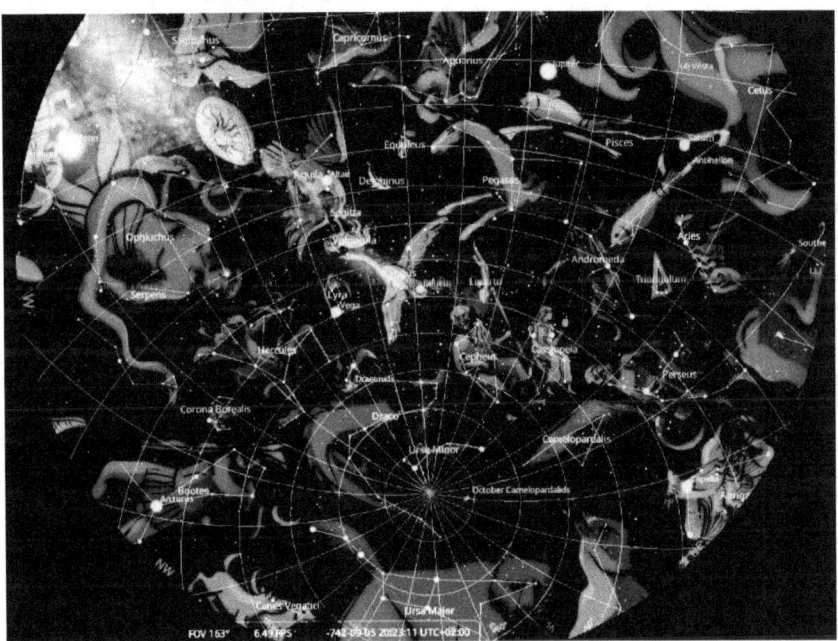

A reconstruction of the sky during May 742 BC from Jerusalem, looking north, showing the constellations, the position of the astronomical north pole, and the positions of the crescent moon and the planet Jupiter. God's throne must be seen as the constellation of Ursa Minor, next to the northern astronomical pole, while the clouds of the Milky Way stretch over the whole sky.

A tentative reconstruction of Isaiah's vision of God's throne between the stars and the "seraphim" was made with the help of a computerized astronomical program above.

In addition, the ancient Greeks saw Mount Olympus, in northern Greece, as the abode of their gods.[47] Likewise, Isa 11: 9 and Isa 65: 25 mention God's "holy mountain" and Isa 2: 2 affirms that God's house is on a high mountain (see also Ps 48: 2–3; Ezek 20: 40; Mic 4: 1).

The "seraphim" are winged angelic creatures and they may be identified with the various constellations of mythological personages surrounding the northern celestial pole. Isaiah wrote about a live or glowing coal that was used to sanitize his sinful lips, which could have been either the moon or a bright planet, such as Jupiter.

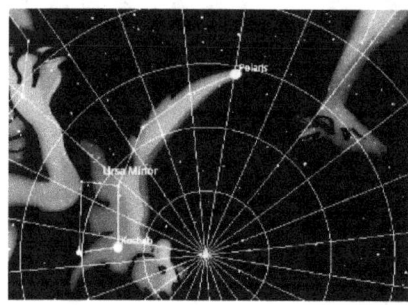

The outlines of Ursa Minor, the Little Bear, next to the astronomical north pole, look like a throne

The smoke that filled the house must have been the Milky Way with its starry clouds, stretching over the whole sky. It is even possible to see the outlines of a throne in the constellation of Ursa Minor, the Little Bear, directly next to the celestial north pole.

The illustrations on the previous page gives an idea of what Isaiah could have seen when "YHWH of hosts" called him.

One must conclude that Isaiah was watching the stars one

---

[47] Cornelius, *Geistesgeschicht,* 13, 35–36; Visser, *De Openbaring,* 5–58.

night in Jerusalem when he was so overwhelmed by the beauty of it all that he experienced it as an appearance of YHWH who called him to become his prophet.

Isaiah was active during a time when the Assyrian Empire threatened the kingdoms of Judah and Israel. His prophecies, therefore, often dealt with current affairs and political issues.

Since the authors of the second and third parts of Isaiah are unknown, nothing can be said about them, except that they wrote their parts during and after the Babylonian Exile.

JEREMIAH

Jeremiah (Hebrew: יִרְמְיָהוּ – *Yirmayahu*, meaning "whom YHWH has appointed") was active during the last years of the kingdom of Judah, before the last king was removed by the conquering Babylonians and the elite of the country was sent into exile.

He hailed from the town of Anatoth and was the son of Hilkia, a member of a priestly family, and was born around 650 BC. Jeremiah was prone to bouts of doubt and depression due to the precarious situation of the kingdom of Judah and the rejection of his warnings by the leaders of his country. Therefore, he never married. He began his career as a young prophet during the thirteenth year of the reign of King Josiah, more or less during 627 BC. This king started a reformation after the Law Book of God had been discovered somewhere in the temple – probably the book of Deuteronomy, or parts of it. Jeremiah urged the successors of Josiah, Jehoahaz, Jehoiakim, Jehoiachin, and Zedekiah, to follow in Josiah's footsteps, but without success because they tolerated the worship of other gods, besides YHWH.

Jeremiah was not only active as a religious reformer, but also as a political commentator. He disagreed with the foreign policies of the kings who tried to resist or rebel against the Babylonian Empire, the dominant power in those days, with the hope that they would be aided by Egypt. This policy eventually led to the destruction of Jerusalem and the exile of the elite of the kingdom to Babylonia.

Jeremiah was abducted by his opponents and critics to Egypt after the fall of Jerusalem in 586 BC, where he later died.

His oracles, dictated to his secretary Baruch, were collected during the Exile and published together with some biographical details and the notes by the final editor of the book.[48]

EZEKIEL

Background

Ezekiel (Hebrew: יְחֶזְקֵאל – *Yechezqe'l*), whose name means "God strengthens", was another prophet who was also a priest, although he never had the privilege of serving in the Jerusalem temple because he was one of the deportees in Babylonia after Jerusalem was conquered for the first time by the Babylonian army in 597 BC.

As a priest, he became the spiritual leader of the exiled Jews at Tel-Abib on the Chebar River, a canal that carried water from the Euphrates to communities further away. It was his task to inspire his fellow-Jews with promises that Israel would be restored by God. The Jews had, though, to understand that God brought the calamity of the second capture of Jerusalem and destruction of the city in 586 BC on them due to their idolatry, iniquities, and impiety.

Ezekiel was called to become a prophet under somewhat extraordinary circumstances by the observation of the starry skies – just as Isaiah. This calling is described in chapter 1 of his book:

The Calling of Ezekiel
Eze 1:1 – 2: 5

---

[48] Boshoff *et al.*, *Geskiedenis*, 144–47; 164–69; Hyatt, "Jeremiah".

1. Now it happened in the thirtieth year, in the fourth [month], in the fifth [day] of the month, as I was among the captives by the river Chebar, that the heavens were opened, and I saw visions of God.
2. In the fifth [day] of the month, which was the fifth year of king Jehoiachin's captivity,
3. the word of YHWH came expressly to Ezekiel the priest, the son of Buzi, in the land of the Chaldeans by the river Chebar; and the hand of YHWH was there on him.
4. I looked, and, behold, a stormy wind came out of the north, a great cloud, with flashing lightning, and a brightness round about it, and out of the midst of it as it were glowing metal, out of the midst of the fire.
5. Out of the midst of it came the likeness of four living creatures. This was their appearance: they had the likeness of a man.
6. Everyone had four faces, and everyone of them had four wings.
7. Their feet were straight feet; and the sole of their feet was like the sole of a calf's foot; and they sparkled like burnished brass.
8. They had the hands of a man under their wings on their four sides; and they four had their faces and their wings [thus]:
9. their wings were joined one to another; they didn't turn when they went; they went everyone straight forward.
10. As for the likeness of their faces, they had the face of a man; and they four had the face of a lion on the right side; and they four had the face of an ox on the left side; they four had also the face of an eagle.

11. Their faces and their wings were separate above; two [wings] of everyone were joined one to another, and two covered their bodies.

12. They went everyone straight forward: where the spirit was to go, they went; they didn't turn when they went.

13. As for the likeness of the living creatures, their appearance was like burning coals of fire, like the appearance of torches: [the fire] went up and down among the living creatures; and the fire was bright, and out of the fire went forth lightning.

14. The living creatures ran and returned as the appearance of a flash of lightning.

15. Now as I saw the living creatures, behold, one wheel on the earth beside the living creatures, for each of the four faces of it.

16. The appearance of the wheels and their work was like a beryl: and they four had one likeness; and their appearance and their work was as it were a wheel within a wheel.

17. When they went, they went in their four directions: they didn't turn when they went.

18. As for their rims, they were high and dreadful; and they four had their rims full of eyes round about.

19. When the living creatures went, the wheels went beside them; and when the living creatures were lifted up from the earth, the wheels were lifted up.

20. Wherever the spirit was to go, they went; there was the spirit to go: and the wheels were lifted up beside them; for the spirit of the living creature was in the wheels.

21. When those went, these went; and when those stood, these stood; and when those were lifted up from the earth, the

wheels were lifted up beside them: for the spirit of the living creature was in the wheels.

22. Over the head of the living creature there was the likeness of an expanse, like the awesome crystal to look on, stretched forth over their heads above.

23. Under the expanse were their wings straight, the one toward the other: everyone had two which covered on this side, and every one had two which covered on that side, their bodies.

24. When they went, I heard the noise of their wings like the noise of great waters, like the voice of the Almighty, a noise of tumult like the noise of a host: when they stood, they let down their wings.

25. There was a voice above the expanse that was over their heads: when they stood, they let down their wings.

26. Above the expanse that was over their heads was the likeness of a throne, as the appearance of a sapphire stone; and on the likeness of the throne was a likeness as the appearance of a man on it above.

27. I saw as it were glowing metal, as the appearance of fire within it round about, from the appearance of his loins and upward; and from the appearance of his loins and downward I saw as it were the appearance of fire, and there was brightness round about him.

28. As the appearance of the bow that is in the cloud in the day of rain, so was the appearance of the brightness round about. This was the appearance of the likeness of the glory of YHWH. When I saw it, I fell on my face, and I heard a voice of one that spoke.

> 1. He said to me, Son of man, stand on your feet, and I will speak with you.
> 2. The Spirit entered into me when he spoke to me, and set me on my feet; and I heard him who spoke to me.
> 3. He said to me, Son of man, I send you to the children of Israel, to nations that are rebellious, which have rebelled against me: they and their fathers have transgressed against me even to this very day.
> 4. The children are impudent and stiff-hearted: I do sent you to them; and you shall tell them, Thus says the Lord YHWH.
> 5. They, whether they will hear, or whether they will forbear, (for they are a rebellious house,) yet shall know that there has been a prophet among them.

This passage was clearly heavily edited by another hand because it mostly contains Ezekiel's own words in the first-person singular ("I"), but verse three refers to him by name and in the third-person singular ("him"). The hand of the editor can also be detected in the repetitions that occur in this passage.

It is no surprise that Ezekiel mentioned winged creatures in his vision because he must have seen many depictions of them in Babylonia. Ezekiel included four such creatures in his description. Although we are told that each one had images of a lion, a bull, an eagle, and a man on them, it is probable that he originally described four living creatures, each one different from the others, and that an editor misunderstood his words.

What Ezekiel saw, were constellations in the starry heaven, probably on 31 July 593 BC in Babylonia, according to the date he supplied. For him, the throne of God must have been situated at the northern astronomical pole – just as Isaiah, John of Patmos, and other ancient people thought.

Babylonian panels of Marduk (center) and other winged creatures

There seems to have been lightning flashes from a thunder storm beyond the horizon because Ezekiel could see the stars, while these flashes also lit up the sky from time to time.

Ezekiel saw four living creatures surrounding God's throne – a lion, a bull, an eagle, and a man. All four were not visible at the same time and only three appeared simultaneously. In the computerized reconstruction of the sky (below), the lion is absent. Ezekiel borrowed these four beings from the Sumerians. The throne of their chief deity, Anu, was surrounded by the following creatures:

- Leo, the Lion, with Regulus as its most prominent star, which was situated at the summer solstice in those days;
- Taurus, the Bull, whose biggest star is Aldebaran, which marked the spring equinox;
- Aquila, the Eagle, with Altair as its principal star, which ruled the winter solstice; and
- Boötes, the Ploughman or Farmer, with Arcturus as his brightest star, which was somewhat askew and did not quite mark the autumn equinox.[49]

---

[49] Cornelius, *Geistesgeschicht,* 13, 35–36; Visser, *De Openbaring,* 57–58.

Ezekiel also saw an "expanse" – the dome of the sky above him. There was a man on a throne, God who ordered him to deliver a message to his people who had rebelled against God.

King Hammurabi of Babylon standing before the winged god Marduk on his throne

Ezekiel described wheels attached to these creatures. In the case of Boötes, it was certainly the constellation of Corona Borealis, the Northern Crown. Taurus' wheel could easily have been the head of Cetus, the Sea Monster. Aquila's wheel may have been either Delphinus, the Dolphin, or Equuleus, the Foal. In the case of Leo, the Lion, the wheel was likely Crater, the Chalice, next to it.

According to Ezekiel, these creatures and their wheels either moved, or stayed stationary, according to what their spirits wanted to do. That was in accordance with the rotation of the stars around the northern celestial pole.

It glowed around God, demonstrating his glory – a description of the bright Milky Way stretching over the whole sky and the thunder flashes beyond the horizon. It must be clear that Ezekiel was deeply influenced by the Babylonian civilization where he lived and worked while being a captive.

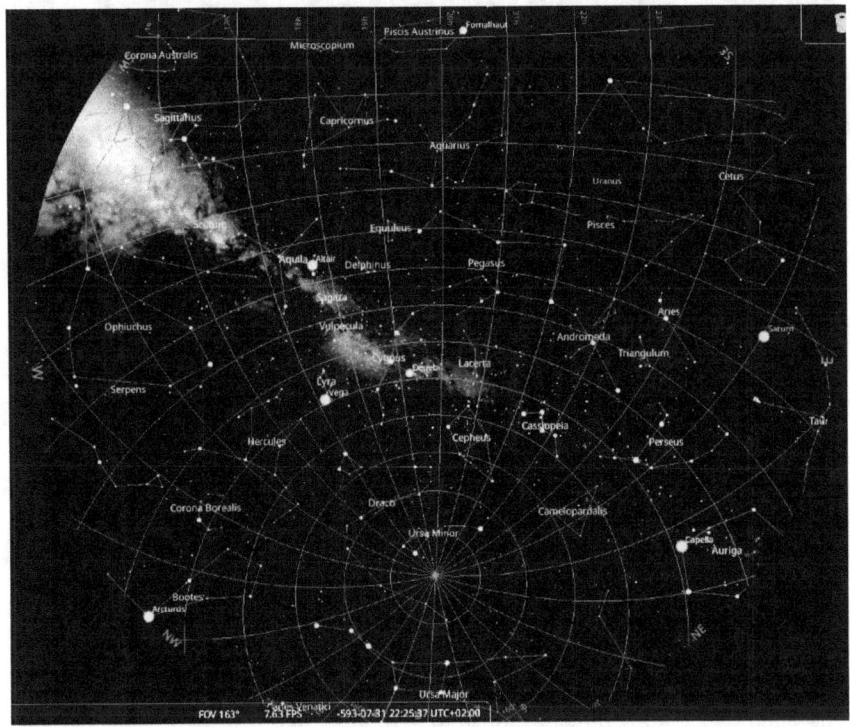

The sky above Babylonia on 31 July 593 BC, showing only the outlines of the constellations. The concentric circles show where the northern astronomical pole with the divine throne was situated. The constellation of Boötes, the Ploughman with its principal star Arcturus, is situated on the north-western horizon, while the constellation of Taurus, the Bull, can be seen rising on the eastern horizon. Aquila, the Eagle with Altair, its brightest star, is situated across the Milky Way.

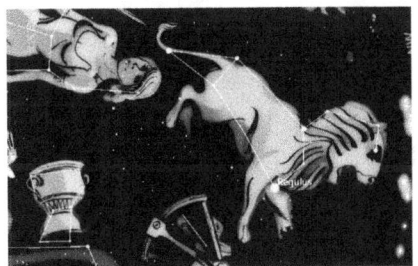

The constellations of Leo and Crater

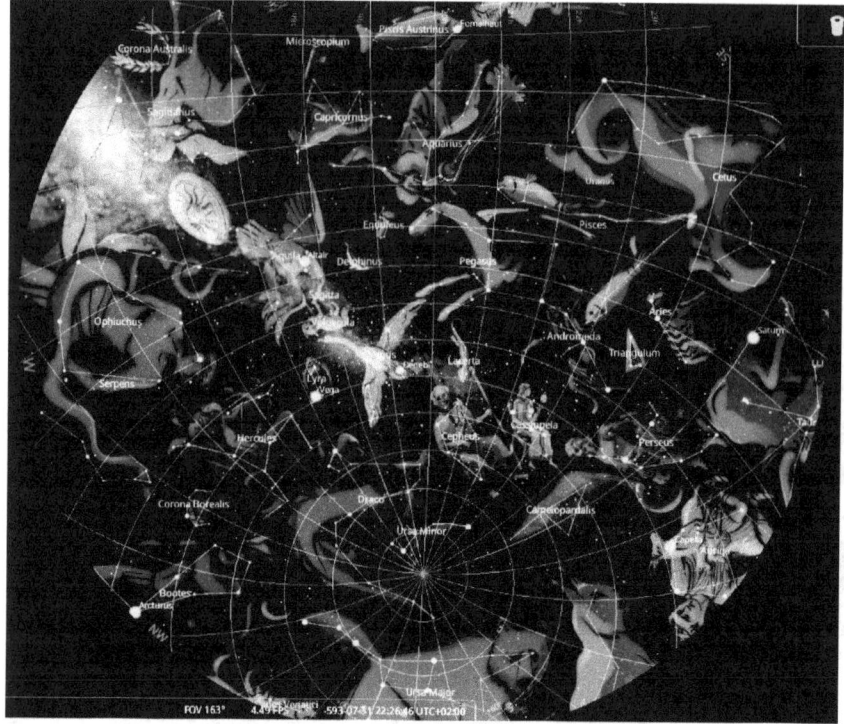

The same scene as the previous illustration, only with the pictures of the various constellations added

ZECHARIAH

The most prominent prophet after the end of the Babylonian Exile when Judea became a Persian province, Zecheriah (Hebrew: זְכַרְיָה – *Zekaryah*), whose name means "YHWH remembers," was the son of Berechiah, the son of Iddo (Zech 1:1). According to the genealogy in Nehemiah, he was born into the priestly line (Neh 12: 1–16).

He was active during the second to the fourth years of King Darius' reign – 520–518 BC (Zech 1: 1 & 7: 1). The book can be divided into two parts: Zech 1–8 and 9–14. The second part differs considerably in style and message from the first part and it was certainly written by an unknown prophet, probably a student or follower of Zechariah.

The first eight chapters contain eight nocturnal visions in which he drew inspiration from the starry skies, as will be explained in the next chapter. The last part warns of dangers from Greece (9: 13) – a reference to Alexander the Great's campaign of conquest. Alexander conquered Palestine during 332 BC and this part of Zechariah seems to date from a period directly before that.[50]

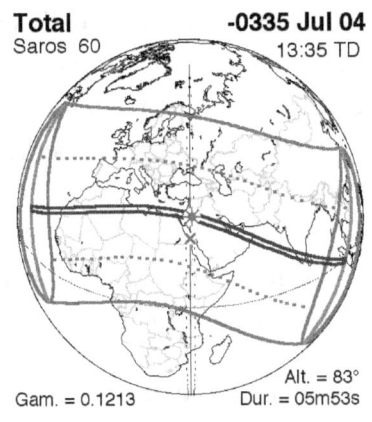

Reconstruction by NASA of the solar eclipse in July 335 BC

A solar eclipse is mentioned in *Zech 14: 6–7* –

> "It shall happen in that day, that there shall not be light; the bright ones shall withdraw themselves: but it shall be one day which is known to YHWH; not day, and not night; but it shall come to pass, that at evening time there shall be light."

Such an eclipse of almost 6 minutes' duration during the afternoon happened on 4 July 335 BC, three years before Alexander's conquest of Palestine.

ENOCH

The idea that Satan was an angel who rebelled against God and was driven from heaven, together with his followers and co-conspirators, does not occur in the Old Testament.[51] This view was found for the first time in the extrabiblical book of I Enoch.

---

[50] Boshoff et al, *Geskiedenis*, 194–97; Enc Brit, "Zechariah, Book of"; Barrett, "Zechariah".

[51] Denova, "The Origin of Satan".

This book purportedly contains the description of the visions and revelations received by the ancient patriarch Enoch. According to Gottheil and Littmann, this book was written to preserve legends and "Jewish folk-lore in the last pre-Christian centuries" about the patriarch Enoch, as well as ideas about the flood in Noah's time, angels, heaven, the netherworld, and hell.[52]

This book was regarded by some early Christians to be part of Holy Scripture. The biblical letter of Jude states the following:

> "To these also Enoch, the seventh from Adam, prophesied, saying, 'Behold, the Lord came with ten thousands of his holy ones, to execute judgment on all, and to convict all the ungodly of all their works of ungodliness which they have done in'" (Jud 1: 14–15).

This is a quotation from I Enoch 1: 9. Jude evidently thought that the book was written by the very ancient Enoch himself – and not by anonymous authors many centuries later.

John of Patmos, the author of Revelation, quoted repeatedly or referred to visions found in Enoch, without naming his source.[53]

No other documents in the New Testament seem to have quoted from Enoch directly, although more than one document made use of ideas found in Enoch. Around AD 300, the church fathers openly and finally rejected Enoch as part of Scripture.[54]

The only groups at present that regard Enoch as Holy Scripture are Ethiopian sects. The only surviving complete text is in Ethiopic, which was translated from Greek, which was, in turn, translated from the original Aramaic.[55] Our knowledge about Enoch,

---

[52] Gottheil and Littmann, "Enoch".
[53] Scholtz, *Revelation,* 27, 33, 47, 64, 67, 190, 281, 295.
[54] Gottheil and Littmann, "Enoch".
[55] Enc Brit, "Enoch".

therefore, depends upon a translation of a translation of a translation. This process of repeated translations could have caused the English translations to be less than accurate or uncertain in certain spots. This Ethiopic text was translated into English by Robert Charles.

Some Aramaic fragments of I Enoch were found in the caves at Qumran containing the Dead Sea Scrolls.[56]

We read the following about the patriarch Enoch in Genesis:

> "Enoch lived sixty-five years, and became the father of Methuselah. Enoch walked with God after he became the father of Methuselah three hundred years, and became the father of sons and daughters. all the days of Enoch were three hundred sixty-five years. Enoch walked with God, and he was not, for God took him" (Gen 5: 21–22).

Since Enoch was such a pious man who walked with God, the anonymous author(s) of the book of I Enoch argued that he must have been walking in heaven with God and the angels. This book is a description of these purported visions and experiences of Enoch, told in the first-person singular at times, but also written about Enoch in the third-person singular.

The book of Enoch consists of five distinct parts:

1. The Book of the Watchers (ch 1–36);
2. The Book of Parables (ch 37–71);
3. The Book of the Heavenly Luminaries (ch 72–82);
4. Two visions of Enoch regarding the Flood and the history of the world (ch 83–90); and
5. A speech by Enoch (ch 91–107).[57]

---

[56] Rylaarsdam, "Biblical Literature"; Wikipedia, "List of the Dead Sea Scrolls".
[57] Rylaarsdam, "Biblical Literature".

The Book of the Watchers or I Enoch, which deals with the fallen angels, can be dated to between 250 and 200 BC, during the Hellenistic period in Israel's history, after various Persian influences from earlier centuries had also been absorbed.[58]

The Book of the Watchers grapples with the question: where do evil, sin, iniquity, arrogance, pride, and violence come from? To answer this question, the author took as his starting point an enigmatic passage in Genesis 6:

> "It happened, when men began to multiply on the surface of the ground, and daughters were born to them, that God's sons saw that men's daughters were beautiful, and they took for themselves wives of all that they chose. YHWH said, 'My spirit will not strive with man forever, because he also is flesh; yet will his days be one hundred twenty years.' The Nephilim were in the earth in those days, and also after that, when God's sons came to men's daughters. They bore children to them: the same were the mighty men who were of old, men of renown" (Gen 6: 1–4).

The Hebrew word for *the Nephilim* (הַנְּפִילִים) is usually translated as "the giants". According to I Enoch, these giants were the offspring of fallen angels, who took human wives. God had to send the flood in Noah's time to drown these creatures, while the fallen angels, who became devils and demons, were banished to the netherworld, awaiting Judgment Day. All the crime, violence, and sin on earth are attributed to their evil influence upon mankind.

It is theorized that I Enoch had its origin amongst the sect of the Essenes of Qumran or its predecessors. After all, the only extant scraps of the original Aramaic text were found among the Dead Sea

---

[58] Denova, "The Origin of Satan".

Scrolls, the hidden and forgotten library of the Essenes. The stance of I Enoch regarding celibacy, the coming Messiah, and the fate of the soul after death seems to correspond with the known convictions of the Essenes.[59]

Another connection between the Essenes – or as they were later known, the Ebionites – and the Book of Enoch, is that only two documents in the New Testament associated with this sect, quoted from it as if it were Scripture, namely the Epistle of Jude and Revelation.[60] The Essenes of Qumran seem to have been unfamiliar with the other parts of Enoch because no fragments of these documents were found among the Dead Sea Scrolls.[61]

JOSEPH

Joseph, the father of Jesus of Nazareth, was not a fully-fledged prophet. We don't have any prophecies attributed to him and we are only told that he received messages from God about Jesus who was to be born. Joseph is sometimes presented as the adopted father of Jesus, since both the Gospels of Matthew and Luke insist that Mary, Jesus' mother, was still a *virgo intacta* when he was born (Matt 1: 22–25; Luke 1: 26–38).

Matthew wrote that a heavenly messenger appeared in a dream to Joseph, the betrothed of Mary, to tell him that his virgin bride was pregnant from the Holy Spirit and that he should not end the engagement. In this respect, one must ask: how did Matthew get this information about Joseph's dream? If Joseph told others of the dream, then we must also ask: is there any independent proof that he really had this dream? After all, dreams are always confined to one

---

[59] Rylaarsdam, "Biblical Literature".
[60] Pretorius, *Jesus of Nazareth*, 103–115; Scholtz, *Revelation*, 16.
[61] Ben-Daniel, "Enoch", 1.

person, the dreamer.

A passage from Isaiah was quoted to prove and explain this virgin birth of Jesus. Matthew often saw prophecies about the Messiah in the Old Testament and decided that something of that sort must have happened in the life of Jesus because it was forecast and, therefore, he invented episodes to fit those purported prophecies in the belief that they simply must have happened.[62]

The quotation from Isaiah regarding the virgin birth rests on a misunderstanding. Isaiah mentioned in chapter 7: 14 of his book that a certain unnamed young woman of his time – not a virgin – would become pregnant. The ancient Greek translation of the Old Testament, used by Matthew and Luke, made a mistake by altering "the young woman" or "maiden" (Hebrew: הָעַלְמָה – *'almah*) to "the virgin" (Greek: ἡ παρθένος – *he parthenos*). There is another Hebrew word for virgin, which was not used in this passage, namely בְּתוּלָה (*bethuwlah*). This passage in Isaiah can, therefore, not be seen as a prediction that Jesus would be born from a virgin.[63]

Joseph is often called Jesus' father in the gospels (Matt 1: 17; 13: 55; Luke 3: 23; 4: 22; John 1: 45; 6: 42). Orthodox scholars who regard the virgin birth as an article of faith usually explain those passages as referring to Joseph as Jesus' adopted father, although those texts do not allow such an interpretation.

Jesus is often called the "son of David" in the gospels (Matt 9: 27; Matt 12: 23; 15: 22; 21: 9; 22: 42–45; Mark 10: 47; 11:10; Luke 18: 38; Rom 1: 3). That could only have been the case if Joseph was his biological father (Luke 3: 23).

It may be added that the Ebionites, the Jewish followers of Jesus of which his brother, James, was the leader, denied the notion

---

[62] Pretorius, *The Gospels,* 389, 401, 403.
[63] Pretorius, *The Gospels,* 391–395, 457–460.

of a virgin birth. They declared that Jesus was the biological son of Joseph and Mary. It may be argued that the Ebionites were in a better position to know the truth than anybody else.[64]

The fact that Jesus became a popular teacher and that the crowds greeted him as their king when he entered Jerusalem on the back of an ass a few days before his execution, suggest that he could not have been born out of wedlock and that his parents must have been legally married before he had been born. After all, we read in *Deut 23: 2* –

> "One whose father and mother are not married may not come into the meeting of the Lord's people, or any of his family to the tenth generation."

If Jesus' parents were not married when he was born, as reported by the gospels, he would have been treated as a social outcast, a pariah. Instead, he was regarded as a charismatic preacher, an eminent teacher and prophet, and a gifted healer who drew large crowds.[65]

Joseph had more dreams – just as his namesake in the Old Testament. According to Matt 2: 13–15, Joseph dreamt that an angel warned him to take Mary and the baby Jesus to Egypt because the killing bands of King Herod were slaughtering all the boys below the age of two years in the vicinity of Bethlehem, where Jesus was born. It is a mystery how Matthew learnt of this dream. Dreams are, by definition, subjective, and only the person who was dreaming may know anything about it.

We must also ask: Why did Joseph not warn other parents of babies of the looming massacre? Why did the angel fail to warn other parents that their babies were in danger? Why did no other

---

[64] Pretorius, *The Gospels,* 74.
[65] Pretorius, *The Gospels,* 393–394; 399–401.

historian write about this outrageous campaign of slaughter?

There are no answers to these questions and we may safely classify Joseph's dreams as devout fiction.

WISE MEN FROM THE EAST

Matthew 2: 1–12 relates that Jesus was born in Bethlehem as the supposed fulfilment of a prophecy of the Old Testament (Mic 5: 2). His parents travelled there from Nazareth, their home town, purportedly to be counted in a census, although people were always counted at their place of residence for tax purposes in those days. It is, therefore, uncertain whether Jesus was really born in Bethlehem.

In any case, star gazers or astrologers from the east, probably Babylonia or Persia, are reported as having visited the baby Jesus in Bethlehem on account of a star they saw. This star gave them the message that a king was born in Judea and they wanted to pay homage to him. The logical place to look for this royal baby was in Jerusalem at the court of King Herod the Great.

Herod – as well the whole of Jerusalem – was ostensibly shocked by this news. Herod asked them to return to him after having visited the baby in Bethlehem where he was supposed to have been born, according to the prophecy, because he wanted to get rid of a possible rival. A heavenly messenger warned the wise men not to return to Jerusalem. In a very mysterious way, the star led them to the place where the baby Jesus was to be found.

There are so many supernatural and improbable elements to this story that most of it may easily be relegated to the realm of myths or legends. We must also ask: where did Matthew gather the information regarding the travels and experiences of these men from a far-away country? He certainly never interviewed them, nor found any people who knew them.

However, there is a possibility that a phenomenon in the sky could have held a message that a king was being born in Judea and many efforts were made to identify this astronomical or astrological event, including an appearance of the comet of Halley.

The three Magi from the East with their gifts for baby Jesus, together with the star they followed (Matt 2: 1). Their traditional names are written above their heads (Balthasar, Melchior, and Gaspar) and they were declared to be saints by the prefix "SCS" – the abbreviation for "Sanctus" (*Saint*) – before each of their names (mosaic from the church of S Apollinare Nuovo in Ravenna, Italy, 6th century).

The most likely explanation is a conjunction of the planets of Jupiter and Saturn on the border between the constellations of Pisces (the Fishes) and Cetus (the Sea Monster) on 23 September, 6 BC. Jupiter was regarded as the royal star, seen as Jupiter or Zeus, the king of the gods in Roman and Greek mythologies. Saturn was the star of specifically Israel. Saturday, the seventh day of the week and the Jewish Sabbath, was named after this seventh planet, Saturn. The constellations of Pisces and Cetus suggested the direction of the Mediterranean Sea to the west of Babylonia.[66] This occurrence may,

---

[66] Allen. *Star Names,* 337.

perhaps, have given some stargazers the message that a king was to be born in Judea.

The Gospel of Matthew doesn't name these wise men, but they were later given the legendary names of Balthasar, Melchior, and Gaspar and they were regarded as kings and saints.[67]

JOHN THE BAPTIST

Another Wild Prophet

Details about the life and work of John the Baptist are to be found in all four gospels of the New Testament, as well as in the writing of the Jewish historian, Flavius Josephus.

Jesus declared after his death that John the Baptist was a resurrected prophet Elijah (Matt 11: 13–14; 17: 12–13). There are indeed some similarities. Both lived in the wilderness – John along the Jordan, where he baptized people. He had a simple lifestyle, being clothed in a basic tunic and living off the land by eating locusts and wild honey. Both were critical of the leaders of their times and John did not hesitate to call the corrupt priests of the party of the Sadducees and the Pharisees "offspring of vipers", implying that they were the children of Satan.

His father, Zecheriah, was a priest and his mother, Elizabeth, was related to Mary, the mother of Jesus. The gospels portray him as a forerunner or herald of Jesus, the Messiah of Israel.

When he criticized Herod Antipas, the son of Herod the Great and ruler of Galilee, of being guilty of adultery by marrying the divorced wife of his half-brother, he was arrested and later decapitated.[68]

---

[67] Enc. Brit. "Magi".
[68] Strugnell, "John the Baptist".

The Essenes

The party or sect of the Essenes was a semi-ascetic group that practiced celibacy in some instances. In cases where their members did get married, they regarded these unions as unbreakable and divorce was forbidden. Several of them were priests who regarded the Jerusalem priesthood of the party of the Sadducees as corrupt and false due to their cooperation with the Roman overlords. Some of them may be described as Nazarites due to their sober and ascetic lifestyles and, according to their own literature, they followed the strict rules imposed upon Nazarites in Num 6. They had strong messianic expectations and awaited royal and priestly messiahs.[69]

Various researchers are of the opinion that John the Baptist had links with this sect, due to his lifestyle and message.[70]

The name "Essenes" (Greek: Ἐσσηνοί, Ἐσσαῖοι, or Ὀσσαῖοι – *Essenoi, Essaioi* or *Ossaioi*) does not occur in the New Testament and many scholars thought that the authors of the gospels simply ignored them and that our knowledge about them is only to be found in the writings of Flavius Josephus, Pliny the Elder, Philo of Alexandria, and other ancient authors.[71]

However, they do appear repeatedly under another name in the New Testament, namely that of the "Nazoreans" (Ναζωραῖοι – *Nazoraioi*).[72] Jesus was a member of this sect.

JESUS OF NAZARETH

Two Perspectives

We often read in the New Testament that Jesus of Nazareth, also

---

[69] Encyclopaedia Britannica, "Essenes"; Rylaarsdam et al., "Biblical Literature".
[70] Pixner, "Jerusalem's Essene Gateway"; Strugnell, "John the Baptist"; see also: Epiphanios, *Panarion,* Liber I, 19:1–6
[71] Duling, "The Jewish World"; Encyclopaedia Britannica, "Essenes".
[72] Pretorius, *Jesus of Nazareth,* 32–33.

known as Jesus the Christ or Messiah, was regarded as a great prophet (Matt 21: 11; Luke 7: 16; 9: 19; 24: 19; John 4: 19; 7: 40; 9: 17; Acts 3: 22; 7: 37; *etcetera*). Of course, a book such as this cannot ignore him.

Jesus may be viewed from two perspectives:

- He may be seen as the Jesus Christ of faith and dogma, who is regarded as the divine Son of God, the second person in the divine Trinity, consisting of a single God, but differentiated into three persons, namely God the Father, God the Son, and God the Holy Spirit. According to mainstream Christianity, he was deemed to have had a dual nature: a divine nature and a human nature, combined in one person. He is also regarded as the savior of sinful mankind.
- Jesus of Nazareth may also be viewed from a purely historical perspective. The sources containing information about his life, deeds, words, execution, and resurrection may be scrutinized critically to construct a historically credible image of him.

This book is written from the second viewpoint mentioned above.

The oldest sources about Jesus, the Q Document, as well as the narrative parts of the Gospel of John, portray Jesus purely as a human being, albeit a very gifted one. The Q Document ignores his execution, while John hints that he did not really die when he was executed on the cross by the Roman authorities, but was nursed back to relative health by his friends (John 19: 38–40).[73]

It was the apostle Paul, who never knew Jesus person-ally and had never read any gospels, who concluded that Jesus was more than just a human being, but the divine Son of God, who was raised with a spiritual body from his grave after his crucifixion and

---

[73] Pretorius, *The Gospels, 87,* 240–41.

ascended into heaven to be with his Father. He based this conviction on a series of visions and revelations he claimed he had received (*vide infra*).

Historical Perspective

The later parts of the gospels, written after the seventies of the first century AD, at least four decades after Jesus' time, repeated Paul's view that Jesus was a divine personage in human form and that he must be regarded as the redeemer of sinners.

One of the most important facts about Jesus' life that is mostly overlooked is that he was a member of the Essene or Nazorean sect. He is often called a Nazorean in the gospels, although translations of the gospels almost always misunderstood this term and confused it with the term "Nazarene" – an inhabitant of the village of Nazareth (Matt 2: 23; 26:71; Luke 18: 37, John 18: 5, 7; 19: 19; Acts 2: 22; 3: 6; 4: 10; 6: 14; 22: 8; and 26: 9). This point is being argued at length in Chapter 5 of this book.

The 17th-cent painting *Christ Crucified* by Diego Velazquez

The King of Israel

To understand the life and message of Jesus of Nazareth, it is necessary to consider that he saw himself in the first place as the Messiah, the legitimate king of Israel. Many Jews of his time agreed with this idea.[74] His teachings, as preserved in the oldest parts of the gospels, must be interpreted against this background. The following facts support this supposition:

- Jesus often called himself the "Son of God" and he called God his "Father" (Matt 6: 9; 11: 27; 16: 27–28; 23: 9; 27: 54; John 3: 35; 5: 21; 6: 46; 8: 18; 8: 42 *etcetera*). The title "Son of God" was used in the Old Testament for the kings from the House of David (2 Sam 7: 14; 1 Chr 17: 13; 1 Chr 22: 10; 1 Chr 28: 6; Ps 2: 6–7, 12; Ps 89: 26–28) and Jesus claimed this title since he was a descendant of King David (Matt 1: 1–17; 21: 9; Luke 3: 23 – 38).
- In John 1: 49–51, the titles "Son of God" and "king of Israel" were used as synonyms and applied to Jesus.
- Jesus' favorite topic in his sermons and parables was the kingdom of God or of Heaven. The conventional explanation is that he meant the heavenly kingdom of God, which his faithful followers would enter in the afterlife. That is, however, certainly not what he meant, since he often assured his audiences that this kingdom would be established very soon, during their lifetimes and before they died (Matt 16: 27–28; 24: 34; 26: 29, 64; Mark 9: 1; 13: 20; Luke 9: 27; 21: 32).
- He taught his disciples to pray: "May your kingdom come. May your will be done, as in heaven, so on earth" (Matt 6: 10). They had, therefore, to pray for the coming of God's kingdom on earth – with Jesus on the throne as David's successor.
- His disciples and even some Pharisees had the expectation that he would restore the Israelite kingdom in the immediate future (Matt 20: 21; Luke 17: 20; 19: 11; Acts 1: 6).

---

[74] Jacobs & Buttenwieser, "Messiah".

- There were people who wanted to "take him by force, to make him king" (John 6: 15).
- He told his disciples, "Most assuredly I tell you, that you who have followed me, in the regeneration when the Son of Man will sit on the throne of his glory, you also will sit on twelve thrones, judging the twelve tribes of Israel" (Matt 19: 28). In other words, they would be judges of Israel and his councilors.
- We read in Matt 25: 31 that he told his disciples: "But when the Son of Man comes in his glory, and all the holy angels with him, then will he sit on the throne of his glory" (see also Matt 16: 27). John 1: 51 reported: "He said to him, 'Most assuredly, I tell you [Nathaniel], hereafter you will see heaven opened, and the angels of God ascending and descending on the Son of Man.'" He expected an army of aggressive angels from heaven to aid him in getting rid of the Roman yoke and re-establish the Israelite monarchy.
- When Jesus entered Jerusalem on the back of a donkey a few days before his crucifixion, he was hailed by the enthusiastic crowd as the Son of David and the king of Israel. He did not contradict them, even when some Pharisees demanded that he silence them. He actually staged this event to fit a prophecy from the Old Testament (Matt 21: 1–11, 15; Mark 11: 1–11; Luke 19: 29–44; John 12: 12–19).
- When he was tried after his arrest by the Roman governor, Pontius Pilate, he confirmed that he was indeed the king of the Jews (Matt 27: 11; Mark 15: 2; Luke 23: 3; and John 18: 33).
- He was sentenced to death precisely because he proclaimed himself king of the Jews without the consent of the emperor in Rome, which warranted the death penalty by crucifixion.
- A notice describing his crime in three languages was placed on the cross: "JESUS THE NAZOREAN, KING OF THE JEWS" (John

19: 19; see also Matt 27: 37; Mark 15: 26; and Luke 23: 38).

Jesus also saw himself as a religious reformer who wanted to lead his people back to the God of their fathers. He was a popular preacher and prophet and many of his sayings, stories, and sermons were recorded in the Gospels.

PAUL OF TARSUS

Biographical Details

The most influential person mentioned in the New Testament, after Jesus of Nazareth, was certainly the Apostle Paul. He was initially known as Saul of Tarsus. His home town was a major Greek city in Asia Minor and a Roman colony, which automatically made him a Roman citizen. He grew up in a Jewish home and belonged to the tribe of Benjamin (Phil 3: 5).

As a youngster, he must have been exposed to the intellectual and mythological heritage of Greece. He was probably familiar with some of the thoughts of the Greek philosopher Aristotle. He also quoted the Stoic philosopher Cleanthes (Κλεάνθης; c 330 BC – c 230 BC), in Tit 1: 12 – "One of them, a prophet of their own, said, 'Cretans are always liars, evil beasts, and idle gluttons.'"

He became known under his Latin name, Paulus (Greek: Παῦλος – *Paulos*). This name, which sounds rather like his Jewish name of Saul, may have been a nickname. "Paulus" in Latin means "small" and that may, perhaps, be an indication that he was not a tall man. When reading about his travels in the book of Acts, as well as his letters, one gets the impression of an energetic, resolute, and strong personality who wrote in good Greek.

According to Acts 22: 3, he sat as a student "at the feet of Gamaliel", a leader and teacher of the party of the Pharisees. His studies made him familiar with the contents of the Hebrew

Scriptures and he often quoted from them in his letters. He was initially also a Pharisee and in his zeal for the Jewish faith, he persecuted the followers of Jesus, who regarded the Pharisees of Jerusalem as frauds and hypocrites.

As a student in Jerusalem, he must have heard stories about Jesus who had been crucified by the Romans. He believed, as most Jews, that Jesus had died a cruel death from his wounds on the cross.

Christian Missionary and Author

Paul's conversion and work as a Christian missionary are described in the second part of the book of Acts, although some of the details differ from the particulars he gave in his own letters.

Paul was a productive writer and copies of some of his letters were collected after his death. His letters form a substantial part of the New Testament and they were probably written in the following order during the fifties and early sixties of the first century AD:

- 1 Thessalonians;
- 1 Corinthians;
- 2 Corinthians;
- Galatians;
- Philippians; and
- Romans

The following letters are regarded as "Deutero-Pauline" – probably written by Paul's followers on his behalf, namely Ephesians, Colossians, and 2 Thessalonians. The so-called pastoral epistles, 1 and 2 Timothy and Titus, are "Trito-Pauline" and were probably also written by members of the Pauline school according to his directives, or a generation after his death.[75]

---

[75] Sanders, "Paul, the Apostle, Saint."

Paul returned to Jerusalem with the money he had raised for the poor followers of Jesus in Jerusalem. There he was arrested and after a series of trials he was sent to Rome. In Chapter 5 of the First Letter of Clement, the bishop of Rome during the nineties of the first century AD, it is told that he and Peter died a martyr's death in Rome during the reign of Emperor Nero.[76]

The Apostle Paul (ceiling mosaic, Archiepiscopal Palace, Ravenna, Italy)

Visions and Revelations

Paul held views that differed substantially from those of the apostles of Jesus in Jerusalem and that led to debates and even clashes. Paul taught that Christians, the followers of Jesus Christ, were freed from the obligation to live according to the Law of Moses because Christ, the eternal and divine Son of God, fulfilled all those obligations on their behalf (Acts 15; 21: 19–30; Gal 1: 22–2: 21, *etcetera*).

This stance was in contrast with the views of Jesus who taught that his followers had to live according to the La of Moses, which Law may not be changed in any way. According to him, the only way to gain eternal life was to obey the Law (Matt 5: 18–19; 19: 17; 22: 36–40; 28: 20; Luke 10: 25–28).

Paul claimed that he had received visions and revelations in which Jesus Christ appeared to him, although there were no independent witnesses to corroborate or confirm these visions and revelations (Gal 1: 11–19; 1 Cor 2: 10; 11: 23; 15: 1–9; 2 Cor 12: 1–5; Eph 3: 3; Col 1: 26–27).

---

[76] 1 Clement, ch 5

Paul's writings were already accepted as "Scriptures" and authoritative at an early date because 2 Pet 3: 15–16 states:

> "Regard the patience of our Lord as salvation; even as our beloved brother Paul also, according to the wisdom given to him, wrote to you; as also in all of his letters, speaking in them of these things. In those are some things hard to be understood, which the ignorant and unsettled twist, as they do also to the *other Scriptures*, to their own destruction" (*emphasis added*).

The word used for "Scripture" is γραφή *(graphe)* – which means "a writing, Scripture, or a biblical book". This word is applied elsewhere in the New Testament to the Hebrew Scriptures.

Paul never met Jesus when he was alive and his knowledge of the life and message of Jesus was second-hand or even third-hand, obtained from the apostles in Jerusalem and other eye-witnesses or people who got their information from them (Acts 9: 26 and 15: 2; Gal 1: 17) – apart from his own subjective and private visions and revelations. The completed gospels were only published after his death and he never read them.

JOHN OF PATMOS

The Author of Revelation
The author of the book Revelation called himself John (Greek: Ἰωάννης – *Ioannes*; Rev 1: 1, 4 & 9; 22: 8). John the Baptist and one of Jesus' apostles also had this name and it was a common name in Palestine in those days. The Hebrew name of *John* is יְהוֹחָנָן or יוֹחָנָן (*Yehochanan* or *Yochanan*) meaning "YHWH is gracious" (2 Chr 17: 17, 2 Chr 23: 1, Neh 12: 22 & 23 and Jer 42: 8).

Certain early Christian authors identified the author of Revelation with the apostle of Jesus with the same name and the author of the Gospel of John and the three epistles of John. Others, however, disputed this.

The tomb of John of Patmos inside the ruins of the ancient basilica of St John the Theologian at Ephesus

The first Christian church historian, Eusebius of Caesarea, who lived in the fourth century AD, states that – according to some earlier authors – John the apostle was the author of Revelation, that he was the leader of the churches in Asia Minor, that he was banished to the island of Patmos for being a witness for Jesus Christ during the reign of Emperor Domitian, that he was released after the death of Domitian and that he died and was buried in Ephesus.[77]

Although one can agree with most of what Eusebius reported, it cannot be confirmed that the author of Revelation and the apostle of Jesus were the same person. This confusion arises

---

[77] Eusebius, *Hist Eccl,* Liber III/XVIII/1–5; XX/10–11; & XXIII/5; Liber V/XXIV/3

from the fact that there is evidence that the apostle John moved to Ephesus with Mary, Jesus' mother, and that he and the author of Revelation, who also lived in Ephesus, were as a result confused with each other and thought to be the same man.[78]

Eusebius adds that, according to Papias, who knew some of the apostles personally, the author of Revelation was known as John the "presbyter" to distinguish him from the apostle. Elsewhere, Eusebius wrote that –

> "There were two persons in Asia that bore the same name [of John], and that there were two tombs in Ephesus, each of which, even to the present day, is called John's. It is important to notice this. For it is probable that it was the second, if one is not willing to admit that it was the first that saw the Revelation, which is ascribed by name to John." [79]

The identification of John of Patmos with the apostle and author of the Gospel and the epistles of John cannot be maintained for various other reasons:

- The style of writing and message of the Apocalypse differs markedly from that in the Gospel and Epistles of John. The Book of Revelation contains many grammatical errors, while the other Johannine writings are written in an elegant Greek.[80]
- The author of Revelation gave no indication that he knew Jesus personally – as could be expected from one of Jesus' apostles.
- John never calls himself an apostle, although he mentions the apostles more than once.

---

[78] Chadwick, "John the Apostle".
[79] Eusebius, *Hist Eccl*, Liber III/XXXXIX/6
[80] Barclay, Revelation, 14.

The only possible conclusion must be that the author of Revelation cannot be the apostle of Jesus or the author of the Gospel. Biblical scholars tend to call him John of Patmos to distinguish him from the apostle. He was most likely a second-generation Christian, young enough during the nineties of the first century AD to be a leader in the church and to survive the hardships of captivity and exile.

Released from Exile

Eusebius also reports that after Emperor Domitian had been assassinated on 18 September AD 96, he was succeeded by the elderly Nerva who ruled for only two years. His chief advisor was also his successor, Trajan. Trajan is remembered for his tolerant attitude towards Christians, as is evidenced by a letter of around AD 112 to his friend Pliny the Younger, governor of Bithynia et Pontus (nowadays in Northern Turkey) in which he advised him not to start any witch hunts against Christians. It is probably due to Trajan's influence during Nerva's reign that the Senate resolved that political and religious exiles, such as the prophet John, were pardoned and allowed to return home.[81]

John regarded himself as a prophet (Rev 22:9) and his book is called a prophecy (Rev 1: 3; 19:10; 22: 7, 10 & 18–19). He frequently remarked that God, Christ, or an angel commanded him to write down what he saw and heard (Rev 1: 19; 2: 1; 14: 13; 19: 9; 21: 5). What he wrote was under the guidance of the Spirit (Rev 1: 10; 4: 2; 17: 3 & 21: 10). From all this, one may conclude that John meant his book to be regarded as Holy Scripture, in the same tradition as the prophetic books of the Old Testament.

John often referred to Jesus Christ, but he nowhere quoted from the gospels what Jesus said and did while alive. It must be noted that John also gave no indication that he knew the epistles of

---

[81] Eusebius, *Hist Eccl,* Liber III/XX/10 & XXXIII/1–4; Hammond, "Trajan".

Paul, the gospels, or any other writings of the New Testament. It is generally accepted that Paul's letters were written during the fifties and early sixties of the first century AD and that the completed gospels appeared during the seventies and eighties of that century. These writings must have been in circulation for quite a while, although John – inexplicably – does not seem to be familiar with them.

John must, surely, have been familiar with the work and writings of Paul. After all, he ministered to the churches in and around Ephesus where Paul also worked (Acts 18: 19–21; 19: 11–29; 20: 17; 1 Tim 1: 3). He simply must have known at least of the epistle of Paul to the church in Ephesus. He agreed with Paul that Jesus Christ is the Son of God, was resurrected from the grave and taken up into heaven. Yet, in the whole book of Revelation there is not a single reference to anything Paul did, said, or wrote.

The only explanation for this somewhat strange state of affairs is that John saw his book as one of a sort – a prophetic book and not a response to problems posed by the churches as found in Paul's letters or a record of the memories of Jesus' life and ministry as found in the gospels. He focused on his own time and the imminent second coming of Christ on Judgment Day.

It is likely that John made preliminary notes of his visions and that he edited those after his release from exile before delivering his book to the seven churches in Asia. That he was no longer an exiled prisoner when he edited his book is apparent from Rev 1: 9 – "I John, ... was [past tense] on the isle that is called Patmos ...."

Natural Phenomena

In the discussion of some of John's visions it will be shown that he 1did not have extra-sensory experiences in which Christ or angels appeared to him as is often assumed, but that he, in fact, described what he saw in the sky with its stars, astrological constellations, and planets – just as Isajah, Ezekiel, Zechariah, and Daniel – as well as other natural phenomena, such as thunder storms, earthquakes, a volcanic outburst, and a locust plague.

Although John's visions were not shared with anybody else, his descriptions are generally convincing, except for the voices he heard. Scholtz has recreated his visions of the stars, planets, and constellations with the help of an astronomical computer program and it seems that he described accurately what was to be seen in the night sky on certain dates during AD 96.[82]

THE CASTING OF LOTS

The casting of lots was a method mentioned in the Bible to determine the will of God. Proverbs 16: 33 declares in this regard: "The lot is cast into the lap, but its every decision is from YHWH."

According to Lev 16: 8, the lot had to be cast to discover which one of two goats had to be sacrificed on the Day of Atonement. The land of Canaan was distributed between the Israelite tribes by casting the lot (Josh 18: 10). After the death of Judas Iscariot, the apostles chose Matthias as his replacement by casting of the lot (Acts 1: 26).

Exodus 28: 6–16, 39: 2–9 and 1 Sam 14: 41 contain instructions for the manufacture and use of an ephod by the Israelite high priest, a breast plate or apron containing the so-called Urim and Thummim, consisting of gem stones, which may have been used to determine innocence or guilt where the factual evidence was not clear enough. The Ephod also contained twelve gem stones with the names of the twelve tribes of Israel and these were somehow used to find the will of God, although it is unclear exactly what had to be done to achieve this goal. It does seem, though, that the use of the ephod made use of the casting of the lot to find God's guidance.

---

[82] Scholtz, *The Prophecies of Revelation*.

The Jewish Encyclopedia explains the Urim and Thummim as "objects connected with the breastplate of the high priest, and used as a kind of divine oracle. Since the days of the Alexandrian translators of the Old Testament it has been asserted that תֻּמִּים אוּרִים mean 'revelation and truth' (δήλωσις καὶ ἀλήθεια), or 'lights and perfections' (φωτισμοὶ καὶ τελεότητες)."[83]

The Jews and Christians were not the only people applying the lot. We read that the prophet Jonah was identified by the lot as the reason why the ship on which he fled was almost wrecked by a storm. He was, therefore, sacrificed by being dumped into the water and the storm blew over (Jonah 1, especially verse 7).

It is difficult to see how the casting of the lot and the use of the ephod is supposed to differ from gambling. Isaiah 65: 11–12 contains this judgment against gamblers:

> "But you who forsake YHWH, who forget my holy mountain, who prepare a table for Fortune, and who fill up mingled wine to Destiny; I will destine you to the sword, and you shall all bow down to the slaughter."

The word used for "Destiny" is גַּד (*gad*), which was used for the goddess of luck. The Hebrew for "Fortune" is מְנִי (*menyi*), which may also mean "Fate", the name of a Babylonian goddess of fortune or fate. Gambling, which depends on pure luck and which is driven by the love for money and greed (Luke 12: 15; Heb 13: 5) is clearly condemned by Isaiah.

The casting of the lot, seen objectively, is also dependent upon pure luck or chance, although it is believed that it reflects the wishes of God. If that is the case, then gambling must also be under the control of God. There can, therefore, be no fundamental

---

[83] Hirsch *et al.*, "Urim and Thumim".

distinction between the casting of the lot (which is allowed) and gambling (which is condemned). This does not make sense and one may verily wonder whether the casting of lots, as practiced in the Bible, really revealed God's will.

MUHAMMAD

Calling as a Prophet

The founder of the religion of Islam, the prophet Muhammad (AD 570–632), left an indelible mark on the world's history because his followers, the Muslims, form the second largest religious group in the world, second only to Christianity.

Muhammad lost his father before he was born and his mother died when he was six years old. Family members then took care of the orphan. He could allegedly trace his ancestry back to the biblical patriarchs Ishmael and Abraham. He married a wealthy woman, 15 years his senior, and she bore him two sons (who died young) and four daughters.

He was a religious man who initially adhered to the traditional pagan religion of the Arabs. He often retreated to the desert for prayer and meditation. When he was 40, he had his first vision of the Archangel Gabriel who commanded him to "recite". Muhammad was initially reluctant to recite anything, but then the first verses of the Qur'an started to flow from his lips.

A bewildered Muhammad told his wife about this experience and she called upon a cousin, a Christian, to guide her husband through this spiritual experience. He regarded this episode as his calling to become Gods messenger. For the next 23 years, Muhammad received many more revelations and visions when the archangel appeared to him or when God spoke directly to him.

He recited his revelations to his family members and friends who learnt them by heart because none of them could read or write.

These revelations were later written down and became the Qur'an. More and more people followed him and accepted him as a prophet.

Muhammad often had contact with Jews and Christians during his travels as a merchant, whom he described as the "People of the Book" (the Bible). There were Jewish and Christian communities in Arabia and Syria from whom Muhammad heard stories from the Bible, which convinced him that there is only one God, called Allah in Arabian.

After the death of his first wife, he married other women, including a slave girl Mary, who was a Christian. The Christians with whom he had contact were mostly Nestorians and Monophysites who held heretical views about the relationship between Jesus' divine and his human natures.

It is also possible that some of these Christians still regarded themselves, even after six centuries, as Nazoreans, the sect to which Jesus also belonged and from which he drew most of his Jewish supporters. The Arab word for Christianity was "Nasraniyah", which seems to be related to or derived from "Nazorean".[84]

There is evidence that Muhammad visited the monastery of Saint Catherine in the Sinai Peninsula and guaranteed its security.[85] It is reasonable to suppose that he also heard some stories from the Bible from the monks in this monastery.

The Qur'an

The revelations of Muhammad were collected after his death into a single document, called the Qur'an. It is the holy book of Islam and it is regarded as the Word of God, dictated by the archangel Gabriel or God himself to Muhammed and, therefore, perfect and without

---

[84] Armstrong. *Muhammad;* Hughes. "Christianity"; Hughes. "Jesus Christ"; Nasr. "Muhammad"; Tisdall. *The Original Sources of the Qur'an,* Chapter IV.
[85] Anon., " Mohammed and the Holy Monastery of Sinai".

any flaw or mistake.

The Qur'an only got its final form several decades after the death of Muhammad. There were several versions, which were suppressed in favor of the final one we have today. It is much shorter than the New Testament and contains 114 chapters or surahs of unequal length. They are arranged haphazardly with no rational order or sequence.[86]

It is only possible to understand the Qur'an adequately with a knowledge of the Bible since this sacred text repeatedly mentions characters from the Bible and their deeds and words. One encounters, for instance, Adam, Abraham, Jacob, Moses, Aaron, David, Solomon, Mary, and especially Jesus. Muhammad did not always understand or remember the stories from the Bible told to him correctly and he made mistakes in this regard. For instance, he confused Jesus' mother Mary with Aaron and Moses' sister, Miriam (Surahs 3: 35–36 and 19: 28).

Although Muslims accept the Qur'an as God's revelation to Muhammad, we only have his word that the Archangel Gabriel or God ever spoke to him – just as there are usually no independent witnesses of the encounters other prophets had with God. Although he seems to have been convinced of the validity of these revelations, these experiences could easily have been hallucinations or the result of Muhammad's own reflections.

CONCLUSION

After this discussion of all the important biblical prophets, as well as Muhammad, it transpired that most or all of them were convinced that they were called by God. However, these events were essentially private, subjective, and unobserved by reliable witnesses. As has been shown, the historical reliability and accuracy of the

---

[86] Jones. *The Koran;* Schimmel. "Islam".

stories of most prophets are subject to skepticism and doubt.

The stories of the prophets were only recorded after their deaths, often centuries later. This makes it difficult to distinguish between fact and legend or fiction.

It is necessary to investigate the most important or typical prophecies, promises, and predictions found in the Scriptures. The following questions must be asked:

- What prompted these prophecies?
- Were they ever fulfilled?

CHAPTER 3
OLD TESTAMENT PROPHECIES REGARDING CURRENT AFFAIRS

There are so many prophecies in the Hebrew Scriptures that it will be an impossible task to pay attention to all of them. The most important of those dealing with the current affairs of their times will be discussed here and summaries of others will be provided.

TEXTS DEALING WITH THE PATRIARCHS

The Fate of Mankind

According to *Gen 2: 17*, God promised the first pair of humans:

> Of every tree of the garden you may freely eat: but of the tree of the knowledge of good and evil, you shall not eat of it: for in the day that you eat of it you will surely die.

This was an empty threat, because they did not fall dead when they ate the fruit from that forbidden tree.

Genesis 3: 14–19

> 14. YHWH God said to the serpent, "Because you have done this, cursed are you above all cattle, and above every animal of the field. On your belly shall you go, and you shall eat dust all the days of your life.

> 15. I will put enmity between you and the woman, and between your offspring and her offspring. He will bruise your head, and you will bruise his heel."
> 16. To the woman he said, "I will greatly multiply your pain in childbirth. In pain you will bring forth children. Your desire will be for your husband, and he will rule over you."
> 17. To Adam he said, "Because you have listened to your wife's voice, and have eaten of the tree, of which I commanded you, saying, `You shall not eat of it,` cursed is the ground for your sake. In toil you will eat of it all the days of your life.
> 18. Thorns also and thistles will it bring forth to you; and you will eat the herb of the field.
> 19. By the sweat of your face will you eat bread until you return to the ground, for out of it you were taken. For you are dust, and to dust you shall return."

These words may be regarded as the earliest prophecy in the Bible, although they were only written centuries after the event. The story of man's fall may safely be regarded as a myth, not as a historical event. It was told to explain where sin and evil came from, together with the hostility between humans and snakes, the painful process of childbirth, and man's need to work hard to earn a living.

The traditional explanation of the snake is that it was Satan in disguise who tempted the woman and her husband to eat from the forbidden fruit. That is how Rev 12: 9 sees it, where Satan is called "the old serpent". However, at the time when this chapter in Genesis was written, the concept of the devil has not yet entered the Hebrew Scriptures – it was only introduced during the third and second centuries BC and it was copied from the Persian religion where a similar figure, Ahriman, was seen as the adversary of the chief deity,

Ahura-Mazda and the originator of evil, untruth, and darkness.[87]

Joseph's Dreams
Gen 37: 3–10

3.	Now Israel loved Joseph more than all his children, because he was the son of his old age, and he made him a coat of many colors.
4.	His brothers saw that their father loved him more than all his brothers, and they hated him, and couldn't speak peaceably to him.
5.	Joseph dreamed a dream, and he told it to his brothers, and they hated him all the more.
6.	He said to them, "Please hear this dream which I have dreamed:
7.	for, behold, we were binding sheaves in the field, and behold, my sheaf arose and also stood upright; and behold, your sheaves came around, and bowed down to my sheaf."
8.	His brothers said to him, "Will you indeed reign over us? Or will you indeed have dominion over us?" They hated him all the more for his dreams and for his words.
9.	He dreamed yet another dream, and told it to his brothers, and said, "Behold, I have dreamed yet another dream: and behold, the sun and the moon and eleven stars bowed down to me."
10.	He told it to his father and to his brothers. His father rebuked him, and said to him, "What is this dream that you have dreamed? Will I and your mother and your brothers indeed come to bow ourselves down to you to the earth?"

---

[87] Pretorius, *To Hell with the Devil*, 132–50.

This report is part of the J Document, which was written during the time of the united monarchy of Israel – several centuries after the episode. There is every reason to believe that the story got distorted and twisted through the centuries. It is quite possible that Joseph had certain dreams, which he mentioned to his family. However, this story was written to prepare the reader for the fact that Joseph became the viceroy of Egypt at a later stage when his brothers had to bow before him, although they initially didn't recognize him as their younger brother whom they had sold into slavery.

It is not clear from this story whether Joseph's dreams could have been the result of divine revelations, although they certainly do boil down to prophetic dreams.

Joseph Interprets Pharaoh's Dreams

The story of how Joseph, who was sold as a slave by his brothers and was a convict at that stage, was taken out of prison to interpret the dreams of Pharaoh, is well known. The core of this story is quoted below:

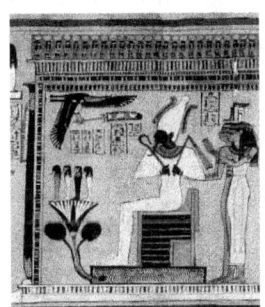

Gen 41: 14 – 37

14.	Then Pharaoh sent and called Joseph, and they brought him hastily out of the dungeon. He shaved himself, changed his clothing, and came in to Pharaoh.
15.	Pharaoh said to Joseph, "I have dreamed a dream, and there is no one who can interpret it. I have heard it said of you, that when you hear a dream you can interpret it."

16. Joseph answered Pharaoh, saying, "It isn't in me: God will give Pharaoh an answer of peace."
17. Pharaoh spoke to Joseph, "In my dream, behold, I stood on the brink of the river:
18. and, behold, there came up out of the river seven cattle, fat-fleshed and well-favored. They fed in the reed-grass,
19. and, behold, seven other cattle came up after them, poor and very ill-favored and lean-fleshed, such as I never saw in all the land of Egypt for badness.
20. The lean and ill-favored cattle ate up the first seven fat cattle,
21. and when they had eaten them up, it couldn't be known that they had eaten them, but they were still ill-favored, as at the beginning. So I awoke.
22. I saw in my dream, and, behold, seven ears came up on one stalk, full and good:
23. and, behold, seven ears, withered, thin, and blasted with the east wind, sprung up after them.
24. The thin ears swallowed up the seven good ears. I told it to the magicians; but there was no one who could explain it to me."
25. Joseph said to Pharaoh, "The dream of Pharaoh is one. What God is about to do he has declared to Pharaoh.
26. The seven good cattle are seven years; and the seven good ears are seven years. The dream is one.
27. The seven lean and ill-favored cattle that came up after them are seven years, and also the seven empty ears blasted with the east wind; they will be seven years of famine.
28. That is the thing which I spoke to Pharaoh. What God is about to do he has showed to Pharaoh.

> 29. Behold, there come seven years of great plenty throughout all the land of Egypt.
> 30. There will arise after them seven years of famine, and all the plenty will be forgotten in the land of Egypt. The famine will consume the land,
> 31. and the plenty will not be known in the land by reason of that famine which follows; for it will be very grievous.
> 32. The dream was doubled to Pharaoh, because the thing is established by God, and God will shortly bring it to pass.
> 33. Now therefore let Pharaoh look for a discreet and wise man, and set him over the land of Egypt.
> 34. Let Pharaoh do this, and let him appoint overseers over the land, and take up the fifth part of the land of Egypt's produce in the seven plenteous years.
> 35. Let them gather all the food of these good years that come, and lay up grain under the hand of Pharaoh for food in the cities, and let them keep it.
> 36. The food will be for a store to the land against the seven years of famine, which will be in the land of Egypt; that the land not perish through the famine."
> 37. The thing was good in the eyes of Pharaoh, and in the eyes of all his servants.

According to Joseph, the dreams of Pharaoh were given to him by God to warn him of a future famine. Joseph gave him the advice to appoint somebody to supervise the gathering of the surplus harvests during the good years and Pharaoh appointed him to this position on account of his wisdom. That made him the second most powerful man in the country.

This report is part of the E Document, which was compiled

in the northern Israelite kingdom, several centuries after the time of Joseph. It is, therefore, unclear whether this story can be regarded as historically accurate or is based on legends. The aftermath of this story demonstrates, though, that Pharaoh's dream was supposed to be an accurate prediction of the future.

MOSES

Most of the books of Exodus, Numbers, Leviticus, and Deuteronomy contain stories about Moses – his actions, but also his conversations, wise advice, and some ethical and ceremonial laws, which he allegedly received from God. Most of the contents of these books may, therefore, be regarded as prophetic in nature, although they are not forecasts and do not deal with future events, but are aimed at the existing conditions of the Israelites. It is an impossible task to discuss all the revelations and wisdom of Moses and only a representative selection will receive attention.

Moses by Michelangelo

The Ten Commandments

It has already been shown in the previous chapter that the Ten Commandments, which is the basis of the covenant between God and his people, could certainly not have been given to Moses while the fugitive Hebrew slaves were camping at the foot of Mount Sinai. The contents of the commandments reflect a sedentary existence where farmers owned land with dwellings, animals, and slaves. The Israelites were repeatedly warned to heed these commandments if they wished to be blessed by YHWH, their God.

Battle against the Amalekites
Ex 17: 8–15

8.	Then Amalek came and fought with Israel in Rephidim.
9.	Moses said to Joshua, "Choose men for us, and go out, fight with Amalek. Tomorrow I will stand on the top of the hill with God's rod in my hand."
10.	So Joshua did as Moses had told him, and fought with Amalek; and Moses, Aaron, and Hur went up to the top of the hill.
11.	It happened, when Moses held up his hand, that Israel prevailed; and when he let down his hand, Amalek prevailed.
12.	But Moses' hands were heavy; and they took a stone, and put it under him, and he sat on it. Aaron and Hur held up his hands, the one on the one side, and the other on the other side. His hands were steady until sunset.
13.	Joshua defeated Amalek and his people with the edge of the sword.
14.	YHWH said to Moses, "Write this for a memorial in a book, and rehearse it in the ears of Joshua: that I will utterly blot out the memory of Amalek from under the sky."
15.	Moses built an altar, and called the name of it YHWH our Banner.

The prophecy that the Amalekites, a nomadic tribe in the southern parts of Palestine, would disappear was fulfilled, but only centuries later during the time of King Hezekiah of Judah (1 Chron 4: 42–43).[88]

It is not unlikely that this report of the battle against the Amalekites was a real historical event. However, the claim that the victory of the Israelites was dependent upon the position and movements of Moses' hands, amounts to a belief in the power of magic or sorcery.

Warnings
Deut 30: 1–5

1.	It shall happen, when all these things are come on you, the blessing and the curse, which I have set before you, and you shall call them to mind among all the nations, where YHWH your God has driven you,
2.	and shall return to YHWH your God, and shall obey his voice according to all that I command you this day, you and your children, with all your heart, and with all your soul;
3.	that then YHWH your God will turn your captivity, and have compassion on you, and will return and gather you from all the peoples, where YHWH your God has scattered you.
4.	If [any of] your outcasts are in the uttermost parts of the heavens, from there will YHWH your God gather you, and from there will he bring you back:
5.	and YHWH your God will bring you into the land which your fathers possessed, and you shall possess it; and he will do you good, and multiply you above your fathers.

---

[88] Enc Brit, "Amalekites".

These words attributed to Moses were echoed by all the other Israelite prophets. The people are warned that calamities would strike them if they did not obey YHWH's commands. There is a hint of the Babylonian Exile, many centuries later, but the promise was also given that Israel would be brought back to their land.

Genocide Ordered
Num 21: 1–3

1.	The Canaanite, the king of Arad, who lived in the South, heard tell that Israel came by the way of Atharim; and he fought against Israel, and took some of them captive.
2.	Israel vowed a vow to YHWH, and said, If you will indeed deliver this people into my hand, then I will utterly destroy their cities.
3.	YHWH listened to the voice of Israel, and delivered up the Canaanites; and they utterly destroyed them and their cities: and the name of the place was called Hormah.

For people of our time, this passage in Scripture seems to be incomprehensible, unacceptable, and even barbaric. How could God approve of the Israelites' vow to commit genocide, to eradicate the pagan inhabitants of the towns in Canaan? This is not an isolated case where genocide was sanctioned or ordered by YHWH through his prophet Moses. We also read in Num 22: 34 and 31: 15–18; Lev 27: 29; Josh 3: 10, 6: 17, 8: 24–26 and 10: 10–14 of divine orders through Moses to commit ethnic cleansing.

Yet, we get this testimony of Moses' character in Num 12: 3 – "Now the man Moses was more gentle than any other man on earth." One can only exclaim in amazement: How is that possible? How could the Israelites start their campaign of the wholesale slaughter of their pagan enemies under the leadership of this supposedly gentle person as their leader and prophet?

Michel Onfrey remarks that God invented "total war". He adds: "Clearly, scorched earth, fire, and wholesale slaughter of populations are not a recent invention."[89]

That is the same God who supposedly also gave the Eighth Commandment: "You shall not murder" (Ex 20: 13) and who condemned all forms of homicide, violence, and retaliation (Gen 9: 6; Num 35: 30–34; Matt 5: 38–47 and 15: 19–20, *etcetera*).

Keith Ward tried to soften this problem by declaring that God did not really command the extermination of the pagans; that was only how the Israelites believed what God would have commanded them to do.[90] This sounds like a reasonable argument, but it boils down to the point of view that we may decide on our own what God said and what he didn't say. That will, inevitably, lead to total arbitrariness regarding biblical exegesis.

Executing a Man Collecting Sticks on the Sabbath
Numbers 15: 32–36

32.	While the children of Israel were in the wilderness, they found a man gathering sticks on the Sabbath day.
33.	Those who found him gathering sticks brought him to Moses and Aaron, and to all the congregation.
34.	They put him in custody, because it had not been declared what should be done to him.
35.	YHWH said to Moses, The man shall surely be put to death: all the congregation shall stone him with stones outside of the camp.

---

[89] Onfrey, *In Defence of Atheism*, 177.
[90] Ward, *Is Religion Irrational?* 146.

> 36. All the congregation brought him outside of the camp, and stoned him to death with stones; as YHWH commanded Moses.

One must ask: was this executed man guilty of some or other ugly or serious or monstruous crime? Did he kill somebody to warrant the death penalty? Did he rape a girl? Dis he steal a fortune? Was he a traitor who sold secrets to the enemy?

The only crime of this man was that he collected sticks on the wrong day of the week to make a fire for his family to keep warm. According to this passage, YHWH gave Moses the message that this man had to be stoned to death, even without a fair trial.

And the worst part of it all is that Moses and all the other Israelites believed God who declared that this man deserved the death penalty for this very minor transgression of a religious law and they willingly and enthusiastically killed him by hurling stones and rocks at him until his body was a lifeless bloody mess.

SAMUEL

It has been mentioned in the previous chapter that the story of Samuel was only recorded in writing about five centuries after his time. Which means that many legendary and fictitious elements could have been included in his story. He was venerated as a great prophet and it is reported in *1 Sam 3: 19–20* as follows:

> Samuel grew, and YHWH was with him, and did let none of his words fall to the ground. All Israel from Dan even to Beersheba knew that Samuel was established to be a prophet of YHWH.

It has already been reported that he foretold the downfall of the house of Eli, the high priest, which did happen (1 Sam 3 and 4).

Some other important prophetic activities of Samuel must be discussed:

Saul Chosen as King of Israel
1 Sam 9: 15–17

> 15. Now YHWH had revealed to Samuel a day before Saul came, saying,
> 16. Tomorrow about this time I will send you a man out of the land of Benjamin, and you shall anoint him to be prince over my people Israel; and he shall save my people out of the hand of the Philistines: for I have looked on my people, because their cry is come to me.
> 17. When Samuel saw Saul, YHWH said to him, Behold, the man of whom I spoke to you! this same shall have authority over my people.

After Samuel had assured Saul that his father's lost donkeys have been found, he had lunch with him and appointed him as future king of Israel. He also told him that he would encounter certain people on his way home, including a group of prophetic apprentices.

After Saul was acclaimed and anointed as king of Israel and thereby became a messiah, an anointed of God, he scored victories over the enemies of Israel. In the end, however, he proved to be a disappointment by disobeying Samuel. We read further in *1 Sam 15: 10–11:*

> Then came the word of YHWH to Samuel, saying, It repents me that I have set up Saul to be king; for he is turned back from following me, and has not performed my commandments. Samuel was angry; and he cried to YHWH all night."

In the meantime, God led Samuel to anoint David as king, although Saul was still occupying the throne (1 Sam 16: 1–13). Saul seemed to have suffered from a psychiatric disorder, probably paranoid schizophrenia, which was attributed to an evil spirit sent by God (1 Sam 16: 14–16). Saul died as a vanquished military leader who took his own life to prevent him from being taken prisoner by his enemies (1 Sam 31). It does seem as if Samuel made a mistake by choosing Saul as king. His choice of David, on the other hand, led to the establishment of a dynasty that lasted four centuries.

NATHAN

David's Dynasty
2 Sam: 7: 8–16

8.	Now therefore thus shall you tell my servant David, Thus says YHWH of Hosts, I took you from the sheep pen, from following the sheep, that you should be prince over my people, over Israel;
9.	and I have been with you wherever you went, and have cut off all your enemies from before you; and I will make you a great name, like the name of the great ones who are in the earth.
10.	I will appoint a place for my people Israel, and will plant them, that they may dwell in their own place, and be moved no more; neither shall the children of wickedness afflict them any more, as at the first,
11.	and [as] from the day that I commanded judges to be over my people Israel; and I will cause you to rest from all your enemies. Moreover YHWH tells you that YHWH will make you a house.
12.	When your days are fulfilled, and you shall sleep with your

> fathers, I will set up your seed after you, who shall proceed out of your bowels, and I will establish his kingdom.
> 13. He shall build a house for my name, and I will establish the throne of his kingdom forever.
> 14. I will be his father, and he shall be my son: if he commit iniquity, I will chasten him with the rod of men, and with the stripes of the children of men;
> 15. but my lovingkindness shall not depart from him, as I took it from Saul, whom I put away before you.
> 16. Your house and your kingdom shall be made sure for ever before you: your throne shall be established forever.

The prophet Nathan gave the promise to King David on behalf of YWHW that his offspring would rule over all the people of Israel forever. Similar promises are to be found in 1 Kgs 2: 4; 1 Kgs 8: 25; Ps 89: 4, 36–77, Isa 9: 5–7, and Jer 33: 17.

It is clear from the subsequent history that this promise of God was not kept. About three decades later, after the time of David's son, Salomon, the biggest part of the nation of Israel broke away from the Davidic dynasty in Jerusalem and established a separate kingdom with Samariah as capital. The result was that the descendants of David did not rule over the whole nation of Israel as God had promised.

The dynasty of David in the kingdom of Judah came to an end when Jerusalem was sacked by the Babylonians in 586 BC. No descendent of David ever sat on a throne in Jerusalem after that.

ELIJAH

After the kingdom of Solomon had been divided into northern and southern parts, Elijah was introduced in 1 Kings 17 as a prophet who told king Ahab of the northern kingdom that a severe drought would come. This had to be seen as God's punishment for Ahab's idiolatry by allowing his wife, a Phoenician princess, to introduce the worship of pagan deities, Baal and Ashera, into the country.

Since Baal was worshipped as the god of rain, lightning, and dew, this drought was a serious challenge to his power as a deity. This drought did happen and it was only broken after Elijah managed to prove that YHWH was the true God by managing to attract a bolt of lightning onto an altar with a sacrifice (1 Kgs 18). Before that, the prophets of Baal who also participated in this ritual, prayed in vain to their god to show his might by igniting their sacrifice on a pile of wood.

Elijah Taken Up in a Chariot of Fire by Giuseppe Angeli, c. 1740/1755

Elijah managed to manipulate the lightning by building his altar on a high point on Mount Carmel and pouring water over the altar built with twelve volcanic rocks, containing lots of iron, while a thunder storm was brewing.[91] The iron in the rocks acted as a lightning

---

[91] Anon. "Mount Carmel's Geology."

discharger, attracting a bolt of lightning from the clouds, thereby demonstrating that YHWH is the only true God.

After this, Elijah had other meetings with Ahab, his wife Jezebel, and Ahab's son and successor, Ahaziah. He prophesied their shameful and inglorious deaths, which happened later (1 Kgs 21 and 2 Kgs 1).

According to the biblical story, Elijah did not die, but was taken up into heaven by a flaming chariot – an incident only witnessed by his successor, Elisha (2 Kgs 2).

AMOS

The prophet Amos, whose career started around 762 BC and who operated in the northern Israelite kingdom, was the first prophet to write down his messages.

The book of Amos can be divided into three parts:

- Prophecies about Israel and her neighboring nations (ch 1–2);
- Comments on the religious scene in Israel (ch 3–6); and
- God's Judgment (ch 7–9).

It is necessary to consider a few key passages of Amos in which he provided a commentary on the political, social, and moral conditions of his time.

Prophecy against Damascus
Amos 1: 3–5)

3.	Thus says YHWH: For three transgressions of Damascus, yes, for four, I will not turn away the punishment of it; because they have threshed Gilead with threshing instruments of iron:
4.	but I will send a fire into the house of Hazael, and it shall

> devour the palaces of Ben-Hadad.
>
> 5. I will break the bar of Damascus, and cut off the inhabitant from the valley of Aven, and him who holds the scepter from the house of Eden; and the people of Syria shall go into captivity to Kir, says YHWH.

The first two chapters of Amos are devoted to prophecies regarding the neighboring nations of Israel, but also to Israel and Judah. The first neighbor to be addressed was the city of Damascus, the ancient capital of Syria, which is the oldest city in the world that has been inhabited without interruption since the third millennium BC.[92] One may, therefore, wonder whether this prophecy of Amos against the capital of the kingdom of the Arameans really did go into fulfilment because there were always people living in that city.

Amos predicted the downfall of the house of Hazael, the monarch of this kingdom, and the destruction of the palace built by King Ben-Hadad, Hazael's father and predecessor. That was meant to be the punishment for the way the Arameans treated the Israelites living in the region of Gilead, on the eastern side of the Jordan, when conquering these parts (2 Kgs 12: 17–18). The region of Gilead was allotted by Moses to the tribes of Gad, Reuben, and the eastern half of Manasseh (Deut 3: 13; Num 32: 40).

Amos wrote these words more or less during 762 BC. The city was indeed sacked by the Assyrians thirty years later and many of the inhabitants were exiled to the country of Kir in Mesopotamia (2 Kgs 16: 9; Isa 22: 6).

Against Israel
Amos 2: 6–16

---

[92] Rabbat, "Damascus".

6. Thus says YHWH: For three transgressions of Israel, yes, for four, I will not turn away the punishment of it; because they have sold the righteous for silver, and the needy for a pair of shoes

7. those who pant after the dust of the earth on the head of the poor, and turn aside the way of the humble: and a man and his father go to the [same] maiden, to profane my holy name:

8. and they lay themselves down beside every altar on clothes taken in pledge; and in the house of their God they drink the wine of such as have been fined.

9. Yet I destroyed I the Amorite before them, whose height was like the height of the cedars, and he was strong as the oaks; yet I destroyed his fruit from above, and his roots from beneath.

10. Also I brought you up out of the land of Egypt, and led you forty years in the wilderness, to possess the land of the Amorite.

11. I raised up of your sons for prophets, and of your young men for Nazirites. Is it not even thus, you children of Israel? says YHWH.

12. But you gave the Nazirites wine to drink, and commanded the prophets, saying, Don't prophesy.

13. Behold, I will press [you] in your place, as a cart presses that is full of sheaves.

14. Flight shall perish from the swift; and the strong shall not strengthen his force; neither shall the mighty deliver himself;

15.	neither shall he stand who handles the bow; and he who is swift of foot shall not deliver [himself]; neither shall he who rides the horse deliver himself;
16.	and he who is courageous among the mighty shall flee away naked in that day, says YHWH.

In this prophecy, Israel is reminded of how their God helped their ancestors to escape from Egypt and to overcome their enemies, the Amorites. It was expected of the Israelites to live according to God's commandments, to love justice, and to show charity towards those in need. The opulent Israelites, however, did the opposite by oppressing the less fortunate and leading immoral lives.

God decided to punish them by allowing them to be defeated during a future war – which happened when the Assyrians conquered their country and abducted the leaders of the nation to strange places in 721 BC, about forty years after the prophecy by Amos.

The first two chapters of Amos also contain prophecies that the cities of the Philistines, the Phoenicians, the Edomites, the Ammonites, the Moabites, and the Judeans would be destroyed – which did happen during the decades and centuries thereafter.

Seek YHWH, and you shall live
Amos 5: 4–9

4.	For thus says YHWH to the house of Israel, Seek you me, and you shall live;
5.	but don't seek Bethel, nor enter into Gilgal, and don't pass to Beersheba: for Gilgal shall surely go into captivity, and Bethel shall come to nothing.

> 6. Seek YHWH, and you shall live; lest he break out like fire in the house of Joseph, and it devour, and there be none to quench it in Bethel.
> 7. You who turn justice to wormwood, and cast down righteousness to the earth,
> 8. [seek him] who makes the Pleiades and Orion, and turns the shadow of death into the morning, and makes the day dark with night; who calls for the waters of the sea, and pours them out on the surface of the earth (YHWH is his name);
> 9. who brings sudden destruction on the strong, so that destruction comes on the fortress.

Amos condemned the rich people in the northern kingdom of Israel who denied justice to those who were wronged and who exploited the poor people. There were peace and prosperity during the reign of King Jeroboam II when Amos spoke out against these social ills and he predicted the downfall of this monarchy – which happened when the Assyrians conquered the country a few decades later in 721 BC.

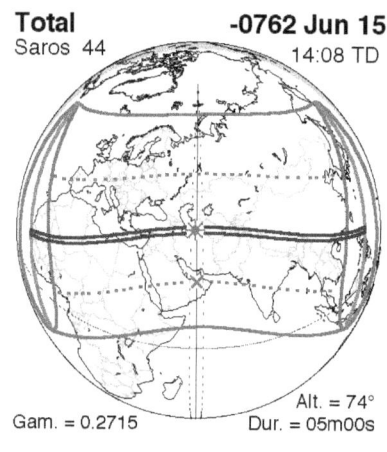

Path of the total solar eclipse of 16 June 762 BC. The moon's shadow fell over northern Israel around noon.

The people of Israel were encouraged to return to YHWH, their God. They were reminded that God is in control of everything, including the waters of the sea and the astrological bodies such as the constellation of Orion and the cluster of the Pleiades inside Taurus, the Bull. They were also required to remember a recent episode when YHWH caused darkness to descend upon the earth during the day (due to a total solar eclipse on 15 June 762 BC).

Justice and Righteousness
Amos 5: 21–27

21.	I hate, I despise your feasts, and I will take no delight in your solemn assemblies.
22.	Yes, though you offer me your burnt offerings and meal-offerings, I will not accept them; neither will I regard the peace-offerings of your fat animals.
23.	Take away from me the noise of your songs; for I will not hear the melody of your viols.
24.	But let justice roll down as waters, and righteousness as a mighty stream.
25.	Did you bring to me sacrifices and offerings in the wilderness forty years, house of Israel?
26.	Yes, you have borne the tent of your king and the shrine of your images, the star of your god, which you made to yourselves.
27.	Therefore will I cause you to go into captivity beyond Damascus, says YHWH, whose name is the God of hosts.

Amos addressed the people of Israel on behalf of "YWHW of hosts", the God who dwells in heaven, between and beyond the host of stars.

God told the Israelites that all their rituals and songs at their sanctuaries didn't impress Him because those rituals were only mechanical actions, only performed out of habit. What God sought was justice and righteousness. Because these values and virtues were lacking, the people were warned that they would face captivity – which happened a few decades later.

Amos saw the danger of the Assyrian empire, which treated the subjugated nations harshly and deporting some of them somewhere else to make place for their own people.[93]

Death and Darkness
Amos 8: 1–3; 7–10

1.	Thus the Lord YHWH showed me: and, behold, a basket of summer fruit.
2.	He said, Amos, what see you? I said, A basket of summer fruit. Then said YHWH to me, The end is come on my people Israel; I will not again pass by them any more.
3.	The songs of the temple shall be wailings in that day, says the Lord YHWH: the dead bodies shall be many: in every place shall they cast them forth with silence.
7.	YHWH has sworn by the excellency of Jacob, Surely I will never forget any of their works.
8.	Shall not the land tremble for this, and everyone mourn who dwells therein? yes, it shall rise up wholly like the River; and it shall be troubled and sink again, like the River of Egypt.
9.	It shall happen in that day, says the Lord YHWH, that I will cause the sun to go down at noon, and I will darken the earth

---

[93] Enc Brit, "Assyria".

> in the clear day.
>
> 10. I will turn your feasts into mourning, and all your songs into lamentation; and I will bring sackcloth on all loins, and baldness on every head; and I will make it as the mourning for an only son, and the end of it as a bitter day.

Amos saw a basket of ripe summer fruit. God made it clear that He intended destroying his sinful people, just as a basket of fruit is consumed. The songs of people will disappear and only cries of anguish will be heard on account of all the corpses lying around.

The Day of YHWH would be a dark day, just as the recent sudden darkness during the day (caused by the total solar eclipse on 15 June 762 BC). This prophecy was fulfilled forty years later when the Assyrians vanquished the Israelite army in 721 BC.

No Escape Possible
Amos 9: 1–10

> 1. I saw the Lord standing beside the altar: and he said, Strike the capitals, that the thresholds may shake; and break them in pieces on the head of all of them; and I will kill the last of them with the sword: there shall not one of them flee away, and there shall not one of them escape.
> 2. Though they dig into Sheol, there shall my hand take them; and though they climb up to heaven, there will I bring them down.
> 3. Though they hide themselves in the top of Carmel, I will search and take them out there; and though they be hid from my sight in the bottom of the sea, there will I command the serpent, and it shall bite them.

4. Though they go into captivity before their enemies, there will I command the sword, and it shall kill them: and I will set my eyes on them for evil, and not for good.
5. For the Lord, YHWH of Hosts, [is] he who touches the land and it melts, and all who dwell therein shall mourn; and it shall rise up wholly like the River, and shall sink again, like the River of Egypt;
6. [it is] he who builds his chambers in the heavens, and has founded his vault on the earth; he who calls for the waters of the sea, and pours them out on the surface of the earth; YHWH is his name.
7. Are you not as the children of the Ethiopians to me, children of Israel? says YHWH. Haven't I brought up Israel out of the land of Egypt, and the Philistines from Caphtor, and the Syrians from Kir?
8. Behold, the eyes of the Lord YHWH are on the sinful kingdom, and I will destroy it from off the surface of the earth; except that I will not utterly destroy the house of Jacob, says YHWH.
9. For, behold, I will command, and I will sift the house of Israel among all the nations, like as [grain] is sifted in a sieve, yet shall not the least kernel fall on the earth.
10. All the sinners of my people shall die by the sword, who say, The evil shall not overtake nor meet us.

This passage contains a message from YHWH, but also comments by the prophet on who and what YHWH really is.

God promised that He would see to it that the leaders of Israel – described as the capitals of the pillars –would die by the sword, although they deemed themselves to be safe. They won't be able to hide anywhere because YHWH of Hosts will find them everywhere – in Sheol (the realm of the dead below the surface of the earth), in the heavens, on a high mountain, or on the bottom of the sea. The "sinful kingdom" would be destroyed. God could do this because He inhabits heaven and rules his creation. He reminded them that they owed their existence as a nation to Him who led them out of Egypt. However, a remnant of the house of Jacob will survive.

This prophecy was fulfilled when the northern kingdom of Israel was vanquished by the Assyrian army a few decades later.

Israel will Vanquish the Edomites
Amos 9: 12–13:

12.	In whose day will I raise up the tent of David who is fallen, and close up the breaches of it; and I will raise up its ruins, and I will build it as in the days of old;
13.	who they may possess the remnant of Edom, and all the nations who are called by my name, says YHWH who does this.

This prophecy was fulfilled many centuries after the Babylonian Exile, during the time when the Hasmonean dynasty ruled Judea. The country of the Edomites was incorporated into Judea and an Edomite, Herod the Great, even became the king of Judea (37–4 BC) after Judea had become a Roman province.[94]

Amos must be classified as a real prophet. He condemned the people of Israel on behalf of God for their sins – a lack of justice, compassion, charity, and righteousness. He exposed the way the rich people exploited the poor. He promised the people that God would punish them by annihilating their prosperous country when a foreign army would overpower them. It is clear that he judged the political and moral circumstances of his time correctly and warned his people

---

[94] Enc Brit, "Herod

appropriately about the dangers confronting them, although his prophecies were only fulfilled decades and even centuries after his time.

MICAH

This Judean prophet acted during the last half of the 8th century BC.

Punishment for Idolatry
Micah 5: 10 –15

10.	It shall happen in that day, says YHWH, that I will cut off your horses out of the midst of you, and will destroy your chariots:
11.	and I will cut off the cities of your land, and will throw down all your strongholds.
12.	I will cut off witchcraft out of your hand; and you shall have no [more] soothsayers:
13.	and I will cut off your engraved images and your pillars out of the midst of you; and you shall no more worship the work of your hands;
14.	and I will pluck up your Asherim out of the midst of you; and I will destroy your cities.
15.	I will execute vengeance in anger and wrath on the nations which didn't listen.

Micah, a contemporary of Amos and Isaiah, gave this prophecy against Judah. The people were warned that their horses and chariots would be destroyed during a future war. They must see it as God's punishment for their idolatry, reliance on soothsaying, and practice of witchcraft. It happened that Jerusalem was destroyed when the Babylonians razed the city during 586 BC, a few decades later.

ISAIAH

Isaiah of Jerusalem, the author of the first 39 chapters of the prophetic book bearing his name, was a somewhat younger contemporary of Amos. His prophecies were directed towards the southern kingdom of Judah. He started his career during the year that King Uzziah died – 742 BC (Isa 6: 1) when he had a vision of God on his throne – as was demonstrated in the previous chapter.

The Earthquake
Isa: 2: 19–22

19.	Men shall go into the caves of the rocks, and into the holes of the earth, from before the terror of YHWH, and from the glory of his majesty, when he arises to shake mightily the earth.
20.	In that day men shall cast away their idols of silver, and their idols of gold, which have been made for them to worship, to the moles and to the bats;
21.	to go into the caverns of the rocks, and into the clefts of the ragged rocks, from before the terror of YHWH, and from the glory of his majesty, when he arises to shake mightily the earth.
22.	Cease you from man, whose breath is in his nostrils; for wherein is he to be accounted of?

The countries of the eastern Mediterranean – Italy, Greece, Turkey, Syria, and Israel – are known for severe seismic activity – earthquakes and even volcanoes.[95] The people of Judah must have experienced an exceptional intense earthquake some time before

---

[95] Volcano Discovery, "Volcanoes of Turkey"; Decker and Decker, "Volcano".

Isaiah wrote these words. He tells of people who sought shelter in caves to escape from the falling rocks. Isaiah possibly referred to the earthquake in Amos 1: 1, which occurred during ±760 BC.

That is how it will be on the day when God will appear in his terror and when He will force people to get rid of their idols.

The Volcano
Isa 4: 5–6

> 5. YHWH will create over the whole habitation of Mount Zion, and over her assemblies, a cloud and smoke by day, and the shining of a flaming fire by night; for over all the glory [shall be spread] a covering.
> 6. There shall be a pavilion for a shade in the day-time from the heat, and for a refuge and for a covert from storm and from rain.

The Day of YHWH will be like the outburst of a recent volcano, which spewed clouds into the sky during the day and caused flames to light up the night sky. This natural disaster must have caused panic in Jerusalem and elsewhere and it is a good illustration of what could be expected on the day when Judah would be destroyed.

A volcano at night (Mount Etna in Sicily)

There are three dormant volcanoes on the Golan Heights in northern Israel. Any one of them could have delivered fireworks during historical times, which would have been visible as far away as Haifa and Damascus.⁹⁶ It is likely that Isaiah saw something like this, which may have been linked to the earthquake.

A Remnant will Return
Isa 10: 20–23

20.	It shall come to pass in that day, that the remnant of Israel, and those who are escaped of the house of Jacob, shall no more again lean on him who struck them, but shall lean on YHWH, the Holy One of Israel, in truth.
21.	A remnant shall return, [even] the remnant of Jacob, to the mighty God.
22.	For though your people, Israel, be as the sand of the sea, [only] a remnant of them shall return: a destruction [is] determined, overflowing with righteousness.
23.	For a full end, and that determined, will the Lord, YHWH of Hosts, make in the midst of all the earth.

Isaiah often predicted that the kingdom of Judah would be conquered, just as the northern kingdom of Israels was subjugated by the Assyrians. However, he also received the promise from God that a remnant of the whole people of Israel would eventually return to their country.

It did happen that many Jews returned to Judea after the Babylonian Exile, but most of those Israelites who were abducted by the Assyrians, were assimilated by the peoples where they were placed. Those who stayed behind in the vicinity of Samaria mingled with pagan settlers from elsewhere and the Jews never accepted the Samaritans as fellow-Israelites (Neh 4; John 4: 9).⁹⁷

---

⁹⁶ Volcano Café, "Ancient Foundations: the Earth of the Bible".
⁹⁷ Enc Brit, "Samaritan".

In other words: this prophecy was only partly fulfilled.

Israel will be Reunited
Isa 11: 11–16

11.	It shall happen in that day, that the Lord will set his hand again the second time to recover the remnant of his people, who shall remain, from Assyria, and from Egypt, and from Pathros, and from Cush, and from Elam, and from Shinar, and from Hamath, and from the islands of the sea.
12.	He will set up an ensign for the nations, and will assemble the outcasts of Israel, and gather together the dispersed of Judah from the four corners of the earth.
13.	The envy also of Ephraim shall depart, and those who vex Judah shall be cut off: Ephraim shall not envy Judah, and Judah shall not vex Ephraim.
14.	They shall fly down on the shoulder of the Philistines on the west; together shall they despoil the children of the east: they shall put forth their hand on Edom and Moab; and the children of Ammon shall obey them.
15.	YHWH will utterly destroy the tongue of the Egyptian sea; and with his scorching wind will he wave his hand over the River, and will strike it into seven streams, and cause men to march over in sandals.
16.	There shall be a highway for the remnant of his people, who shall remain, from Assyria; like as there was for Israel in the day that he came up out of the land of Egypt

In Isaiah 11 it is foretold that the remnants of the people of Israel, who were exiled after the fall of Samaria in 772 BC, would return to the Holy Land and enjoy peace under a future king. Christians regard this as another prophecy regarding Jesus Christ's reign as eternal king in heaven. Isaiah is, however, explicit that his prophecy deals with the real people of Israel, not very long after his own time – not some hypothetical future millennium.

History tells us, though, that those Israelites who were taken away in exile by the Assyrians just vanished. They were simply assimilated by the nations where they were held and they never returned to Palestine.[98] This prophecy of Isaiah was, therefore, never fulfilled. It did happen, though, that the neighboring nations of the Philistines, Edomites, Moabites, and Ammonites disappeared, although the Egyptians did not suffer the same fate.

Destruction of Damascus
Isa 17: 1–4

1.	The burden of Damascus. Behold, Damascus is taken away from being a city, and it shall be a ruinous heap.
2.	The cities of Aroer are forsaken; they shall be for flocks, which shall lie down, and none shall make them afraid.
3.	The fortress shall cease from Ephraim, and the kingdom from Damascus, and the remnant of Syria; they shall be as the glory of the children of Israel, says YHWH of Hosts.
4.	It shall happen in that day, that the glory of Jacob shall be made thin, and the fatness of his flesh shall wax lean.

This prophecy envisaged the destruction of the capital of Syria, Damascus, because of cruelties perpetrated against Ephraim, the northern Israelite kingdom. The destruction would be so complete that the site would become farm land where sheep would graze.

This prophecy was never fulfilled and Damascus was never

---

[98] Jones, *In the Blood*, 142.

destroyed. However, the city fell like other capitals of the region to foreign conquerors—to the Assyrians in the 8th century, to the Babylonians in the 7th century, to the Persians in the 6th century, to the Greeks in the 4th century, and to the Romans in the 1st century BC. Damascus is the oldest continuously inhabited city in the world and it didn't become a heap of ruins as foretold.[99]

The Fate of Edom
Isa 34: 5–15

5.	For my sword has drunk its fill in the sky: behold, it shall come down on Edom, and on the people of my curse, to judgment.
6.	The sword of YHWH is filled with blood, it is made fat with fatness, with the blood of lambs and goats, with the fat of the kidneys of rams; for YHWH has a sacrifice in Bozrah, and a great slaughter in the land of Edom.
7.	The wild-oxen shall come down with them, and the bulls with the bulls: and their land shall be drunken with blood, and their dust made fat with fatness.
8.	For YHWH has a day of vengeance, a year of recompense for the cause of Zion.
9.	The streams of [Edom] shall be turned into pitch, and the dust of it into sulfur, and the land of it shall become burning pitch.
10.	It shall not be quenched night nor day; the smoke of it shall go up for ever; from generation to generation it shall lie waste; none shall pass through it forever and ever.
11.	But the pelican and the porcupine shall possess it; and the owl and the raven shall dwell therein: and he will stretch

---

[99] Enc Brit, "Damascus".

> 12. They shall call the nobles of it to the kingdom, but none shall be there; and all its princes shall be nothing.
> 13. Thorns shall come up in its palaces, nettles and thistles in the fortresses of it; and it shall be a habitation of jackals, a court for ostriches.
> 14. The wild animals of the desert shall meet with the wolves, and the wild goat shall cry to his fellow; yes, the night-monster shall settle there, and shall find her a place of rest.
> 15. There shall the dart-snake make her nest, and lay, and hatch, and gather under her shade; yes, there shall the kites be gathered, everyone with her mate.

Isaiah foresaw a very dark future for the kingdom of Edom. War with an enemy was due to break out and many people, including the royal family, would be killed by the sword. The country would become desolate, inhabited by wild animals, and weeds would grow in their palaces and fortresses in Bozrah, the capital of Edom.

History knows of various clashes between the Edomites and the Israelites, which started during the Exodus from Egypt when the wandering Israelites were denied permission to travel on the highway through their country. The western parts of the Edomite kingdom were often occupied and annexed by the Israelites and Judeans. The Edomite language was like ancient Hebrew.[100]

The Edomites were later vanquished by the Babylonians, but they survived as a nation. The western parts of their territory were taken over by the Judeans at the time of the Hasmonean monarchy during the second century BC. The Edomite or Idumean Antipater

---

[100] McCarter, "Edomite in 12 Easy Lessons".

even succeeded in being appointed as governor of Judea by the Romans. His son, Herod the Great, was appointed king of Palestine by the Romans.[101] The eastern parts of Edom were conquered by the Nabateans, who built the ancient city of Petra.[102]

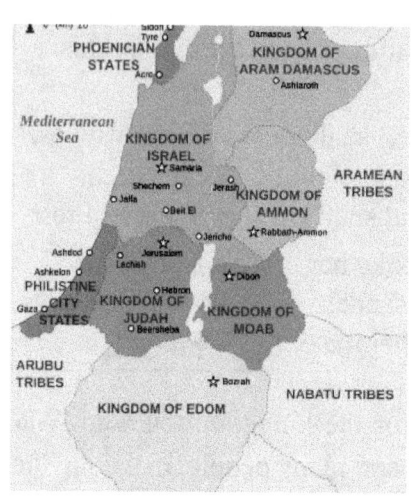

There is evidence that the name of the chief deity of the Edomites, Qos/Quas (קוס), was another name for YHWH. That explains why the Idumeans were so easily absorbed by the Jews in the first century BC.[103] We read in Ezra 2: 53 and Neh 7: 55 of "the children of Barkos" (בְּנֵי־בַרְקוֹס – *beney barqos*) who returned from Babylon. There was, therefore, at least one Jew called "son of Qos".

It does seem as if Isaiah's prophecy was not fulfilled in all respects.

NAHUM

The prophet Nahum operated during the seventh century BC in the kingdom of Judah and after the northern Israelite kingdom had been conquered by the Assyrians. The theme of his book is the judgment of YHWH against the Assyrian capital, Nineveh.[104] The following excerpt is typical of this short book with only three chapters:

---

[101] Enc Brit, "Antipater".
[102] Enc Brit, "Petra".
[103] Burnett, Joel S. "Ammon, Moab and Edom"; Rylaarsdam et al. "Biblical Literature"; Enc Brit, "Edom".
[104] Boshoff, *Geskiedenis*, 140.

Against Nineveh
Nah 1: 7–11

7.	YHWH is good, a stronghold in the day of trouble; and he knows those who take refuge in him.
8.	But with an overflowing flood, he will make a full end of her place, and will pursue his enemies into darkness.
9.	What do you plot against YHWH? He will make a full end. Affliction won't rise up the second time.
10.	For entangled like thorns, and drunken as with their drink, they are consumed utterly like dry stubble.
11.	There is one gone forth out of you, who devises evil against YHWH, who counsels wickedness.

Those who seek YHWH will be blessed, but the enemies of YHWH, the people of Assyria who demolished the northern Israelite kingdom, are doomed. Nineveh was indeed later destroyed by the Babylonians. It is unclear whether the Assyrians ever took note of this prophecy, but it was meant as a warning to the people of Jerusalem that they must not neglect to serve YHWH.

ZEPHANIAH

The prophet Zephaniah delivered his oracles against Jerusalem during the end of the seventh century BC. He demanded in the name of YHWH that the elite of the kingdom return to their God and do what is right.

The Day of YHWH is Near
Zeph 1: 7–18

7. Be silent at the presence of the Lord YHWH, for the day of YHWH is at hand. For YHWH has prepared a sacrifice. He has consecrated his guests.

8. It will happen in the day of YHWH's sacrifice, that I will punish the princes, the king's sons, and all those who as are clothed with foreign clothing.

9. In that day, I will punish all those who leap over the threshold, who fill their master's house with violence and deceit.

10. In that day, says YHWH, there will be the noise of a cry from the fish gate, a wailing from the second quarter, and a great crashing from the hills.

11. Wail, you inhabitants of Maktesh, for all the people of Canaan are undone! All those who were laden with silver are cut off.

12. It will happen at that time, that I will search Jerusalem with lamps, and I will punish the men who are settled on their dregs, who say in their heart, "YHWH will not do good, neither will he do evil."

13. Their wealth will become a spoil, and their houses a desolation. Yes, they will build houses, but won't inhabit them. They will plant vineyards, but won't drink their wine.

14. The great day of YHWH is near. It is near, and hurries greatly, the voice of the day of YHWH. The mighty man cries there bitterly.

15. That day is a day of wrath, a day of distress and anguish, a day of trouble and ruin, a day of darkness and gloom, a day of clouds and blackness,

16.	a day of the trumpet and alarm, against the fortified cities, and against the high battlements.
17.	I will bring distress on men, that they will walk like blind men, because they have sinned against YHWH, and their blood will be poured out like dust, and their flesh like dung.
18.	Neither their silver nor their gold will be able to deliver them in the day of YHWH's wrath, but the whole land will be devoured by the fire of his jealousy; for he will make an end, yes, a terrible end, of all those who dwell in the land.

According to Zeph 1: 1, Zephaniah lived during the time of King Josiah of Judah (reigned *c.* 640–609 BC), although he seems to have been active only after this king's reign. The theme of this book is "the Day of YHWH" or Judgment Day, when the sinners in Jerusalem will be punished.

One of his key passages is quoted here. It must be noted that it is not possible to distinguish the prophet's comments from the message he has received from YHWH. However, it is clear that he warned the people of Jerusalem, the sons of the king, and the people of Maktesh (a suburb of Jerusalem where rich people lived) of God's wrath, which happened later when Jerusalem was destroyed by the Babylonians. All their riches won't help on that terrible day.

Against Jerusalem
Zeph 3: 1–7

1.	Woe to her who is rebellious and polluted, the oppressing city!
2.	She didn't obey the voice. She didn't receive correction. She didn't trust in YHWH. She didn't draw near to her God.

3.	Her princes in the midst of her are roaring lions. Her judges are evening wolves. They leave nothing until the next day.
4.	Her prophets are arrogant and treacherous people. Her priests have profaned the sanctuary. They have done violence to the law.
5.	YHWH, in the midst of her, is righteous. He will do no wrong. Every morning he brings his justice to light. He doesn't fail, but the unjust know no shame.
6.	I have cut off nations. Their battlements are desolate. I have made their streets waste, so that no one passes by. Their cities are destroyed, so that there is no man, so that there is no inhabitant.
7.	I said, "Just fear me. Receive correction, so that her dwelling won't be cut off, according to all that I have appointed concerning her." But they rose early and corrupted all their doings.

Zephaniah had harsh words for the people who have forgotten their God. There are dishonest princes, unjust judges, false prophets, and corrupt priests. Because YHWH is a God of justice and He has demonstrated his might by destroying nations, it is clear that the people of Jerusalem need correction.

The quoted passage seems to an accurate description of conditions in Jerusalem at that time.

JEREMIAH

Jeremiah operated during the last years of the Judean monarchy in Jerusalem, after the northern Israelite kingdom had been demolished by the Assyrians. He was aware of the danger posed by the Babylonian Empire after its conquest of Assyria. He warned the people of Judah not to rely on any help from Egypt. A selection of his prophecies is discussed below:

Jeremiah a Childless Bachelor
Jer 22: 30

> Thus says YHWH, Write you this man childless, a man who shall not prosper in his days; for no more shall a man of his seed prosper, sitting on the throne of David, and ruling in Judah.

This text confirms that Jeremiah was unmarried and had no children, which could be attributed to his unhappy life and all the animosity he experienced. His childlessness was a symbol of the expected downfall of the house of David.

Sacrifices not Ordered
Jer 7: 22–23

> 22. For I didn't speak to your fathers, nor command them in the day that I brought them out of the land of Egypt, concerning burnt offerings or sacrifices:
> 23. but this thing I commanded them, saying, Listen to my voice, and I will be your God, and you shall be my people; and walk you in all the way that I command you, that it may be well with you.

The books of Exodus, Numbers, Leviticus, and Deuteronomy contain numerous indications how the Israelites had to worship their God, YHWH, including the way burnt offerings and sacrifices had to be performed. These orders were given to the Israelites through their leader, the prophet Moses.

However, the prophet Jeremiah denies in the words quoted from his book that God ever gave such orders. According to him,

God wished that his people should listen to his voice, worship Him as their God, and respect his commands by doing what is right and avoiding that which is wrong.

One is forced to ask: did God command the Israelites to bring animal sacrifices, or did He not? Jeremiah flatly contradicted all the prescriptions in the books of Moses regarding sacrifices. This is a serious case of contradictory elements in the Hebrew Scriptures.

It must be remembered, though, that the Pentateuch, containing the books from Genesis to Deuteronomy, was only finalized after the Babylonian Exile and that Jeremiah could not have been aware of the contents of these books.

False Prophets
Jer 14: 11–18

11.	YHWH said to me, Don't pray for this people for [their] good.
12.	When they fast, I will not hear their cry; and when they offer burnt offering and meal-offering, I will not accept them; but I will consume them by the sword, and by the famine, and by the pestilence.
13.	Then said I, Ah, Lord YHWH! behold, the prophets tell them, You shall not see the sword, neither shall you have famine; but I will give you assured peace in this place.
14.	Then YHWH said to me, The prophets prophesy lies in my name; I didn't send them, neither have I commanded them, neither spoke I to them: they prophesy to you a lying vision, and divination, and a thing of nothing, and the deceit of their own heart.
15.	Therefore thus says YHWH concerning the prophets who prophesy in my name, and I didn't send them, yet they say,

> Sword and famine shall not be in this land: By sword and famine shall those prophets be consumed.
>
> 16. The people to whom they prophesy shall be cast out in the streets of Jerusalem because of the famine and the sword; and they shall have none to bury them-them, their wives, nor their sons, nor their daughters: for I will pour their wickedness on them.
>
> 17. You shall say this word to them, Let my eyes run down with tears night and day, and let them not cease; for the virgin daughter of my people is broken with a great breach, with a very grievous wound.
>
> 18. If I go forth into the field, then, behold, the slain with the sword! and if I enter into the city, then, behold, those who are sick with famine! for both the prophet and the priest go about in the land, and have no knowledge.

According to this prophecy, YHWH was angry at the prophets who declared that peace and abundance would be given by God to the people of Judah. These prophets received no messages from Him in this regard and their promises amount to lies. The sins of the people would certainly be punished and they would suffer war, famine, and destruction.

The Exiles will Return

Jer 30: 18–24

> 18. Thus says YHWH: Behold, I will turn again the captivity of Jacob's tents, and have compassion on his dwelling-places; and the city shall be built on its own hill, and the palace shall be inhabited after its own manner.

19.	Out of them shall proceed thanksgiving and the voice of those who make merry: and I will multiply them, and they shall not be few; I will also glorify them, and they shall not be small.
20.	Their children also shall be as before, and their congregation shall be established before me; and I will punish all who oppress them.
21.	Their prince shall be of themselves, and their ruler shall proceed from the midst of them; and I will cause him to draw near, and he shall approach to me: for who is he who has had boldness to approach to me? says YHWH.
22.	You shall be my people, and I will be your God.
23.	Behold, the tempest of YHWH, [even his] wrath, is gone forth, a sweeping tempest: it shall burst on the head of the wicked.
24.	The fierce anger of YHWH shall not return, until he has executed, and until he have performed the intents of his heart: in the latter days you shall understand it.

This prophecy was recorded long after the prophecy quoted from Jer 14 (see above). These words were meant for those Judeans who were taken away in exile by the Babylonians after Jerusalem had surrendered to the hostile army. Jeremiah gave them the promise on behalf of YHWH that they would be allowed to return in due course and that their God hasn't forgotten them.

Jeremiah promised that the good times would return and the nation would again be ruled by their own prince. It did happen that the exiled Jews were allowed to return to Judea some decades later and that a prince, Zerubbabel, was appointed as governor of the country. It took a long time, though, before the good times returned.

Warning against Egypt
Jer 42: 7–16

7.	It happened after ten days, that the word of YHWH came to Jeremiah.
8.	Then called he Johanan the son of Kareah, and all the captains of the forces who were with him, and all the people from the least even to the greatest,
9.	and said to them, Thus says YHWH, the God of Israel, to whom you sent me to present your supplication before him:
10.	If you will still abide in this land, then will I build you, and not pull you down, and I will plant you, and not pluck you up; for I repent me of the evil that I have done to you.
11.	Don't be afraid of the king of Babylon, of whom you are afraid; don't be afraid of him, says YHWH: for I am with you to save you, and to deliver you from his hand.
12.	I will grant you mercy, that he may have mercy on you, and cause you to return to your own land.
13.	But if you say, We will not dwell in this land; so that you don't obey the voice of YHWH your God,
14.	saying, No; but we will go into the land of Egypt, where we shall see no war, nor hear the sound of the trumpet, nor have hunger of bread; and there will we dwell:
15.	now therefore hear you the word of YHWH, O remnant of Judah: Thus says YHWH of Hosts, the God of Israel, If you indeed set your faces to enter into Egypt, and go to sojourn there;
16.	then it shall happen, that the sword, which you fear, shall overtake you there in the land of Egypt; and the famine,

> whereof you are afraid, shall follow hard after you there in Egypt; and there you shall die.

Jeremiah was approached by the chief of the remnant of the Judahite army, Johanan, and other important officers to inquire about YHWH's advice regarding the continuing danger from Babylonia. They wanted to know whether they would be safe in Egypt.

Jeremiah did well to warn them against such a rash move and advised them to stay in Jerusalem and accept the Babylonian domination after Jerusalem had surrendered to the Babylonians during March 597 BC.

A few years previously, the son of the Babylonian king, prince Nebuchadrezzar, inflicted a crushing defeat on the Egyptians during the battle of Carchemish. When his father died shortly afterwards, he returned to Babylon to ascend the throne.

In 604 Nebuchadrezzar took the Philistine city of Ashkelon. He attacked the Egyptians again in 601 but was forced to retire after a bloody, undecide battle. After battles against the Syrians, he attacked Judea at the end of 598, forcing the surrender of Jerusalem a few months later. King Jehoiakim died during the siege and his son, King Johoiachin, together with at least 3,000 Jews, was led into exile in Babylonia. Zedekiah became the new king.

Jeremiah's advice was not followed and Judah rebelled in 589, and Jerusalem was placed under siege. The city fell in 587/586 and was completely destroyed and thousands of the Jews were taken to Babylonia as exiles.[105] The book of Lamentations describes the hopeless situation of those who survived the war.

Jeremiah was afraid that those who fled from Jerusalem before the revolt would die in Egypt by the sword. After Jerusalem

---

[105] End Brit, "Mesopotamia, History of".

had been taken by the Babylonian army he was, nevertheless, abducted by some of his opponents to Egypt, where he later died. The Babylonians did not subdue Egypt as Jeremiah had prophesied.[106]

Warning against Moving to Egypt
Jer 44: 11 – 18

11.	Therefore thus says YHWH of Hosts, the God of Israel: Behold, I will set my face against you for evil, even to cut off all Judah.
12.	I will take the remnant of Judah, that have set their faces to go into the land of Egypt to sojourn there, and they shall all be consumed; in the land of Egypt shall they fall; they shall be consumed by the sword and by the famine; they shall die, from the least even to the greatest, by the sword and by the famine; and they shall be an object of horror, [and] an astonishment, and a curse, and a reproach.
13.	For I will punish those who dwell in the land of Egypt, as I have punished Jerusalem, by the sword, by the famine, and by the pestilence;
14.	so that none of the remnant of Judah, who have gone into the land of Egypt to sojourn there, shall escape or be left, to return into the land of Judah, to which they have a desire to return to dwell there: for none shall return save such as shall escape.
15.	Then all the men who knew that their wives burned incense to other gods, and all the women who stood by, a great

---

[106] Enc Brit, "Jeremiah".

> assembly, even all the people who lived in the land of Egypt, in Pathros, answered Jeremiah, saying,
>
> 16. As for the word that you have spoken to us in the name of YHWH, we will not listen to you.
>
> 17. But we will certainly perform every word that is gone forth out of our mouth, to burn incense to the queen of the sky, and to pour out drink-offerings to her, as we have done, we and our fathers, our kings and our princes, in the cities of Judah, and in the streets of Jerusalem; for then had we plenty of victuals, and were well, and saw no evil.
>
> 18. But since we left off burning incense to the queen of the sky, and pouring out drink-offerings to her, we have wanted all things, and have been consumed by the sword and by the famine.
>
> 19. When we burned incense to the queen of the sky, and poured out drink-offerings to her, did we make her cakes to worship her, and pour out drink-offerings to her, without our husbands?

Although Jeremiah warned the people who wanted to settle in Egypt after the fall of Jerusalem, they refused to listen. They even declared that they would continue the worship of the Queen of the Sky, the goddess Astarte or Ishtar, the planet Venus, the goddess of fertility.

Jeremiah's warning that all these Judeans would perish in Egypt never came to pass and a flourishing Jewish community was established in Egypt during the ensuing centuries – especially in the city of Alexandria and on the island of Elephantine on the Nile where some Jewish mercenaries built a temple devoted to YHWH.[107]

---

[107] Josephus, *Wars of the Jews,* VII/407–436; Evelina G, "The Fascinating Story of the Jews in Egypt"; Steinmeyer, "A Jewish Curse Text".

God's People will Return
Jer 31: 10–14

10.	Hear the word of YHWH, you nations, and declare it in the isles afar off; and say, He who scattered Israel will gather him, and keep him, as shepherd does his flock.
11.	For YHWH has ransomed Jacob, and redeemed him from the hand of him who was stronger than he.
12.	They shall come and sing in the height of Zion, and shall flow to the goodness of YHWH, to the grain, and to the new wine, and to the oil, and to the young of the flock and of the herd: and their soul shall be as a watered garden; and they shall not sorrow any more at all.
13.	Then shall the virgin rejoice in the dance, and the young men and the old together; for I will turn their mourning into joy, and will comfort them, and make them rejoice from their sorrow.
14.	I will satiate the soul of the priests with fatness, and my people shall be satisfied with my goodness, says YHWH.

These words were written after many Jews were abducted to Babylonia after the defeat of the army of Judah. The Jews were given the promise that their God hasn't forgotten them and that they would be able to return home. It will be a happy and prosperous time.

These words were generally fulfilled, but only a few decades later when the Babylonian Empire was overthrown by the Persians and the Jews were allowed to return to their country in 539 BC. After they had managed to get settled again, a generally peaceful time ensued and they were allowed to manage their own affairs. The promised prosperity, however, did not materialize because the Persians taxed all the countries under their domination heavily.[108]

The Fall of Babylon
Jer 50: 29–32

29.	Call together the archers against Babylon, all those who bend the bow; encamp against her round about; let none of it escape: recompense her according to her work; according to all that she has done, do to her; for she has been proud against YHWH, against the Holy One of Israel.
30.	Therefore shall her young men fall in her streets, and all her men of war shall be brought to silence in that day, says YHWH.
31.	Behold, I am against you, you proud one, says the Lord, YHWH of Hosts; for your day is come, the time that I will visit you.
32.	The proud one shall stumble and fall, and none shall raise him up; and I will kindle a fire in his cities, and it shall devour all who are round about him.

Jer 51: 51–57

51.	We are confounded, because we have heard reproach; confusion has covered our faces: for strangers are come into the sanctuaries of YHWH's house.
52.	Therefore, behold, the days come, says YHWH, that I will execute judgment on her engraved images; and through all her land the wounded shall groan.
53.	Though Babylon should mount up to the sky, and though she should fortify the height of her strength, yet from me

---

[108] Boshoff, *Geskiedenis*, 144–47.

> shall destroyers come to her, says YHWH.
> 54. The sound of a cry from Babylon, and of great destruction from the land of the Chaldeans!
> 55. For YHWH lays Babylon waste, and destroys out of her the great voice; and their waves roar like many waters; the noise of their voice is uttered:
> 56. for the destroyer is come on her, even on Babylon, and her mighty men are taken, their bows are broken in pieces; for YHWH is a God of recompenses, he will surely requite.
> 57. I will make drunk her princes and her wise men, her governors and her deputies, and her mighty men; and they shall sleep a perpetual sleep, and not wake up, says the King, whose name is YHWH of Hosts.

These two passages are part of a long prophecy at the end of the book of Jeremiah. He foresaw the destruction and downfall of Babylon, the place where many Jewish exiles were being held.

It is possible that Jeremiah knew about the growing might of the Persian kingdom under Cyrus the Great, which eventually defeated the Babylonian Empire in 539 BC.

EZEKIEL

Ezekiel, the priest, was the spiritual leader of a group of the exiled Judeans in Babylonia. His messages were later collected and preserved in a single book.

False Prophets
Ezek 13: 1–5

> 1. The word of YHWH came to me, saying,

2.	Son of man, prophesy against the prophets of Israel who prophesy, and say you to those who prophesy out of their own heart, Hear you the word of YHWH:
3.	Thus says the Lord YHWH, Woe to the foolish prophets, who follow their own spirit, and have seen nothing!
4.	Israel, your prophets have been like foxes in the waste places.
5.	You have not gone up into the gaps, neither built up the wall for the house of Israel, to stand in the battle in the day of YHWH.

There were many prophets in Israel whose names have never been recorded. Their messages did not always agree and some prophets branded those who differed from them as false and foolish prophets – just as Ezekiel has done in this passage.

According to Ezekiel, these false prophets have not had any visions and they cannot speak on behalf of YHWH. It is unclear how the difference between genuine and false prophets could be determined since all of them claimed to be God's messengers.

We are left in the dark about what type of messages these false prophets brought to the people.

No Exodus
Ezek 16: 1–3

1.	Again the word of YHWH came to me, saying,
2.	Son of man, cause Jerusalem to know her abominations;
3.	and say, Thus says the Lord YHWH to Jerusalem: Your birth and your birth is of the land of the Canaanite; the Amorite was your father, and your mother was a Hittite.

The Biblical book of Exodus contains the story of how the Hebrew slaves were able to escape from Egypt under the leadership of Moses, and how they wandered through the desert until they eventually settled in the Promised Land, Canaan.

Ezekiel, the prophet spoke on behalf of YHWH, the national God of Israel, reminding the people of their real ancestry: they were the offspring of the Canaanites, the original inhabitants of Canaan, as well of the Amorites, a neighboring Semitic nation.

According to Finkelstein and Silberman, there is no archaeological evidence that the Exodus ever happened and they concluded that the Israelites were simply an indigenous group of Canaanites who started to worship YHWH and thereby acquired an own identity.[109]

It seems as if Ezekiel's words confirm these two authors' conclusion that the Exodus didn't happen as described in the book of Exodus.

Against Jerusalem
Ezek 16: 48–58

48.	As I live, says the Lord YHWH, Sodom your sister has not done, she nor her daughters, as you have done, you and your daughters.
49.	Behold, this was the iniquity of your sister Sodom: pride, fullness of bread, and prosperous ease was in her and in her daughters; neither did she strengthen the hand of the poor and needy.
50.	They were haughty, and committed abomination before me: therefore I took them away as I saw [good].

---

[109] Finkelstein and Silberman, *The Bible Unearthed*, 48–122.

> 51. Neither has Samaria committed half of your sins; but you have multiplied your abominations more than they, and have justified your sisters by all your abominations which you have done.
> 52. You also, bear you your own shame, in that you have given judgment for your sisters; through your sins that you have committed more abominable than they, they are more righteous that you: yes, be you also confounded, and bear your shame, in that you have justified your sisters.
> 53. I will turn again their captivity, the captivity of Sodom and her daughters, and the captivity of Samaria and her daughters, and the captivity of your captives in the midst of them;
> 54. that you may bear your own shame, and may be ashamed because of all that you have done, in that you are a comfort to them.
> 55. Your sisters, Sodom and her daughters, shall return to their former estate; and Samaria and her daughters shall return to their former estate; and you and your daughters shall return to your former estate.
> 56. For your sister Sodom was not mentioned by your mouth in the day of your pride,
> 57. before your wickedness was uncovered, as at the time of the reproach of the daughters of Syria, and of all who are round about her, the daughters of the Philistines, who do despite to you round about.
> 58. You have borne your lewdness and your abominations, says YHWH.

The sins and abominations of the people of Jerusalem are depicted in the worst way possible: the prophet tells them that YHWH declared that the sins of Sodom and Samaria were less serious than those of the people of Jerusalem – idolatry, pride, haughtiness, injustice, and exploiting the poor people. They have brought their misfortunes upon themselves by their sins.

Against Egypt
Ezek 29: 6–14

6.	All the inhabitants of Egypt shall know that I am YHWH, because they have been a staff of reed to the house of Israel.
7.	When they took hold of you by your hand, you did break, and did tear all their shoulders; and when they leaned on you, you broke, and mad all their loins to be at a stand.
8.	Therefore thus says the Lord YHWH: Behold, I will bring a sword on you, and will cut off from you man and animal.
9.	The land of Egypt shall be a desolation and a waste; and they shall know that I am YHWH. Because he has said, The river is mine, and I have made it;
10.	therefore, behold, I am against you, and against your rivers, and I will make the land of Egypt an utter waste and desolation, from the tower of Seveneh even to the border of Ethiopia.
11.	No foot of man shall pass through it, nor foot of animal shall pass through it, neither shall it be inhabited forty years.
12.	I will make the land of Egypt a desolation in the midst of the countries that are desolate; and her cities among the cities that are laid waste shall be a desolation forty years; and I will scatter the Egyptians among the nations, and will disperse them through the countries.

> 13. For thus says the Lord YHWH: At the end of forty years will I gather the Egyptians from the peoples where they were scattered;
> 14. and I will bring back the captivity of Egypt, and will cause them to return into the land of Pathros, into the land of their birth; and they shall be there a base kingdom.

This prophecy of Ezekiel was never fulfilled. The prophet declared that the country of Egypt would lay desolate for forty years after the inhabitants have been taken into exile by an unnamed enemy. This state of affairs had to be seen as God's punishment for the way the Egyptians treated the "house of Israel" by being unreliable allies during the war with the Babylonians.

It never happened that Egypt became an "utter waste" and uninhabitable.

Against Egypt
Ezek 30: 1–5

> 1. The word of YHWH came again to me, saying,
> 2. Son of man, prophesy, and say, Thus says the Lord YHWH: Wail you, Alas for the day!
> 3. For the day is near, even the day of YHWH is near; it shall be a day of clouds, a time of the nations.
> 4. A sword shall come on Egypt, and anguish shall be in Ethiopia, when the slain shall fall in Egypt; and they shall take away her multitude, and her foundations shall be broken down.
> 5. Ethiopia, and Put, and Lud, and all the mingled people, and Cub, and the children of the land that is in league, shall fall with them by the sword.

Ezekiel warned the Egyptians and their southern neighbors that the Day of YHWH was nearby. That would be when these countries would be devastated by war.

It is understandable that this prophet would harbor negative feelings regarding Egypt and predict its defeat because this country was never a friend of Israel. It did happen that Egypt was taken over by Alexander the Great in 332 BC – a considerable time after Ezekiel's time. However, Ethiopia was never conquered by Alexander.

Israel's Great Future
Ezek: 37: 21–28

21.	Say to them, Thus says the Lord YHWH: Behold, I will take the children of Israel from among the nations, where they are gone, and will gather them on every side, and bring them into their own land:
22.	and I will make them one nation in the land, on the mountains of Israel; and one king shall be king to them all; and they shall be no more two nations, neither shall they be divided into two kingdoms any more at all;
23.	neither shall they defile themselves any more with their idols, nor with their detestable things, nor with any of their transgressions; but I will save them out of all their dwelling-places, in which they have sinned, and will cleanse them: so shall they be my people, and I will be their God.
24.	My servant David shall be king over them; and they all shall have one shepherd: they shall also walk in my ordinances, and observe my statutes, and do them.
25.	They shall dwell in the land that I have given to Jacob my servant, in which your fathers lived; and they shall dwell

> therein, they, and their children, and their children's children, forever: and David my servant shall be their prince for ever.
>
> 26. Moreover I will make a covenant of peace with them; it shall be an everlasting covenant with them; and I will place them, and multiply them, and will set my sanctuary in the midst of them forevermore.
>
> 27. My tent also shall be with them; and I will be their God, and they shall be my people.
>
> 28. The nations shall know that I am YHWH who sanctifies Israel, when my sanctuary shall be in the midst of them forevermore.

This prophecy by Ezekiel promised the following:

- All the Israelites who were abducted to other countries would return to their land;
- All the Israelites would be united in a single kingdom;
- This kingdom would be ruled by a monarch from the house of David; and
- All the Israelites would serve YHWH willingly and with enthusiasm.

None of this ever became true.

DEUTERO-ISAIAH

The unknown author of the second part of the book of Isaiah wrote his messages during the Babylonian Exile.

A Light to the Gentiles
Isa 49: 1 – 7

1.	Listen, isles, to me; and listen, you peoples, from far: YHWH has called me from the womb; from the bowels of my mother has he made mention of my name:
2.	and he has made my mouth like a sharp sword; in the shadow of his hand has he hid me: and he has made me a polished shaft; in his quiver has he kept me close:
3.	and he said to me, You are my servant; Israel, in whom I will be glorified.
4.	But I said, I have labored in vain, I have spent my strength for nothing and vanity; yet surely the justice [due] to me is with YHWH, and my recompense with my God.
5.	Now says YHWH who formed me from the womb to be his servant, to bring Jacob again to him, and that Israel be gathered to him (for I am honorable in the eyes of YHWH, and my God is become my strength);
6.	yes, he says, It is too light a thing that you should be my servant to raise up the tribes of Jacob, and to restore the preserved of Israel: I will also give you for a light to the Gentiles, that you may be my salvation to the end of the earth.
7.	Thus says YHWH, the Redeemer of Israel, [and] his Holy One, to him whom man despises, to him whom the nation abhors, to a servant of rulers: Kings shall see and arise; princes, and they shall worship; because of YHWH who is faithful, [even] the Holy One of Israel, who has chosen you.

The prophet was convinced that he was called to be a prophet even before he was born. He was called to lead the descendants of Jacob back to YHWH, their national God and their "Redeemer", but who would also be "a light to the Gentiles, that you [YHWH] may be my salvation to the end of the earth."

That means that he was supposed to tell the Babylonians, who had abducted him and other Jews, about who and what YHWH is. He had to call them to repentance, just as the fictitious prophet Jonah did in Nineveh.

One is compelled to ask: why is there no evidence that this prophet embarked on a missionary drive in Babylonia? If YHWH really wanted to be worshipped by all peoples on earth, as stated in this passage, why did He focus all his attention only on Israel – and not also on the Egyptians, Assyrians, Greeks, Medes, Persians, and other nations? Why were all the prophets in the service of YHWH exclusively Hebrew-speaking?

This is, yet, another misguided prophecy.

TRITO-ISAIAH

The last part of the book of Isaiah (ch 56–66), called the Third Isaiah or Trito-Isaiah, was written by an unknown author after the end of the Babylonian Exile – probably a former student of Isaiah of Jerusalem.

YHWH will be Worshipped in Jerusalem
Isa 60: 1–12

1.	Arise, shine; for your light is come, and the glory of YHWH is risen on you.
2.	For, behold, darkness shall cover the earth, and gross darkness the peoples; but YHWH will arise on you, and his glory shall be seen on you.
3.	Nations shall come to your light, and kings to the brightness of your rising.

OLD TESTAMENT PROPHECIES REGARDING CURRENT AFFAIRS

4.	Lift up your eyes round about, and see: they all gather themselves together, they come to you; your sons shall come from far, and your daughters shall be carried in the arms.
5.	Then you shall see and be radiant, and your heart shall thrill and be enlarged; because the abundance of the sea shall be turned to you, the wealth of the nations shall come to you.
6.	The multitude of camels shall cover you, the dromedaries of Midian and Ephah; all they from Sheba shall come; they shall bring gold and frankincense, and shall proclaim the praises of YHWH.
7.	All the flocks of Kedar shall be gathered together to you, the rams of Nebaioth shall minister to you; they shall come up with acceptance on my altar; and I will glorify the house of my glory.
8.	Who are these who fly as a cloud, and as the doves to their windows?
9.	Surely the isles shall wait for me, and the ships of Tarshish first, to bring your sons from far, their silver and their gold with them, for the name of YHWH your God, and for the Holy One of Israel, because he has glorified you.
10.	Foreigners shall build up your walls, and their kings shall minister to you: for in my wrath I struck you, but in my favor have I had mercy on you.
11.	Your gates also shall be open continually; they shall not be shut day nor night; that men may bring to you the wealth of the nations, and their kings led captive.
12.	For that nation and kingdom that will not serve you shall perish; yes, those nations shall be utterly wasted.

This prophecy contains a very optimistic promise: the Judeans could expect that the people from all nations on earth, even from remote islands, would flock to Jerusalem to worship YHWH there. These peoples were expected to bring valuable gifts, which would make the people of Judea very rich. Jerusalem would be such a safe place under YHWH's favor that the city gates would stay open all night.

This optimism was never realized. The book of Nehemia contains the report of how the people of Jerusalem had to struggle to restore and strengthen the city walls and defense works due to the dangers and threats posed by neighboring peoples.

Honor instead of Suffering
Isa 61: 1–7

1.	The Spirit of the Lord YHWH is on me; because YHWH has anointed me to preach good news to the humble; he has sent me to bind up the broken-hearted, to proclaim liberty to the captives, and the opening [of the prison] to those who are bound;
2.	to proclaim the year of YHWH's favor, and the day of vengeance of our God; to comfort all who mourn;
3.	to appoint to those who mourn in Zion, to give to them a garland for ashes, the oil of joy for mourning, the garment of praise for the spirit of heaviness; that they may be called trees of righteousness, the planting of YHWH, that he may be glorified.
4.	They shall build the old wastes, they shall raise up the former desolations, and they shall repair the waste cities, the desolations of many generations.
5.	Strangers shall stand and feed your flocks, and foreigners shall be your plowmen and your vine-dressers.

6.	But you shall be named the priests of YHWH; men shall call you the ministers of our God: you shall eat the wealth of the nations, and in their glory shall you boast yourselves.
7.	Instead of your shame [you shall have] double; and instead of dishonor they shall rejoice in their portion: therefore in their land they shall possess double; everlasting joy shall be to them.

The author of the third part of Isaiah saw it as his calling to provide the returning exiles from Babylon with hope for the future. With this goal in mind, he wrote this prophecy and other similar prophecies to sketch a wonderful future waiting for the people of God.

History tells us that it took some time for the Judeans to rebuild their lives, but the Persian period in the history of the Jews seems to have been generally a peaceful and relatively prosperous time. The book of Job, which was written during this period, for instance, tells the story of the experiences of a prosperous landowner.

The Wrath of YHWH
Isa 63: 1–6

1.	Who is this who comes from Edom, with dyed garments from Bozrah? this who is glorious in his clothing, marching in the greatness of his strength? I who speak in righteousness, mighty to save.
2.	Why are you red in your clothing, and your garments like him who treads in the wine vat?
3.	I have trodden the winepress alone; and of the peoples there was no man with me: yes, I trod them in my anger, and

> trampled them in my wrath; and their lifeblood is sprinkled on my garments, and I have stained all my clothing.
> 4. For the day of vengeance was in my heart, and the year of my redeemed is come.
> 5. I looked, and there was none to help; and I wondered that there was none to uphold: therefore my own arm brought salvation to me; and my wrath, it upheld me.
> 6. I trod down the peoples in my anger, and made them drunk in my wrath, and I poured out their lifeblood on the earth.

This prophecy quoted the words of YHWH who expressed his anger against those in Edom and Judea who did not take his messages seriously enough. These ungrateful people who disbelieved or ignored his promises had to know that He has the power to crush them, just as a wine farmer crushes the grapes in a wine press.

OBADIAH

It is uncertain when this book was written, but a post-exilic date is a possibility. The prophet was critical of the Edomites who neglected to help Israel against common enemies.

Against Edom
Obad 1: 1–4

> 1. The vision of Obadiah. This is what the Lord YHWH says about Edom. We have heard news from YHWH, and an ambassador is sent among the nations, saying, "Arise, and let's rise up against her in battle.
> 2. Behold, I have made you small among the nations. You are greatly despised.

> 3. The pride of your heart has deceived you, you who dwell in the clefts of the rock, whose habitation is high, who says in his heart, 'Who will bring me down to the ground?'

The Edomites, who lived "in the cleft of the rock" – the ancient city of Petra in present southern Jordan – are told that Israel's God would humiliate them. It happened many centuries later when the Edomites or Idumeans were absorbed into Judah and adopted the religion of Israel. The king of Judea at the time when Jesus was born, Herod the Great, was of Idumean descent.

The entrance to the ancient city of Petra through the narrow passage in the mountain – "in the cleft in the rock"

ZECHARIAH

The prophecies of the book of Zecheriah are particularly interesting since it is possible to reconstruct the scenes in the starry skies that the prophet described and used as inspirations for his comments on the circumstances in and around Judea after the return of some exiles from Babylon and the rebuilding of the temple.

The Four Horsemen of Zechariah
Zech 1: 7 – 15

7.	On the four and twentieth day of the eleventh month, which is the month Shebat, in the second year of Darius, came the word of YHWH to Zechariah the son of Berechiah, the son of Iddo, the prophet, saying,
8.	I saw in the night, and, behold, a man riding on a red horse, and he stood among the myrtle-trees that were in the bottom; and behind him there were horses, red, sorrel, and white.
9.	Then said I, my lord, what are these? The angel who talked with me said to me, I will show you what these are.
10.	The man who stood among the myrtle-trees answered, These are they whom YHWH has sent to walk back and forth through the earth.
11.	They answered the angel of YHWH who stood among the myrtle-trees, and said, We have walked back and forth through the earth, and, behold, all the earth sits still, and is at rest.
12.	Then the angel of YHWH answered, Oh YHWH of Hosts, how long will you not have mercy on Jerusalem and on the cities of Judah, against which you have had indignation these seventy years?
13.	YHWH answered the angel who talked with me with good words, [even] comfortable words.

> 14. So the angel who talked with me said to me, Cry you, saying, Thus says YHWH of Hosts: I am jealous for Jerusalem and for Zion with a great jealousy.
>
> 15. I am very sore displeased with the nations that are at ease; for I was but a little displeased, and they helped forward the affliction.

Zechariah gave an exact date when he had his first vision, namely "On the four and twentieth day of the eleventh month, which is the month Shebat, in the second year of Darius." It is possible to calculate exactly when that was according to our Gregorian calendar.

Darius (Hebrew: דָּרְיָוֶשׁ – *Dar'yavesh*) ascended the throne in September 522 BC. His second year, therefore, ended in September 520 BC. The month Shebat started on 14 January 520 BC with the new moon. The 24th day of this month, therefore, fell on 7 February 520 BC.

Zechariah observed four horsemen who had the task of reporting on the condition of the world. They found that the world was at rest and peaceful – certainly due to the rule of King Darius of Persia at that time. God was, however, not satisfied with this situation because his people in the Persian province of Judea lived in poverty.

It is possible to recreate Zechariah's vision on 7 February 520 BC with the help of a computerized astronomical program. Zechariah saw these four horsemen as constellations in the starry skies, shortly before dawn. The first one, on a red horse, was Pegasus, the winged horse, lying on the horizon, visible between some myrtle trees. The Jews knew this constellation as Nimrod's Horse.[110] He is described as red because of the first rays of daybreak

---

[110] Allen, *Star Names*, 323.

behind him. Next to him was the constellation of Equuleus, the Foal, a faint constellation, which also glowed red.

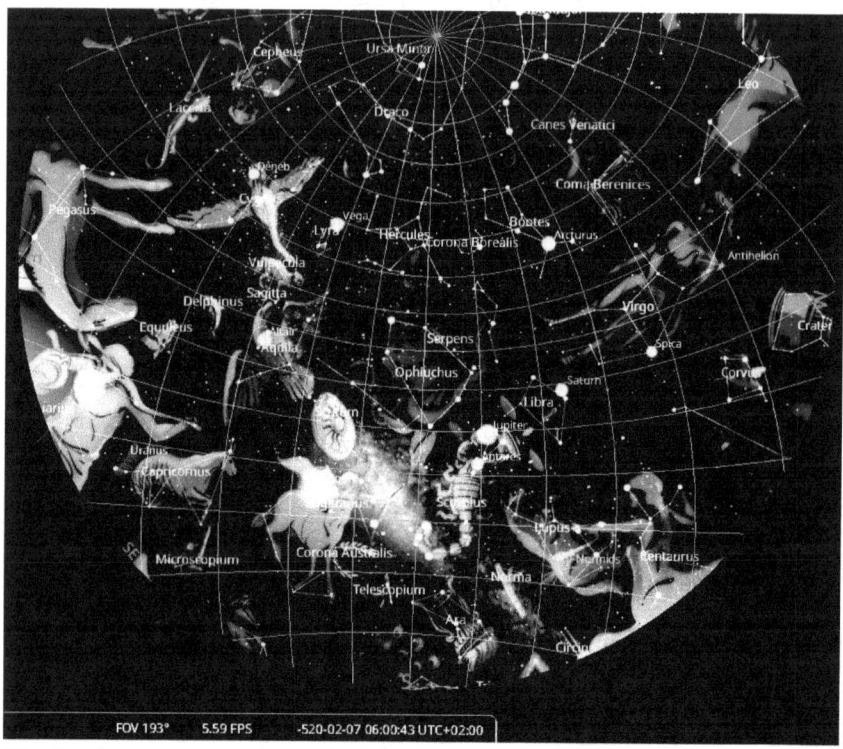

The four horsemen seen by Zechariah on 7 February 520 BC, at 06:00 local time, looking south: Pegasus and Equuleus (the two red horses), Sagittarius, and Centaurus. The angel who spoke was the moon (26% illuminated) in Sagittarius.

Pegasus as drawn by Johannes Hevelius. Equuleus is faintly visible next to Pegasus.

Sagittarius and Centaurus, as drawn by Johannes Hevelius

On the southern horizon the other two horsemen were seen: Sagittarius, the Archer, and Centaurus, the Centaur. Both represented Greek mythological figures, but the Jews avoided their pagan connotations and only regarded them as men on horseback.[111]

Hachlili reports that the Jewish depictions of Sagittarius were always that of a man holding a bow and arrow. They "felt that the centaur was a pagan hybrid figure and consequently would not want to use it ..."[112]

Zechariah saw YHWH of Hosts, most probably at the celestial north pole – just as Isaiah some centuries previously (Isa 6). The angel who spoke to him must have been the crescent moon inside the constellation of Sagittarius – at that stage, the brightest object in the sky. The moon was also peeping through some myrtle trees on the horizon as Zechariah was standing at a spot outside Jerusalem.

The Four Horns
Zech 1: 18–21

18.	I lifted up my eyes, and saw, and, behold, four horns.
19.	I said to the angel who talked with me, What are these? He

---

[111] Allen, *Star Names,* 151 & 354.
[112] Hachlili, "The Zodiac", 224.

> answered me, These are the horns which have scattered Judah, Israel, and Jerusalem.
> 20. YHWH showed me four smiths.
> 21. Then said I, What come these to do? He spoke, saying, These are the horns which scattered Judah, so that no man did lift up his head; but these are come to terrify them, to cast down the horns of the nations, which lifted up their horn against the land of Judah to scatter it.

During his second vision, Zechariah saw four horns. Horns are the weapons of a horned animal that has two of them. These two animals symbolized kingdoms that have harmed the Israelites severely. The first one was Egypt where the Israelites were slaves long ago, but also when the Judean army was destroyed during the battle of Megiddo in 609 BC when king Josiah fell. The other kingdom was Babylonia of which the army destroyed Jerusalem in 586 BC, after which many Jews were deported to Babylonia.[113]

The four smiths (or craftsmen) whom the prophet also saw, who overthrew the oppressive empires and came to the aid of the Judeans, must have been the following Persian kings:

- Cyrus II (the Great) the conqueror of the Median Empire in 550 BC and the Babylonian Empire in 539 BC, and who allowed the exiled Jews to return to Judea;
- Cambyses I, who ruled during the early 6th century–559 BC; he was the founder of the Achaemenid Dynasty;
- Cambyses II, who ruled during 530–522 BC; and
- Darius I (the Great) who ruled during 522–486 BC.[114]

---

[113] Perowne, "Jerusalem".
[114] Young, "Iran, Ancient".

The relief stone of Darius the Great in the Behustum Inscription

Zechariah had this vision when he again observed the night sky. He saw two constellations of animals with two horns each: Taurus, the Bull, and Aries, the Ram. The four craftsmen or smiths are to be found in the nearby constellations of Orion (the Hunter), Gemini (the Twins), and Perseus (the Champion). The Jews identified Orion with Nimrod, the Twins were associated with Esau and Jacob, and Perseus was seen as David with the head of Goliath.[115]

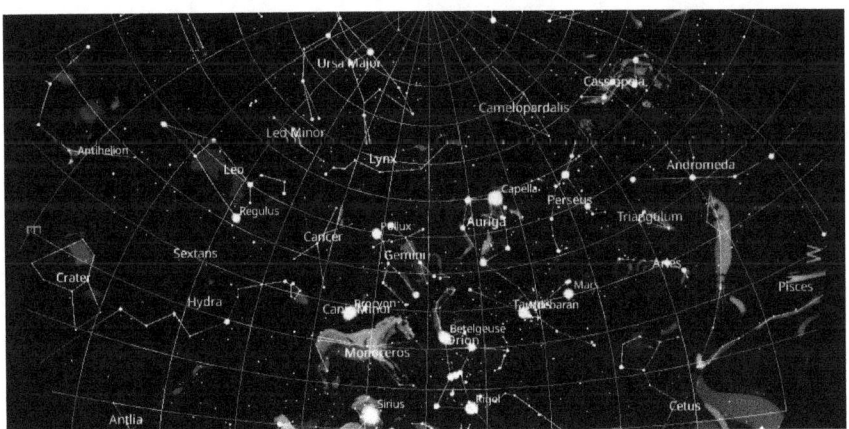

Taurus, the Bull with its two horns, and Aries, the Ram also with two horns, lying next to each other during February 520 BC after sunset. The warriors watching them are Orion, the Hunter, Gemini, the Twins, and Perseus, the Hero. The planet Mars lies within Taurus.

---

[115] Allen, *Star Names*, 224, 309, 331.

Taurus, the Bull, and Aries, the Ram, as illustrated by Johannes Hevelius

 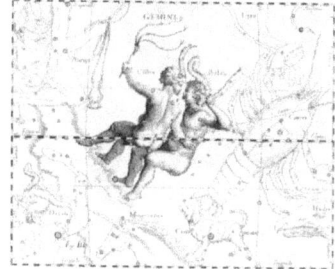

Orion, the Hunter, and Gemini, the Twins, as drawn by Hevelius

Perseus, the Hero, with the head of Medusa, as illustrated by Hevelius

The Man with the Measuring Line
Zech 2: 1 – 8

1.	I lifted up my eyes, and saw, and, behold, a man with a measuring line in his hand.
2.	Then said I, Where go you? He said to me, To measure Jerusalem, to see what is the breadth of it, and what is the length of it.

> 3. Behold, the angel who talked with me went forth, and another angel went out to meet him,
> 4. and said to him, Run, speak to this young man, saying, Jerusalem shall be inhabited as villages without walls, by reason of the multitude of men and cattle therein.
> 5. For I, says YHWH, will be to her a wall of fire round about, and I will be the glory in the midst of her.
> 6. Ho, ho, flee from the land of the north, says YHWH; for I have spread you abroad as the four winds of the sky, says YHWH.
> 7. Ho Zion, escape, you who dwell with the daughter of Babylon.
> 8. For thus says YHWH of hosts: After glory has he sent me to the nations which plundered you; for he who touches you touches the apple of his eye.

In yet another vision, Zecheriah watched a man with a measuring tape, measuring the city of God, Jerusalem. At that time, Jerusalem had few inhabitants, namely the people who survived the war against the Babylonians and some returned exiles. The goal of the measuring exercise was to plan for the future, when more people would return from Babylonia.

God gave the promise that Jerusalem would be protected because He would dwell there. There would be so many people, with their animals, that many would live outside the city walls because the city would become too small for all of them.

Zechariah received inspiration for this scene from YHWH of Hosts, God who is living between the hosts of stars. The man with the measuring line was the constellation of Ophiuchus, also known as Serpentarius, which the prophet watched shortly before dawn.

Ophiuchus is always pictured as grasping a long snake – the measuring tape in this vision.

Jerusalem was represented by the constellation of Virgo, the Virgin. Israel is often called the wife or woman of God in the Old Testament (Isa 54: 5–8; Ezek 16: 8–21; Jer 3: 6–8; Amos 3: 1–2) and that must be how Zechariah saw Virgo as Jerusalem. The planet Saturn was lying next to Virgo's feet. This planet, the seventh moving body in the sky, had a special connection with the people of Israel who worshipped God especially on the seventh day of the week. The Hebrew word for "Shabbath" and the name of "Saturn" are related [Hebrew: שַׁבְּתַאי (Shabray – Saturn) and שַׁבָּת (Shabbath)]. The English name of "Satur(n)day" for the seventh day of the week is still a reminder of the day of Saturn.

The angel who addressed Zechariah must have been the crescent moon in the west.

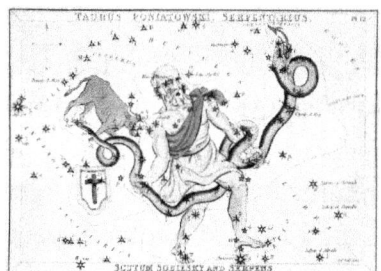 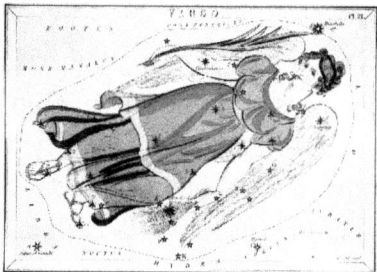

The constellations of Ophiuchus with Serpens and Virgo, as drawn by Hevelius

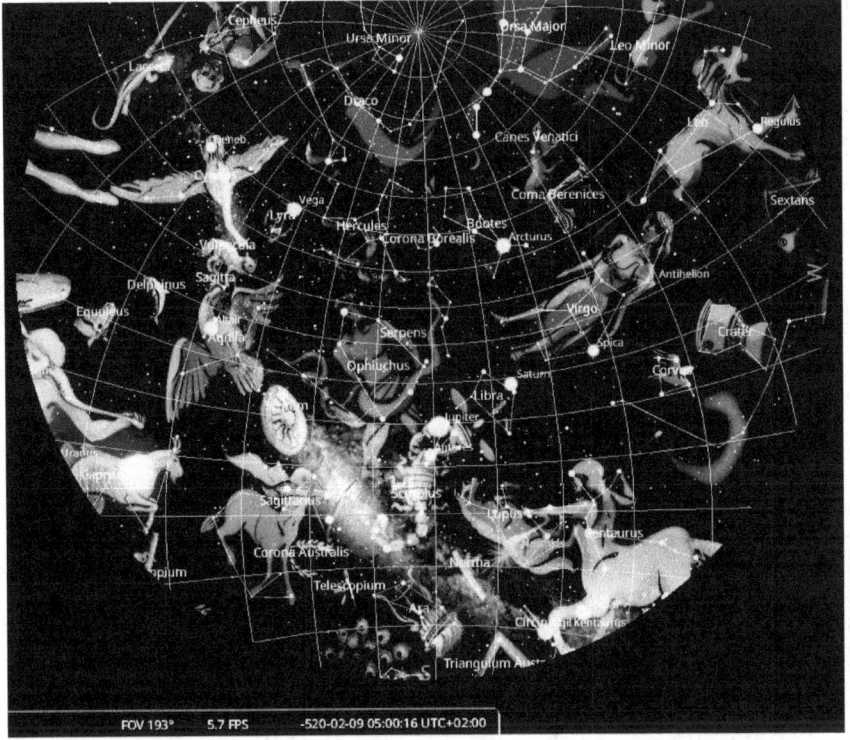

The night sky over Jerusalem during February 520 BC, before daybreak. The constellations Ophiuchus or Serpentarius with Serpens (the man with the measuring line) and Virgo (Jerusalem) situated next to each other. The planet Saturn lies next to the feet of Virgo and a crescent moon is visible in the east, inside Capricornus.

Satan and Joshua

Zech 3: 1–10

1.	He showed me Joshua the high priest standing before the angel of YHWH, and Satan standing at his right hand to be his adversary.
2.	YHWH said to Satan, YHWH rebuke you, Satan; yes, YHWH that has chosen Jerusalem rebuke you: is not this a brand plucked out of the fire?

> 3. Now Joshua was clothed with filthy garments, and was standing before the angel.
> 4. He answered and spoke to those who stood before him, saying, Take the filthy garments from off him. To him he said, Behold, I have caused your iniquity to pass from you, and I will clothe you with rich clothing.
> 5. I said, Let them set a clean mitre on his head. So they set a clean mitre on his head, and clothed him with garments; and the angel of YHWH was standing by.
> 6. The angel of YHWH protested to Joshua, saying,
> 7. Thus says YHWH of hosts: If you will walk in my ways, and if you will keep my charge, then you also shall judge my house, and shall also keep my courts, and I will give you a place of access among these who stand by.
> 8. Hear now, Joshua the high priest, you and your fellows who sit before you; for they are men who are a sign: for, behold, I will bring forth my servant the Branch.
> 9. For, behold, the stone that I have set before Joshua; on one stone are seven eyes: behold, I will engrave the engraving of it, says YHWH of Hosts, and I will remove the iniquity of that land in one day.
> 10. In that day, says YHWH of hosts, shall you invite every man his neighbor under the vine and under the fig-tree.

Zecheriah watched two figures: the high priest, Joshua, and Satan, his adversary or accuser.

The name "Satan" is used here as a personal name, but also in its literal meaning of "accuser" or "adversary". Satan makes only three appearances in the Old Testament:

- In the book of Job, where he is depicted as one of the "sons of God" or an angel who executed God's orders (Job 1 and 2);
- In 1 Chr 21: 1–2 where he coaxed King David into holding a census in his country; and
- Here in Zech 3.

In this scene, Satan is not the devil of the New Testament, the adversary or enemy of God and the source of all evil. In this scene, he merely criticized Joshua's dirty clothes, a symbol of his sins. YHWH rebuked him for being so critical. This Satan is not a demonic figure, but a heavenly personage who has direct access to YHWH.

There is, however, an angel or messenger of YHWH standing by and he orders that Joshua be supplied with clean clothes as a sign that his sins were forgiven. He was even given a clean mitre or head dress.

YHWH then addressed Joshua and admonished him to obey his commandments. He would be made a judge or leader of his people. A stone with seven all-seeing eyes was given to him as a sign that his sins and the sins of his people in Jerusalem were forgiven by God who can see everything.

God also promised that his servant, "the Branch", would appear. This expression is also used in Zech 6:12 where it is applied to Zerubbabel, the governor of Judea, who had to supervise the rebuilding of the temple. He was the grandson of Jehoiachin, the penultimate king of Judah and leader of the first group of exiles who were allowed by Cyrus the Great to return to Judea (Ezra 2: 1–2, 64;3: 8; 5: 2).

The Hebrew word for "Branch" is צֶמַח (*Tsemach*), which means "sprout, growth, branch", is derived from a verb which means "to sprout, spring up, grow up". This expression was used elsewhere to denote descendants of David – such as Zerubbabel (Zech 6: 12;

Isa 4: 2; 11:1; 53: 2; Jer 23: 5; 33: 15; Ezek 17: 22–24; 34: 29).

Zecheriah found the figures of Joshua and Satan between the stars. The constellation of Boötes represented the high priest. His head dress lies next to him, the constellation of Corona Borealis, the Northern Crown. In Zech 6: 11 it is explicitly stated that Joshua was to be crowned.

The stone with seven eyes must be the constellation of Coma Berenices, the Hair of Berenice, a cluster of faint stars. The angel before whom the high priest was standing, was Ophiuchus, the Snake Catcher, below his feet.

Satan as a heavenly figure is to be found in the constellation of Hercules, to the right-hand side of Joshua. The ancient Jews saw this constellation as the biblical hero of Samson.[116]

---

[116] Allen, *Star Names,* 242.

The sky before dawn in February 520 BC as seen from Jerusalem – a wide view and a narrower view, looking northwards. Boötes represents the high priest Joshua with a crown (Corona Borealis) and Hercules must be seen as Satan. Virgo depicts Jerusalem. The angel of YHWH is again the planet Jupiter inside Scorpius (outside the illustration above).

The constellations of Boötes and Hercules, as drawn by Hevelius

Jerusalem is also mentioned and that city is identified with the figure of Virgo, the Virgin, with the planet Saturn at her feet – a depiction of the bride of YWHW.

The Flying Scroll and the Woman in a Bucket
Zech 5: 1–11

1. Then again I lifted up my eyes, and saw, and, behold, a flying scroll.
2. He said to me, What see you? I answered, I see a flying scroll; the length of it is twenty cubits, and the breadth of it ten cubits.
3. Then said he to me, This is the curse that goes forth over the surface of the whole land: for everyone who steals shall be cut off on the one side according to it; and everyone who swears shall be cut off on the other side according to it.
4. I will cause it to go forth, says YHWH of Hosts, and it shall enter into the house of the thief, and into the house of him who swears falsely by my name; and it shall abide in the midst of his house, and shall consume it with the timber of it and the stones of it.
5. Then the angel who talked with me went forth, and said to me, Lift up now your eyes, and see what is this that goes forth.
6. I said, What is it? He said, This is the ephah that goes forth. He said moreover, This is their appearance in all the land
7. (and, behold, there was lifted up a talent of lead); and this is a woman sitting in the midst of the ephah.
8. He said, This is Wickedness: and he cast her down into the midst of the ephah; and he cast the weight of lead on the mouth of it.
9. Then lifted I up my eyes, and saw, and, behold, there came forth two women, and the wind was in their wings; now

> they had wings like the wings of a stork; and they lifted up the ephah between earth and the sky.
> 10. Then said I to the angel who talked with me, Where do these bear the ephah?
> 11. He said to me, To build her a house in the land of Shinar: and when it is prepared, she shall be set there in her own place.

This chapter contains two visions, which may have occurred shortly after each other, namely the vision of the flying scroll and the vision of the woman inside the ephah or bucket.

As happened previously, Zechariah watched the sky before dawn during February 520 BC. The bright Milky Way, that stretched over the whole sky, caught his attention. He interpreted it as a long and broad scroll on which all the sins of mankind were written – theft, lies, adultery, and whatever else. YHWH gave him the promise that the sins of thieves and liars will haunt them and that they will have to bear the curses that result from their sins.

In the scene of the ephah and the woman the angel who usually spoke to him, let him see a woman sitting in an ephah or bucket in which a measure of grain was measured. This woman personified wickedness and her fate was sealed. Two winged females took her and the ephah to the country of Shinear, which is in the far east, in Mesopotamia. That amounted to a promise that God would rid this earth of wickedness and sin.

The woman, who represented wickedness, is clearly the constellation of Virgo, next to the constellation of Crater, which may represent a bucket. The winged creatures to the east of these two, the constellations of Aquiula, the Eagle, and Cygnus, the Swan, swept down with their big wings, grabbed this woman and the ephah to fly away to the east.

The angel who showed the prophet these scenes must have been the bright planet, Jupiter, inside Scorpius.

The night sky before dawn during February 520 BC with only the outlines of the constellations shown. The Milky Way is clearly visible, and also Virgo, Crater, Aquila and Cygnus. Jupiter lies in Scorpius.

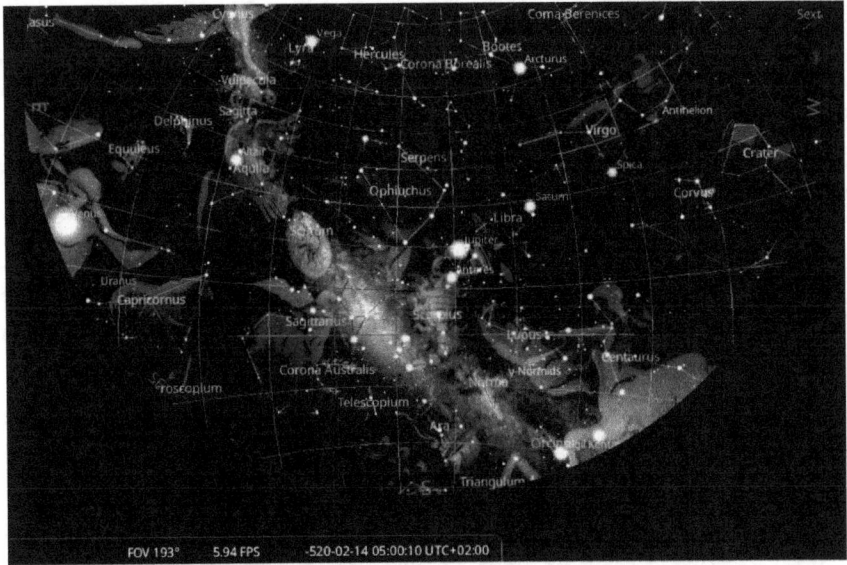

The same scene as in the previous illustration, but with the pictures of the different constellations added.

The Four Chariots
Zech 6: 1–8

1.	Again I lifted up my eyes, and saw, and, behold, there came four chariots out from between two mountains; and the mountains were mountains of brass.
2.	In the first chariot were red horses; and in the second chariot black horses;
3.	and in the third chariot white horses; and in the fourth chariot grizzled strong horses.
4.	Then I answered the angel who talked with me, What are these, my lord?
5.	The angel answered me, These are the four winds of the sky, which go forth from standing before the Lord of all the earth.

> 6. [The chariot] in which are the black horses goes forth toward the north country; and the white went forth after them; and the grizzled went forth toward the south country.
> 7. The strong went forth, and sought to go that they might walk back and forth through the earth: and he said, Get you hence, walk back and forth through the earth. So they walked back and forth through the earth.
> 8. Then cried he to me, and spoke to me, saying, Behold, those who go toward the north country have quieted my spirit in the north country.

Zechariah described something impossible: four chariots, each filled with horses. A chariot in those days, called a מֶרְכָּבָה (*Merkabah*) in Hebrew, was a war vehicle drawn by one or more horses and usually carrying one or two soldiers, usually the charioteer and an archer.

There was nothing in the heavens visible from Jerusalem during 520 BC that resembled a chariot. There were, however, four horses: Pegasus, Equuleus, Sagittarius, and Centaurus – the animals also described in Zech 1. They came out from two mountains that shone like brass with their yellow rocks. Jerusalem lies in a hilly part of Palestine and there are several hills to the east, from which direction Pegasus and Equuleus rose from behind the horizon.

A chariot with two horses and two warriors on an ancient Greek drinking vessel, dating from ca 510 BC

The constellations of Pegasus and Equuleus are rising in the east, while Sagittarius and Centaurus lay towards the south. The Jews regarded the last two as ordinary horsemen, not mythological figures. Pegasus was known as the Horse of Nimrod. Jupiter, inside Scorpius, was the brightest object in the sky.

According to Zechariah, they moved in different directions. The angel who spoke to him (probably Jupiter in Scorpius) told him that these four chariots received orders from God and that they symbolized the four winds or wind directions of the earth. That meant that all the forces on earth, whether they be military, political, or part of the natural world, are under the direction of God.

Three Revelations
Zech 7: 1–14

1.	It happened in the fourth year of king Darius, that the word of YHWH came to Zechariah in the fourth [day] of the ninth month, even in Chislev.

2.	Now [they of] Bethel had sent Sharezer and Regem-Melech, and their men, to entreat the favor of YHWH,
3.	[and] to speak to the priests of the house of YHWH of Hosts, and to the prophets, saying, Should I weep in the fifth month, separating myself, as I have done these so many years?
4.	Then came the word of YHWH of Hosts to me, saying,
5.	Speak to all the people of the land, and to the priests, saying, When you fasted and mourned in the fifth and in the seventh [month], even these seventy years, did you at all fast to me, even to me?
6.	When you eat, and when you drink, do not you eat for yourselves, and drink for yourselves?
7.	[Should you] not [hear] the words which YHWH cried by the former prophets, when Jerusalem was inhabited and in prosperity, and the cities of it round about her, and the South and the lowland were inhabited?
8.	The word of YHWH came to Zechariah, saying,
9.	Thus has YHWH of Hosts spoken, saying, Execute true judgment, and show kindness and compassion every man to his brother;
10.	and don't oppress the widow, nor the fatherless, the sojourner, nor the poor; and let none of you devise evil against his brother in your heart.
11.	But they refused to listen, and pulled away the shoulder, and stopped their ears, that they might not hear.
12.	Yes, they made their hearts as an adamant stone, lest they should hear the law, and the words which YHWH of Hosts

> had sent by his Spirit by the former prophets: therefore there came great wrath from YHWH of Hosts.
>
> 13. It is come to pass that, as he cried, and they would not hear, so they shall cry, and I will not hear, said YHWH of Hosts;
>
> 14. but I will scatter them with a whirlwind among all the nations which they have not known. Thus the land was desolate after them, so that no man passed through nor returned: for they laid the pleasant land desolate.

This chapter in the book of Zechariah contains three separate revelations, each one starting with the words "the word of YHWH came to Zechariah, saying…" The first one (vs 1–3) is dated precisely and it may be assumed that the other two followed shortly afterwards. It is dated during the fourth year of Darius, which was 518 BC. The month Chislev, the ninth month, always fell during November and December. The fourth day after the start of this month at new moon turns out to be 17 November 518 BC.

These communications from YHWH to the prophet, to the people of Bethel, and to the rest of the country cannot be connected to any vision inspired by the night sky and they were somehow directly revealed to Zechariah.

In the first communication, YHWH reminded his people that He wept in the past due to their sins. The second communication (vs 4–7) dealt with the rituals of fasting and weeping of the people and whose hearts were not involved with these actions.

In the third message (vs 8–14), God expected of his people to practice social justice, charity, compassion with the helpless, and justice. With this, Zecheriah continued in the footsteps of Amos with his comments on the social ills of his time.

The Shepherds
Zech 10: 1–12

1. Ask you of YHWH rain in the time of the latter rain, [even of] YHWH who makes lightnings; and he will give them showers of rain, to everyone grass in the field.
2. For the teraphim have spoken vanity, and the diviners have seen a lie; and they have told false dreams, they comfort in vain: therefore they go their way like sheep, they are afflicted, because there is no shepherd.
3. My anger is kindled against the shepherds, and I will punish the male goats; for YHWH of Hosts has visited his flock, the house of Judah, and will make them as his goodly horse in the battle.
4. From him shall come forth the corner-stone, from him the nail, from him the battle bow, from him every ruler together.
5. They shall be as mighty men, treading down [their enemies] in the mire of the streets in the battle; and they shall fight, because YHWH is with them; and the riders on horses shall be confounded.
6. I will strengthen the house of Judah, and I will save the house of Joseph, and I will bring them back; for I have mercy on them; and they shall be as though I had not cast them off: for I am YHWH their God, and I will hear them.
7. [They of] Ephraim shall be like a mighty man, and their heart shall rejoice as through wine; yes, their children shall see it, and rejoice; their heart shall be glad in YHWH.
8. I will hiss for them, and gather them; for I have redeemed them; and they shall increase as they have increased.

OLD TESTAMENT PROPHECIES REGARDING CURRENT AFFAIRS

> 9. I will sow them among the peoples; and they shall remember me in far countries; and they shall live with their children, and shall return.
>
> 10. I will bring them again also out of the land of Egypt, and gather them out of Assyria; and I will bring them into the land of Gilead and Lebanon; and [place] shall not be found for them.
>
> 11. He will pass through the sea of affliction, and will strike the waves in the sea, and all the depths of the Nile shall dry up; and the pride of Assyria shall be brought down, and the scepter of Egypt shall depart.
>
> 12. I will strengthen them in YHWH; and they shall walk up and down in his name, says YHWH.

The first three verses of this chapter amount to a condemnation of false prophets, soothsayers, and those who rely on their teraphim or domestic idols. They can be compared with wayward shepherds who neglected their flocks, which made YHWH angry.

However, He reminds the people that He is YHWH, their God, and he will make sure that all those who have been strewn all over the world will return to their country. Those who fled to Egypt and those of the old northern kingdom, called Ephraim in this chapter, will come back to Gilead and the Lebanon. God will see to it that a great leader, called a "corner stone", will be available and he will lead other rulers or chiefs and a great army consisting of fighters who will cause the cavalry of the enemy to be ashamed.

This prophecy was only partly fulfilled during 110 BC when the Jews successfully threw off the yoke of the Greek kings of Syria and established an own kingdom for a few decades.[117] It never

---

[117] Knight, "Maccabees".

happened that all those who were strewn all over the world ever returned to Palestine. The Israelites who were deported by the Assyrians were absorbed by the nations where they were settled. Ephraim and the other tribes of the northern kingdom became known as the "lost tribes of Israel".[118]

The Jewish community in Egypt endured many centuries without returning to Judea. Most of them adopted Greek as their home language, although they retained their links with the Judaism. There was even a famous Jewish school in Alexandria with Philo Judaeus as its most famous professor during the first century AD.[119]

HAGGAI

A More Beautiful Temple
Hag 2: 6–9

6.	For this is what YHWH of Hosts says: "Yet once, it is a little while, and I will shake the heavens, the earth, the sea, and the dry land;
7.	and I will shake all nations. The precious things of all nations will come, and I will fill this house with glory," says YHWH of Hosts.
8.	"The silver is mine, and the gold is mine," says YHWHG of Hosts.
9.	"The latter glory of this house will be greater than the former," says YHWH of Hosts; "and in this place will I give peace," says YHWH of Hosts.

It was the task of the prophet Haggai to encourage the returning Jews

---

[118] Enc Brit, "Ephraim".
[119] Enc Brit, "Philo Judaeus."

from Babylonia to rebuild the Jerusalem temple and rebuild their lives. In the passage quoted above, he promised that the rebuilt temple would surpass the temple of Solomon in glory.

According to Ezra 3: 12, there was joy when the foundation stone of the new temple was laid, but there were also those who wept. According to Simensky, the people who wept were the older generation who remembered Solomon's temple and compared the new more modest building with that edifice.[120] That means that the prophecy of Haggai was inaccurate.

Pure-Hearted Builders
Hag 2: 10–19

10.	In the twenty-fourth day of the ninth month, in the second year of Darius, the Word of YHWH came by Haggai the prophet, saying,
11.	"Thus says YHWH of Hosts: Ask now the priests concerning the law, saying,
12.	'If someone carries holy meat in the fold of his garment, and with his fold touches bread, stew, wine, oil, or any food, will it become holy?'" The priests answered, "No."
13.	Then Haggai said, "If one who is unclean by reason of a dead body touch any of these, will it be unclean?" The priests answered, "It will be unclean."
14.	Then Haggai answered, "'So is this people, and so is this nation before me,' says YHWH; 'and so is every work of their hands. That which they offer there is unclean.
15.	Now, please consider from this day and backward, before a stone was laid on a stone in the temple of YHWH.

---

[120] Sinensky, "Ezra Chapter 3".

16.	Through all that time, when one came to a heap of twenty measures, there were only ten. When one came to the wine vat to draw out fifty, there were only twenty.
17.	I struck you with blight, mildew, and hail in all the work of your hands; yet you didn't turn to me,' says YHWH.
18.	'Consider, please, from this day and backward, from the twenty-fourth day of the ninth month, since the day that the foundation of YHWH's temple was laid, consider it.
19.	Is the seed yet in the barn? Yes, the vine, the fig-tree, the pomegranate, and the olive tree haven't brought forth. From this day will I bless you.'"

Haggai gave an exact date when he had this vision, namely "In the twenty-fourth day of the ninth month, in the second year of Darius." It is possible to calculate exactly when that was according to our Gregorian calendar, namely 17 October 520 BC.

YHWE was dissatisfied with his people who had to rebuild his temple due to their impurity of heart. He wanted them to be devoted to Him totally – not half-way.

DANIEL

The book of Daniel presents itself as the story of one Daniel, who lived during the Babylonian Exile, during the sixth century BC. The book was, however, only written during the second century BC and it used imaginary prophecies in a historical setting to comment on current affairs.

Nebuchadnezzar's Dream
Dan 2: 31–45

OLD TESTAMENT PROPHECIES REGARDING CURRENT AFFAIRS

31. You, O king, saw, and, behold, a great image. This image, which was mighty, and whose brightness was excellent, stood before you; and the aspect of it was awesome.

32. As for this image, its head was of fine gold, its breast and its arms of silver, its belly and its thighs of brass,

33. its legs of iron, its feet part of iron, and part of clay.

34. You saw until a stone was cut out without hands, which struck the image on its feet that were of iron and clay, and broke them in pieces.

35. Then was the iron, the clay, the brass, the silver, and the gold, broken in pieces together, and became like the chaff of the summer threshing floors; and the wind carried them away, so that no place was found for them: and the stone that struck the image became a great mountain, and filled the whole earth.

36. This is the dream; and we will tell the interpretation of it before the king.

37. You, O king, are king of kings, to whom the God of heaven has given the kingdom, the power, and the strength, and the glory;

38. and wherever the children of men dwell, the animals of the field and the birds of the sky has he given into your hand, and has made you to rule over them all: you are the head of gold.

39. After you shall arise another kingdom inferior to you; and another third kingdom of brass, which shall bear rule over all the earth.

> 40. The fourth kingdom shall be strong as iron, because iron breaks in pieces and subdues all things; and as iron that crushes all these, shall it break in pieces and crush.
> 41. Whereas you saw the feet and toes, part of potters' clay, and part of iron, it shall be a divided kingdom; but there shall be in it of the strength of the iron, because you saw the iron mixed with miry clay.
> 42. As the toes of the feet were part of iron, and part of clay, so the kingdom shall be partly strong, and partly broken.
> 43. Whereas you saw the iron mixed with miry clay, they shall mingle themselves with the seed of men; but they shall not cling to one another, even as iron does not mingle with clay.
> 44. In the days of those kings shall the God of heaven set up a kingdom which shall never be destroyed, nor shall the sovereignty of it be left to another people; but it shall break in pieces and consume all these kingdoms, and it shall stand forever.
> 45. Because you saw that a stone was cut out of the mountain without hands, and that it broke in pieces the iron, the brass, the clay, the silver, and the gold; the great God has made known to the king what shall happen hereafter: and the dream is certain, and the interpretation of it sure.

The purported dream of the king involved a huge statue with a head of gold, a breast and arms of silver, a belly and thighs of brass, legs of iron and feet of iron mixed with clay. A stone rolled down the mountain and smashed the statue.

Daniel explained that the successive parts of the statue represented different kingdoms, starting with the Babylonian Empire, which was succeeded by the Median Empire, the Persian

Empire, and finally the Greek Empire of Alexander the Great and his successors. The stone that pulverized the statue represented the Jewish revolt against Antiochus IV Epiphanius of Syria, that was destined to succeed with the help of God. Indirectly, it also pointed to the eternal kingdom of God at the end of time, which would endure into eternity.

The author of Daniel demonstrated with this tale that the Babylonian, Median, and Persian Empires have already perished and that the current Greek kingdom was doomed.

The Four Animals
Dan 7: 1–10

1.	In the first year of Belshazzar king of Babylon Daniel had a dream and visions of his head on his bed: then he wrote the dream and told the sum of the matters.
2.	Daniel spoke and said, I saw in my vision by night, and, behold, the four winds of the sky broke forth on the great sea.
3.	Four great animals came up from the sea, diverse one from another.
4.	The first was like a lion, and had eagle's wings: I saw until the wings of it were plucked, and it was lifted up from the earth, and made to stand on two feet as a man; and a man's heart was given to it.
5.	Behold, another animal, a second, like a bear; and it was raised up on one side, and three ribs were in its mouth between its teeth: and they said thus to it, Arise, devour much flesh.

> 6. After this I saw, and, behold, another, like a leopard, which had on its back four wings of a bird; the animal had also four heads; and dominion was given to it.
> 7. After this I saw in the night-visions, and, behold, a fourth animal, awesome and powerful, and strong exceedingly; and it had great iron teeth; it devoured and broke in pieces, and stamped the residue with its feet: and it was diverse from all the animals that were before it; and it had ten horns.
> 8. I considered the horns, and, behold, there came up among them another horn, a little one, before which three of the first horns were plucked up by the roots: and, behold, in this horn were eyes like the eyes of a man, and a mouth speaking great things.
> 9. I saw until thrones were placed, and one who was ancient of days sat: his clothing was white as snow, and the hair of his head like pure wool; his throne was fiery flames, [and] the wheels of it burning fire.
> 10. A fiery stream issued and came forth from before him: thousands of thousands ministered to him, and ten thousand times ten thousand stood before him: the judgment was set, and the books were opened.

This purported nocturnal vision of the legendary prophet Daniel is clearly based on a description of four astrological constellations, together with God's throne at the northern celestial pole, and the Milky Way.

The first two constellations can be identified with ease: Leo, the Lion, and Ursa Major, the Great Bear. The leopard (Aramaic: נְמַר (*nenar*, meaning a leopard or a panther) is not so easy to identify, until it is discovered that the ancient Jewish name for Lupus, the Wolf, was the Panther.[121]

The fourth animal was none other than Scorpius, the Scorpion. It has ten horns, the constellation of Libra, the Scales, directly in front of it.

The throne of God was, as always, situated at the northern astronomical pole. God was, of course, invisible and he is described as if he were visible and looking like an ancient wise man with pure white clothes to emphasize his holiness and perfection. The fiery stream in front of him, consisting of thousands of worshippers, was certainly the Milky Way.

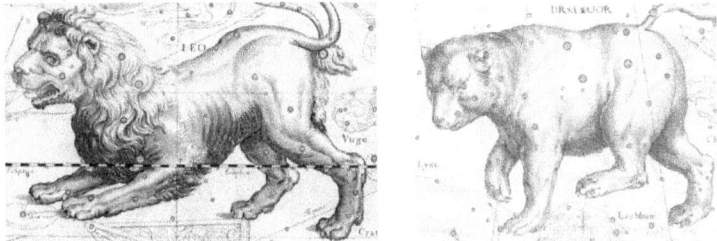

Drawing of the constellations of Leo and Ursa Major by Hevelius

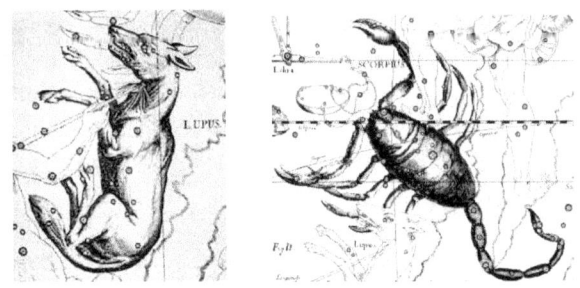

The constellations of Lupus and Scorpius, as drawn by Hevelius

---

[121] Allen, *Star Names,* 179.

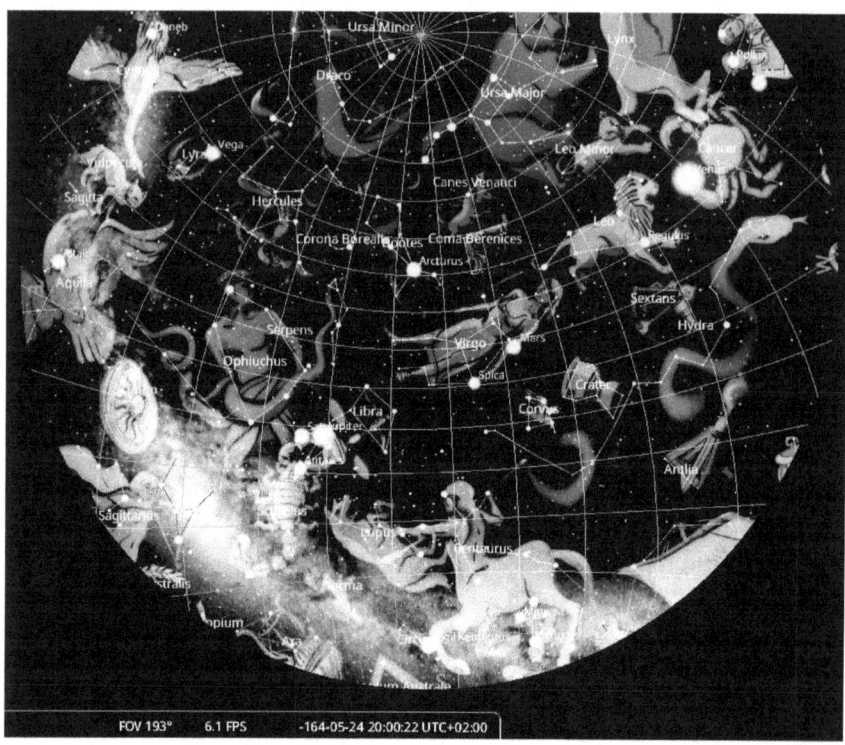

The night sky how it may have looked at the time (May, 164 BC, 20:00 local time) when the author of Daniel described his vision. The following constellations were observed: Leo, the Lion, Ursa Major, the Great Bear, Lupus, the Wolf/Panther, and Scorpius, the Scorpion. The ten horns of the fourth animal are formed by the constellation of Libra, the Scales, directly in front of it. The horn that pushed away the other horns was likely the planet Jupiter. The Milky Way is clearly visible above the south-eastern horizon.

According to the rest of the chapter, these four animals represented four successive kingdoms: the Babylonian, Median, Persian, and Greek kingdoms. Palestine was at that time part of the Greek kingdom of Syria. The "horn" that replaced the other "horns" was Antiochus IV Epiphanes, who tried to replace the worship of YHWH with the worship of Zeus in the Jerusalem temple. He was likely represented by the planet Jupiter.

The Ram and the Goat
Dan 8: 3 – 12

3.	Then I lifted up my eyes, and saw, and, behold, there stood before the river a ram which had two horns: and the two horns were high; but one was higher than the other, and the higher came up last.
	I saw the ram pushing westward, and northward, and southward; and no animals could stand before him, neither was there any who could deliver out of his hand; but he did according to his will, and magnified himself.
5.	As I was considering, behold, a male goat came from the west over the surface of the whole earth, and didn't touch the ground: and the goat had a notable horn between his eyes.
6.	He came to the ram that had the two horns, which I saw standing before the river, and ran on him in the fury of his power.
7.	I saw him come close to the ram, and he was moved with anger against him, and struck the ram, and broke his two horns; and there was no power in the ram to stand before him; but he cast him down to the ground, and trampled on him; and there was none who could deliver the ram out of his hand.
8.	The male goat magnified himself exceedingly: and when he was strong, the great horn was broken; and instead of it there came up four notable [horns] toward the four winds of the sky.
9.	Out of one of them came forth a little horn, which grew exceeding great, toward the south, and toward the east, and toward the glorious [land].

> 10. It grew great, even to the host of the sky; and some of the host and of the stars it cast down to the ground, and trampled on them.
> 11. Yes, it magnified itself, even to the prince of the host; and it took away from him the continual [burnt offering], and the place of his sanctuary was cast down.
> 12. The host was given over [to it] together with the continual [burnt offering] through disobedience; and it cast down truth to the ground, and it did [its pleasure] and prospered.

The two animals who fought each other in this scene, the ram and the goat, are the constellations of Aries, the Ram, and Capricornus, the Goat – both part of the Zodiac. That a scene from the starry skies is described, is apparent from verse 10 where the stars are explicitly mentioned.

The ram represented Egypt. Palestine was initially part of the kingdom of the Egyptian Ptolomies after the death of Alexander the Great. The Seleucids of Syria, represented by the goat, however, succeeded in conquering Palestine. The blasphemous horn was the king, Antiochus IV Epiphanes, who wanted to convert the Jerusalem temple into a sanctuary dedicated to Zeus and which the Jews, of course, found unacceptable and they rose up in revolt.

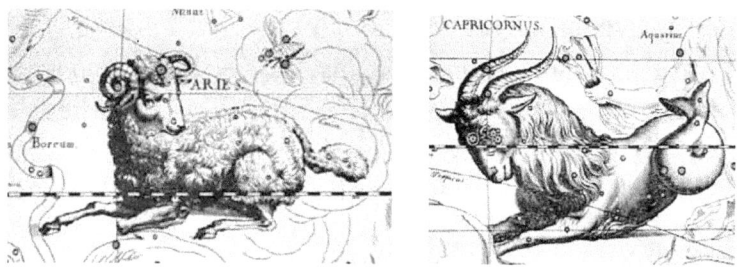

The constellations of Aries and Capricornus, by Hevelius

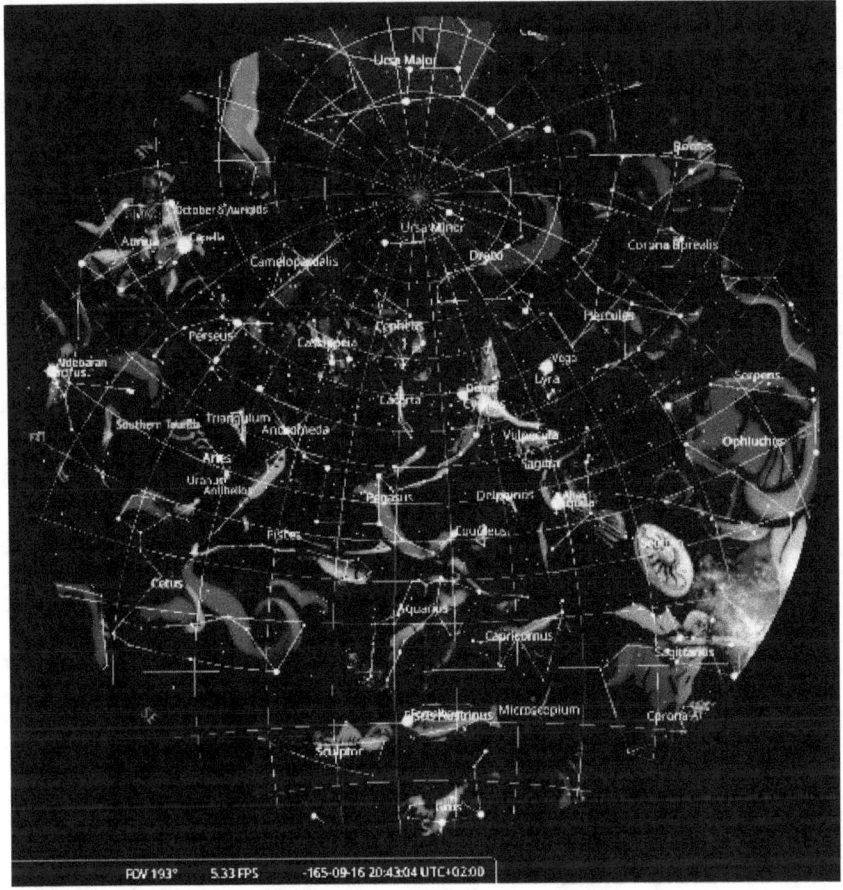

A likely recreation of the scene described in Dan 8, containing Aries, the Ram (on the left, between the Bull and the Fishes) and Capricornus, the Goat (on the bottom, right), as seen during September 165 BC from Jerusalem.

ENOCH

The idea that Satan was an angel who rebelled against God and was driven from heaven, together with his followers and co-conspirators, does not occur in the Old Testament.[122] This view was found for the

---

[122] Denova, "The Origin of Satan".

first time in the extrabiblical book of Enoch. This book grappled with the question: where do evil, sin, iniquity, arrogance, pride, and violence come from?

The Zodiac on the mosaic floor of the Beth Alpha Synagogue in Israel (5th Century AD). Capricornus, the Goat, is partly obscured at the bottom by a damaged part, while Aries, the Ram, is clearly visible at the right, next to Pisces, the Fishes.

The first part of the Book of Enoch, the Book of Watchers, can be regarded as an effort to expand on the following enigmatic passage in Genesis 6:

> "It happened, when men began to multiply on the surface of the ground, and daughters were born to them, that God's

sons saw that men's daughters were beautiful, and they took for themselves wives of all that they chose. YHWH said, 'My spirit will not strive with man forever, because he also is flesh; yet will his days be one hundred twenty years.' The Nephilim were in the earth in those days, and also after that, when God's sons came to men's daughters. They bore children to them: the same were the mighty men who were of old, men of renown" (Gen 6: 1–4).

The name *"the Nephilim"* (Hebrew: הַנְּפִילִים) mentioned in this passage is often translated as "the giants".

The following passages from the Book of the Watchers can be regarded as prophetic utterances to explain current affairs, namely the sinful nature of man and to exonerate God as the author of all that is bad, catastrophic, or disastrous.

The Angels who Took Human Women
1 Enoch 5: 1–9

> And it came to pass when the children of men had multiplied that in those days were born unto them beautiful and comely daughters. And the angels, the children of the heaven, saw and lusted after them, and said to one another: 'Come, let us choose us wives from among the children of men and beget us children.' And Semjaza, who was their leader, said unto them: 'I fear ye will not indeed agree to do this deed, and I alone shall have to pay the penalty of a great sin.' And they all answered him and said: 'Let us all swear an oath, and all bind ourselves by mutual imprecations not to abandon this plan but to do this thing.' Then sware they all together and bound themselves by mutual imprecations upon it. And they were in all two hundred; who descended in the days of Jared on the summit of Mount Hermon, and they called it Mount Hermon, because they

> had sworn and bound themselves by mutual imprecations upon it. And these are the names of their leaders: Samlazaz, their leader, Araklba, Rameel, Kokablel, Tamlel, Ramlel, Danel, Ezeqeel, Baraqijal, Asael, Armaros, Batarel, Ananel, Zaqiel, Samsapeel, Satarel, Turel, Jomjael, Sariel. These are their chiefs of tens.

1 Enoch 7: 1–5

> And all the others together with them took unto themselves wives, and each chose for himself one, and they began to go in unto them and to defile themselves with them, and they taught them charms and enchantments, and the cutting of roots, and made them acquainted with plants. And they became pregnant, and they bare great giants, whose height was three thousand ells: Who consumed all the acquisitions of men. And when men could no longer sustain them, ...

Some of the angels or watchers saw the beautiful daughters of men on earth and lusted after them. They formed a secret clique to which they were bound by an oath. This was the start of the rebellion against God because these angels preferred to live on earth and leave heaven. These sex-obsessed angels mated with mortal females and their offspring were giants. These giants demanded so much food that humans could not continue to feed them and they suffered famine themselves. These passages were obviously inspired by Gen 6: 1–4.

The group of watchers had twenty leaders and each one of them led ten members. That means that 200 angels took part in this thrust and incursion to earth. Samlaza was the top leader.

Men were Taught Secret Knowledge
1 Enoch 8: 1–4

> And Azâzêl taught men to make swords, and knives, and shields, and breastplates, and made known to them the metals of the earth and the art of working them, and bracelets, and ornaments, and the use of antimony, and the beautifying of the eyelids, and all kinds of costly stones, and all coloring tinctures. And there arose much godlessness, and they committed fornication, and they were led astray, and became corrupt in all their ways. Semjâzâ taught enchantments, and root-cuttings, Armârôs the resolving of enchantments, Barâqijâl, taught astrology, Kôkabêl the constellations, Ezêqêêl the knowledge of the clouds, Araqiêl the signs of the earth, Shamsiêl the signs of the sun, and Sariêl the course of the moon. ...

1 Enoch 9: 6–9

> Thou seest what Azâzêl hath done, who hath taught all unrighteousness on earth and revealed the eternal secrets which were preserved in heaven, which men were striving to learn: And Semjâzâ, to whom Thou hast given authority to bear rule over his associates. And they have gone to the daughters of men upon the earth, and have slept with the women, and have defiled themselves, and revealed to them all kinds of sins. ...

Azazel, one of the chief watchers, taught men secret knowledge: how to produce instruments of war, cosmetics to make women more sexually attractive and to be able to seduce men more easily, and knowledge about sorcery and astrology. This all resulted in hatred, fighting, and fornication on earth.

These ideas from Enoch had a profound influence upon the early Christians who wrote the various books of the New Testament. The idea of devils or satans who are the enemies of God, was copied from the Persian religion where an evil spirit, Ahriman, was seen as the enemy of the chief god, Ahura-Mazda.[123]

THE MODERN STATE OF ISRAEL

Certain fundamentalist Christians, especially those who entertain a belief in a literal millennium or Christian Empire of a thousand years when Jesus is expected to return, are of the opinion that many prophecies in the Bible foretold the mass conversion of the Jews to Christianity, as well as the creation of the modern state of Israe in 1948.

Two examples of authors who have propagated this point of view are as follows: Dr. Michael Rydelnik of Chosen People Ministries[124] and Thomas D. Ice of Liberty University.[125]

Many biblical texts are usually cited to support this point of view and it is necessary to investigate four typical passages carefully.

Israelites will Return
Isa. 11: 11–12

11.	It shall happen in that day, that the Lord will set his hand again the second time to recover the remnant of his people, who shall remain, from Assyria, and from Egypt, and from Pathros, and from Cush, and from Elam, and from Shinar, and from Hamath, and from the islands of the sea.
12.	He will set up an ensign for the nations, and will assemble the outcasts of Israel, and gather together the dispersed of Judah from the four corners of the earth.

---

[123] Pretorius, *To Hell with the Devil*, 45–47.
[124] Rydelnik, "Is the Modern State of Israel the Fulfillment of Prophecy?"
[125] Ice, "Is Modern Israel Fulfilling Prophecy?"

These words certainly look as if they can be applied to the modern state of Israel. When this state was created in 1948 it drew settlers from all over Europa, the Middle East, Africa, and elsewhere.

Isaiah, however, never thought about events more than two thousand years in the future, which would have had no value for the people of his own time. He only foresaw the return of Israelites who were taken prisoner by the Assyrians when the northern Israelite kingdom was conquered, as well as all those Israelites who fled to other countries during that war.

The Birth of a Nation
Isa 66: 8–11

8.	Who has heard such a thing? who has seen such things? Shall a land be born in one day? shall a nation be brought forth at once? for as soon as Zion travailed, she brought forth her children.
9.	Shall I bring to the birth, and not cause to bring forth? says YHWH: shall I who cause to bring forth shut [the womb]? says your God.
10.	Rejoice you with Jerusalem, and be glad for her, all you who love her: rejoice for joy with her, all you who mourn over her;
11.	that you may suck and be satisfied with the breasts of her consolations; that you may milk out, and be delighted with the abundance of her glory.

These words were written during the Persian period in Israel's history, after the end of the Babylonian Exile. The returning exiles needed hope for the future and that was what these sentences provided. They were given the promise that YHWH would oversee the birth of a new nation and adopt the role of wet nurse for the new nation.

The people to whom these words were directed, would not have able to find any consolation or hope in a promise that their descendants would return to the country of Israel more than two thousand years after their time. This prophecy cannot be applied to the modern Israel and it was also never fulfilled.

Statistics from 2022 reveal the following: There are currently about 15 million Jewish people in the world. The countries with the highest Jewish population are the United States of America with 7.3 million and Israel, with 7.1 million Jews.[126] In other words: less than half of the world's Jews live in Israel – the rest live elsewhere, mostly in America. It has never happened that all the Jews have returned to the Promised Land as this and other prophecies have envisaged.

The People will Return to the Land of their Father
Jer 16: 14–16

14.	Therefore, behold, the days come, says YHWH, that it shall no more be said, As YHWH lives, who brought up the children of Israel out of the land of Egypt;
15.	but, As YHWH lives, who brought up the children of Israel from the land of the north, and from all the countries where he had driven them. I will bring them again into their land that I gave to their fathers.
16.	Behold, I will send for many fishermen, says YHWH, and they shall fish them up; and afterward I will send for many hunters, and they shall hunt them from every mountain, and from every hill, and out of the clefts of the rocks.

---

[126] Statista, "Countries with the largest Jewish population 2022".

According to Jeremiah, who wrote his prophecies during the final years of the kingdom of Judah, YHWH promised to bring all the exiles and fugitives back to their own land. He compared God with a fisherman who makes sure that he catches his fish or a hunter who catches his prey.

This promise was never fulfilled. The exiles from the northern Israelite kingdom were absorbed by the peoples where they were placed. This promise can certainly not be applied to the modern state of Israel.

A New Heart for Israel
Ezek 36: 24–26

24.	For I will take you from among the nations, and gather you out of all the countries, and will bring you into your own land.
25.	I will sprinkle clean water on you, and you shall be clean: from all your filthiness, and from all your idols, will I cleanse you.
26.	A new heart also will I give you, and a new spirit will I put within you; and I will take away the stony heart out of your flesh, and I will give you a heart of flesh.

This prophecy promises that the Israelites would be brought back from *all* the countries – which never happened. There are more Jews outside Israel than living inside the country.

In perhaps the most important prophecy in the Old Testament, to be found in Genesis 15, YHWH promised Abraham the whole of the Middle East as the Promised Land, everything between the Nile in Egypt and the Euphrates in Babylonia. The Jews base their ownership of the country of Israel on this spurious prophecy. This promise by God was never honored.

SOME PRELIMENARY DEDUCTIONS

This analysis of some prophecies from the Old Testament showed that –

- The biblical prophets often criticized other prophets for being false prophets, but the difference between genuine and false prophets was not always very clear, except that the words and writings of the prophets who were deemed to be genuine were preserved in the Scriptures;
- When the biblical prophets commented on the moral, social, political, and military matters of their times, they were often accurate with their analyses and warnings, especially when they saw the dangers their people faced from the Assyrian and the Babylonian Empires;
- Prophecies about the fate of various foreign kingdoms were either fulfilled at a much later date, or not at all;
- When the prophets made promises about a bright future for the Israelites and later for the Judeans after the Babylonian Exile, including a reunification of the whole nation of Israel under a single monarchy, history usually proved them wrong;
- When various prophets promised that the house of David would rule in Jerusalem into the very far future, even after the end of the Babylonian Exile, they had it wrong;
- The modern state of Israel was never envisaged by the Old Testament prophets; and
- It is a serious theological problem: how could God order Moses and the Israelites to commit genocide and murder?

CHAPTER 4
NEW TESTAMENT PROPHECIES REGARDING CURRENT AFFAIRS

There are many prophetic pronouncements in the New Testament regarding current affairs, issues that occupied the minds of people at that stage and had to be explained. The most important prophecies in this regard will be discussed more or less in chronological order:

ZACHERIAH

The oldest prophecy found in the New Testament was spoken by Zacheriah, the father of John the Baptist. It will be followed by prophecies from John the Baptist, Jesus of Nazareth, Paul, and John of Patmos.

Zacheriah's Prophecy
Luke 1: 67–80

67.	His father, Zacharias, was filled with the Holy Spirit, and prophesied, saying,
68.	"Blessed be the Lord, the God of Israel, for he has visited and worked redemption for his people;
69.	Has raised up a horn of salvation for us in the house of his servant David
70.	(As he spoke by the mouth of his holy prophets who have been from of old),

71.	Salvation from our enemies, and from the hand of all who hate us;
72.	To show mercy towards our fathers, to remember his holy covenant,
73.	The oath which he spoke to Abraham, our father,
74.	To grant to us that we, being delivered out of the hand of our enemies, should serve him without fear,
75.	In holiness and righteousness before him all the days of our life.
76.	And you, child, will be called a prophet of the Most High, For you will go before the face of the Lord to make ready his ways,
77.	To give knowledge of salvation to his people by the remission of their sins,
78.	Because of the tender mercy of our God, whereby the dawn from on high will visit us,
79.	To shine on those who sit in darkness and the shadow of death; to guide our feet into the way of peace."
80.	The child grew, and grew strong in spirit, and was in the desert until the day of his public appearance

Zachariah supposedly composed this Psalm after the birth of his son. Before this, he was struck with aphasia for being skeptical about the announcement of John's birth by an angel.

The Psalm attributed to Zacharias is presented by Luke as a prophecy, although it actually described history. John became a prophet in a time when the Jews longed for a Messiah, somebody who would free them from their Roman oppressors. This song – probably written by Luke – retained some memories of Jesus' campaign to restore the kingdom of David.

It is noteworthy that Luke reported that John grew up in the desert while his parents lived in a town in the hilly countryside of Judea. This may mean that John received his education at Qumran, the headquarters of the Essene sect near the Dead Sea. That would explain his lifestyle as an adult, his message of repentance, and his criticism of the rich religious authorities in Jerusalem.

JOHN THE BAPTIST

John's Preaching
Luke 3: 7–9 (Matt 3: 7–9)

7.	John said to the crowds that came out to be baptized by him, "You brood of vipers! Who warned you to flee from the wrath to come?
8.	Bear fruits worthy of repentance. Do not begin to say to yourselves, 'We have Abraham as our ancestor'; for I tell you, God is able from these stones to raise up children to Abraham.
9.	Even now the axe is lying at the root of the trees; every tree therefore that does not bear good fruit is cut down and thrown into the fire".

Luke 3: 16–17 (Matt 3: 11–12)

16.	John answered all of them by saying, "I baptize you with water; but one who is more powerful than I is coming; I am not worthy to untie the thong of his sandals. He will baptize you with the Holy Spirit and fire.
17.	His winnowing fork is in his hand, to clear his threshing floor and to gather the wheat into his granary; but the chaff he will burn with unquenchable fire."

John followed the example of Old Testament prophets by calling upon the people to repent and return to God, otherwise they could expect the wrath and punishment of God. He even called them a "brood of vipers" – that is, children of the devil. According to him, the Messiah was due to come and he would execute God's judgment.

John the Baptist's Appearance
John 1: 6, 19–27

6.	There came a man, sent from God, whose name was John.
19.	This is John's testimony, when the Jews sent priests and Levites from Jerusalem to ask him, "Who are you?"
20.	He confessed, and didn't deny, but he confessed, "I am not the Christ."
21.	They asked him, "What then? Are you Elijah?" He said, "I am not." "Are you the prophet?" He answered, "No."
22.	They said therefore to him, "Who are you? Give us an answer to take back to those who sent us. What do you say about yourself?"
23.	He said, "I am the voice of one crying in the wilderness, 'Make straight the way of the Lord,' as Isaiah the prophet said."
24.	The ones who had been sent were from the Pharisees.
25.	They asked him, "Why then do you baptize, if you are not the Christ, nor Elijah, nor the Prophet?"
26.	John answered them, "I baptize in water, but among you stands one whom you don't know,
27.	he who comes after me, whose sandal strap I'm not worthy to untie."

The "Jews" from Jerusalem, members of the Judean elite and Pharisees, did not trust this rough prophet named John, due to his connections to the Essenes and who criticized the priests at the temple for being frauds and false priests, although his father was also a priest. The report of John's denial that he was the Messiah and his affirmation that he only prepared the way for the Messiah, was meant to convince the disciples and followers of John after his death – probably during AD 30 – that Jesus was the real expected Messiah.

Salome with the head of John the Baptist, by Caravaggio, National Gallery, London, c 1607–10.

The Death of John the Baptist
Mark 6: 14–29 (Matt 14: 1–12; Luke 9: 7–9)

14.	King Herod heard this, for his name had become known, and he said, "John the Baptizer has risen from the dead, and therefore these powers work in him."
15.	But others said, "It is Elijah." Others said, "It is the Prophet, or like one of the prophets."

16.	But Herod, when he heard this, said, "This is John, whom I beheaded. He has risen from the dead."
17.	For Herod himself had sent out and laid hold on John, and bound him in prison for the sake of Herodias, his brother Philip's wife, for he had married her.
18.	For John said to Herod, "It is not lawful for you to have your brother's wife."
19.	Herodias set herself against him, and desired to kill him, but she couldn't,
20.	for Herod feared John, knowing that he was a righteous and holy man, and kept him safe. When he heard him, he did many things, and he heard him gladly.
21.	When a convenient day had come, that Herod on his birthday made a supper for his lords, and the high captains, and the chief men of Galilee;
22.	and when the daughter of Herodias herself came in and danced, she pleased Herod and those reclining with him. The king said to the young lady, "Ask me whatever you want, and I will give it to you."
23.	He swore to her, "Whatever you shall ask of me, I will give you, up to half of my kingdom."
24.	She went out, and said to her mother, "What shall I ask?" She said, "The head of John the Baptizer."
25.	She came in immediately with haste to the king, and asked, "I want you to give me right now the head of John the Baptizer on a platter."
26.	The king was exceedingly sorry, but for the sake of his oaths, and of his dinner guests, he didn't wish to refuse her.

> 27. Immediately the king sent forth a soldier of his guard, and commanded to bring John's head, and he went and beheaded him in the prison,
> 28. and brought his head on a platter, and gave it to the young lady; and the young lady gave it to her mother.
> 29. When his disciples heard this, they came and took up his corpse, and laid it in a tomb.

Mark 6: 17 records that Herod Antipas, the tetrarch or ruler of Galilee, married his sister-in-law, Herodias, the divorced wife of his half-brother Philip. We are also told that John the Baptist acted as a proper prophet by criticizing him for this sin. However, Herodias was not the ex-wife of Philip, but of Herod Archelaus, another half-brother and ruler of Judea after the death of their father, Herod the Great. Archelaus was removed from his position by the Romans due to his incompetence and mismanagement.[127]

The superstitious Herod Antipas believed that Jesus was a revived or resurrected John the Baptist, although he had him beheaded to please his wife and step-daughter. He had made a rash promise after having ingested too much Palestinian wine, which made him reckless. Poor John paid with his life for being a prophet.

JESUS OF NAZARETH

Almost all the recorded teachings and parables of Jesus of Nazareth may be regarded as prophetic in nature because he recruited people to support his campaign to establish God's kingdom with him on the throne as the Messiah and King David's successor. It was also his goal and task as Messiah to lead his people back to God.

---

[127] Josephus, *Antiquities*, XVIII/v/4.

Jesus' Hour has not yet Come
John 2: 1–4

1.	The third day, there was a marriage in Cana of Galilee. Jesus' mother was there.
2.	Jesus also was invited, with his disciples, to the marriage.
3.	When the wine ran out, Jesu'' Mother said to him, "They have no wine."
4.	Jesus said to her, "Woman, what does that have to do with you and me? My hour has not yet come."

Jesus' remark to his mother, "My hour has not yet come," is repeated in John 7: 6 & 30; 8: 20; 12:23; and 13:1. It is usually interpreted that the time for Jesus to be crucified and be resurrected has not yet arrived. A more plausible explanation is that he meant to make it clear that the time was not yet ripe to re-establish the monarchy in Israel and drive the hated pagan Romans away.

It is told in verse 11 that this first "sign" (Greek: σημεῖον – *semeion*, meaning "sign" or "miracle") of Jesus had the result that it "revealed his glory" so that "his disciples believed in him." The idea of belief in Jesus as the Messiah occurs often in John's Gospel.

People of our age may accept that Jesus really attended a wedding, but that he magically turned water into wine, does seem incredible and even impossible. There is, though, the possibility that the story later got distorted and that Jesus somehow got hold of a new supply of wine without performing any magic.

Cleansing of the Temple
John 2: 12–25

12.	After this, he went down to Capernaum, he, and his mother, his brothers, and his disciples; and there they stayed not many days.

13.	The Passover of the Jews was at hand, and Jesus went up to Jerusalem. He found in the temple those who sold oxen, sheep, and doves, and the changers of money sitting.
15.	He made a whip of cords, and threw all out of the temple, both the sheep and the oxen; and he poured out the changers' money, and overthrew their tables.
16.	To those who sold the doves, he said, "Take these things out of here! Don't make my Father's house a marketplace!"
17.	His disciples remembered that it was written, "Zeal for your house will eat me up."
18.	The Jews therefore answered him, "What sign do you show to us, seeing that you do these things?"
19.	Jesus answered them, "Destroy this temple, and in three days I will raise it up."
20.	The Jews therefore said, "Forty-six years was this temple in building, and will you raise it up in three days?"
21.	But he spoke of the temple of his body.
22.	When therefore he was raised from the dead, his disciples remembered that he said this, and they believed the Scripture, and the word which Jesus had said.
23.	Now when he was in Jerusalem at the Passover, during the feast, many believed in his name, observing his signs which he did.
24.	But Jesus didn't trust himself to them, because he knew all people,
25.	and because he didn't need for anyone to testify concerning man; for he himself knew what was in man

Jesus seemed to have made Capernaum the headquarters of his campaign of becoming the king of Israel. At this stage, he did not trust the Judeans of Jerusalem yet to support him and, therefore, he did not campaign openly there, although he became well-known enough on account of the "signs" he had performed there. Most probably, the Essene community in Jerusalem supported him, but the temple elite did not.

The story of the throwing out of the dishonest merchants and money exchangers placed this event at the beginning of Jesus' ministry, according to John's Gospel – in contrast with the other gospels, where it took place shortly before the crucifixion.

It must be noted that the temple authorities did not stop Jesus, probably because he was already a popular figure due to all his signs. These businessmen put up their stalls on the temple mount, but not inside the temple itself. The Sanhedrin or Jewish Council had no jurisdiction there and, therefore, did not intervene.[128]

Jesus' announcement about the temple of his body that would be destroyed and restored three days later, was probably meant to prepare the readers of this gospel for the passion. There are also signs in the Synoptic Gospels that Jesus anticipated his crucifixion by the Romans, but that he and some helpers conspired to rescue him from the cross to bolster his claim to be the Messiah.

Blind Guides
Luke 6: 39–40 (Matt 15: 14; 10: 24–25)

39.	He also told them a parable: "Can a blind person guide a blind person? Will not both fall into a pit?
40.	A disciple is not above the teacher, but everyone who is fully qualified will be like the teacher.

---

[128] Cohn, *The Trial and Death of Jesus*, 54–59.

The blind guides and teachers mentioned in this passage were evidently the Jewish elite in Jerusalem of Jesus' time. The Essenes accused them of distorting the Scriptures and regarded the priests at the temple as frauds and false priests. Jesus repeated this sentiment.

Messengers for the Coming Kingdom
Luke 10: 2–12 (Matt 9: 37–38; 10: 7–16)

2.	He said to them, "The harvest is plentiful, but the laborers are few; therefore ask the Lord of the harvest to send out laborers into his harvest.
3.	Go on your way. See, I am sending you out like lambs into the midst of wolves.
4.	Carry no purse, no bag, no sandals; and greet no one on the road.
5.	Whatever house you enter, first say, 'Peace to this house!'
6.	And if anyone is there who shares in peace, your peace will rest on that person; but if not, it will return to you.
7	Remain in the same house, eating and drinking whatever they provide, for the laborer deserves to be paid. Do not move about from house to house.
8.	Whenever you enter a town and its people welcome you, eat what is set before you;
9.	cure the sick who are there, and say to them, 'The kingdom of God has come near to you.'
10.	But whenever you enter a town and they do not welcome you, go out into its streets and say,
11.	Even the dust of your town that clings to our feet, we wipe off in protest against you. Yet know this: the kingdom of God has come near.'
12.	I tell you, on that day it will be more tolerable for Sodom than for that town.

Jesus sent his disciples and followers out on a recruitment drive to increase the number of his followers – laborers to gather the harvest, the harvest of new recruits. They had to concentrate on other Essenes, who would provide them with lodging and food, as the Essenes were known to do towards other members of their sect. They had to distribute the news that God's kingdom was near – in other words: the time was almost ripe to restore the Israelite monarchy (and drive the Romans away).

If the inhabitants of certain towns refused to provide hospitality, the disciples were told to shake off the dust of that town from their feet and keep on announcing that the kingdom was nearby.

The Fate of Galilean Towns
Luke 10: 13–16 (Matt 11: 21–24)

13.	"Woe to you, Chorazin! Woe to you, Bethsaida! For if the deeds of power done in you had been done in Tyre and Sidon, they would have repented long ago, sitting in sackcloth and ashes.
14.	But at the judgment it will be more tolerable for Tyre and Sidon than for you. And you, Capernaum, will you be exalted to heaven? No, you will be brought down to Hades.
16.	Whoever listens to you listens to me, and whoever rejects you rejects me, and whoever rejects me rejects the one who sent me."

The Galilean towns of Chorazin, Bethsaida, and Capernaum refused to provide hospitality to Jesus' messengers and to accept Jesus' teaching that the kingdom was due to be restored soon. Jesus cursed them in his role as a prophet for failing to support him and his helpers. Jesus was convinced that he was called by God to restore the monarchy of Israel. If people did not accept his message (such as the three towns in Galilee), it meant that they rejected God who had sent him.

Against the Pharisees. Scribes, and Teachers of the Law
Luke 11: 34–36 (Matt 6: 22–23)

34.	Your eye is the lamp of your body. If your eye is healthy, your whole body is full of light; but if it is not healthy, your body is full of darkness.
35.	Therefore consider whether the light in you is not darkness.
36.	If then your whole body is full of light, with no part of it in darkness, it will be as full of light as when a lamp gives you light with its rays."

This short parable is a hidden rebuke of the religious authorities in Jerusalem who opposed Jesus' teachings. According to Jesus, they were blind and lived in darkness – in contrast with those who have seen the validity of his message and who lived in the light as a result.

Luke 11: 42 (Matt 23: 23)

"But woe to you Pharisees! For you tithe mint and rue and herbs of all kinds, and neglect justice and the love of God; it is these you ought to have practiced, without neglecting the others.

The Pharisees were known for their strict obedience to the Law of Moses. Jesus pointed out that they even followed the smallest requirements of the Law, but neglected the most important issues, namely justice and love towards God.

Luke 11: 39–41 (Matt 23: 25–27)

39.	Then the Lord said to him, "Now you Pharisees clean the outside of the cup and of the dish, but inside you are full of greed and wickedness.

> 40. You fools! Did not the one who made the outside make the inside also?
> 41. So give for alms those things that are within; and see, everything will be clean for you.

According to Jesus, the Pharisees were only interested in the outward appearance of their piety, including giving alms to the poor, while their hearts were not filled with love, mercy, and compassion towards the poor.

Luke 11: 43 (Matt 23: 6)

> Woe to you Pharisees! For you love to have the seat of honor in the synagogues and to be greeted with respect in the marketplaces.

Jesus – just as the Essenes – preferred a humble and simple lifestyle – in contrast with some Pharisees, members of the Sanhedrin, the Jewish Council – who loved to occupy seats of honor at meetings to display their importance.

Luke 11: 44 (Matt 23: 27–28)

> "Woe to you! For you are like unmarked graves, and people walk over them without realizing it."

This saying was an insult aimed at the Pharisees who were members of the Sanhedrin who were compared with an unmarked tomb full of rotting corpses.

Luke 11: 46 (Matt 23: 4)

> "Woe also to you lawyers! For you load people with burdens hard to bear, and you yourselves do not lift a finger to ease them.

Jesus had no respect for the teachers of the Law who entangled the people in clever-sounding interpretations of Moses' Law, while they disregarded their own teachings.

The Tombs of the Prophets
Luke 11: 47–48 (Matt 23: 29–32)

47.	"Woe to you! For you build the tombs of the prophets whom your ancestors killed.
48.	So you are witnesses and approve of the deeds of your ancestors; for they killed them, and you build their tombs."

Jesus added to the preceding passage that the prophet Zechariah was killed by the ancestors of the teachers of the Law and the Pharisees. Jesus probably thought of Jer 2: 30 that reported that the people of Israel "mocked the messengers of God, and despised his words, and scoffed at his prophets, until the wrath of the Lord arose against his people." Something similar appears in 2 Chr 30: 16. Jesus accused, in effect, the teachers of the Law and the Pharisees of condoning the sins of their ancestors by building tombs for the prophets.

The Wisdom of God
Luke 11: 49–51 (Matt 23: 34–36)

49.	"Therefore also the Wisdom of God said, 'I will send them prophets and apostles, some of whom they will kill and persecute,'
50.	so that this generation may be charged with the blood of all the prophets shed since the foundation of the world,
51.	from the blood of Abel to the blood of Zechariah, who perished between the altar and the sanctuary. Yes, I tell you, it will be charged against this generation."

The "Wisdom of God" is described in Prov 8–9, but Jesus may also have thought of the apocryphal book of Ecclesiasticus where "Wisdom" is personified in Chapter 24.

Wisdom is quoted as having promised to send prophets and apostles who were due to be killed. No such promise is to be found in the Old Testament or the apocrypha and it must be a case where the memories of the informants of the author(s) of the Q Document became confused, while Jesus said something quite different.

Nevertheless, the stoning of the prophet Zechariah is described in 2 Chr 24: 20–22. Jesus emphasized his view that the wrath of God would rest upon those Jews who opposed him, just as it angered God that the prophets were mocked and killed.

The Key of Knowledge
Luke 11: 52 (Matt 23: 13)

> "Woe to you lawyers! For you have taken away the key of knowledge; you did not enter yourselves, and you hindered those who were entering."

With these words, Jesus accused the lawyers of misrepresenting the Scriptures, preventing the common folk to understand that Jesus himself was promised in the Scriptures as *the* Messiah.

The Rich Man
Mark 10: 17–31 (Matt 19: 16–30; Luke 18: 18–30)

> 17. As he was going forth into the way, one ran to him, kneeled to him, and asked him, "Good Teacher, what shall I do that I may inherit eternal life?"
> 18. Jesus said to him, "Why do you call me good? No one is good except one — God.

19. You know the commandments: "Do not murder' 'Do not commit adultery,' 'Do not steal,' 'Do not give false testimony,' 'Do not defraud,' 'Honor your father and mother.'"
20. He said to him, "Teacher, all these things have I observed from my youth."
21. Jesus looking at him loved him, and said to him, "One thing you lack. Go, sell whatever you have, and give to the poor, and you will have treasure in heaven; and come, follow me, taking up the cross."
22. But his face fell at that saying, and he went away sorrowful, for he was one who had great possessions.
23. Jesus looked around, and said to his disciples, "How difficult it is for those who have riches to enter into the kingdom of God!"
24. The disciples were amazed at his words. But Jesus answered again, "Children, how hard is it for those who trust in riches to enter into the kingdom of God!
25. It is easier for a camel to go through the needle's eye, than for a rich man to enter into the kingdom of God."
26. They were exceedingly astonished, saying to him, "Then who can be saved?"
27. Jesus, looking at them, said, "With men it is impossible, but not with God, for all things are possible with God."
28. Peter began to tell him, "Behold, we have left all, and have followed you."
29. Jesus said, "Most assuredly I tell you, there is no one who has left house, or brothers, or sisters, or father, or mother,

> or wife, or children, or land, for my sake, and for the gospel's sake,
>
> 30. but he will receive one hundred times now in this time, houses, brothers, sisters, mothers, children, and land, with persecutions; and in the age to come eternal life.
>
> 31. But many who are first will be last; and the last first."

According to Jesus, one could find eternal life by obeying all of God's commandments. As a good Essene, Jesus also thought that opulence led one away from God and, therefore, he advised the rich man who consulted him to get rid of his belongings and follow him, even to the cross, which awaited him. In effect, he invited the rich man to become an Essene himself.

Thereupon, Jesus told a joke. He asked his audience to imagine an absurd situation, namely a camel crawling through the eye of a needle, to demonstrate how impossible it was for a rich man to join his kingdom.

The Way to Eternal Life
Luke 10: 25–28

> 25. Behold, a certain lawyer stood up and tested him, saying, "Teacher, what will I do to inherit eternal life?"
>
> 26. He said to him, "What is written in the law? How do you read it?"
>
> 27. He answered, "You shall love the Lord your God with all your heart, with all your soul, with all your strength, and with all your mind; and your neighbor as yourself."
>
> 28. He said to him, "You have answered correctly. Do this, and you will live."

Jesus told the lawyer or teacher of the Law who engaged him in a conversation that the way to inherit eternal life was to love Gd and to love one's neighbor. This is in stark contrast with the stance of Paul who propagated the view that one should have faith in Christ as the Savior of the world to enter eternal life after death.

The Law of Moses

Matt 5: 19

> Whoever then goes against the smallest of these laws, teaching men to do the same, will be named least in the kingdom of heaven; but he who keeps the laws, teaching others to keep them, will be named great in the kingdom of heaven.

Luke 16: 17

> But it is easier for heaven and earth to pass away, than for one tiny stroke of a pen in the law to fall.

Jesus, as a religious reformer, wanted to lead his people back to God and he often condemned those leaders of the people who acted against the intentions of the Law of Moses by living in luxury and cooperating with the pagan occupiers of their country.

For that reason, Jesus emphasized the immutability and permanence of the Law of Moses. He expected of his followers to always adhere to these laws – just as the prophets of the Old Testament did.

Jesus Predicts Peter's Denial

Mark 14: 27–31 (Matt 26: 31–35; Luke 22: 31–34; John 13: 36–38)

> 27. Jesus said to them, "All of you will be made to stumble because of me tonight, for it is written, 'I will strike the shepherd, and the sheep will be scattered.'

28.	However, after I am raised up, I will go before you into Galilee."
29.	But Peter said to him, "Although all will be offended, yet I will not."
30.	Jesus said to him, "Most assuredly I tell you, that you today, even this night, before the cock crows twice, you will deny me three times."
31.	But he spoke all the more, "If I must die with you, I will not deny you." Likewise, they all said so.

Jesus evidently knew Peter with his compulsive personality well enough and predicted that he would deny knowing Jesus during the following night before daybreak when events would come to a head and Jesus was arrested. The prediction of the denial of Peter is also mentioned in John. According to the synoptics, Jesus based his prediction of Zech 13: 7 – although this verse never had the denial of Peter in mind when it was written.

Jesus certainly had a plan to survive the expected crucifixion and he announced that he would go to Galilee after that.

The Angels of God
Luke 12: 8–9 (Matt 10: 32–33)

8.	And I tell you, everyone who acknowledges me before others, the Son of Man also will acknowledge before the angels of God;
9.	but whoever denies me before others will be denied before the angels of God.

This saying was traditionally interpreted as a description of Judgment Day. A more plausible explanation, though, is that Jesus expected a legion of angels of God to drive the Romans away and allow him to ascend the throne in Jerusalem as the Son of Man, the Messiah (Matt 25: 31; Mark 8: 38; 14: 62; Luke 9: 26; 22: 69; John 1: 49–51). That event would reveal people's support for Jesus. Those who opposed him, would be exposed to the vengeance of the angels, while those who openly sided with him would be honored in the presence of the angels from heaven.

Lament over Jerusalem
Luke 13: 34–35 (Matt 23: 37–39)

34.	Jerusalem, Jerusalem, the city that kills the prophets and stones those who are sent to it! How often have I desired to gather your children together as a hen gathers her brood under her wings, and you were not willing!
35.	See, your house is left to you. And I tell you, you will not see me until the time comes when you say, 'Blessed is the one who comes in the name of the Lord.'"

Jesus clearly felt let down that the Jerusalem elite did not take him seriously and even rejected and opposed him because Jerusalem was meant to be the capital of the restored Israelite kingdom. He promised that the day will come when he would be welcomed as *the* Messiah, sent by God.

Luke 19: 41–44

41.	When he drew near, he saw the city and wept over it,
42.	saying, "If you, even you, had known today the things which belong to your peace! But now, they are hidden from your eyes.
43.	For the days will come on you, when your enemies will throw up a barricade against you, surround you, hem you in on every side,

> 44. and will dash you and your children within you to the ground. They will not leave in you one stone on another, because you didn't know the time of your visitation."

Luke presented these words of lament over Jerusalem by Jesus as a prophecy regarding the destruction of the city by the Romans, four decades later. It is unlikely that Jesus ever spoke these words because they are a good description of what happened much later. Jesus saw himself as the legitimate king of Israel and Jerusalem was supposed to be his capital, not a destroyed city.

The Need to be Watchful
Luke 21: 34–38

> 34. "So be careful, or your hearts will be loaded down with carousing, drunkenness, and cares of this life, and that day will come on you suddenly.
> 35. For it will come like a snare on all those who dwell on the surface of all the earth.
> 36. Therefore be watchful all the time, asking that you may be counted worthy to escape all these things that will happen, and to stand before the Son of Man."
> 37. Every day Jesus was teaching in the temple, and every night he went out, and spent the night on the mountain that is called Olivet.
> 38. All the people came early in the morning to him in the temple, to hear him.

The first part of this passage was again presented as a prophecy by Jesus regarding the destruction of Jerusalem, which amounts to a description of what happened decades later. It follows Luke's variation of the purported prophecy by Jesus of the destruction of the temple and the fall of Jerusalem, which was taken from Mark.

The Day of the Son of Man
Luke 17:22–24, 26–30, 34–35, 37 (Matt 24: 26–28, 37, 39–41)

22.	Then he said to the disciples, "The days are coming when you will long to see one of the days of the Son of Man, and you will not see it.
23.	They will say to you, 'Look there!' or 'Look here!' Do not go, do not set off in pursuit.
24.	For as the lightning flashes and lights up the sky from one side to the other, so will the Son of Man be in his day.
26.	Just as it was in the days of Noah, so too it will be in the days of the Son of Man.
27.	They were eating and drinking, and marrying and being given in marriage, until the day Noah entered the ark, and the flood came and destroyed all of them.
28.	Likewise, just as it was in the days of Lot: they were eating and drinking, buying and selling, planting and building,
29.	but on the day that Lot left Sodom, it rained fire and sulfur from heaven and destroyed all of them
30.	— it will be like that on the day that the Son of Man is revealed.
34.	I tell you, on that night there will be two in one bed; one will be taken and the other left.
35.	There will be two women grinding meal together; one will be taken and the other left."
37.	Then they asked him, "Where, Lord?" He said to them, "Where the corpse is, there the vultures will gather."

This passage is usually interpreted as a prophecy about Judgment Day and the so-called rapture when certain people will be taken up to heaven and others left behind.

It must, rather, be seen as the day on which Jesus, as the Son of Man, as the Messiah, re-established the kingdom of Israel with the help of a brigade of angels from heaven. It was meant to be a sudden event, not expected by the people. Some will become part of this kingdom, while others will be left out, or rather, leave this earth through death.

The corpse and the vultures mentioned in the rather enigmatic saying at the end of this passage, only makes sense when it is understood to be either the corpse of the Roman Empire, or the corpse of the corrupt Sadducees and priests in Jerusalem, which will be devoured by vultures, the hungry and angry angels from heaven.

Matthew added this comment at the end of this passage: "Watch therefore, for you don't know in what hour your Lord comes" (Matt 24: 38).

Jesus Talks to the Women of Jerusalem
Luke 23: 27–31

27.	A great multitude of the people followed him, including women who also mourned and lamented him.
28.	But Jesus, turning to them, said, "Daughters of Jerusalem, don't weep for me, but weep for yourselves and for your children.
29.	For behold, the days are coming in which they will say, Blessed are the barren, the wombs that never bore, and the breasts that never nursed.
30.	Then will they begin to tell the mountains, Fall on us! and to the hills, Cover us.

> 31. For if they do these things in the green tree, what will be done in the dry?"

It is hard to imagine how Jesus could have been able to address the women of Jerusalem with a rather lengthy speech while he was being led away to be crucified and he was guarded by a company of soldiers.

His words to them amounted to a prophecy about the destruction of Jerusalem decades later, which Jesus certainly never foresaw. This episode must be an invention, either of Luke or one of his sources. It seems to be an embellishment of Mark's story that Jesus, the great prophet, must have predicted the destruction of Jerusalem and the temple.

Albrecht Dürer. Christ Carrying his Cross (1512)

The statement that there were women who "mourned and lamented him" is at odds with the story that the crowd outside the place where Jesus was tried called for his death.

ACTS

The Coming of the Holy Spirit
Acts 2: 1–13

1. Now when the day of Pentecost had come, they were all with one accord in one place.
2. Suddenly there came from the sky a sound like the rushing of a mighty wind, and it filled all the house where they were sitting.
3. Tongues like fire appeared and were distributed to them, and it sat on each one of them.
4. They were all filled with the Holy Spirit, and began to speak with other languages, as the Spirit gave them the ability to speak.
5. Now there were dwelling at Jerusalem Jews, devout men, from every nation under the sky.
6. When this sound was heard, the multitude came together, and were bewildered, because everyone heard them speaking in his own language.
7. They were all amazed and marveled, saying to one another, "Behold, aren't all these who speak Galileans?
8. How do we hear, everyone in our own native language?
9. Parthians, Medes, Elamites, and people from Mesopotamia, Judea, Cappadocia, Pontus, Asia,
10. Phrygia, Pamphylia, Egypt, the parts of Libya around Cyrene, visitors from Rome, both Jews and proselytes,
11. Cretans and Arabians: we hear them speaking in our languages the mighty works of God!"
12. They were all amazed, and were perplexed, saying one to another, "What does this mean?"
13. Others, mocking, said, "They are filled with new wine."

There is a perfectly natural explanation for the strange and seemingly mysterious events on that day of Pentecost. Luke wrote that a strong wind was heard and that "tongues like fire" were seen on all those present, which caused them to speak in strange languages about "the mighty works of God". They were, in effect, transformed into prophets at that time.

The explanation is simple: those "tongues like fire" were sparks of static electricity, caused by a very dry desert wind and a dust storm blowing over Jerusalem from the east. A professor in physics explains: "The dry winter months are high season for an annoying downside of static electricity – electric discharges like tiny lightning zaps whenever you touch door knobs..."[129]

When two objects are rubbed together, especially if the surrounding air is dry, the objects acquire equal and opposite electrical charges and an attractive force develops between them. The object that loses electrons becomes positively charged, and the other becomes negatively charged, which causes sparks to fly between them when the opposite charges are neutralized.[130]

Phenomena like this are not strange in the country of Israel. The Jerusalem Post published a report a few years ago of the owner of a motor vehicle who was filling the vehicle with fuel at a filling station when sparks of static electricity, caused by a strong dry wind, ignited the fumes of the fuel, which caused the vehicle to go up in flames. A photo showed the wrecked motor car.[131]

If Jesus was crucified on 3 April AD 33, this incident of static electricity sparks must have taken place fifty days later, namely on 23 May – in the season for dry easterly or southerly desert winds

---

[129] Deffner, "Static Electricity's Tiny Sparks".
[130] Enc Brit, "Static Electricity".
[131] Jerusalem Post, 28 November 2016.

with dust storms – and static electricity.[132]

Albrecht Dürer: Outpouring of the Holy Spiri

Those who were affected on that day of Pentecost found this experience strange and even magical and they must have called out their amazement and surprise. Some of them may have been pilgrims from elsewhere and they used their home languages – creating the impression of a language miracle. Outsiders thought they drank too much wine. These bystanders, who also were pilgrims from other countries, heard those hysterical people speaking in their own languages.

The strong wind was interpreted as the Spirit or breath of God that took hold of these people. After all, the Greek language uses the same word for "wind", "breath", and "spirit", namely πνευμα (*pneuma*).

PAUL OF TARSUS

Most of Paul's teachings in his epistles to Christian communities in Asia Minor, Greece, and Rome, can be regarded as prophetic in nature. Hy claimed that his insights were based on visions and revelations he had received. His most important prophecies

---

[132] Weather Spark, "Climate and Average Weather Year Round in Jerusalem Israel".

regarding his authority as an apostle and prophet and the current situation in which his readers found themselves are presented in the paragraphs that follow.

The Conversion of St Paul by Caravaggio

The Gospel Revealed to Paul
Gal 1: 6–12

6.	I marvel that you are so quickly deserting him who called you in the grace of Christ to a different gospel;

> 7. and there isn't another gospel. Only there are some who trouble you, and want to pervert the gospel of Christ.
> 8. But even though we, or an angel from heaven, should preach to you any gospel other than that which we preached to you, let him be cursed.
> 9. As we have said before, so I now say again: if any man preaches to you any gospel other than that which you received, let him be cursed.
> 10. For am I now seeking the favor of men, or of God? Or am I striving to please men? For if I were still pleasing men, I wouldn't be a servant of Christ.
> 11. But I make known to you, brothers, concerning the gospel which was preached by me, that it is not according to man.
> 12. For neither did I receive it from man, nor was I taught it, but it came to me through revelation of Jesus Christ.

Paul was convinced that his message was based on revelations of Jesus Christ he had received. He cursed those who contradicted him, including the apostle Peter whom he rebuked when they met in Antioch (Gal 2: 11). He also called those who differed from him "false brothers" (Gal 2: 4).

It is important to note that Paul never met Jesus when he was spreading his message in Galilee and Judea. The apostles, including Peter, followed him during the three years before his crucifixion and it may be assumed that they could remember Jesus' message very well. It is no surprise that they differed from Paul who distorted Jesus' teachings, according to them.

It will be shown in the last chapter that Paul evidently suffered from hallucinations, which he took as divine revelations.

Paul's Visions

Eph 3: 3–5

3.	...how that by revelation the mystery was made known to me, as I wrote before in few words,
4.	whereby, when you read, you can perceive my understandding in the mystery of Christ;
5.	which in other generations was not made known to the sons of men, as it has now been revealed to his holy apostles and prophets in the Spirit;

Paul claimed to have received revelations "in the Spirit" regarding the "mystery of Christ". His knowledge about Jesus, therefore, depended primarily upon supernatural messages and not information received from eye-witnesses or personal experience. These visions and revelations were, by their very nature, subjective and could not be confirmed independently. When he fell on the Damascus Road, only he could see and hear Christ speaking to him.

Eph 3: 8 12

8.	To me, the very least of all saints, was this grace given, to preach to the Gentiles the unsearchable riches of Christ,
9.	and to make all men see what is the administration of the mystery which for ages has been hidden in God, who created all things through Jesus Christ;
10.	to the intent that now through the assembly the manifold wisdom of God might be made known to the principalities and the powers in the heavenly places,
11.	according to the eternal purpose which he purposed in Christ Jesus, our Lord;

| 12. | in whom we have boldness and access in confidence through our faith in him. |

Although Paul called himself "the very least of all saints", he claimed the "grace" to preach to the Gentiles about the mysteries of a cosmic or metaphysical Christ through whom all creation was brought about – a mystery that was hidden, even to Jesus' closest followers, until it was revealed to Paul.

The Hymn on Christ
Phil 2: 5–11

5.	Have this in your mind, which was also in Christ Jesus,
6.	who, existing in the form of God, didn't consider it robbery to be equal with God,
7.	but emptied himself, taking the form of a servant, being made in the likeness of men.
8.	Being found in human form, he humbled himself, becoming obedient to death, yes, the death of the cross.
9.	Therefore God also highly exalted him, and gave to him the name which is above every name;
10.	that at the name of Jesus every knee would bow, of those in heaven, those on earth, and those under the earth,
11.	and that every tongue would confess that Jesus Christ is Lord, to the glory of God, the Father.

Paul quoted this hymn to encourage the readers of his letter to be humble, gentle, and generous – just as Christ was.

This hymn, that must have been known to his readers, may even have been composed by Paul himself. It is a poem in three parts:

- Christ as God;
- Christ as man; and
- Christ in glory.[133]

This song is a good expression of Paul's views regarding Christ who had a pre-existence with his Father, his equal, but who humbled himself by becoming a human and being executed on a cross. He was, though, resurrected, taken up into heaven so that all creation would recognize him as the Lord, as God himself.

Attention must be drawn to the primitive and prescientific world view of Paul where he mentions the three layers of creation, populated by "those in heaven, those on earth, and those under the earth" – in other words: the angels and demons (stars in the sky), people on earth, and the deceased souls in Hades below the surface of the earth.[134]

A Hymn on Christ
Col 1: 13–20

13.	[The Father] who delivered us out of the power of darkness, and translated us into the kingdom of the Son of his love;
14.	in whom we have our redemption through his blood, the forgiveness of our sins.
15.	He is the image of the invisible God, the firstborn of all creation.
16.	For in him were all things created, in the heavens and on the earth, things visible and things invisible, whether thrones or dominions or principalities or powers; all things have been created through him, and to him.

---

[133] Bright, "Letter of Joy".
[134] Pretorius. *Who, What, and Were is God?* 5–58.

> 17. He is before all things, and in him all things are held together.
> 18. He is the head of the body, the assembly, who is the beginning, the firstborn from the dead; that in all things he might have the preeminence.
> 19. For all the fullness was pleased to dwell in him;
> 20. and through him to reconcile all things to himself, having made peace through the blood of his cross.
> Through him, I say, whether things on the earth, or things in the heavens.

This passage contains an old hymn on Christ (vs 15–18), dealing with three aspects:

- Christ's relationship with God (1:15);
- His relationship with creation (1:16–17); and
- His relationship with the church (1:18).[135]

The two verses preceding this old hymn mention the kingdom of Christ, which is clearly thought to be a spiritual or heavenly kingdom – not a kingdom with Jerusalem as its capital.

The hymn itself reminds one of the prologue to John's gospel where we read:

> "In the beginning was the Word, and the Word was with God, and the Word was God. The same was in the beginning with God. All things were made through him. Without him was not anything made that has been made" (John 1: 1–3).

This passage in John harks back to Genesis 1 where God's creative

---

[135] MacArthur, *Bible Introductions – Colossians*..

word called the creation into being. The same theme appears in this hymn. Christ is introduced as the visible presentation of God who is invisible. As firstborn of the creation, he is not part of creation but the agent through which creation came about. As such, he is the head of the church. His death and resurrection are also mentioned as the act through which the believers are redeemed.[136]

Because this passage deals with Christ on a metaphysical level, no real biographical details are given, except for his blood on the cross and that he was the firstborn from the dead. On the other hand, his divinity is emphasized. These views are consistent with the visions and revelations Paul has received and of which he convinced his converts.

It is almost as if Jesus of Nazareth was not a man of flesh and blood, but an ethereal being who briefly visited mankind on earth and who rules his church, his spiritual kingdom, from heaven.

Christ a Manifestation of God
Col 2: 8–12

8.	Be careful that you don't let anyone rob you through his philosophy and vain deceit, after the tradition of men, after the elements of the world, and not after Christ.
9.	For in him all the fullness of the Godhead dwells bodily,
10.	and in him you are made full, who is the head of all principality and power;
11.	in whom you were also circumcised with a circumcision not made with hands, in the putting off of the body of the sins of the flesh, in the circumcision of Christ;

---

[136] Pocock, "Christ has Everything you Need."

> 12. having been buried with him in baptism, in which you were also raised with him through faith in the working of God, who raised him from the dead.

This passage also introduces a metaphysical Christ. The readers of the letter are warned against strange doctrines, with which pagan religions, Greek philosophical schools, and Jewish religious ideas may have been meant. Christ, as a human being with a physical body, was actually a manifestation of God. As such, he holds all power in heaven and on earth and rules over all principalities, angels, and demons.

The Christian baptism, which replaced the Jewish circumcision, amounts to a symbolic or spiritual burial together with Christ who was buried after having died, but also to a symbolic or spiritual resurrection from death, together with Christ.

Paul's Differences with the Apostles of Jesus
Gal 2: 1–21

> 1. Then after a period of fourteen years I went up again to Jerusalem with Barnabas, taking Titus also with me.
> 2. I went up by revelation, and I laid before them [the apostles] the gospel which I preach among the Gentiles, but privately before those who were respected, for fear that I might be running, or had run, in vain.
> 3. But not even Titus, who was with me, being a Greek, was compelled to be circumcised.
> 4. This was because of the false brothers secretly brought in, who stole in to spy out our liberty which we have in Christ Jesus, that they might bring us into bondage;

5. to whom we gave no place in the way of subjection, not for an hour, that the truth of the gospel might continue with you.

6. But from those who were reputed to be important (whatever they were, it makes no difference to me; God doesn't show partiality to man) – they, I say, who were respected imparted nothing to me,

7. but to the contrary, when they saw that I had been entrusted with the gospel for the uncircumcision, even as Peter with the gospel for the circumcision

8. (for he who appointed Peter to the apostleship of the circumcision appointed me also to the Gentiles);

9. and when they perceived the grace that was given to me, James and Cephas and John, they who were reputed to be pillars, gave to me and Barnabas the right hand of fellowship, that we should go to the Gentiles, and they to the circumcision.

10. They only asked us to remember the poor – which very thing I was also zealous to do.

11. But when Peter came to Antioch, I resisted him to the face, because he stood condemned.

12. For before some people came from James, he ate with the Gentiles. But when they came, he drew back and separated himself, fearing those who were of the circumcision.

13. The rest of the Jews joined him in his hypocrisy; so much that even Barnabas was carried away with their hypocrisy.

14. But when I saw that they didn't walk uprightly according to the truth of the gospel, I said to Cephas before them all, "If

> you, being a Jew, live as the Gentiles do, and not as the Jews do, why do you compel the Gentiles to live as the Jews do?
> 15. "We, being Jews by nature, and not Gentile sinners,
> 16. yet knowing that a man is not justified by the works of the law but through the faith of Jesus Christ, even we believed in Christ Jesus, that we might be justified by faith in Christ, and not by the works of the law, because no flesh will be justified by the works of the law.
> 17. But if, while we sought to be justified in Christ, we ourselves also were found sinners, is Christ a servant of sin? God forbid!
> 18. For if I build up again those things which I destroyed, I prove myself a law-breaker.
> 19. For I, through the law, died to the law, that I might live to God.
> 20. I have been crucified with Christ, and it is no longer I that live, but Christ living in me. That life which I now live in the flesh, I live by faith in the Son of God, who loved me, and gave himself up for me.
> 21. I don't make void the grace of God. For if righteousness is through the law, then Christ died for nothing!"

This passage contains Paul's recollections of his debates and differences with the apostles of Jesus, including Peter.

We also read in Acts 15 another version of the meeting Paul and Barnabas had with the apostles and elders in Jerusalem regarding the question whether new converts to the Jesus Movement had to be circumcised as Jews and to keep the Law of Moses as was required of Jews.

Paul defended the stance that Christians are not justified of their sins by living according to the laws of Moses and being circumcised, but by having faith in Jesus Christ. He clashed with the apostles, especially Peter, whom he called "false brothers" who defended the point of view of Jesus that the Law of Moses had to be upheld in all respects by all Jesus' followers.

Redemption through Christ
Gal 3: 13–14

28.	Christ redeemed us from the curse of the law, having become a curse for us. For it is written, "Cursed is everyone who hangs on a tree,"
29.	that the blessing of Abraham might come on the Gentiles through Christ Jesus; that we might receive the promise of the Spirit through faith.

Gal 4: 4–5

1.	But when the fullness of the time came, God sent forth his Son, born to a woman, born under the law,
2.	that he might redeem those who were under the law, that we might receive the adoption of sons.

Paul quoted from Deut 21: 23, which required that an executed criminal's "body shall not remain all night on the tree, but you shall surely bury him the same day; for he who is hanged is accursed of God."

The point he wished to make is that Christ suffered the curse of God to free believers from that curse.

Rom 3: 19–26

19.	Now we know that whatever things the law says, it speaks to those who are under the law, that every mouth may be

> closed, and all the world may be brought under the judgment of God.
> 20. Because by the works of the law, no flesh will be justified in his sight. For through the law comes the knowledge of sin.
> 21. But now apart from the law, a righteousness of God has been revealed, being testified by the law and the prophets;
> 22. even the righteousness of God through faith in Jesus Christ to all and on all those who believe. For there is no distinction,
> 23. for all have sinned, and fall short of the glory of God;
> 24. being justified freely by his grace through the redemption that is in Christ Jesus;
> 25. whom God set forth to be an atoning sacrifice, through faith, in his blood, to show his righteousness because of the passing over of the sins done before, in the forbearance of God;
> 26. for the showing of his righteousness at this present time; that he might himself be just, and the justifier of him who has faith in Jesus.

Paul certainly never had the opportunity of reading the earliest documents containing the teachings of Jesus, the Q Document and the narrative parts of John's Gospel, which were written somewhat earlier than his letters, or at the same time, namely two or three decades after the time of Jesus. If Paul had read these, he would have seen that Jesus clearly declared that his followers should live according to the Law of Moses if they wanted to inherit eternal life.

Paul claimed that he had received the revelation that the Law of Moses was not the route to justification or forgiveness of sins.

The only value of the Law was that it exposed the sins of all sinners. When Jesus died on the cross as an innocent victim of the Romans, he fulfilled all the requirements of the Law and it is only required of his followers, the Christians, to accept his sacrifice in faith to be justified of their sins.

Divisions in the Church
1 Cor 1: 10–17

10.	Now I beg you, brothers, through the name of our Lord, Jesus Christ, that you all speak the same thing and that there be no divisions among you, but that you be perfected together in the same mind and in the same judgment.
11.	For it has been reported to me concerning you, my brothers, by those who are from Chloe's household, that there are contentions among you.
12.	Now I mean this, that each one of you says, "I follow Paul," "I follow Apollos," "I follow Cephas," and, "I follow Christ."
13.	Is Christ divided? Was Paul crucified for you? Or were you baptized into the name of Paul?
14.	I thank God that I baptized none of you, except Crispus and Gaius,
15.	so that no one should say that I had baptized you into my own name.
16.	(I also baptized the household of Stephanas; besides them, I don't know whether I baptized any other.)
17.	For Christ sent me not to baptize, but to preach the gospel -- not in wisdom of words, so that the cross of Christ wouldn't be made void.

Paul lamented the news he had received that there were divisions and different parties in the Christian community in the Greek city of Corinth. He found this situation so disturbing that this is the first issue that he dealt with in this letter.

It seems that there were four parties in the church in Corinth:

- The followers of Paul – most probably former pagans he converted to his brand of Christianity. He mentions three names of people whom he had baptized, people with Greek and Roman names.
- The followers of Apollos – people who revered John the Baptist and regarded him as the most important prophet of the recent past, even more important than Jesus of Nazareth.
- Those who followed Cephas or Peter – most probably Jewish members of the Jesus Movement who lived in the Greek city of Corinth and didn't agree with all Paul's ideas. They followed Peter since he and Paul had clashed in the past about the obligation of believers to adhere to the Law of Moses, including the rule about circumcision.
- The party who belonged to Christ – it is not quite clear who these people were, but they were probably believers who tried to reconcile the ideas of Paul and Peter.

This situation, as described by Paul, is a sign that the followers of Jesus of Nazareth, the first Christians, certainly did not form a single and united movement. The differences between previous pagans who believed in Jesus as the Messiah and those who supported Jesus' campaign to resurrect the Israelite kingdom and of which Jesus' brother, James, became the leader after he had left the scene, is described in the book of Acts, especially Acts 15 and Acts 21: 27 – 24: 27.

The history of Christianity through the centuries demonstrates that there were always divisions and competing parties and sects within Christianity. Paul's comments and lament in this regard did nothing to remedy this situation, although Paul's theology won the battle in a certain sense by becoming the orthodox view.

JAMES

The author of the Epistle of James introduces himself as "James, a servant of God and of the Lord Jesus Christ" (Jas 1: 1).

Experts agree that this letter of James originated in a Jewish "Christian" community. It is, after all, addressed "to the twelve tribes which are in the Dispersion" (Jas 1: 1) – by which the Jewish followers of Jesus inside and outside of Palestine must have been meant. The followers of Jesus, who were mostly recruited from the party of the Essenes, regarded themselves as the true Israel – hence they are called "the twelve tribes which are in the Dispersion".

In Jas 2: 2 an "assembly" is mentioned, where the word "synagogue" (Greek: συναγωγή – *synagoge*) is actually used. That means that James' readers gathered in (Jewish) synagogues of their own. There are many allusions to the Old Testament and the author seems to have assumed that his readers knew the Hebrew Scriptures.

All this point to the Essenes or Ebionites as the intended recipients.

There is no agreement as to who the author was and when it was written. Some experts date it late in the first century AD or even later when James, the brother of Jesus and leader of the Ebionites in Jerusalem, was already deceased. According to Josephus, he was killed in AD 62.[137]

There are also those who believe that the author was, in fact,

---

[137] Josephus, *Antiquities*, Liber XX/IX;

James, Jesus' brother. The book of Acts presents James as the leader of the Jerusalem congregation and as the successor of Jesus as leader of the Jesus Movement (Acts 12: 17; 15: 13–21; 21: 18). Paul mentions "James and Cephas and John, they who were reputed to be pillars" of the community in Jerusalem (Gal 2: 9). According to Eusebius, he was called "James the Just" on account of his piety.[138]

The fact that the epistle was clearly addressed to the Ebionites, certainly points to James, Jesus' brother, as the author. This letter, which deals mainly with ethical issues, often referred to poverty and riches – which agrees with the idea that it originated within an Ebionite community, the Jewish followers of Jesus.[139]

In this letter, no mention is made of the destruction of the Jerusalem temple. The social situation also seems to mirror the period before the Jewish War with the destruction of Jerusalem during AD 66–70 when rich landowners exploited the poor (Jas 1: 10; 2: 1–7; 5: 1–6). Therefore, this letter must have been written before AD 62 when James died.

There is a possibility that Jesus was still alive after his miraculous survival of the crucifixion and the medical care he received from his friends while in the tomb (John 19: 38–40) at the time when this epistle was written because James twice warns his readers to await the "coming of the Lord" (James 5: 7–8).

Partiality against the Poor
Jas 2: 1–7

1.	My brothers, don't hold the faith of our Lord Jesus Christ, [the Lord] of glory, with respect of persons.

---

[138] Eusebius, *Historia Ecclesiastica,* Liber II/XXIII.
[139] Enc Brit, "James, the letter of"; Rylaarsdam *et al.,* "Biblical Literature"; Gaum, *Kernensiklopedie,* 510–11.

2.	For if a man with a gold ring, in fine clothing, comes into your assembly, and there come in also a poor man in filthy clothing;
3.	and you pay special attention to him who wears the fine clothing, and say, "Sit here in a good place;" and you tell the poor man, "Stand there," or "Sit by my footstool;"
4.	haven't you shown partiality among yourselves, and become judges with evil thoughts?
5.	Listen, my beloved brothers. Didn't God choose those who are poor in this world to be rich in faith, and heirs of the kingdom which he promised to those who love him?
6.	But you have dishonored the poor man. Don't the rich oppress you, and personally drag you before the courts?
7.	Don't they blaspheme the honorable name by which you are called?

The Essenes were known for their abhorrence of riches and opulence and that sentiment is mirrored in this passage.

The followers of Jesus, who regarded him as the Messiah, are encouraged not to look down on poor people and not treat rich people with golden rings and fine clothes better than others. James evidently followed in the footsteps of Amos who also warned the rich people of his time not to trample upon the poor people.

The Fate of Rich People
Jas 5: 1–6

1.	Come now, you rich, weep and howl for your miseries that are coming on you.
2.	Your riches are corrupted and your garments are moth-eaten.

> 3. Your gold and your silver are corroded, and their corrosion will be for a testimony against you, and will eat your flesh like fire. You have laid up your treasure in the last days.
> 4. Behold, the wages of the laborers who mowed your fields, which you have kept back by fraud, cries out, and the cries of those who reaped have entered into the ears of the Lord of Hosts.
> 5. You have lived delicately on the earth, and taken your pleasure. You have nourished your hearts as in a day of slaughter.
> 6. You have condemned, you have murdered the righteous one. He doesn't resist you.

James sounds just like an Old Testament prophet, especially where he mentions "the Lord of Hosts". In Greek this expression is Κύριος Σαβαώθ (*Kurios Sebaoth*), which comes from the Hebrew יְהוָה צְבָאוֹת – (*YHWH Tsebaoth*).

In true Essene or Ebionite form, he condemned rich people in general and called for the judgment of God on them.

JOHN OF PATMOS

A Prophetic Book

The book of Revelation, written by John of Patmos, is the only exclusively prophetic book in the New Testament, containing bizarre visions, which amount to a commentary on the circumstances under which John and his fellow-Christians in Asia Minor lived during the nineties of the first century AD.

John wrote this book with the Christians of his own time in mind – not people who would live centuries or millennia after his time. He explicitly addressed his book to the seven existing churches in Asia Minor, including his home town of Ephesus (Rev 1: 4 and Rev 2 & 3). He wanted to convey a message to these Christians in their difficult circumstances.

Revelations can, therefore, not be seen as a detailed prediction about the far future – except for a description of Judgment Day and the New Jerusalem, the dwelling of God and his angels. It comments on events during the final decade of the first century AD, together with promises that God would not forget the faithful and that the second coming of Christ on Judgment Day was imminent. After all, in Rev 1: 1, 3 & 19; 4: 1; 10: 6; and 22: 6–7, 10 and 12, John repeatedly reminded his readers that he was remarking on events in the present and the immediate foreseeable future.

Many commentaries on Revelation did not take this aspect into consideration and they tried to predict what people can expect in the decades and centuries still to come. Of course, all the predictions about the date of Judgment Day so far have proved to be misguided. The prophecies of Revelation, therefore, deal mostly with the current affair of John's own time. In a later chapter, his description of Judgment Day and the New Jerusalem will receive attention.

An analysis of John's visions, coupled with a knowledge of ancient astrology, reveals that John did not describe extra-sensory sights or supernatural dreams, but the starry skies and other natural phenomena – just as the Old Testament books of Ezekiel, Zechariah, and Daniel did. In the pages that follow, a selection of his disclosures will be quoted, together with an explanation of his experiences and messages.

The Four Living Creatures
Rev 4: 1–11

1. After these things I looked and saw a door opened in heaven, and the first voice that I heard, like a trumpet speaking with me, was one saying, "Come up here, and I will show you the things which must happen after this."

2. Immediately I was in the Spirit. Behold, there was a throne set in heaven, and one sitting on the throne

3. that looked like a jasper stone and a sardius. There was a rainbow around the throne, like an emerald to look at.

4. Around the throne were twenty-four thrones. On the thrones were twenty-four elders sitting, dressed in white garments, with crowns of gold on their heads.

5. Out of the throne proceed lightnings, sounds, and thunders. There were seven lamps of fire burning before the throne, which are the seven Spirits of God.

6. Before the throne was something like a sea of glass, like a crystal. In the midst of the throne, and around the throne were four living creatures full of eyes before and behind.

7. The first creature was like a lion, and the second creature like a calf, and the third creature had a face like a man, and the fourth creature was like a flying eagle.

8. and the four living creatures, having each one of them six wings, are full of eyes around about and within. They have no rest day and night, saying, Holy, holy, holy is the Lord God, the Almighty, who was and who is and who is to come.

9. When the living creatures give glory, honour, and thanks to him who sits on the throne, to him who lives forever and ever,

10. the twenty-four elders fall down before him who sits on the

> throne, and worship him who lives forever and ever, and will throw their crowns before the throne, saying,
>
> 11. "Worthy are you, our Lord and our God, to receive the glory, the honour, and the power, for you created all things, and because of your desire they existed, and were created."

What John saw

John gazed at night at the stars during the beginning of February AD 96 from his vantage point on the small island of Patmos. There must have been a thunder storm earlier and lightning was still to be seen at a distance. There must also have been a rainbow after the storm had passed. A rainbow is always seen at a part of the sky opposite the sun.[140] In John's case, the sun set over Patmos on 2 February around 19:00 and the rainbow could, therefore, still be seen shortly before the onset of darkness. The trumpet he heard could have been the thunder connected with the storm.

Something similar happened when Moses and the people of Israel were encamped at the foot of Mount Sinai:

> "It happened on the third day, when it was morning, that there were thunders and lightnings, and a thick cloud on the mountain, and the sound of an exceedingly loud trumpet; and all the people who were in the camp trembled. (....) Mount Sinai, the whole of it, smoked, because YHWH descended on it in fire; and its smoke ascended like the smoke of a furnace, and the whole mountain quaked greatly" (Ex 19: 16 & 18).

John saw a door opened in the vault of the sky. This is accordance with the beliefs of the ancients that the heavens had doors or windows through which the waters above the vault of the sky fell

---

[140] Enc Brit, "Rainbow".

onto the earth as rain. Ps 148: 4 tells us of "waters that are above the heavens". These were thought to be the storage places of the rain and, therefore, the heaven and the sky had to have windows through which this water could be poured down onto the earth (Gen 1: 7; Gen 7: 11; 2 Kgs 7: 2; Mal 3: 10).

He also heard a voice like a trumpet. Trumpets are military musical instruments used to convey the orders of a general to troops on a battle field. We are not told who was speaking but it may be assumed that the voice belonged to God or Christ.

John saw the throne of God/Christ at the north celestial pole, just as Isaiah, Ezekiel, and Zechariah, although he didn't see anything representing God or Christ Himself. The seven Spirits of God were the seven prominent stars on the body of the constellation of Draco, forming an arc below the heavenly north pole. He most probably used his imagination to picture Christ sitting on the right side of God because there is nothing around the northern celestial pole that could serve as a representation of Christ.

He described the throne as surrounded by a rainbow that looked like an emerald, a green stone, often with blue and yellow hues. That must have been the bright Milky Way, not far from the north celestial pole and stretching over the whole sky from the north-western horizon to the south-eastern horizon. The occupant of the throne was compared to a jasper stone and a sardius – both are reddish and even multicolored stones that can be polished to a high gloss and these stones were worn as expensive jewelry. John wanted to emphasize God's glory with this comparison.

Before the throne he saw "a sea of glass, like a crystal." That must have been the Aegean Sea on which the light of the stars was reflected, which is visible from any point on the small island of Patmos. Ezekiel saw something similar: "And the likeness of the firmament upon the heads of the living creature was as the color of the terrible crystal, stretched forth over their heads above" (Ezek 1: 22).

He observed four living creatures: a lion, a calf or a bull, a man, and an eagle in flight. The number of four is significant, it being the number symbolizing the earth and creation. The ancients thought that the earth and the heavens were composed of four elements: earth, water, air, and fire. Earth also had four corners and wind directions – north, east, south, and west. These four creatures, therefore, symbolized the earth and creation.

Each of these creatures had six wings. That is almost a repetition of Isa 6: 1–2 – "In the year that king Uzziah died I saw the Lord sitting on a throne, high and lifted up; and his train filled the temple. Above him stood the seraphim: each one had six wings; with two he covered his face, and with two he covered his feet, and with two he did fly."

These four living beings are also mentioned in Ezek 1.

The god of the heavens of the ancient Sumerians, Anu, had his throne at the northern celestial pole and his throne was also surrounded by a lion, a bull, a man, and an eagle. The following constellations were involved –

- Leo, the Lion, with Regulus as its most prominent star, which was situated at the summer solstice in those days;
- Taurus, the Bull, whose biggest star is Aldebaran, which marked the spring equinox;
- Aquila, the Eagle, with Altair as its principal star, which ruled the winter solstice; and
- Boötes, the Ploughman or Farmer, with Arcturus as his biggest star, which was somewhat askew and did not quite mark the autumn equinox.[141]

---

[141] Cornelius, 1962: 13, 3 5–36; Visser, 1972: 57–58

John certainly held the same view as the old Sumerians. It must be noted that the Aramaic astrological calendar found at Qumran used a name for the constellation of Taurus that literally means "bull, ox or steer". In Aramaic script it is תורא (*tora*), which sounds almost the same as the Greek Ταυρος (*Tauros* = bull) or the Latin Taurus (= bull).[142]

In addition, John observed 24 elders, surrounding the central throne. It is not quite possible to identify these constellations or stars precisely, since there are so many of them. It is not possible that the number of 24 (12 X 2 = 24) had any relation to the twelve signs of the Zodiac since two figures on the Zodiac, the Lion and the Bull, were already part of the quartet of living creatures. It is probable, though, that John saw a connection between the 24 elders and the 24 hours of the day – 12 hours during daylight and 12 hours during the night. It is also possible that he thought of a combination of the twelve patriarchs of Israel and the twelve apostles of Christ. They would then be the representatives of the faithful from the time before Christ and the time after Christ. Another possibility is that he thought of the 24 divisions of the priests serving in the temple (1 Chr 24).

The accompanying computer-generated images depict the sky above Patmos during early February 96 AD, showing the four living creatures at different times during the same night.

John's message
The 24 elders are frequently encountered in Revelation and they are to be found on the following places:

- Rev 5: 5 – an elder consoled John when he wept when he didn't immediately see somebody who could open the seven seals.

---

[142] Jacobus, "The Zodiac Sign Names", 317

- Rev 5: 8 – each of the elders received a harp and they and the four living creatures sang a hymn in praise of the Lamb.
- Rev 5: 14 – the elders fell down and worshipped the Lamb.
- Rev 7: 11 – the elders worshipped God.
- Rev 7: 14 – one of the elders explains a scene to John.
- Rev 8: 16 – the elders fell on their faces and worshipped God.
- Rev 14: 3 – the elders are in front of God's throne.
- Rev 19: 4 – the elders worshipped God.

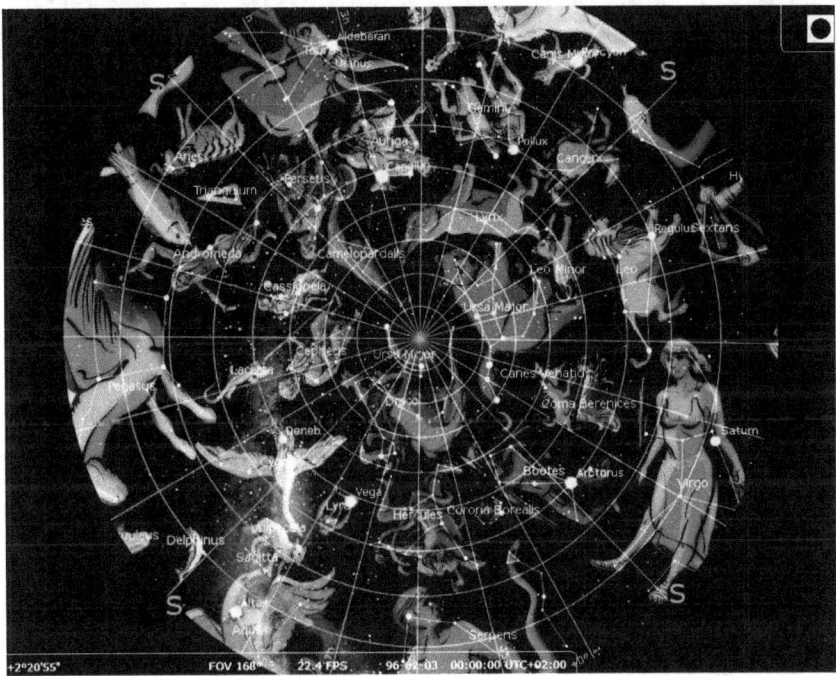

The view of the sky at the terrestrial north pole showing the distribution of the four living creatures around the pole. Taurus (the Bull) is at the upper left, Leo (the Lion) is at the upper right, Aquila (the Eagle) is at the lower left and Boötes (the Ploughman) is situated at the lower right. The sky is also divided into 24 segments – one for each hour of the day.

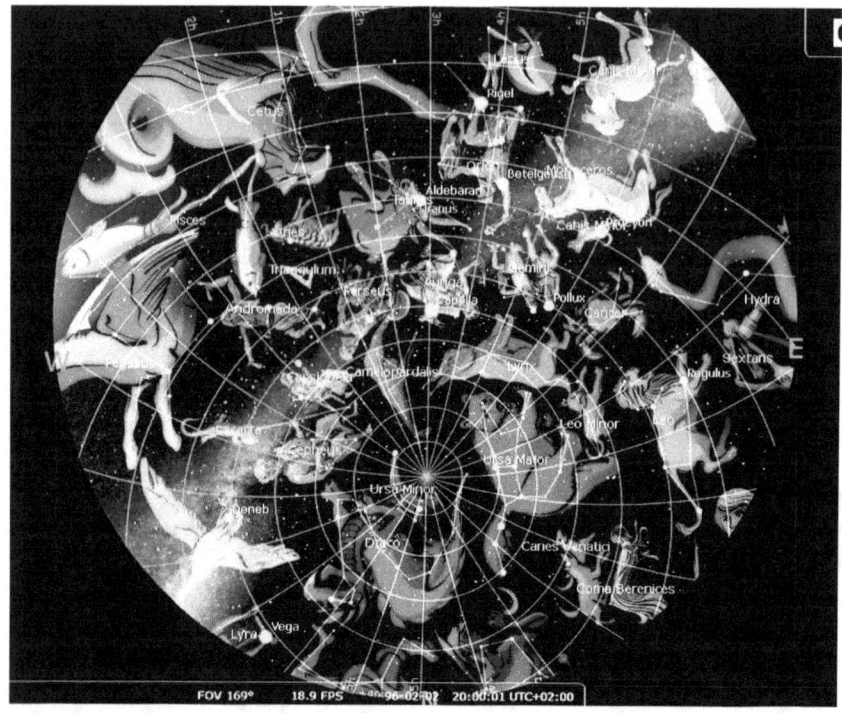

A computer-generated image of the sky as it appeared at the beginning of February AD 96, at about 20:00 local time from Patmos, looking north. Three of the four living beings are visible: Leo (the Lion) can be seen on the right, in the east; Taurus (the Bull) is on top in the south, and a part of Boötes (the Ploughman – holding a sickle in his hand) can be seen on the lower right in the northeast. The lines radiating from the celestial north pole – where the divine throne is situated – divide the sky into 24 parts – each 15° wide.

The number of 24 elders is, of course, symbolic. They could each have represented a separate hour of the day. The custom of dividing the day into 24 hours seems to have originated with the ancient Egyptians who divided the duration of daylight and the duration of darkness each into twelve parts – with the result that the lengths of hours varied from season to season.[143] If the number of 24 elders refers to the hours of the day, then John intended to convey the

---

[143] Enc Brit, "Hour".

message that God and Jesus Christ control every hour of the day and that they have to be worshipped 24 hours per day. This must be a never-ceasing activity.

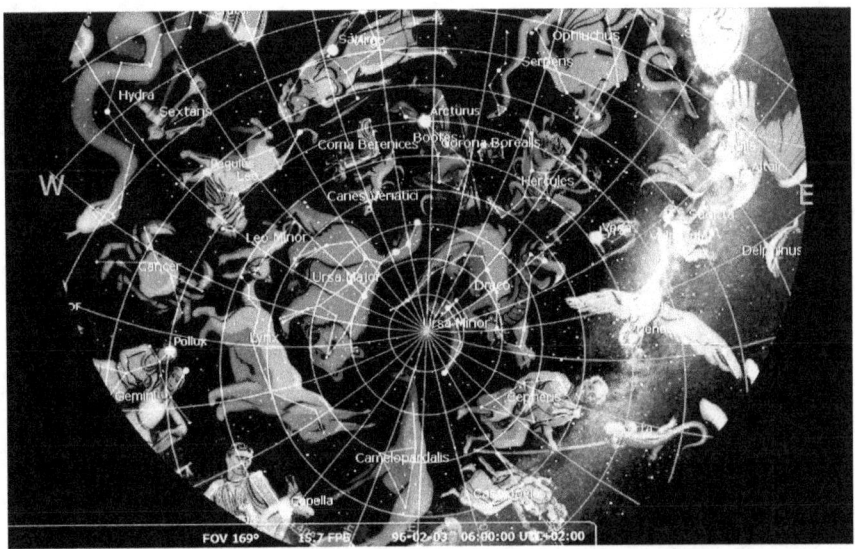

The fourth living creature, Aquila (the Eagle) appeared near the eastern horizon in the early morning, before daybreak. Boötes and Leo were situated respectively to the south and the west at this time of the night.

The number of 24 is also the sum of 12 + 12. Israel had twelve patriarchs and Jesus had twelve apostles, each of them representing one of the tribes of Israel. These 24 elders are, therefore, the representatives of the faithful from the time of the Old Testament, as well as of the New Testament. They are all equally the people of God and all will find a place in heaven. The idea espoused by some Bible students that the people of Israel or the Jews are still the special people of God and that gentile believers come in second place, cannot be maintained in the light of John's vision that believers from the time before Christ and the faithful of the time after Christ are all equally the chosen of God.

The four living beings also played an active role in the rest of John's narrative and they always surrounded God's throne. They are often mentioned in conjunction with the elders. We meet them on the following occasions:

- They are always near God's throne (Rev 4: 6; 5: 6 and 14: 3);
- They are constantly engaged in worship and praise (Rev 4: 8; 5: 8; 5: 14; 7: 11 and 19: 4);
- They invite the horrible wrath of God to appear (Rev 6:1 and 6: 7); and
- One of them hands over the vials of God's wrath (Rev 15: 7).

Although the four living beings can be identified in the starry heaven as constellations, they are also symbols or representatives of the whole of God's creation. The Lion is the king of the wild animals. The bull is the strongest of the domesticated animals. The eagle is the bird that flies higher than other birds. The human being is the crown of God's creation. These four figures are also the representtatives of the four equinoxes and solstices, the four seasons, the four basic elements and the four wind directions or corners of the earth.

In other words: according to John, the whole of creation sings God's praise and worships Him. This is an echo of Ps 19: 1–2 – "The heavens declare the glory of God. The expanse shows his handiwork. Day after day they pour forth speech, and night after night they display knowledge."

The Four Horsemen
Rev 6: 1–11

1.	I saw that the Lamb opened one of the seven seals, and I heard one of the four living creatures saying, as with a voice of thunder, "Come and see!"

2.	I saw, and behold, a white horse, and he who sat on it had a bow. A crown was given to him, and he came forth conquering, and to conquer.
3.	When he opened the second seal, I heard the second living creature saying, "Come!"
4.	Another came forth, a red horse. To him who sat on it was given to take peace from the earth, and that they should kill one another. There was given to him a great sword.
5.	When he opened the third seal, I heard the third living creature saying, "Come and see!" I saw, and behold, a black horse. He who sat on it had a balance in his hand.
6.	I heard a voice in the midst of the four living creatures saying, "A choenix of wheat for a denarius, and three choenix of barley for a denarius! Don't damage the oil and the wine!"
7.	When he opened the fourth seal, I heard the voice of the fourth living creature saying, "Come and see!"
8.	I saw, and behold, a pale horse. He who sat on him, his name was Death. Hades followed with him. Authority over one fourth of the earth, to kill with the sword, with famine, with death, and by the wild animals of the earth was given to them.
9.	When he opened the fifth seal, I saw underneath the altar the souls of those who had been killed for the word of God, and for the testimony which they held.
10.	They cried with a loud voice, saying, "How long, Master, the holy and true, do you not judge and avenge our blood on those who dwell on the earth?"

> 11. There was given to each one of them a white robe. It was said to them that they should rest yet for a little time, until their fellow servants and their brothers, who would also be killed even as they were, had been fulfilled.

What John saw

John saw the Lamb, Jesus Christ, on the throne, at the celestial north pole, breaking open seven seals in succession. These seals were the seven stars of Ursa Minor, the Little Bear, next to the celestial north pole. The breaking of each seal introduced a new scene.

Then he heard the voice of one of the four living creatures sounding like thunder, calling upon him to watch a new scene. It is quite possible that a passing thunderstorm occurred on that particular night.

John thereafter saw four horsemen. He often incorporated war horses in his visions (Rev 9: 17-19; 18:13; 19: 11, 14 & 21) and we may presume that he saw detachments of Roman cavalry in action during the Jewish War of AD 66–90.

He describes the first horseman as seated on a white horse, holding a bow and receiving a crown. This is clearly the constellation of Sagittarius, the Archer, in the south – traditionally depicted with a bow and arrow – together with the constellation of Corona Australis, the Southern Crown. Sagittarius is traditionally depicted as a centaur, a being with the upper body of a man and the rump and legs of a horse. John, with his convictions rooted in the Old Testament, would not have seen in Sagittarius this Greek mythological figure but a real horseman or knight on his steed.

The nearest living being to Sagittarius is Boötes, the Ploughman, and it must be this celestial figure that called to John.

The second horseman appeared after the breaking of the second seal and a second living being had called upon John to come and watch. This red horse can only be Pegasus, the Winged Horse. The sword given to this horseman can be identified as one of the fishes in the constellation of Pisces (the Fishes), just above Pegasus' back. It is easy to imagine the outlines of the fish to represent a sword. The living being that called to John must be Taurus, the Bull.

The third (black) horse that appeared after the breaking of the third seal is none other than Centaurus, the creature with the upper body of a man and the lower body of a horse. John would have regarded this constellation, just as in the case of Sagittarius, as a rider on his horse. This horseman held a pair of scales, the constellation of Libra, the Scales, directly to his east. The living being that called John, must be Leo, the Lion, which lies to the west of Centaurus. Although only the upper part of Centaurus was visible above the horizon in Patmos, one may assume that John was familiar with the whole constellation if he previously had lived further south in Judea where the whole of Centaurus, together with the Southern Cross, would have risen above the horizon.

John heard a voice calling on all those present to be prepared for a famine. This may be perhaps linked to the fact that John suffered from a poor diet as a poor exile on a small barren island.

The fourth horse that came forth after the breaking of the fourth seal, a pale horse, is the constellation of Equuleus, the Foal. It is a faint constellation and only the head of this animal is usually depicted in illustrations. It lies directly in front of Pegasus and the living being that called to John must be Aquila, the Eagle, directly next to it.

According to John, this last horse was called Death. Hades (Greek: ᾅδης) – the abode of the dead – was following it and that can only be the red planet Mars that lay almost next to it, inside the constellation of Capricornus, the Goat. Mars, or Ares (Ἀρης) as he was called in Greek, was the god of warfare and since there are always casualties during a war Mars was an appropriate choice to symbolize the realm of the dead. John must have had vivid memories of the Jewish War of AD 66–70 when more than a million people perished or were sold as slaves.[144]

The inspiration for the horsemen came from Zech 1: 8 –

> "I saw in the night, and, behold, a man riding on a red horse, and he stood among the myrtle-trees that were in the bottom; and behind him there were horses, red, sorrel, and white."

Something similar is described in Zech 6: 1–3 –

> "Again I lifted up my eyes, and saw, and, behold, there came four chariots out from between two mountains; and the mountains were mountains of brass. In the first chariot were red horses; and in the second chariot black horses; and in the third chariot white horses; and in the fourth chariot grizzled strong horses."

It has already been explained in the previous chapter what Zechariah meant by his visions. It is clear, though, that John had his own ideas in this regard.

When the fifth seal was broken by the Lamb, John saw some martyrs under the altar. The altar must be sought in the constellation of Ursa Major, the Great Bear, with a clear square forming its body. The Milky Way lies not too far from the northern celestial pole and that can be seen as a crowd of martyrs.

John's message

The four horsemen symbolized for John four different aspects of the world in which he and his fellow Christians were living. Each one

---

[144] Eusebius, Hist Eccl, Liber II/XXVI/1-2 & Liber III/V & VII/3).

became visible after one of the seals had been broken. These successive seals on the scroll are the unfolding of God's vision and plans for the world and how this world with its godlessness and blasphemy had to be dealt with.

The sky over Patmos during the early morning hours in March AD 96. Ursa Minor (the Little Bear) with its seven stars (the seven seals) are to be found next to the celestial north pole. Sagittarius (the Archer – the white horse) and Corona Australis (the Southern Crown) are in the south. Pegasus (the winged horse – the red horse), and Equuleus (the Foal – the pale horse), are visible in the east. The red planet Mars (Hades), is to be seen in the south-east inside Capricornus (the Goat). The following living beings are present: Boötes (the Ploughman) and Aquila (the Eagle), while Leo (the Lion), is disappearing in the west.

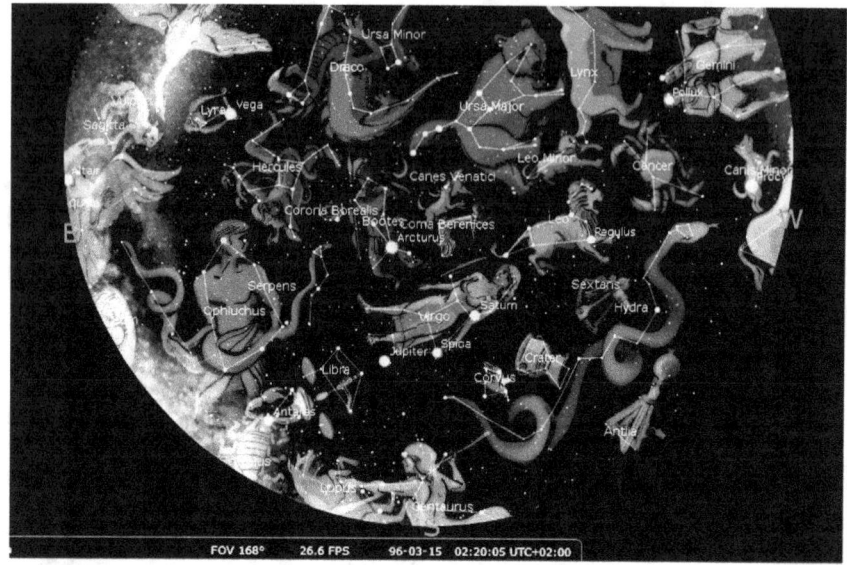

Centaurus (the black horse) and Libra (the Scales) visible in the south in March AD 96, late at night, as seen from Patmos. Leo (the Lion), one of the living beings, is also visible in the middle of the sky.

The first horseman sat on a white horse, held a bow, received a crown, and went out to conquer. That can only be a depiction of Christ and his message. The color white was a symbol of purity and sinlessness – and that may be applicable to Christ. He proved to be more powerful than all the evil forces in creation with his resurrection from death and ascension into heaven and, therefore, he was crowned as king of kings. John meant to convey the insight that nobody and nothing could stop the progress of the Gospel of Jesus Christ and that it was inevitable that more and more people would heed the message of salvation.

The second horse was described as red – the color of blood. Its rider held a sword and it was his task to take away the peace from earth. This horseman represented the military might and cruelty of the Roman Empire that held many nations and peoples under its rule through its army that was stationed in all parts of the empire and that had to defend its borders against aggression from outside and insurrection from inside.

The Roman regime was a bloodthirsty regime that was constantly at war somewhere. Its best-known victim was Jesus of Nazareth who was crucified in Jerusalem by Roman soldiers after having been sentenced to death by a Roman governor. Many Christians also died a martyr's death during the reigns of Nero and Domitian as emperors. John must also have had the wholesale slaughter especially at the end of the Jewish revolt of AD 66–70 by the Roman army in Judea in mind.

The black horse with the pair of scales that followed was a symbol of famine. The Roman system of taxation left many people destitute and that was one of the reasons why the Jews rebelled against Roman rule in AD 66.

The citadel of Jerusalem was overpowered by the Roman military might in AD 70 after the inhabitants had been cut off from the outside world through a siege and the result was that they suffered starvation before the Romans broke through their defenses. Eusebius wrote regarding those who were holed up in Jerusalem during the siege: "Many, indeed, secretly sold their possessions for one measure of wheat, if they belonged to the wealthier class, of barley if they were poorer." [145]

Many Christians in Asia Minor, who refused to participate in the veneration and adoration of the emperor as a living god, had to endure hardship. They were excluded from the trade guilds of their cities and they had to endure unjust discrimination, and that led to poverty in many cases.

John heard a voice calling out: "Don't damage the oil and the wine!" That may be a reference to the habit of Roman armies to

---

[145] Eusebius, *Hist Eccl*, Liber III/VI/5

destroy the crops, orchards, and vineyards of vanquished people as a form of punishment or vengeance.

The four horsemen of the Apocalypse, together with Hades, which is devouring a dead king, by the German artist, Albrecht Dürer (ca 1497).

A silver denarius coin minted during the reign of Emperor Domitian. At the opening of the third seal, one of these coins – approximately one day's wage of a laborer – was said to be needed to buy a single ration of wheat.[146]

The fourth horse had a pale color that reminds one of the color of putrefying corpses. Its rider was appropriately called Death. Hades, the realm of the dead, was following it. This was a reminder that the fate of death awaited all human beings, but it was also a sign that the cruel Roman regime caused the death of many of its subjects, especially those who were considered to be political and religious undesirables. People were to be killed through the following four causes: "with the sword, with famine, with death, and by the wild animals of the earth". Four is the symbolic number of the earth with its four wind directions and thereby John wanted to convey the message that all the possible causes of death were included. These causes were also characteristic of Roman rule: people were killed by the sword during war or gladiatorial games, but also when they were executed. Famine was often the result of war or heavy taxation. Wild animals were encountered in circuses where gladiators and martyrs had to fight them.[147]

    The life of an individual did not count for much in those days, even though Rome had an exemplary legal system, but that system worked only for Roman citizens. Criminals, war prisoners, and rebels were dealt with harshly, usually death by crucifixion as

---

[146] Franz, "The King and I".   [147] Enc Brit, 2010: Gladiator

the history during 73–71 BC of Spartacus and his band of rebellious fellow-slaves demonstrates.[148] Thousands upon thousands of Jewish captives were killed by the sword or were crucified after Jerusalem had been taken by the Roman army in August AD 70. In total, more than a million people perished during the war, while ninety thousand youths were sold as slaves.[149]

The fifth seal introduced the souls of the martyrs who were waiting to be avenged. They were seen under the altar – a symbol of having been sacrificed. Their white robes demonstrated that all their sins were wiped away through the death and resurrection of Jesus Christ. They got the assurance that God would avenge their violent deaths but that they had to wait for their number to be complete at the arrival of Judgment Day before God would finally avenge them. Many Christians lost their lives under Roman rule, but also through the ages that followed.

The Entrance to Hades
Rev 6: 12–17

12.	I saw when he opened the sixth seal, and there was a great earthquake. The sun became black as sackcloth made of hair, and the whole moon became as blood.
13.	The stars of the sky fell to the earth, as a fig tree drops its unripe figs when it is shaken by a great wind.
14.	The sky was removed as a scroll when it is rolled up. Every mountain and island were moved out of their places.
15.	The kings of the earth, the princes, the commanding officers, the rich, the strong, and every slave and freeman, hid themselves in the caves and in the rocks of the mountains.

---

[148] Enc Brit, "Spartacus".
[149] Eusebius, *Hist Eccl,* Liber II (XXVI/1-2) & Liber III (V & VII/3)

> 16. They told the mountains and the rocks, "Fall on us, and hide us from the face of him who sits on the throne, and from the wrath of the Lamb,
> 17. for the great day of his wrath has come; and who is able to stand?"

What John saw

It is tempting to explore the possibility of a solar and/or lunar eclipse during the nineties of the first century AD when reading these verses since John reported that the sun became black and the moon became red when the sixth seal was opened. However, an investigation of NASA's website on solar eclipses during the first century AD reveals that no solar eclipse was visible from the Mediterranean during the nineties. There was only one lunar eclipse that may perhaps arouse interest. That was the penumbral eclipse of 26 April AD 96, which was not visible from the eastern Mediterranean.

We may take John on his word that a violent earthquake occurred and that the mountains and islands were moved and shaken. The Aegean Sea and western coastal region of Asia Minor – nowadays Turkey – is known for periodic seismic activities, namely earthquakes and volcanic outbursts. A violent earthquake, causing widespread damage and casualties in the Aegean, especially on the island of Kos and the Turkish coastal town of Bodrum, occurred as recently as 21 July 2017.[150]

Decker and Decker declare: "There is a clear correspondence between the geographic distribution of volcanoes and major earthquakes..."[151] The following cities mentioned in John's letters to the seven churches in Asia Minor have been wrecked by violent

---

[150] Volcano Discovery, "Volcanoes of Turkey".
[151] Decker and Decker, "Volcano".

earthquakes at various times: Sardis, Philadelphia, and Laodicea.[152] Acts 16: 26 reports an earthquake in Philippi in Macedonia where Paul and Silas were being held in prison.

It has been shown in the previous chapter that the prophets Amos and Isaiah mentioned earthquakes in their time and that Isaiah described a volcanic outburst.

One can only conclude that John did experience a violent earthquake that shook the island of Patmos and that he did witness a volcanic event. The steam, dust clouds, ash, toxic vapors, and the smoke of wildfires generated by the glowing volcanic rocks must have obscured the sun and the moon, as well as a large part of the sky. The glowing blobs of lava and rocks flying skywards and falling back must have looked like stars crashing onto the earth. There can be no doubt that people witnessing the event must have been struck by panic and tried to hide from the falling debris.

The book of Revelation records at least five earthquakes:

- during the sixth seal, a "great earthquake" occurred (Rev 6:12);
- during the breaking of the seventh seal (Rev 8:5);
- after the resurrection of the two witnesses, a "great earthquake" happened when 7,000 men were killed (Rev 11:13);
- during the blowing of the seventh trumpet (Rev 11:19); and
- the final one, during the seventh bowl judgment, described as "a great earthquake, such a mighty and great earthquake as had not occurred since men were on the earth" (Rev 16:18).

A website dealing with 'Volcanoes in Greece' reports: "Greece has a large volcanic arch, which was created millions of years ago by the sinking of the African lithosphere (Oceania) under the Eurasiatic plate (mainland). This volcanic arch of Greece had an especially

---

[152] Scholtz, *Revelation*, 73–101.

intense volcanic activity in the past and created the volcanic landscapes that we come across in many regions and islands around Greece. Most of the volcanoes in Greece and the Greek islands are extinct, however there are some still active. The most important active volcanoes in Greece are situated on Santorini island, Nisyros island, Methana and Milos Island, receiving thousands of visitors every year."[153]

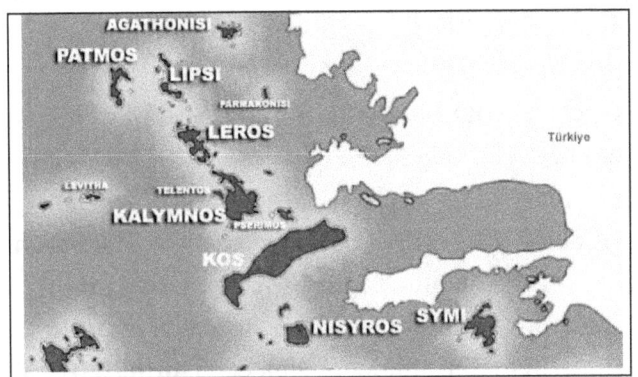

A map of the Aegean Sea, showing the relative positions of Patmos and Nisyros as members of the Dodecanese.

The volcano on the island of Nisyros (Greek: Νίσυρος), about 90 km from Patmos to the south-east as the crow flies, is most likely the volcano that John saw.

The Department of Geology of the Oregon State University reported on Nisyros: "It is suspected that the volcano erupted in 1422. In 1871, an eruption was accompanied by earthquakes, detonations, and red and yellow flames. Ash and lapilli [small stones] were erupted and covered the floor of Ramos, destroying the fruit gardens there. During a three-day-long eruption in 1873, a 20–25 foot (6–7 m) diameter crater formed and ash and blackish mud

---

[153]Greeka, "Volcanoes in Greece & the Islands".

was ejected. The bottom of Lakki and Ramos was transformed into a lake by hot saline water that overflowed the crater. The most recent eruption was in 1888. This strong eruption threw out a cylindrical pipe of volcanic material at least 80 feet (25 m) in diameter. Mud, lapilli, and steam were also ejected."[154]

The volcano on Nisyros is a popular tourist destination where low-grade volcanic activity is still going on. A tourist guide states that "occasional bubbles are seen and the sulphureous smell is often overpowering." There are also frequent "subterranean rumbling noises."[155]

No record could be found of an eruption of Nisyros during the first century AD, but such an event cannot be ruled out either, since this volcano has erupted at various times and geological evidence of at least 13 eruptions in the past could be found. Kinvig *et al.* report: "There is no record of any fatalities on the island of Nisyros.... It is important to consider, however that there may have been fatalities that were undocumented." During 2010 there were concerns that the volcano could erupt at any time again.[156]

The fireworks on Nisyros at night would have been clearly visible from Patmos – especially if the observer stood on one of the low hills on Patmos. The glowing lava, dust, ash, gas, steam, stones, and other material ejected from the volcano could have showered on places as far as 300 km away.[157]

If the tradition is correct that John lived in a cave on Patmos then it is quite probable that some inhabitants of Patmos fled to the safety of his cave.

---

[154] Volcano World, "Nisyros".
[155] Sattin & Franquet, *Greek Islands,* 160
[156] Kinvig *et al.* "Analysis og Volcanic Threat", 1101 & 1108
[157] Kinvig *et al.* "Analysis og Volcanic Threat", 1108

An aerial photo of the Greek island of Nisyros with its volcanic crater.

A volcanic eruption at night: Stromboli, the small volcanic island located north of Sicily. This volcano has been erupting periodically for hundreds of years to produce a lightshow that gives rise to its nickname, the "Lighthouse of the Mediterranean". John of Patmos must have witnessed something similar from afar.

Volcanic outbursts often take weeks and even months before they come to an end.[158] It is clear from John's descriptions that volcanic activity continued several weeks and Patmos suffered the effects of this natural disaster for a long time.

It must be remembered that people in the ancient world did not have the faintest idea of what causes earthquakes or volcanoes to erupt. Just as they attributed diseases to supernatural causes, such as the influence of evil spirits or magic, they regarded earthquakes and volcanoes as supernatural events, caused by the gods. It is no wonder that John incorporated a seismic event into his visions and regarded the volcano as the entrance to the netherworld or Hades.

The position of Nisyros to the south-east of Patmos, almost directly opposite the northern celestial pole where John visualized the throne of God, would have had added significance for him. It would have been obvious to him that the entrance to the abyss of Hades must have been as far away from God's throne as possible.

John's message

John meant to give a description of the prelude to Judgment Day and the second coming of Christ. Various parts of Scripture foresaw cosmic catastrophes and calamities connected to this event.

All these texts must have inspired John to see the outburst of the volcano as an illustration of what would happen when Judgment Day arrives – and also that Judgment Day was imminent.

John mentioned seven classes or categories of people affected by the cosmic catastrophes: kings, princes, war lords, rich people, strong people, slaves, and freemen. The sacred number of seven tells us that God was in control and that no single class of people was exempted from his revenge.

As a child of his time, John would have shared the ancient

---

[158] Decker & Decker, "Volcano".

world-view of a stationary flat earth, three heavens above, and a netherworld below. This netherworld contained the abode of the dead and the prison where Satan and his demons were locked up. The only explanation for a volcanic outburst would have been that the flames of hell were spilling over onto the surface of the earth.

The pregnant woman and the dragon
Rev 12: 1–17

1.	A great sign was seen in heaven: a woman clothed with the sun, and the moon under her feet, and on her head a crown of twelve stars.
2.	She was with child. She cried out, labouring and in pain, giving birth.
3.	Another sign was seen in heaven. Behold, a great red dragon, having seven heads and ten horns, and on his heads seven crowns.
4.	His tail drew one third of the stars of the sky, and threw them to the earth. The dragon stood before the woman who was about to give birth, so that when she gave birth he might devour her child.
5.	She gave birth to a son, a male child, who is to rule all the nations with a rod of iron. Her child was caught up to God, and to his throne.
6.	The woman fled into the wilderness, where she has a place prepared by God, that there they may nourish her one thousand two hundred sixty days.
7.	There was war in the sky. Michael and his angels made war on the dragon. The dragon and his angels made war.
8.	They didn't prevail, neither was a place found for him any more in heaven.

9. The great dragon was thrown down, the old serpent, he who is called the Devil and Satan, the deceiver of the whole world. He was thrown down to the earth, and his angels were thrown down with him.

10. I heard a loud voice in heaven, saying, "Now is come the salvation, the power, and the kingdom of our God, and the authority of his Christ; for the accuser of our brothers has been thrown down, who accuses them before our God day and night.

11. They overcame him because of the Lamb's blood, and because of the word of their testimony. They didn't love their life, even to death.

12. Therefore rejoice, heavens, and you who dwell in them. Woe for the earth and for the sea, because the devil has gone down to you, having great wrath, knowing that he has but a short time."

13. When the dragon saw that he was thrown down to the earth, he persecuted the woman who gave birth to the male child.

14. Two wings of the great eagle were given to the woman, that she might fly into the wilderness to her place, where she was nourished for a time, and times, and half a time, from the face of the serpent.

15. The serpent spewed water out of his mouth after the woman like a river, that he might cause her to be carried away by the stream.

16. The earth helped the woman, and the earth opened its mouth and swallowed up the river which the dragon spewed out of his mouth.

> 17. The dragon grew angry with the woman, and went away to make war with the rest of her seed, who keep God's commandments and hold Jesus' testimony.

What John saw

Enough details are supplied in this chapter to attach a specific date and time to the vision that John had, namely 17 June AD 96, more or less from half-past ten at night, local time, until later that night. What John saw was indeed a great sign, involving at least five prominent constellations in the sky: Virgo, Coma Berenices, Scorpius, Ophiuchus, and Serpens. The moon and the planets Jupiter and Saturn were also part of the scene.

When John started to gaze at the stars, the last faint rays of the summer sun were still visible in the west, directly above the head of the constellation of Virgo, the Virgin – the woman seen by John. She was, in other words, clothed by the sun.

Detail of the antique zodiac mosaic floor at Hamat Tiberias Synagogue National Park, Tiberias, Galilee, Israel (4th century) showing Virgo (the Virgin), called בְּתוּלָה (*Bethulah*) in Hebrew

This constellation was known under various names by the ancients. Belmont explains: "This includes Ishtar (Babylonian mythology), Isis (Egyptian mythology), Ceres (Roman mythology), and Demeter (Greek mythology). The constellation Virgo is thought to be a woman holding a spike of wheat, thus reinforcing the Harvest Mother mythology".[159] The Jews knew it under name of *Bethulah,* the Virgin (Hebrew: בְּתוּלָה) and the Hebrew name for the brightest star in Virgo, Spica, is שִׁבֹּלֶת (*Shibbolet*), meaning an ear of wheat.[160]

To the north of Virgo lies the constellation of Coma Berenices, the Crown or Hair of Berenice. It consists of several faint stars – the crown of twelve stars on the head of the woman. The idea of the crown of the woman comes from Is 62: 3 where the people of Israel are told: "You shall also be a crown of beauty in the hand of YHWH, and a royal diadem in the hand of your God." The twelve stars symbolized the twelve tribes of Israel.

John adds that she had the moon at her feet. On 17 June AD 96, 64% of the surface of the moon was illuminated as it lay at the feet of the constellation of Virgo.

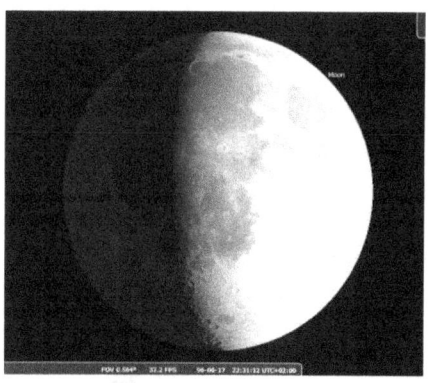

The moon with 64% of its surface illuminated as it appeared at the feet of Virgo on 17 June AD 96.

We are informed that the woman was pregnant and that she brought a son into the world. This son must be the planet Jupiter, the king of the planets – also known as Zeus, Baal, or Marduk to the ancients. This planet was also at Virgo's feet – the position the infant would have been in, directly after having been born. This male child was for John none other than Jesus Christ. The woman with the crown of twelve stars symbolized the people of Israel – the

---

[159] Belmont, "The Virgo Myth".
[160] Jacobs & Eisenstein, "Zodiac"; Jacobus, "The Zodiac Sign Names", 320

people from which Jesus was born.

John lived in the Greco-Roman world in which the Egyptian goddess Isis was also venerated and it seems possible that he copied some of her attributes into his description of the woman who was clothed by the sun and who had a male child – although he was vehemently opposed to paganism. There are various depictions known of Isis with the disc of the sun on her head and a child on her lap – very much in the same way that the Virgin Mary was later depicted with the infant Jesus. Butler observes: "Statues of Isis holding Horus to her breast look the same as statues created of Mary holding the baby Jesus to her breast. This similarity of iconography between the two is generally accepted by scholars."[161]

The fact that the planet Saturn was in Virgo also at that time is a confirmation of the identification of this constellation with Israel and/or Jerusalem. John would have known that Saturn was associated by ancient astrologers with the nation of Israel since the Israelites regarded Saturday, the day devoted to Saturn, as their Sabbath or holy day. The Hebrew name for Saturn is שַׁבְתַאי (shabtay) and it is derived from the word for Sabbath (שַׁבָּת).[162]

There is good reason to identify Jesus Christ with the planet Jupiter. The Hebrew name for Jupiter is "*Tzedeq* (צֶדֶק)", which means "justice" or "righteousness"[163] – a much more appropriate identification for Christ, the cosmic Judge (Rev 20: 11–15). John would have remembered that it is emphasized in Zech 9: 9 that the Messiah would be a man of "justice". Isa 11: 5 has this prediction about the Messiah: "Righteousness shall be the belt of his waist, and faithfulness the belt of his loins."

The red dragon that John saw is clearly the constellation of

---

[161] Butler, "The Cult of Isis", 76
[162] Stieglitz, "The Hebrew Names", 135–37; Zucker, "Hebrew Names of the Planets", 304
[163] Stieglitz, "The Hebrew Names", 135

Scorpius, the Scorpion. The Jews saw in this constellation a dragon or a snake[164] and John explicitly calls the dragon the "old serpent" and identifies him as Satan (Rev 12: 9). The main star in this constellation is Antares (also known as α Sco), a distinctly red star and, therefore, John described the dragon as a red beast.

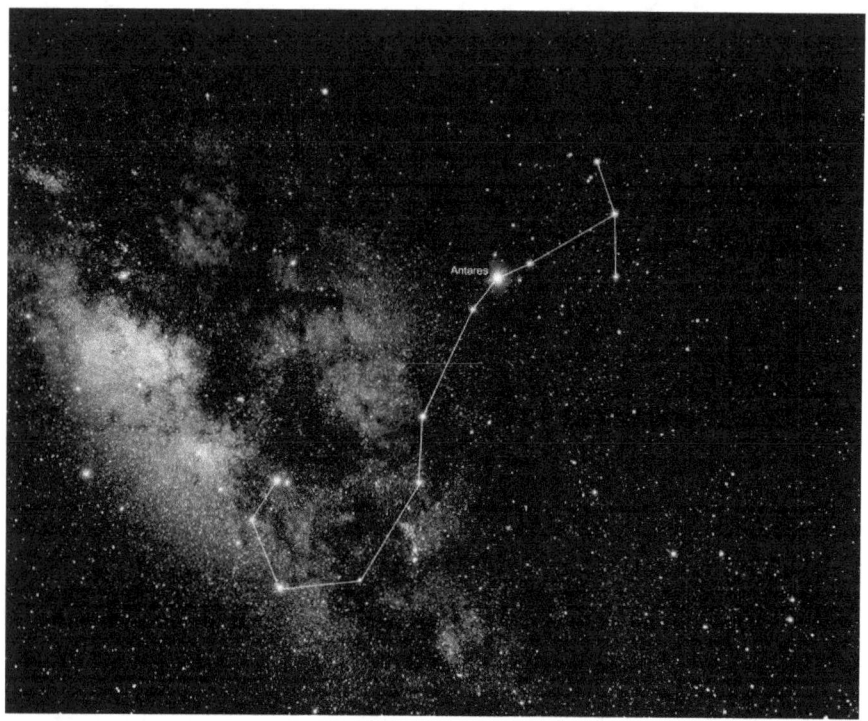

A photo of the constellation of Scorpius with its outlines marked, against the background of the Milky Way. Dark areas in the Milky Way, due to dense dust clouds, obscure the stars behind them. The impression can be created that the Scorpion/Dragon swept several stars away with its tail.

The dragon had seven crowned heads, the seven stars in its front part [Alpha, Beta, Delta, Epsilon, Nu, Sigma and Tau (α, β, δ, ε, ν, σ & τ) Scorpii]. Its ten horns are the stars in Libra, the Scales, which was seen as the claws of the Scorpion in ancient times (see illustration).

---

[164] Allen, *Star Names,* 361–62.

We are told that the dragon threw a third of the stars to the earth with his tail. Above is a photo of the constellation of Scorpius, together with a dark area in the Milky Way, next to its tail. This dark spot is formed by dense dust clouds in the Milky Way, obscuring the light from stars further away. It looks indeed as if the tail of Scorpius is sweeping a few stars away.

For John, it would not have been a coincidence that Scorpius, the dragon or Satan, was situated at that time on the southern horizon – the spot exactly opposite from the northern celestial pole with the throne of God.

The woman was able to flee to the desert, while her Son was taken up to God's throne in the north – the ascension of Jesus Christ after his resurrection. That happened when the constellation of Virgo set in the west and disappeared later that night. The woman received the wings of an eagle to enable her to flee. The people of Israel got a similar promise from God in Ex 19: 4 – "You have seen what I did to the Egyptians, and how I bore you on eagles' wings, and brought you to myself." The constellation of Corvus, the crow, lies next to Virgo and John must have thought of the wings of this bird that aided the woman in her flight. Aquila, the Eagle, was also visible, but was too far away to be of any assistance to the 'woman.

The leader of the archangels, Michael, fought with the dragon and his angels – in other words: his demons. This archangel is also encountered in Dan 10: 21, Dan 12:1 and Jude 1:9. In Enoch 24: 6 Michael is called the leader of the archangels. Jesus also referred to "the devil and his angels" in Matt 25: 41. Michael is clearly the constellation of Ophiuchus, the Snake Catcher, also called Serpentarius in olden days. Ophiuchus lies directly to the north of Scorpius. The dragon was thrown down onto the earth – that happened when Scorpius disappeared behind the western horizon later that night.

It was also stressed, "Woe for the earth and for the sea,

because the devil has gone down to you..." In other words: Scorpius disappeared into the Aegean Sea or behind a part of the island of Patmos to the south-west later that night, as seen from John's vantage point on Patmos. His evil angels were also thrown down and they must be sought in the star clouds of the Milky Way behind the tail of Scorpius.

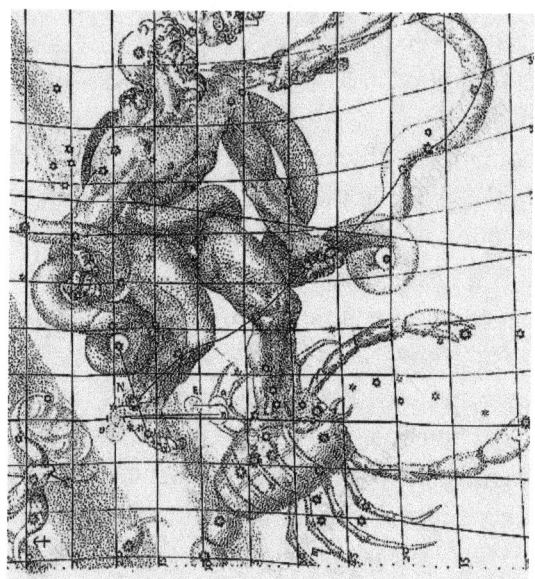

An illustration from an old star atlas showing the following constellations: Ophiuchus/Serpentarius (the Serpent Catcher), Serpens (the Serpent – the only constellation consisting of two separate parts) and Scorpius (the Scorpion or Dragon).

The river that the serpent sent after the woman may be equated with the constellation of Hydra, the Water Snake. It does resemble a river. This constellation was disappearing behind the south-western horizon and, therefore, it could be said that the earth swallowed the water of this stream (Rev 12: 16).

In the illustrations that follow, a reconstruction of the night sky over Patmos on the night of 17 June AD 96 is given. In the first illustration, only the stars and the outlines of the constellations are shown. The second illustration includes pictures of the personages, animals and objects represented by the relevant constellations. Depictions of Ophiuchus, and Serpens from an old star atlas give an idea how these constellations were perceived in the past.

The message of John

Chapter 12 contains a brief biography of Jesus Christ, written in symbolic language. Jesus was born as a member of the nation of Israel and destined to become a king, since his mother had a royal status with her crown of twelve stars, symbolizing the twelve tribes of Israel.

The people of Israel were called the wife of God in the Old Testament. In Is 54: 5-6 one reads:

> "For your Maker is your husband; YHWH of Hosts is his name: and the Holy One of Israel is your Redeemer; the God of the whole earth shall he be called. For YHWH has called you as a wife forsaken and grieved in spirit, even a wife of youth, when she is cast off, says your God."

The twelve stars in the woman's crown symbolized the twelve tribes of Israel.

The male child – Jesus Christ – was destined to rule the nations with a rod of iron – a reference to Ps 2: 9, as well as Ps 17 of the Psalms of Solomon.

The dragon threw one third of the stars from the sky with his tail. That is a reference to the fact that Satan managed to recruit several angels to support his rebellion against God and that they were thrown out of heaven and were turned into evil spirits or demons. This thought is repeated in Jud 1: 6 – "Angels who didn't keep their first domain, but deserted their own dwelling place, He [God] has kept in everlasting bonds under darkness for the judgment of the great day" (see also 2 Pet 2: 4).

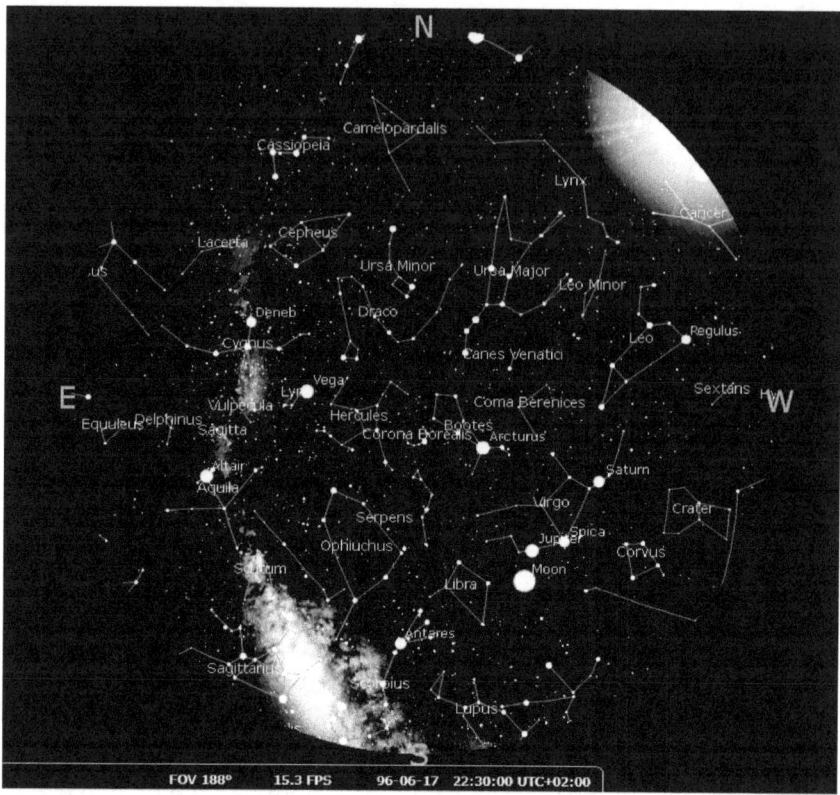

The moon, Jupiter and Saturn in Virgo (the Virgin), with the last rays of the sun in the north-west, together with Scorpius (the Scorpion) and Ophiuchus (the Serpent Catcher) to the south – 17 June AD 96, as seen from Patmos. Also visible are Coma Berenices (the Crown or Hair of Berenice), Serpens (the Serpent), Corvus (the Crow) and Hydra (the Water Snake – partly behind the south-western horizon).

Virgo (the Virgin) with the moon and Jupiter at her feet on 17 June AD 96, after sunset – as seen from Patmos. To her north, the constellation of Coma Berenices (the Hair or Crown of Berenice) can be seen. To the south, Scorpius (the Scorpion), as well as Ophiuchus (the Serpent Catcher), together with Serpens (the Serpent), lie next to the Milky Way. Corvus (the Crow) is to be found next to Virgo's left arm and Hydra (the Water Snake) was lying directly on the south-western horizon.

During earlier centuries, it happened that the woman of Rev 12 was seen as Mary, the mother of Jesus. She was often depicted with a crown of twelve stars and a crescent moon at her feet. This identification cannot be maintained.

A wooden statue of Mary, the mother of Jesus, and her child, with a crown with 12 stars on her head and a crescent moon at her feet, by the medieval sculptor Tilman Riemenschneider (*ca* 1490). This statue is meant to be a depiction of the woman featured in Rev 12 and she is shown as the queen of heaven. As has been shown in the explanation of Rev 12, the woman seen by John cannot be identified with Mary, although she was the biological mother of Jesus. For John, the woman in the sky symbolized the people of Israel, the people who brought the Messiah forth.

Satan did his best to destroy Jesus, which happened when Herod the Great had all the male children below two years of age killed in Bethlehem, but also when Jesus was crucified and his life blood flowed away. However, Jesus did not stay dead but was resurrected and taken up into heaven. This was a fulfilment of the first prophecy in the Bible, namely Gen 3: 15, where God told the snake: "I will put enmity between you and the woman, and between your offspring and her offspring. He will bruise your head, and you will bruise his heel."

This amounted to a victory over the powers of darkness and

Satan was defeated – although he was not totally annihilated. The woman, symbolizing all the faithful from Israel, as well as the New Testament, had to flee to the desert – a harsh and difficult environment. The faithful were persecuted by the dark powers, but God looked after his children, even though they had to endure hardship. Satan tried to persecute all her offspring.

The desert was seen as a desolate and forlorn place – the condition in which the church found herself during the time of John. The desert of Rev 12 is, of course, also a symbol of the desert through which the Israelites trekked when they fled slavery in Egypt en route to the Promised Land; in other words – a place where they were under God's protection and looking forward to the Promised Land of heaven.

The stay in the desert was "for a time, and times, and half a time." This expression also occurs in Rev 11: 2–3 and 13: 5 and there it is explained as a period of three-and-a half years, 42 months, or 1 260 days. It is also a quotation from Dan 7: 25 – "He [the beast that represents the fourth king] shall speak words against the Most High, and shall wear out the saints of the Most High; and he shall think to change the times and the law; and they shall be given into his hand until a time and times and half a time."

This period of 42 months is the product of 7 X 6. The sacred number of seven symbolizes God's work; there were seven days of Creation, for instance. Six symbolizes sinful and godless man's unsuccessful endeavor to deify himself and to reach seven. Mankind was also created on the sixth day of creation, according to Gen 1: 26–31. This period is therefore the time in which God is busy with mankind until the final Judgment arrives – a limited time that is sure to end but which is characterized by man's rebellion against God.

It is important to note that John gave a clear indication exactly who the "seed" or offspring of the woman were: The "rest of her seed" – apart from the male child that was born – are those "who keep God's commandments and hold Jesus' testimony" (Rev

12: 17). In other words: everybody who obeys God and accepts Jesus as Messiah is to be regarded as a member of God's people and part of the "seed" of the woman who symbolized Israel. This privilege does not apply only to the descendants of Abraham, but equally to all believers. Those who argue that the Jews still occupy a special place in God's kingdom cannot find any justification in Revelation. This is also in line with Paul's declaration: "There is neither Jew nor Greek, there is neither slave nor free man, there is neither male nor female; for you are all one in Christ Jesus. If you are Christ's, then you are Abraham's seed, heirs according to promise" (Gal 3: 28–29).

CONCLUSIONS

This chapter dealt with the way various prophets of the New Testament commented on their own times:

- Jesus of Nazareth was mainly concerned about the resistance he received from the Jewish elite in Jerusalem in his bid to resurrect the kingdom of Israel as its Messiah. It must be noted that he never directly called for the overthrow of the Roman occupation of his country because that would have been too dangerous. He merely hinted about that possibility at times by promising that he would be able to ascend the throne in Jerusalem with the aid of a host of angels from heaven.
- As a religious reformer, Jesus stressed the importance of living according to the Law of Moses.
- The people who gathered on the day of Pentecost interpreted a natural phenomenon as a spiritual event, which caused them to cry out in amazement and talk about God's actions.
- Paul of Tarsus endeavored to marry Judaism with Greek paganism by introducing Jesus, the Messiah, as the eternal divine Son of God. He also lamented the fact that his message

wasn't accepted by the apostles in Jerusalem and that there were various parties and divisions under those who regarded themselves as followers of Jesus.
- Paul's thoughts about the Law of Moses, including the requirement to be circumcised, differed from those of Jesus. To find eternal life, one only had to believe in Jesus Christ as the Savior who died on the cross for the sins of repentant sinners. Observance of the Mosaic Law was not required.
- Jesus, on the other hand, declared more than once that one could inherit eternal life by living according to the Ten Commandments. This point of view actually made his vicarious death on the cross unnecessary because his followers could reach heaven in the afterlife by obeying the Law of Moses.
- The Epistle of James contained social comments. The followers of Jesus were warned not to discriminate against poor people and rich people must know that they will have to face God's judgment. The expected return of Jesus from his hiding place was imminent – which didn't happen.
- John of Patmos, although a former Jewish priest, totally supported Paul's idea that Jesus was the eternal divine Son of God. He studied the stars at night, as well as other natural phenomena, such as the outburst of a volcano, and he interpreted these sights against his background with a primitive and pre-scientific view of the world. He read various spiritual messages in the stars. Although he never mentioned the Roman Empire or emperor directly, his visions were, nevertheless, hidden references to the cruelties and detestable paganism of this pagan and harsh empire. God as ruler of the universe received much attention to contrast him with the Roman emperor.

This chapter has demonstrated there were differing and even contradictory ideas held by the various prophets whose ideas were recorded in the New Testament – Jesus of Nazareth, the apostles, Paul of Tarsus, James, and John of Patmos.

CHAPTER 5
OLD TESTAMENT PROPHECIES REGARDING THE MESSIAH

It is a Christian article of faith that the Old Testament prophecies regarding Jesus as the expected Messiah of Israel are trustworthy and clear. The Creed of Nicaea declares: "On the third day he [Jesus] rose again in accordance with the Scriptures." Article 5 of the Belgic Confession, a doctrinal standard of Reformed Churches, deals with "the Authority of Scripture". It is states that "even the blind themselves are able to see that the things predicted in them do happen."

Chapter VII of the Westminster Confession says in paragraph V: "This covenant was differently administered in the time of the law, and in the time of the Gospel; under the law it was administered by *promises, prophecies*, sacrifices, circumcision, the paschal lamb, and other types and ordinances delivered to the people of the Jews, all foresignifying Christ to come…" (*emphasis added*).

Various texts in the New Testament declared with confidence that prophets of the Old Testament predicted that Jesus of Nazareth would be the ultimate Messiah of Israel – as will be shown below.

It must be asked: are all these claims correct and accurate?

It is, first of all, necessary to explain the meaning of the title of "Messiah". It is derived from the Hebrew מָשִׁיחַ (*mashiyach*), which means "anointed" and is rendered in English as "Messiah". There were various anointed persons in the Old Testament –kings, priests, or prophets. There was also the expectation that a special

Messiah or liberator of Israel would appear.[165]

Most authors of parts of the New Testament thought that details of the life, death, resurrection, and ascent into heaven of Jesus of Nazareth were foretold in the Old Testament. It cannot be denied: there are indeed many prophecies in the Old Testament about a future Messiah. There are also many prophecies that have erroneously been viewed as being messianic prophecies by Christian theologians and preachers.

It is necessary to investigate these prophecies in historical order. The following questions must be answered:

- Did some of the messianic prophecies of the Old Testament have specifically Jesus of Nazareth in mind?
- Were the birth, ministry, messages, miracles, execution, and resurrection of Jesus as described in the Gospels predicted in the Hebrew Scriptures?

TEXTS DEALING WITH THE PERIOD OF THE PATRIARCHS

Hostility between the Woman's Seed and the Serpent
Gen 3: 14–16

14.	YHWH God said to the serpent, "Because you have done this, cursed are you above all cattle, and above every animal of the field. On your belly shall you go, and you shall eat dust all the days of your life.
15.	I will put enmity between you and the woman, and between your offspring and her offspring. He will bruise your head, and you will bruise his heel."

---

[165] Jacobs & Buttenwieser, "Messiah".

> 16. To the woman he said, "I will greatly multiply your pain in childbirth. In pain you will bring forth children. Your desire will be for your husband, and he will rule over you."

Verse 15 in this passage is very often seen as a prophecy about the death of Jesus on the cross where Satan managed to wound him seriously, although he vanquished Satan in the end.

It has been shown that the concept of Satan was absent from the oldest parts of the Old Testament and played only a very minor role in the youngest parts. Satan was only introduced into the Hebrew Scriptures and the New Testament by the book of I Enoch during the late third century BC.[166]

This passage in Genesis 3 merely contains a mythological talking snake to explain man's disobedience towards God's commands. The woman's "seed" includes all human beings who are afraid of serpents.

Everlasting Covenant
Gen 17: 19–20

> 19. God said, "No, but Sarah, your wife, will bear you a son. You shall call his name Isaac. I will establish my covenant with him for an everlasting covenant for his seed after him.
> 20. As for Ishmael, I have heard you. Behold, I have blessed him, and will make him fruitful, and will multiply him exceedingly. He will become the father of twelve princes, and I will make him a great nation."

The "seed" of Abraham in verse 19 was often taken to refer to the future Messiah. That is certainly not what this text says. It is clear

---

[166] Pretorius, *To Hell with the Devil*, 94–100.

from the context that the nation of Israel is meant, just as the next verse refers to the offspring of Ishmael, which was also due to develop into a mighty nation.

Judah's Offspring will Rule
Gen 49: 9–10

9.	Judah is a lion's whelp. From the prey, my son, you have gone up. He stooped down, he couched as a lion, As a lioness. Who will rouse him up?
10.	The scepter will not depart from Judah, nor the ruler's staff from between his feet, until Shiloh comes. To him will the obedience of the peoples be.

This chapter in Genesis is part of the J Document, written during the time of the unified monarchy of Israel – a few centuries after the event it described. This chapter is an effort to link each of the twelve tribes to a sign of the Zodiac, according to the Babylonian astrology. The tribe of Judah's sign is Leo, the Lion (see Rev 5: 5).

An old drawing by Johannes Hevelius (1611–1687) of the constellation of Leo, the Lion

These verses were composed to legitimize the monarchy of the house of David. This monarchy did not endure, despite this prophecy. The ultimate Israelite Messiah was certainly not meant, although some Christians would have been tempted to see this as a prophecy of Christ's eternal kingship in heaven.

The Brass Serpent on a Pole
Num 21: 6–9

6.	YHWH sent fiery serpents among the people, and they bit the people; and much people of Israel died.
7.	The people came to Moses, and said, We have sinned, because we have spoken against YHWH, and against you; pray to YHWH, that he take away the serpents from us. Moses prayed for the people.
8.	YHWH said to Moses, "Make you a fiery serpent, and set it on a standard: and it shall happen, that everyone who is bitten, when he sees it, shall live."
9.	Moses made a serpent of brass, and set it on the standard: and it happened, that if a serpent had bitten any man, when he looked to the serpent of brass, he lived.

It is a mystery how people could have been cured from snake bites by merely gazing at a brass serpent on a pole. This brass serpent has been seen as a foreshadowing of Jesus who was hanging from a wooden cross to becoming the redeemer of sinful and repentant mankind (John 3:14–15). It is hard to see any connection between that snake and Jesus. When Moses fabricated that brass snake, he certainly didn't have a future Messiah in mind. He only wanted to help the victims of those poisonous reptiles with some magic.

Balaam's Prophecy
Num 24: 17

> I see him, but not now; I see him, but not near: There shall come forth a star out of Jacob, a scepter shall rise out of Israel, shall strike through the corners of Moab, break down all the sons of tumult.

These words by Balaam, a pagan prophet, look superficially like a prophecy about the Messiah who would be born from Israel. Many Christians have used these words to declare that even a pagan prophet predicted the coming of Jesus Christ as *the* Messiah.

This prophecy of Balaam is part of the E Document and it was only composed during the eighth century BC after the northern Israelite kingdom broke away from the house of David – four centuries after the Exodus and the time of Balaam. The Assyrian Empire, which only came into being long after the Exodus, is named in verses 22 and 24 of this chapter as a current threat – a clear anachronism.

Nobody recorded this pagan prophet's words when he blessed the Israelites, instead of cursing them, as required by Balak, the king of Moab. When the whole chapter is scrutinized, it becomes clear from verses 7 and 19 that the quoted words apply to the Israelite king at the time when this passage was written. It is a mistake to see these words as a messianic prophecy.

A Prophet like Moses
Deut 18: 15–18

15.	YHWH your God will raise up to you a prophet from the midst of you, of your brothers, like me; to him you shall listen;
16.	according to all that you desired of YHWH your God in Horeb in the day of the assembly, saying, Let me not hear again the voice of YHWH my God, neither let me see this great fire any more, that I not die.
17.	YHWH said to me, They have well said that which they have spoken.

> 18. I will raise them up a prophet from among their brothers, like you; and I will put my words in his mouth, and he shall speak to them all that I shall command him.

These words are part of the book of Deuteronomy, which was written towards the end of the Judean monarchy and completed during the Babylonian Exile. It is theorized that the final editor was Baruch, the secretary of Jeremiah. The prediction of a future prophet in the quoted passage may probably be applied to Jeremiah or any of the other great prophets of the Old Testament – and certainly not the expected Messiah.

The Captain of God's Army
Josh 5: 14–15

> 14. He said, No; but [as] prince of the host of YHWH am I now come. Joshua fell on his face to the earth, and did worship, and said to him, What says my lord to his servant?
> 15. The prince of YHWH's host said to Joshua, Put off your shoe from off your foot; for the place whereon you stand is holy. Joshua did so.

The translation from which this quotation was taken, translated the Hebrew expression שַׂר־צְבָא יְהוָה (*shar tseba YHWH*) as "the prince of the host of YWHW". Another translation reads: "the captain of the Lord's army". It has been shown in a previous chapter that the word "host" is used for God's angels, who were also equated with the stars.

This passage has often been interpreted as an appearance of Christ before the time when he was born as a human being. The context makes it clear, though, that only one of God's angels is being meant – not the Mesiah who made a preliminary appearance.

TEXTS FROM THE TIME OF THE MONARCHY

The House of David to Rule Forever
2 Sam 7: 12–16

> 12. And when the time comes for you to go to rest with your fathers, I will put in your place your seed after you, the offspring of your body, and I will make his kingdom strong.
> 13. He will be the builder of a house for my name, and I will make the seat of his authority certain for ever.
> 14. I will be to him a father and he will be to me a son: if he does wrong, I will give him punishment with the rod of men and with the blows of the children of men;
> 15. But my mercy will not be taken away from him, as I took it from him who was before you.
> 16. And your family and your kingdom will keep their place before me for ever: the seat of your authority will never be overturned.

These words are part of an oracle spoken on behalf of God by the prophet Nathan to King David. This monarch was promised that his offspring would rule into eternity. This story is repeated in 1 Chr 17.

This prophecy was certainly not fulfilled in a literal sense. Jerusalem was destroyed by the Babylonians in 586 BC, about four centuries after the time of David. That brought about the end of the house of David.

Christians argue that Jesus of Nazareth, as a descendant of David, is an eternal king on his throne in heaven. This idea is in accordance with the subjective and unverifiable visions and revelations of the Apostle Paul – which were likely hallucinations – but it cannot be verified historically. The oldest parts of the gospels, the Q Document and the narrative parts of the Gospel of John, did not portray Jesus as a divine being, only as an ordinary mortal who survived his crucifixion due to the medical care given to him by his friends (John 19: 38–42). The latter parts of the gospels, written at least forty years after Jesus' time, followed the questionable visions of Paul by portraying Jesus as the divine and eternal Son of God.[167]

It is doubtful whether Nathan meant the eternal kingship of Jesus with his oracle. He merely flattered David by exaggerating the durability of his kingdom and dynasty, which did endure four centuries.

The King of Israel
Ps 45: 6–8

6.	Your throne, God, is forever and ever. A scepter of equity is the scepter of your kingdom.
7.	You have loved righteousness, and hated wickedness. Therefore God, your God, has anointed you with the oil of gladness above your fellows.
8.	All your garments smell like myrrh, aloes, and cassia. Out of ivory palaces stringed instruments have made you glad.

A superficial reading of these verses may look like a prophecy regarding Christ's eternal rule as God. That is, however, not what this Psalm is about.

The first verse of this Psalm clearly indicates that it is dedicated to the king of Israel from the house of David. The title "God" in verses 6 and 7 is ambiguous and may also be translated as "ruler" or "judge", otherwise verse 7 would not make sense. This verse ought to be read as "therefore, oh Ruler, your God…"

---

[167] Pretorius, *The Gospels,* passim.

David's Eternal Kingdom
Ps 89: 34–37

34.	I will not break my covenant, nor alter what my lips have uttered.
35.	Once have I sworn by my holiness, I will not lie to David.
36.	His seed will endure forever, his throne like the sun before me.
37.	It will be established forever like the moon, the faithful witness in the sky

These words are often seen as a prophecy about the eternal kingdom of Christ, the "seed" of King David. But did the original poet think about the future Messiah when composing this song? It seems very unlikely.

The house of David endured about four centuries and more than five centuries elapsed after that before the time of Jesus. This Psalm implied that there would be a continuous succession of David's offspring – and not the big gap before Jesus appeared.

The promise in this Psalm that the house of David would endure forever amounts to a pious wish and nothing more.

King David Playing the Harp by Gerard van Honthorst (1622)

The Cornerstone
Ps 118: 17–24

17.	I will not die, but live, and declare Yah's works.
18.	Yah has punished me severely, but he has not given me over to death.
19.	Open to me the gates of righteousness. I will enter into them. I will give thanks to Yah.
20.	This is the gate of YHWH; the righteous will enter into it.
21.	I will give thanks to you, for you have answered me, and have become my salvation.
22.	The stone which the builders rejected has become the head of the corner.
23.	This is YHWH's doing. It is marvelous in our eyes.
24.	This is the day that YHWH has made. We will rejoice and be glad in it!

The composer or poet of this song praised God on behalf of the whole Israel. The people of God have endured hardships, but YHWH preserved them. This Psalm was traditionally seen as messianic in nature. The cornerstone mentioned in verse 22 is regarded as a prophecy of Christ's life and work (see Eph 2: 19–21; 1 Pet 2: 6). However, if the context is taken into regard, it is clear that the poet meant that all the people of Israel, who were despised and trampled upon by their enemies, became an essential part of God's plans.

David's Offspring
Ps 132: 10–16

10.	For your servant David's sake, don't turn away the face of your anointed one.

> 11. YHWH has sworn to David in truth. He will not turn from it: "I will set the fruit of your body on your throne.
> 12. If your children will keep my covenant, My testimony that I will teach them, their children also will sit on your throne forevermore."
> 13. For YHWH has chosen Zion. He has desired it for his habitation.
> 14. "This is my resting place forever. Here I will live, for I have desired it.
> 15. I will abundantly bless her provision. I will satisfy her poor with bread.
> 16. Her priests I will also clothe with salvation. Her saints will shout aloud for joy."

Christians often focus on verses 11 and 12 where David was promised that his descendants – including the Messiah – would stay on the throne forever.

It must be remembered that God also promised that He would reside on Zion in Jerusalem's temple into eternity. This Psalm, therefore, deals with more than only David's offspring.

These promises were not kept. The temple in Jerusalem was finally destroyed on 30 August AD 70 by the Romans and never rebuilt. No king of Judah sat on a throne since 586 BC when Jerusalem was conquered by the Babylonians. The Messiah cannot be regarded as part of this song.

Wisdom's Eternity
Prov 8: 23

> I was set up from everlasting, from the beginning, before the earth existed.

These words are part of a song in which Lady Wisdom is praised and her eternity as a quality of the all-knowing God is pointed out.

According to Paul, "to those who are called, both Jews and Greeks, Christ is the power of God and the wisdom of God" (I Cor 1: 24). Because of this, theologians have seen the sentence in Proverbs as a prophecy proclaiming the eternity of a divine Christ.

When Paul mentioned God's wisdom, he meant to tell his readers that his message regarding Christ as the Son of God must satisfy the Greek philosophers who seek wisdom and insight. After all, the word "philosophy" (φιλοσοφία – *philosophia*) is a Greek word, which means "the love of wisdom". The Hebrew concept of wisdom is illustrated clearly in the book of Proverbs. It has nothing to do with Greek philosophy, but means good practical judgment or common sense.

Therefore, the words in Proverbs never had the Messiah in mind and cannot be applied to Jesus Christ.

ISAIAH

Isaiah lived in turbulent times when the kingdom of Judah was threatened by the Assyrian Empire after the sister-kingdom, Israel or Ephraim, had been overrun by the Assyrian army. Some passages from his book dealt with messianic figures.

Immanuel
Isa 7: 10–17

10. YHWH spoke again to Ahaz, saying,
11. Ask you a sign of YHWH your God; ask it either in the depth, or in the height above.
12. But Ahaz said, I will not ask, neither will I tempt YHWH.

> 13. He said, "Listen now, house of David: Is it a small thing for you to weary men, that you will weary my God also?
> 14. Therefore the Lord himself will give you a sign: behold, a virgin shall conceive, and bear a son, and shall call his name Immanuel.
> 15. Butter and honey shall he eat, when he knows to refuse the evil, and choose the good.
> 16. For before the child shall know to refuse the evil, and choose the good, the land whose two kings you abhor shall be forsaken.
> 17. YHWH will bring on you, and on your people, and on your father's house, days that have not come, from the day that Ephraim departed from Judah [even] the king of Assyria."

Isaiah approached King Ahaz of Judah with the message that it wouldn't be necessary for the Judeans to rely on alliances with other countries to stay safe and that they may trust that YHWH would protect them against their enemies. To support this message, he invited his majesty to ask for any sign from God to prove this point. Ahaz declined the invitation with the excuse that he didn't want to worry God unduly.

Thereupon, Isaiah told him that YHWH would send his own sign to support his promise. A certain young woman would become pregnant soon and name her son Immanuel. He would grow up in a prosperous time, eating butter and honey.

It has already been shown in Chapter 2 that the Gospels of Matthew and Luke used the faulty Greek translation of Isa 7: 14 to conclude that Jesus' mother must have been a virgin when he was born. The original Hebrew merely mentions a certain unnamed young woman who would bear a child. The Hebrew word is הָעַלְמָה

(*Ha-almah*) and it denotes any female of marriageable age, not necessarily a virgin. The definitive article "the" (Hebrew: ה – *Ha*) is an indication that Ahaz was supposed to know who this young woman would be – probably a member of his household. The mother of Jesus, who lived centuries later, was certainly never meant.[168]

A Royal Child
Isa 9: 6–7

6.	For to us a child is born, to us a son is given; and the government shall be on his shoulder: and his name shall be called Wonderful, Counselor, Mighty God, Everlasting Father, Prince of Peace.
7.	Of the increase of his government and of peace there shall be no end, on the throne of David, and on his kingdom, to establish it, and to uphold it with justice and with righteousness from henceforth even forever. The zeal of YHWH of Hosts will perform this.

This passage is generally held to be a prophecy of Jesus of Nazareth as the Messiah. However, it is nowhere quoted in the New Testament as proof that these words predicted the coming of Jesus.

When the context of these words is investigated it becomes certain that Isaiah foresaw the appearance of a great and ideal king from the house of David of a unified Israel in the foreseeable future – not a Messiah of far-away centuries.[169]

This passage is often used to prove the divine status of Jesus Christ because this child is called a "Mighty God". The Hebrew word is אֵל (*El*), which may mean "god", but may also be translated

---

[168] Jacobs & Mittenwieler, "Messiah".
[169] Jacobs & Buttenwieser, "Messiah".

as mighty one, man of rank, mighty hero".

Although this passage has a clear messianic flavor, it cannot be applied to Jesus of Nazareth.

The Messiah as a Judge
Isa 11: 1–10

1.	There shall come forth a shoot out of the stock of Jesse, and a branch out of his roots shall bear fruit.
2.	The Spirit of YHWH shall rest on him, the spirit of wisdom and understanding, the spirit of counsel and might, the spirit of knowledge and of the fear of YHWH.
3.	His delight shall be in the fear of YHWH; and he shall not judge after the sight of his eyes, neither decide after the hearing of his ears;
4.	but with righteousness shall he judge the poor, and decide with equity for the humble of the earth; and he shall strike the earth with the rod of his mouth; and with the breath of his lips shall he kill the wicked.
5.	Righteousness shall be the belt of his waist, and faithfulness the belt of his loins.
6.	The wolf shall dwell with the lamb, and the leopard shall lie down with the kid; and the calf and the young lion and the fattened calf together; and a little child shall lead them.
7.	The cow and the bear shall feed; their young ones shall lie down together; and the lion shall eat straw like the ox.
8.	The sucking child shall play on the hole of the asp, and the weaned child shall put his hand on the adder's den.
9.	They shall not hurt nor destroy in all my holy mountain; for the earth shall be full of the knowledge of YHWH, as the waters cover the sea.

> 10. It shall happen in that day, that the root of Jesse, who stands for an ensign of the peoples, to him shall the nations seek; and his resting-place shall be glorious.

This song or poem in Isaiah is usually interpreted as a prophecy regarding the eternal kingship of Christ, who would be the judge on Judgment Day, as portrayed in Matt 25: 31–46 and Rev 20: 11–15. It must be granted: this prophecy does deal with an expected offspring of Jesse, the father of King David. The gospels and the letters of Paul all confirm that Jesus was indeed a descendant of David and Jesse.

This song also tells us of the perfect and peaceful conditions that were expected to prevail after Judgment Day.

Isaiah of Jerusalem, the author of the first 39 chapters of the book of Isaiah, operated as prophet during the eighth century BC, several centuries before the time of Jesus.[170] He had no inkling of the destruction of Jerusalem by the Babylonians during 586 BC, the resulting Exile, the conquest of Palestine by Alexander the Great in 332 BC or the annexation of Palestine by the Romans. He took it for granted that the Israelite monarchy with the house of David would endure till the end of time, when Judgment Day would arrive and that YWHW would appoint this king as a judge.

Although this passage must be seen as a prophecy about the Messiah of Israel, a description of the ideal king, there is no indication that it was meant to predict the appearance of Jesus of Nazareth, who never occupied the throne of David in Jerusalem, although he unsuccessfully aspired to become the king of the Jews.

The Key to the House of David
Isa 22: 22–23

---

[170] Boshoff et al., *Geskiedenis*, 135–37.

> 22. The key of the house of David will I lay on his shoulder; and he shall open, and none shall shut; and he shall shut, and none shall open.
> 23. I will fasten him as a nail in a sure place; and he shall be for a throne of glory to his father's house.

Although these verses may superficially look like a messianic prophecy, namely that the Messiah would control the house of David, the kingdom of Judea, they are, in fact, addressed to Elyakim, the royal steward of King Hezekiah. As steward, he kept the keys to the palace. A future Messiah did not feature.

JEREMIAH

The Branch of David
Jer 23: 5–8

> 5. Behold, the days come, says YHWH, that I will raise to David a righteous Branch, and he shall reign as king and deal wisely, and shall execute justice and righteousness in the land.
> 6. In his days Judah shall be saved, and Israel shall dwell safely; and this is his name whereby he shall be called: YHWH our righteousness.
> 7. Therefore, behold, the days come, says YHWH, that they shall no more say, As YHWH lives, who brought up the children of Israel out of the land of Egypt;
> 8. but, As YHWH lives, who brought up and who led the seed of the house of Israel out of the north country, and from all the countries where I had driven them. They shall dwell in their own land.

In the rest of this chapter, Jeremiah cursed the false prophet in Israel who have led the people astray. Their wrong deeds will be rectified by a future king under whose rule Israel would flourish. This prophecy certainly predicted the appearance of a Messiah, a king from the house of David, who would restore justice in the land.

It must be clear that this prophecy cannot be applied to Jesus of Nazareth, even though he was a descendant of David. Although he aspired to ascend the throne in Jerusalem, he received a death sentence before he could achieve that.

The promise that the people of the northern kingdom who were abducted by the Assyrians, would return to their land, was an empty promise. The king predicted by Jeremiah never appeared because the Babylonians destroyed Jerusalem a few years later and abolished the monarchy in Judah permanently.

The Branch of David
Jer 33: 12–18

12.	Thus says YHWH of Hosts: Yet again shall there be in this place, which is waste, without man and without animal, and in all the cities of it, a habitation of shepherds causing their flocks to lie down.
13.	In the cities of the hill-country, in the cities of the lowland, and in the cities of the South, and in the land of Benjamin, and in the places about Jerusalem, and in the cities of Judah, shall the flocks again pass under the hands of him who numbers them, says YHWH.
14.	Behold, the days come, says YHWH, that I will perform that good word which I have spoken concerning the house of Israel and concerning the house of Judah.

> 15. In those days, and at that time, will I cause a Branch of righteousness to grow up to David; and he shall execute justice and righteousness in the land.
> 16. In those days shall Judah be saved, and Jerusalem shall dwell safely; and this is [the name] whereby she shall be called: YHWH our righteousness.
> 17. For thus says YHWH: David shall never want a man to sit on the throne of the house of Israel;
> 18. neither shall the priests the Levites want a man before me to offer burnt offerings, and to burn meal-offerings, and to do sacrifice continually.

At a first glance, it seems as if this prophecy from the last days of the kingdom of Judah and which is rather like the previous prophecy, predicted the coming of Jesus of Nazareth as a righteous descendant of David. This is, however, not the case.

This prophecy foresaw a time of peace and prosperity during which the future righteous king or Messiah, a descendant of David, was destined to provide justice and who would secure his people's safety. Such a king never ruled over the people of Israel and the promised peace and prosperity never materialized since Jerusalem was destroyed shortly afterwards. This prophecy amounted to mere pious wishful thinking.

HABAKKUK

The Anointed People of God
Hab 3: 12–13

> 12. You marched through the land in wrath. You threshed the nations in anger.

> 13. You went forth for the salvation of your people, For the salvation of your anointed. You crushed the head of the land of wickedness. You stripped them head to foot. Selah.

In this passage, the people of Israel are explicitly called the "anointed" or "messiah" of God. That indicates the special status of Israel in the world filled with other nations.

In other words: the concept of a "messiah" is wider than simply a liberator of Israel. It may also be the nation of Israel herself (see also Ps. 28: 8 and 84: 9).

MICAH

The prophet Micah was active during the same period as Isaiah and Amos and he worked in the southern kingdom of Judah.

A Ruler from Bethlehem
Mic 5: 1–8

> 1. Now shall you gather yourself in troops, daughter of troops: he has laid siege against us; they shall strike the judge of Israel with a rod on the cheek.
> 2. But you, Bethlehem Ephrathah, which are little to be among the thousands of Judah, out of you shall one come forth to me that is to be ruler in Israel; whose goings forth are from of old, from everlasting.
> 3. Therefore will he give them up, until the time that she who travails has brought forth: then the residue of his brothers shall return to the children of Israel.
> 4. He shall stand, and shall feed [his flock] in the strength of YHWH, in the majesty of the name of YHWH his God: and

	they shall abide; for now shall he be great to the ends of the earth.
5.	This [man] shall be [our] peace. When the Assyrian shall come into our land, and when he shall tread in our palaces, then shall we raise against him seven shepherds, and eight principal men.
6.	They shall waste the land of Assyria with the sword, and the land of Nimrod in the entrances of it: and he shall deliver us from the Assyrian, when he comes into our land, and when he treads within our border.
7.	The remnant of Jacob shall be in the midst of many peoples as dew from YHWH, as showers on the grass, that don't wait for man, nor wait for the sons of men.
8.	The remnant of Jacob shall be among the nations, in the midst of many peoples, as a lion among the animals of the forest, as a young lion among the flocks of sheep; who, if he go through, treads down and tears in pieces, and there is none to deliver.

When verse 2 in the quoted passage is taken on its own, it does seem as if Micah predicted a Messiah who was to hail from Bethlehem, the town of David, a king who would rule into all eternity over Israel. This verse was interpreted by authors of the New Testament as a prophecy that Jesus Christ would be born in Bethlehem and that he would rule his people for all eternity from heaven (Matt 2: 3–6; John 7: 42).

This type of superficial interpretation fails to take the context into consideration. Micah addressed the people of his country who lived in fear for the might of Assyria, the empire that has already vanquished the northern Israelite kingdom a few decades earlier. He predicted that a king from the house of David, who hailed from Bethlehem, would overcome the might of the Assyrians.

Micah also foresaw the return of those Israelites who were abducted by the Assyrians when Samaria was razed in 772 BC (verse 3).

It is said of this promised ruler, that his "goings forth are from of old, from everlasting." That simply means that God has often promised that the house of David would rule forever (2 Sam: 7: 16; Ps 89: 36; Isa 9: 7), which did not happen.

It is true that the Assyrian Empire came to an end during the last years of the seventh century BC when it was destroyed by the Babylonians. Josiah, the king of Judah, tried to stop the Egyptian army from joining the Assyrians during a battle at Megiddo, but to no avail and he fell during the battle (2 Kgs 23: 28–30). Judah was defeated by the Babylonians a few years later and Jerusalem was eventually destroyed in 586 BC.[171]

Apart from the fact that this prophecy in Micah does not promise a final Messiah for Israel, his prediction of the future proved to be misguided.

TEXTS FROM THE EXILIC AND POST-EXILIC PERIODS

The Servant of the Lord
Isa 42: 1–4

1.	Behold, my servant, whom I uphold; my chosen, in whom my soul delights: I have put my Spirit on him; he will bring forth justice to the Gentiles.
2.	He will not cry, nor lift up his voice, nor cause it to be heard in the street.

---

[171] Bosgoff *et al. Geskiedenis,* 156–57.

> 3. A bruised reed will he not break, and a dimly burning wick will he not quench: he will bring forth justice in truth.
> 4. He will not fail nor be discouraged, until he have set justice in the earth; and the isles shall wait for his law.

A hasty reading of these verses may lead to the conclusion that the Messiah, Jesus Christ, is being meant. According to Matt 12: 18–23, these words were fulfilled in Jesus.

These words are spoken about God's servant, which servant in the book of Isaiah is always the people of Israel, not the expected Messiah (see Isa 49: 3 & 6).[172]

Cyrus the Anointed of YHWH
Isa 45: 1–7

> 1. Thus says YHWH to his anointed, to Cyrus, whose right hand I have held, to subdue nations before him, and I will loose the loins of kings; to open the doors before him, and the gates shall not be shut:
> 2. I will go before you, and make the rough places smooth; I will break in pieces the doors of brass, and cut in sunder the bars of iron;
> 3. and I will give you the treasures of darkness, and hidden riches of secret places, that you may know that it is I, YHWH, who call you by your name, even the God of Israel.
> 4. For Jacob my servant's sake, and Israel my chosen, I have called you by your name: I have surnamed you, though you have not known me.

---

[172] Boshoff *et al.*, *Gesmkiedenis*, 182.

> 5. I am YHWH, and there is none else; besides me there is no God. I will gird you, though you have not known me;
> 6. that they may know from the rising of the sun, and from the west, that there is none besides me: I am YHWH, and there is no one else.
> 7. I form the light, and create darkness; I make peace, and create evil. I am YHWH, who does all these things.

It is unlikely that Cyrus the Great, the king of Persia, ever took note of this prophecy about him in which he is called the "anointed" or "Messiah" of YHWH. He would, anyway, have been flattered and would have appreciated these words. As a Persian whose religion was Zoroastrianism, he was a monotheist who worshipped the god Ahura-Mazda, the creator of the world and the source of light and all that is good and commendable. He would have seen similarities between his religion and that of the Judeans.[173]

The four-winged guardian figure of Cyrus, bas-relief on a doorway pillar from Pasargadae. An inscription says "I am Cyrus the King, an Achaemenian."

After he defeated the Babylonian Empire in 539 BC, he issued an edict, allowing the Jewish exiles to return to Judea. His edict is quoted in 2 Chron 36: 22–23: "Thus says Cyrus king of Persia, All the kingdoms of the earth has YHWH, the God of heaven,

---

[173] König, "Zoroaster".

given me; and he has charged me to build him a house in Jerusalem, which is in Judah. Whoever there is among you of all his people, YHWH his God be with him, and let him go up."

This passage in Isaiah is the clearest indication that the title of Messiah in the Old Testament was given to living people. It is also noteworthy that Deutero-Isaiah described YHWH as if He and Ahura-Mazda were the same deity.

Suffering Servant of YHWH
Isa 52: 13 – 53: 12

13.	Behold, my servant shall deal wisely, he shall be exalted and lifted up, and shall be very high.
14.	Like as many were astonished at you (his visage was so marred more than any man, and his form more than the sons of men),
15.	so shall he sprinkle many nations; kings shall shut their mouths at him: for that which had not been told them shall they see; and that which they had not heard shall they understand.
1.	Who has believed our message? and to whom has the arm of YHWH been revealed?
2.	For he grew up before him as a tender plant, and as a root out of a dry ground: he has no form nor comeliness; and when we see him, there is no beauty that we should desire him.
3.	He was despised, and rejected of men; a man of sorrows, and acquainted with grief: and as one from whom men hide their face he was despised; and we didn't respect him.
4.	Surely he has borne our infirmities, and carried our sorrows; yet we esteemed him stricken, struck of God, and afflicted.

5. But he was wounded for our transgressions, he was bruised for our iniquities; the chastisement of our peace was on him; and with his stripes we are healed.

6. All we like sheep have gone astray; we have turned everyone to his own way; and YHWH has laid on him the iniquity of us all.

7. He was oppressed, yet when he was afflicted he didn't open his mouth; as a lamb that is led to the slaughter, and as a sheep that before its shearers is mute, so he didn't open his mouth.

8. By oppression and judgment he was taken away; and as for his generation, who [among them] considered that he was cut off out of the land of the living for the disobedience of my people to whom the stroke [was due]?

9. They made his grave with the wicked, and with a rich man in his death; although he had done no violence, neither was any deceit in his mouth.

10. Yet it pleased YHWH to bruise him; he has put him to grief: when you shall make his soul an offering for sin, he shall see [his] seed, he shall prolong his days, and the pleasure of YHWH shall prosper in his hand.

11. He shall see of the travail of his soul, [and] shall be satisfied: by the knowledge of himself shall my righteous servant justify many; and he shall bear their iniquities.

12. Therefore will I divide him a portion with the great, and he shall divide the spoil with the strong; because he poured out his soul to death, and was numbered with the transgressors: yet he bore the sin of many, and made intercession for the transgressors.

Paul wrote in I Cor 15: 3 that "the Scriptures" foretold the death and resurrection of Christ, but that is not correct. The only part of the Old Testament where something of the sort is seemingly written is Isa 52: 13–15 and 53: 1–12 where a description of the suffering "servant of YHWH" is given. This passage is often mentioned in the New Testament as a prophecy of the Messiah that was purportedly fulfilled in Jesus Christ who was crucified (Luke 22: 37; 24: 26–27; Acts 3: 18; 8: 26–40; 26: 22–23; Rom 15: 21; Phil 2: 7–11; Eph 5: 2; 1 Pet 2: 22–25; 3: 18).

The most plausible explanation of this passage in Isaiah is that the "servant of YHWH" must be seen as the nation of Israel, not the promised Messiah, as Christians believe.

Hirsch analyzed the whole of the Old Testament and found that the expression "servant of YHWH" was applied to the patriarch Jacob and his descendants, the people of Israel as a whole, as well as other leaders of Israel like Joshua, David, or the prophets. The promised Messiah was never linked to this expression.

For example: Ezek 28: 25 contains these words:

> "Thus says the Lord YHWH: When I shall have gathered the house of Israel from the peoples among whom they are scattered, and shall be sanctified in them in the sight of the nations, then shall they dwell in their own land which I gave to *my servant Jacob*" (*emphasis added*).

In Isa 41: 8–9 we read:

> "But you, *Israel, my servant, Jacob* whom I have chosen, the seed of Abraham my friend, you whom I have taken hold of from the ends of the earth, and called from the corners of it, and said to you, you are *my servant*, I have chosen you and not cast you away" (*emphasis added*).

Isaiah 44: 1 states:

> "Yet now hear, *Jacob my servant, and Israel*, who I have chosen"[174] (*emphasis added*).

Professor Mordechai ben–Tziyyon of the University of Jerusalem concurs with Hirsch regarding the meaning of the expression "servant of YHWH" in Isa 52–53. He adds that the nation of Israel has indeed suffered much during the centuries, and he reminds his readers that most Jewish scholars through the ages held this view.

It must be remembered: this passage was written during the Babylonian Exile, exactly at a time when the people of Israel were experiencing the utmost hardship and suffering because of their sins and failure to worship their God wholeheartedly.

Ben-Tziyyon accuses Christian translators of the Old Testament of making deliberate mistakes with the goal of creating the impression that the passage in Isa 52–53 refers to "the christian man-god" (*i e* Jesus Christ). An example is Isa 53: 8 as he translated it, which contains a clear reference to Israel's exile in Babylonia –

> "Now that they have been released from detention and judgement, who could have imagined such a generation? for they were removed far from the land where they lived, and a plague came upon them through the transgression of my people."

The Hebrew word translated by "stroke" or "plague" (נֶגַע – *Nega*) actually means "leprosy" – something Jesus never suffered from. This verse also refers to the people of Israel who suffered because the verbs are in the plural, not the singular as Christian translations have it.

---

[174] Hirsch, "Servant of God".

Professor Ben–Tziyyon wrote that Isa 52–53 may also refer to a specific pious person of that time who experienced suffering due to the sins of the people of Israel, but certainly not to the promised Messiah of the future.[175]

It must be concluded that Paul's statement that "the Scriptures" – especially Isa 52–53 – contain prophecies regarding Jesus Christ's death and resurrection cannot be supported.

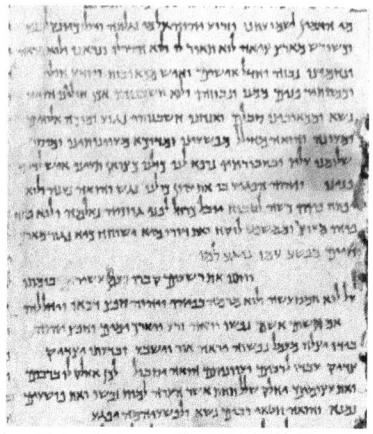

Isaiah 53 in the Great Isaiah Scroll, the best preserved of the biblical scrolls found at Qumran from the second century BC

A Redeemer for Zion
Isa 59: 16–21

16.	He [YHWH] saw that there was no man, and wondered that there was no intercessor: therefore his own arm brought salvation to him; and his righteousness, it upheld him.
17.	He put on righteousness as a breastplate, and a helmet of salvation on his head; and he put on garments of vengeance for clothing, and was clad with zeal as a mantle.
18.	According to their deeds, accordingly he will repay, wrath to his adversaries, recompense to his enemies; to the islands he will repay recompense.

---

[175] Ben–Tziyyon, "The 'Suffering Servant' in ch.53 of *Y'shayahu*".

> 19. So shall they fear the name of YHWH from the west, and his glory from the rising of the sun; for he will come as a rushing stream, which the breath of YHWH drives.
> 20. A Redeemer will come to Zion, and to those who turn from disobedience in Jacob, says YHWH.
> 21. As for me, this is my covenant with them, says YHWH: my Spirit who is on you, and my words which I have put in your mouth, shall not depart out of your mouth, nor out of the mouth of your seed, nor out of the mouth of your seed's seed, says YHWH, from henceforth and forever.

The first part of this chapter deals with all the sins of the people of Israel. They are reminded of why YHWH allowed them to be carried away as captives during the Exile. However, God promised in this passage that He would send a redeemer, an intercessor, to lead the people back to Him.

The descendants of Jacob were reminded of God's covenant with them, which meant that they could rely on his promises. This Redeemer can be seen as a messianic figure, but no further details are given about who he would be and when he would appear. It must be noted that this prophecy failed to link this messianic figure to the house of David; it merely promised that one of more leaders and religious reformers would certainly appear to lead the offspring of Jacob back to God.

That did happen when figures like Zerubbabel, the high priest Jeshua, Ezra, and Nehemiah appeared after the end of the Exile.

Israel will have David as a King
Jer 30: 8–10

> 8. It shall come to pass in that day, says YHWH of Hosts, that I will break his yoke from off your neck, and will burst your bonds; and strangers shall no more make him their bondservant;
> 9. but they shall serve YHWH their God, and David their king, whom I will raise up to them.
> 10. Therefore don't you be afraid, O Jacob my servant, says YHWH; neither be dismayed, Israel: for, behold, I will save you from afar, and your seed from the land of their captivity; and Jacob shall return, and shall be quiet and at ease, and none shall make him afraid.

These words were written after the Judean elite had been taken away to Babylon in captivity. Jeremiah gave them the promise that the yoke of the oppressor would be broken, that the exiled people would return to their land and live in peace, and that they would live under a king from the house of David, a Messiah.

It did happen that the Jews in Babylonia were given the opportunity to return to their country after the Persians had conquered the Babylonian Empire in 539 BC. The two centuries after this were generally peaceful, until Alexander the Great defeated the Persians and the Egyptians in 332 BC and took over Palestine in the process.

However, no king from the house of David ever reigned again in Jerusalem. Christians may be tempted to say that Jesus of Nazareth was that promised king. His campaign of more than three years to resurrect the Israelite monarchy failed when he was crucified and h disappeared from the scene in April AD 33.

The Cedar Branch
Ezek 17: 22–24

> 22. Thus says the Lord YHWH: I will also take of the lofty top of the cedar, and will set it; I will crop off from the topmost of its young twigs a tender one, and I will plant it on a high and lofty mountain:
> 23. in the mountain of the height of Israel will I plant it; and it shall bring forth boughs, and bear fruit, and be a goodly cedar: and under it shall dwell all birds of every wing; in the shade of the branches of it shall they dwell.
> 24. All the trees of the field shall know that I, YHWH, have brought down the high tree, have exalted the low tree, have dried up the green tree, and have made the dry tree to flourish; I, YHWH, have spoken and have done it.

Ezekiel employed figurative language to describe the future Messiah of Israel. He compared him with a tender branch from a cedar tree that had been transplanted and developed into a big tree on top of a high mountain, from where it could look down on the other trees. The birds who sought shelter in this tree were the people of God who were protected by this messianic figure.

This prophecy lacks specifics and it is impossible to determine how Ezekiel visualized the messiah of Israel.

The King of Tyre as an Anointed Cherub
Ezek 28: 12–19

> 12. Son of man, take up a lamentation over the king of Tyre, and tell him, Thus says the Lord YHWH: You seal up the sum, full of wisdom, and perfect in beauty.
> 13. You were in Eden, the garden of God; every precious stone was your covering, the sardius, the topaz, and the diamond, the beryl, the onyx, and the jasper, the sapphire, the

> emerald, and the emerald, and gold: the workmanship of your tambourines and of your pipes was in you; in the day that you were created they were prepared.
>
> 14. You were the anointed cherub who covers: and I set you, [so that] you were on the holy mountain of God; you have walked up and down in the midst of the stones of fire.
>
> 15. You were perfect in your ways from the day that you were created, until unrighteousness was found in you.
>
> 16. By the abundance of your traffic they filled the midst of you with violence, and you have sinned: therefore I have cast you as profane out of the mountain of God; and I have destroyed you, covering cherub, from the midst of the stones of fire.
>
> 17. Your heart was lifted up because of your beauty; you have corrupted your wisdom by reason of your brightness: I have cast you to the ground; I have laid you before kings, that they may see you.
>
> 18. By the multitude of your iniquities, in the unrighteousness of your traffic, you have profaned your sanctuaries; therefore have I brought forth a fire from the midst of you; it has devoured you, and I have turned you to ashes on the earth in the sight of all those who see you.
>
> 19. All those who know you among the peoples shall be astonished at you: you are become a terror, and you shall nevermore have any being.

Certain aspects of this prophecy don't seem to make sense. The most enigmatic is the statement that the pagan king of Tyre, whose downfall is announced, is called "the anointed cherub who covers [protectively]". The Hebrew expression (כְּרוּב מִמְשַׁח – *keroub mimashiach*) clearly says that this king was an anointed heavenly being, a celestial messiah.

This prophecy does not tally with known history if it is understood literally. The Phoenician city of Tyre was at the time of Ezekiel – during the Babylonian Exile that started in 586 BC – a flourishing harbor city and commercial hub. The city, which was partly built on an island, successfully withstood a long siege by the Babylonian army of King Nebuchadrezzar during 585–573 BC, exactly at the time when Ezekiel was writing his prophecy. The city only became part of the Persian Empire after the fall of Babylon in 538 BC. The city was only partially destroyed in 332 BC by Alexander the Great, long after the time of Ezekiel.[176]

It is also said of this king of Tyre that he was in "Eden, the garden of God". One is reminded of *Gen 3: 24* by these words, and also by Ezekiel's description of this king as an "anointed cherub":

> "So He [God] drove out the man; and he placed Cherubs at the east of the garden of Eden, and the flame of a sword which turned every way, to guard the way to the tree of life."

The enigmas disappear when one applies this prophecy to the patron deity of Tye, namely Melqart. This name in the Phoenician language means "king of the city". That is near enough to Ezekiel's name in Hebrew, namely מֶלֶךְ צוֹר (*Melek Tsor* – King of Tyre). Melqart can be identified with the Canaanite or Phoenician god of Baal, but also with the Greek hero of Hercules.[177]

When one looks at a computerized recreation of the night sky at Babylon when Ezekiel was writing his prophecies, it becomes clear where he got the inspiration for this prophecy.

---

[176] Enc Brit, "Tyre".
[177] Enc Brit, "Melqart".

The sky above Babylonia on 31 July 593 BC, as seen during Ezekiel's first vision, showing the constellations, including Hercules (Melqart) on the lower left of the illustration. The concentric circles show where the northern astronomical pole with the divine throne was situated and the Milky Way can be equated with the Garden of God, Eden.

The constellation of Hercules lay very near to the northern celestial pole, where God's throne is situated. It can, therefore, be said that he was on God's holy mountain before his fall. He was covered by nine different types of colorful precious stones, the stars in the sky. The Garden of Eden must be sought in the nearby Milky Way with its fields of star clouds. Hercules disappeared behind the western horizon during the night and when his place was taken by the bright sun, the "stones of fire".

It is important to note that this Phoenician deity, Melqart, is described as an "anointed cherub" or messianic angel who became proud and full of iniquities and the city's "unrighteousness of your traffic" or dishonest commercial practices. Ezekiel, therefore, prophesied that this pagan deity would disappear – which did happen many centuries later when Tyre became a Christian city.[178] This means that the term "messiah" was used by Ezekiel in a very broad sense, without referring to a champion and liberator for Israel.

A Shepherd for Israel
Ezek 34: 23–25

23.	I will set up one shepherd over them, and he shall feed them, even my servant David; he shall feed them, and he shall be their shepherd.
24.	I, YHWH, will be their God, and my servant David prince among them; I, YHWH, have spoken it.

"The Good Shepherd" mosaic, 5th century, Mausoleum of Galla Placidia, Ravenna, Italy

In the rest of this chapter, Ezekiel pointed out on behalf of YHWH that the people have been led astray by false prophets and shepherds. The quoted words contain a promise that God would send a true shepherd, a descendant of David, who would feed the people. It is true that Jesus was called the Good Shepherd (John 10: 14), but he never ruled over Israel as promised in this prophecy.

Ezekiel's assurance that the house of David would rule in future proved to be wrong and no descendant of David ever sat on a throne again. It amounted to a case of pious wishful thinking.

---

[178] Enc Brit, "Tyre".

The Yearning for a King
Ezek 37: 24–28

> 24. My servant David shall be king over them; and they all shall have one shepherd: they shall also walk in my ordinances, and observe my statutes, and do them.
> 25. They shall dwell in the land that I have given to Jacob my servant, in which your fathers lived; and they shall dwell therein, they, and their children, and their children's children, forever: and David my servant shall be their prince for ever.
> 26. Moreover I will make a covenant of peace with them; it shall be an everlasting covenant with them; and I will place them, and multiply them, and will set my sanctuary in the midst of them forevermore.
> 27. My tent also shall be with them; and I will be their God, and they shall be my people.
> 28. The nations shall know that I am YHWH who sanctifies Israel, when my sanctuary shall be in the midst of them forevermore.

Ezekiel promised the people of Israel on behalf of YHWH that a resurrected David, or one of his descendants, would rule over a united nation that would live in peace and in accordance with God's ordinances.

According to Jacobs and Buttenwieser, "after the fall of the nation, the Jews of the Exile dreamed of the coming of a second David, who would reestablish them as a glorious nation. So, Ezekiel lays emphasis on the fact that the future Israel is to be a united nation as it was under David of old."

This passage is merely an expression of the Jews' "hope in

the return of David."[179]

This promise of YHWH was never kept. Although Jesus was called the "Good Shepherd" (John 10: 14), he never became the promised shepherd of a reunited Israel. Jesus was convinced that this prophecy was aimed at him, but he was wrong.

Zerubbabel Chosen
Hag 2: 20–23

20.	The Word of YHWH came the second time to Haggai in the twenty-fourth day of the month, saying,
21.	"Speak to Zerubbabel, governor of Judah, saying, 'I will shake the heavens and the earth.
22.	I will overthrow the throne of kingdoms. I will destroy the strength of the kingdoms of the nations. I will overthrow the chariots, and those who ride in them. The horses and their riders will come down, everyone by the sword of his brother.
23.	In that day, says YHWH of Hosts, will I take you, Zerubbabel, my servant, the son of Shealtiel,' says YHWH, 'and will make you as a signet, for I have chosen you,' says YHWH of Hosts."

God tasked Haggai to deliver a message to the governor of Judea after the end of the Babylonian Exile, Zerubbabel, to inform him of the following:

- YHWH approved of his position as governor
- The earth would be shaken – just as Amos and Zecheriah experienced earth tremors; and
- Kingdoms would fall.

---

[179] Jacobs and Buddenwieser, "Messiah".

The only kingdoms worthy to be mentioned at that time were the Persian and Egyptian kingdoms. Both were conquered two centuries later by the Greek king, Alexander the Great.

God's Messenger
Mal 3: 1

> Behold, I send my messenger, and he shall prepare the way before me: and the Lord, whom you seek, will suddenly come to his temple; and the messenger of the covenant, whom you desire, behold, he comes, says YHWH of hosts.

John the Baptist applied these words to himself when he explained that he was sent to prepare the way for the Messiah (Mark 1: 2).

The important question here is: who is supposed to be this messenger? When one reads this verse in the original Hebrew it is immediately clear that the prophet Malachi had himself in mind. The expression "my messenger" (Hebrew: מַלְאָכִי – *Mal'akyi*) is precisely the proper name of the prophet Malachi. He never thought about John the Baptist and the Messiah several centuries after his time.

Elijah the Prophet
Mal 4: 5–6

> 5. Behold, I will send you Elijah the prophet before the great and terrible day of YHWH come.
> 6. He shall turn the heart of the fathers to the children, and the heart of the children to their fathers; lest I come and strike the earth with a curse.

Jesus applied these words to John the Baptist after his death, implying that there were striking similarities between Elijah and John and that John can almost be seen as a resurrected Elijah (Matt

11: 14). However, a deputation from Jerusalem also asked John whether he was the promised Elijah, which he denied (John 1: 21).

What did Malachi mean with this prophecy? One must conclude in the light of Mal 3: 1 that he saw himself as a successor of Elijah who had to warn the people that the "terrible day of YHWH", Judgment Day, was to be expected. His words have, strictly speaking, nothing to do with Johan the Baptist or the Messiah.

The Golden Lamp Stand
Zech 4: 1–14

1.	The angel who talked with me came again, and waked me, as a man who is wakened out of his sleep.
2.	He said to me, What see you? I said, I have seen, and, behold, a lampstand all of gold, with its bowl on the top of it, and its seven lamps thereon; there are seven pipes to each of the lamps, which are on the top of it;
3.	and two olive-trees by it, one on the right side of the bowl, and the other on the left side of it.
4.	I answered and spoke to the angel who talked with me, saying, What are these, my lord?
5.	Then the angel who talked with me answered me, Don't you know what these are? I said, No, my lord.
6.	Then he answered and spoke to me, saying, This is the word of YHWH to Zerubbabel, saying, Not by might, nor by power, but by my Spirit, says YHWH of Hosts.
7.	Who are you, great mountain? before Zerubbabel [you shall become] a plain; and he shall bring forth the top stone with shouts of Grace, grace, to it.
8.	Moreover the word of YHWH came to me, saying,

> 9. The hands of Zerubbabel have laid the foundation of this house; his hands shall also finish it; and you shall know that YHWH of Hosts has sent me to you.
> 10. For who has despised the day of small things? for these seven shall rejoice, and shall see the plummet in the hand of Zerubbabel; [these are] the eyes of YHWH, which run back and forth through the whole earth.
> 11. Then answered I, and said to him, What are these two olive-trees on the right side of the lampstand and on the left side of it?
> 12. I answered the second time, and said to him, What are these two olive-branches, which are beside the two golden spouts, that empty the golden [oil] out of themselves?
> 13. He answered me and said, "Don't you know what these are?" I said, No, my lord.
> 14. Then said he, These are the two anointed ones, that stand by the Lord of the whole earth.

Zechariah had this vision during the middle of the night, because he was woken from his sleep to watch the heavens.

During this vision, he saw a lamp stand with seven arms, reminding him of the Menorah that used to stand in the Jerusalem Temple. He saw two olive trees on both sides of the lamp and an angel explained that these trees were "anointed ones" – in other words: messiahs. They represented Zerubbabel, the governor who was overseeing the completion of the temple, and Joshua, the high priest. Zerubbabel was to follow a peaceful policy by avoiding violence with those who opposed his work and to rely on God's spirit to guide him.

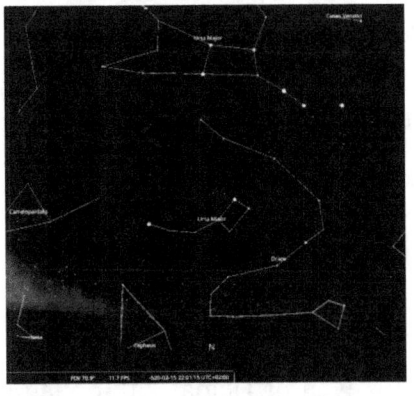

The arc of seven stars of the constellation of Draco, resembling the Menorah. The bowl containing the oil is represented by Ursa Minor

Olive trees are useful trees. Their fruit is edible and the oil pressed from the berries is used for illumination, the preparation of food, and the soothing of wounds, but also for anointing people. These olive trees symbolized the important roles and functions of these two anointed men.

A reconstruction of the Menorah of the Temple in Jerusalem manufactured by the Temple Institute.

Zechariah watched the sky just above the northern horizon where he saw the constellation of Draco, of which seven stars form an arc around the northern celestial pole where the throne of God was thought to be situated. Within this arc, there is the constellation of Ursa Minor, the Little Bear, representing the lamp's bowl of oil.

He watched these stars while sitting in an olive grove and he looked at the stars with two olive trees on both sides of these constellations. He must have seen real olive trees since there are no starry constellations that could depict anything looking like olive trees.

Crowning the High Priest
Zech 6: 9–15

9.	The word of YHWH came to me, saying,
10.	Take of them of the captivity, even of Heldai, of Tobijah, and of Jedaiah; and come you the same day, and go into the house of Josiah the son of Zephaniah, where they are come from Babylon;
11.	yes, take [of them] silver and gold, and make crowns, and set them on the head of Joshua the son of Jehozadak, the high priest;
12.	and speak to him, saying, Thus speaks YHWH of Hosts, saying, Behold, the man whose name is the Branch: and he shall grow up out of his place; and he shall build the temple of YHWH;
13.	even he shall build the temple of YHWH; and he shall bear the glory, and shall sit and rule on his throne; and he shall be a priest on his throne; and the counsel of peace shall be between them both.
14.	The crowns shall be to Helem, and to Tobijah, and to Jedaiah, and to Hen the son of Zephaniah, for a memorial in the temple of YHWH.
15.	Those who are far off shall come and build in the temple of YHWH; and you shall know that YHWH of hosts has sent me

> to you. [This] shall happen, if you will diligently obey the voice of YHWH your God.

Some Bible students see a prophecy about the ultimate Messiah in verses 12 and 13. That is stretching the words of this passage too far. But it cannot be denied that some sort of a messiah was meant in those two verses. The whole chapter deals with Joshua, the high priest, and the man called "Branch", who was destined to supervise the rebuilding of the Jerusalem temple. He is called the "Branch", a name that is also used in Zech 3: 8.

In other parts of the Old Testament, a descendant of David was called a "Branch" (Isa 4: 2; 11: 1; 53: 2 Jer 23: 5; 33: 15). In this case, it is applied to Zerubbabel, who descended from David. The Hebrew word for "Branch" is צֶמַח (*Tsemach*), which means "sprout, growth, branch" and it is derived from a verb which means "to sprout, spring up, grow up", suggesting a descendant.

The Righteous King on a Donkey
Zech 9: 9–10

> 9. Rejoice greatly, daughter of Zion; shout, daughter of Jerusalem: behold, your king comes to you; he is just, and having salvation; lowly, and riding on a donkey, even on a colt the foal of a donkey.
> 10. I will cut off the chariot from Ephraim, and the horse from Jerusalem; and the battle bow shall be cut off; and he shall speak peace to the nations: and his dominion shall be from sea to sea, and from the River to the ends of the earth.

These two verses form a unit on their own, without direct links to the preceding and following verses.

This is one of the clearest Old Testament prophecies regarding an expected Messiah. These words were written almost two centuries after the end of the Exile, at a time when Alexander the Great was conquering one country after the other. The throne of David in Jerusalem had been empty for a few centuries and the Jews longed for a restoration of the monarchy and their independence.

The promised king would be riding an ass, instead of a war horse. This has often been interpreted as a sign of humility, but that is not necessarily the case. Other important figures in the Old Testament also made use of donkeys: Abraham (Gen 22: 3), the wife of Moses (Ex 4: 20), the sons of Jacob on their way to Egypt (Ex 42: 26), Balaam (Num 22), and Abigail (1 Sam 25: 20–23). Jacob sent a gift of thirty donkeys to his brother Esau (Gen 32: 5). Saul, the future king of Israel, was sent with a servant to find the stray asses of his father, when he met the prophet Samuel (1 Sam 9: 3–14). In other words: donkeys were seen as valuable, dependable, and industrious animals. The association of this king with this animal demonstrated also his dependability and diligence.

The promised king would be just when judging the people. He would deliver salvation from oppression and hardship. Resistance could be expected from Ephraim, the country to the north of Jerusalem, as well as from Jerusalem itself. This king would, however, prevail over all hostile forces.

This prophecy is a summary of Ps 72 where Israel is also given the promise that their future king would rule "from sea to sea, from the River to the ends of the earth" (Ps 72: 8). That would be a universal rule.

It is clear from Zecheriah and the Psalm that this Messiah was expected at the end of time, on Judgment Day. They expected a "royal son" (Ps 72: 1), a heavenly figure. It must be remembered, though, that YHWH is frequently called the king of Israel (Ps 5: 2;

24: 10; 44: 4; 74: 12; Isa 6: 5; 8: 21; Jer 10:7 *etcetera*) – and that is also the case here in Zech 9: 9). That YHWH is meant to be the expected king, the Messiah himself, is to be seen in verse 10 where the prophet quotes God in the first-person singular: "I will cut off the chariot from Ephraim, and the horse from Jerusalem."

Zech 9: 9 contains an echo of Zech 2: 10 – "Sing and rejoice, daughter of Zion; for, behold, I come, and I will dwell in the midst of you, says YHWH." In other words: YHWH would dwell with his people and, therefore, they may rejoice because Judgment Day and eternal bliss would arrive.

Jesus of Nazareth staged and choreographed an entry into Jerusalem a few days before his crucifixion by organizing a donkey on which he could ride into the city (John 12: 12–19; Mark 11: 4–11). The crowds were warned beforehand and they lined the streets to greet him as their king. They certainly knew of this prophecy of the king on a donkey in Zecheriah and they applied it to Jesus, as he had intended, by calling out: "Hosanna! Blessed is he who comes in the name of the Lord, the King of Israel!" (John 12: 13).

It must be concluded that Psalm 72 and Zech 9: 9–10 never had Jesus in mind, since these prophecies clearly dealt with the final victory of God over the forces of evil at the end of time – not the time when Jesus was alive.

The Spirit of Grace and Supplication
Zech 12: 10–14

10.	I will pour on the house of David, and on the inhabitants of Jerusalem, the spirit of grace and of supplication; and they shall look to me whom they have pierced; and they shall mourn for him, as one mourns for his only son, and shall be in bitterness for him, as one who is in bitterness for his firstborn.

11.	In that day shall there be a great mourning in Jerusalem, as the mourning of Hadadrimmon in the valley of Megiddon.
12.	The land shall mourn, every family apart; the family of the house of David apart, and their wives apart; the family of the house of Nathan apart, and their wives apart;
13.	the family of the house of Levi apart, and their wives apart; the family of the Shimeites apart, and their wives apart;
14.	all the families who remain, every family apart, and their wives apart.

A cursory glance at these verses may lead to the idea that we find here a prophecy regarding Jesus as the son of God who was pierced when he was crucified. However, Zecheriah never meant something like that.

It must be emphasized: the prophet told his people on behalf of God that they had pierced Him by rejecting and disobeying Him, which led to the destruction of Jerusalem and the Exile. Th prophet also explained that the people would mourn for God's only son – the people of Israel who have gone astray. Israel is often called the son of God in the Old Testament, including this passage (see Ex 4: 22; Deut 14: 1; Ps 82: 6; Jer 31: 9; Hos 11: 1). This mourning would be universal and can be compared with the mourning when king Josiah of Judah fell during a battle against the Egyptians (2 Kgs 23: 29–30).

However, there is a promise: God will send to them a spirit of repentance, while they are mourning their fate and sins.

The Son of Man
Dan 7: 13–14

> 13. I saw in the night-visions, and, behold, there came with the clouds of the sky one like a son of man, and he came even to the ancient of days, and they brought him near before him.
> 14. There was given him dominion, and glory, and a kingdom, that all the peoples, nations, and languages should serve him: his dominion is an everlasting dominion, which shall not pass away, and his kingdom that which shall not be destroyed.

These words follow Daniel's description of four terrible animals – a lion, a bear, a leopard, and a vicious monster (see Chapter 3). They symbolized four successive kingdoms, all of which would come to an end. These two verses may certainly be regarded as a prophecy about a future Messiah who would receive his power from God. His reign would be everlasting and would, therefore, only come to pass at the end of days, at Judgment Day. He would, in other words, not be a figure in Israel's future.

The rest of the chapter discloses the identity of this messiah:

The Saints
Dan 7: 16–18

> 16. I came near to one of those who stood by, and asked him the truth concerning all this. So he told me, and made me know the interpretation of the things.
> 17. These great animals, which are four, are four kings, who shall arise out of the earth.
> 18. But the saints of the Most High shall receive the kingdom, and possess the kingdom forever, even forever and ever.

In other words: the Messiah would not be a certain identifiable person, but the collection of the "saints of the Most High", the faithful Jews.

One can concur with Jacobs and Buttenwieser: "These constitute the earthly representatives of God in the 'civitas Dei,' and in contrast to the other nations of the world, who are represented under the figures of animals, they are represented under the figure of a man in order to signify that in them the divine ideal of manhood has preserved itself most faithfully.[180]

The Coming of a Messiah
Daniel 9: 20–27

20.	While I was speaking, and praying, and confessing my sin and the sin of my people Israel, and presenting my supplication before YHWH my God for the holy mountain of my God;
21.	yes, while I was speaking in prayer, the man Gabriel, whom I had seen in the vision at the beginning, being caused to fly swiftly, touched me about the time of the evening offering.
22.	He instructed me, and talked with me, and said, Daniel, I am now come forth to give you wisdom and understanding.
23.	At the beginning of your petitions the commandment went forth, and I am come to tell you; for you are greatly beloved: therefore consider the matter, and understand the vision.
24.	Seventy weeks are decreed on your people and on your holy city, to finish disobedience, and to make an end of sins, and to make reconciliation for iniquity, and to bring in everlasting righteousness, and to seal up vision and prophecy, and to anoint the most holy.

---

[180] Jacobs and Buttenwieser, "Messiah".

> 25. Know therefore and discern, that from the going forth of the commandment to restore and to build Jerusalem to the Anointed One, the prince, shall be seven weeks, and sixty-two weeks: it shall be built again, with street and moat, even in troubled times.
>
> 26. After the sixty-two weeks the Anointed One shall be cut off, and shall have nothing: and the people of the prince who shall come shall destroy the city and the sanctuary; and the end of it shall be with a flood, and even to the end shall be war; desolations are determined.
>
> 27. He shall make a firm covenant with many for one week: and in the midst of the week he shall cause the sacrifice and the offering to cease; and on the wing of abominations [shall come] one who makes desolate; and even to the full end, and that determined, shall [wrath] be poured out on the desolate.

The first part of this chapter contains the prayer of Daniel on behalf of his people, asking God's forgiveness for all their sins.

After that, the Archangel Gabriel, who was already encountered in Dan 8: 16,[181] came with a message for Daniel. The prophet saw him during the early evening and it is possible that he saw this winged figure in some or other constellation in the night sky. The name *Gabriel* (Hebrew: גַּבְרִיאֵל) means "Warrior of God".

Gabriel told him that YHWH had allotted seventy weeks to Israel before Judgment Day, the point in time "to make an end of sins, and to make reconciliation for iniquity, and to bring in everlasting righteousness." The "seventy weeks" must be seen as a

---

[181] Daniel found the figure of Gabriel in the earlier First Book of Enoch (Pretorius, *To Hell with the Devil*, 137).

symbolic period of time. The Hebrew word for "week" is שבוע (*Shabuwa*), which means "a unit, period, seven, period of seven (days or years)". The number of 70 must be seen as the product of the symbolic numbers of 7 and 10. The number seven is connected to God's work when he created the world in seven days, according to Genesis 1 and Exodus 20. According the ancients, there were seven planets or moving bodies in the sky. Ten is the number of completeness – just as there were Ten Commandments and ten plagues in Egypt. The ten fingers on two hands are a reminder of the ability to work and to accomplish something. These seventy weeks or periods are, therefore, the time determined by God before Judgment Day when all sin and iniquity will be wiped away.

These seventy periods were due to start at that same time, the moment when the Persian king gave the command that Jerusalem had to be rebuilt and that the exiles in Babylon be allowed to return home.

During his prayer, Daniel alluded to Jeremiah who predicted that the Jews would be subjugated to the king of Babylon for seventy years (Jer 25:11,12 and 29:10). This may have prompted him to describe the period before the deliverance of the Jews as seventy periods or weeks. The command to rebuild the city would be given to an "Anointed one, a prince," It is tempting to see in this figure, called a מָשִׁיחַ (*Mashiyach* or Messiah) in Hebrew, as a prophecy of Jesus Christ. For that reason, many translations call him "*the* Anointed One, *the* prince." However, the definite article, "the", is absent and it denotes an unidentified figure in the future who would rebuild Jerusalem.

The restoration of Jerusalem was due to begin within seven periods, a time under the control of God. The remaining 63 periods had to be divided into 62 plus one. The Messianic figure would be "cut off" when the people of another prince would come to destroy the city again. This "prince" or ruler would "cause the sacrifice and the offering to cease; and on the wing of abominations [shall come] one who makes desolate." In other words, the people of God would be persecuted.

When one remembers that the Book of Daniel was written around 165 BC, it is clear that the author really described what had already happened. Jerusalem was, indeed, rebuilt when the Jewish leadership was taken over by Esra and Nehemiah. After the conquest of Palestine by the army of Alexander the Great in 332 BC and his death in 323 BC, his empire was divided among his generals. The ruler of Syria, the great-grandson of the original king, Antiochus IV Epiphanes, who ruled between 175 and164/163 BC, tried to force the Jews to worship the Greek chief deity of Zeus in the Jerusalem temple and the temple was violated. That led to a successful revolt under the Maccabees. The victory of the Jews over the army of Antiochus was seen by Daniel as a day of judgment over the pagan forces of darkness – not the final Judgment at the end of time.[182]

Because Daniel, in fact, described history, the quoted verses of chapter 9 do not contain a prophecy of Jesus of Nazareth as a future Messiah.

ENOCH

The Son of Man and the Messiah
2 Enoch 48: 1–10

1.	And in that place I saw the fountain of righteousness Which was inexhaustible: And around it were many fountains of wisdom; And all the thirsty drank of them, And were filled with wisdom,

---

[182] Boshoff, *Geskiedenis*, 232–235; Rylaarsdam *et al.* " Biblical Literature".

      And their dwellings were with the righteous and holy and elect.

2. And at that hour that Son of Man was named In the presence of the Lord of Spirits,
And his name before the Head of Days.

3. Yea, before the sun and the signs were created,
Before the stars of the heaven were made,
His name was named before the Lord of Spirits.

4. He shall be a staff to the righteous whereon to stay themselves and not fall,
And he shall be the light of the Gentiles,
And the hope of those who are troubled of heart.

5. All who dwell on earth shall fall down and worship before him,
And will praise and bless and celebrate with song the Lord of Spirits.

6. And for this reason hath he been chosen and hidden before Him,
Before the creation of the world and for evermore.

7. And the wisdom of the Lord of Spirits hath revealed him to the holy and righteous;
For he hath preserved the lot of the righteous,
Because they have hated and despised this world of unrighteousness,
And have hated all its works and ways in the name of the Lord of Spirits:
For in his name they are saved,
And according to his good pleasure hath it been in regard to their life.

8. In these days downcast in countenance shall the kings of the earth have become,

	And the strong who possess the land because of the works of their hands; For on the day of their anguish and affliction they shall not (be able to) save themselves.
9.	And I will give them over into the hands of Mine elect: As straw in the fire so shall they burn before the face of the holy: As lead in the water shall they sink before the face of the righteous, And no trace of them shall any more be found.
10.	And on the day of their affliction there shall be rest on the earth, And before them they shall fall and not rise again: And there shall be no one to take them with his hands and raise them: For they have denied the Lord of Spirits and His Anointed. The name of the Lord of Spirits be blessed.

This chapter in 2 Enoch clearly describes a messianic figure – the Son of Man and the Anointed of the Lord of Spirits.

His appearance will not only benefit Israel; his presence will benefit all by being "the light of the Gentiles". He will be the judge on Judgment Day, which will usher in a perfect existence with perfect wisdom and righteousness.

This Messiah is, somehow, a divine figure because he existed before the creation of the sun, the "signs" (constellations), and the stars. The blessed souls will worship him. Although he is, somehow, a divine figure, he is not identical with God, "the Lord of Spirits". It is difficult to gather where Enoch got this figure from because nobody like this appears in the Old Testament. Perhaps Enoch thought of one of the archangels as the "Elect One".

The Elect One
2 Enoch 52: 1–9

1. And the mountain of gold, and the mountain of soft metal, and the mountain of lead,
2. All these shall be in the presence of the Elect One
   As wax: before the fire,
   And like the water which streams down from above [upon those mountains],
3. And they shall become powerless before his feet.
   And it shall come to pass in those days that none shall be saved,
4. Either by gold or by silver,
   And none be able to escape.
5. And there shall be no iron for war,
   Nor shall one clothe oneself with a breastplate.
6. Bronze shall be of no service,
   And tin [shall be of no service and] shall not be esteemed,
   And lead shall not be desired.
7. And the mountain of gold, and the mountain of soft metal, and the mountain of lead,
   All these shall be in the presence of the Elect One
   As wax: before the fire,
8. And like the water which streams down from above [upon those mountains],
9. And they shall become powerless before his feet.
   And it shall come to pass in those days that none shall be saved,
   Either by gold or by silver,
   And none be able to escape.

Enoch was shown mountains containing various metals. An angel informed him that all these metals – sources of wealth and material for armaments – would have no value when the Elect One or Messiah of the Lord of Spirits appears on Judgment Day.

SUMMARY

This lengthy discussion and analysis of the most important texts in the Hebrew Scriptures that can be linked to the expected Messiah of Israel, demonstrates without the slightest doubt that no prophecy in the Old Testament ever envisaged the appearance of Jesus of Nazareth as the ultimate Messiah of Israel.

No single prophecy of those quoted from the Old Testament ever foresaw that any Messiah would be executed, as happened with Jesus. Since the execution of the Messiah was never foreseen, it goes without saying that his resurrection from the dead could not have received any attention.

There were certainly some messianic figures – God Himself, a king from the house of David, other unidentifiable personages, or the nation of Israel herself. In many cases, these figures would be involved with Judgment Day at the end of time when this sinful world would be judged and cleansed.

Jacobs and Buttenwieser describe the hopes of the Jews during the time of Jesus as follows: "Not until after the fall of the Maccabean dynasty, when the despotic government of Herod the Great and his family, and the increasing tyranny of the Roman empire had made their condition ever more unbearable, did the Jews seek refuge in the hope of a personal Messiah. They yearned for the promised deliverer of the house of David, who would free them from the yoke of the hated foreign usurper, would put an end to the impious Roman rule, and would establish His own reign of peace and justice in its place."[183]

---

[183] Jacobs and Buttenwieser, "Messiah".

Jesus did not fulfil the prophecies about the expected Messiah of Israel for the following reasons:

- The Messiah was expected to free Israel from foreign domination;
- The Messiah was supposed to bring all the Jewish exiles home;
- The Messiah was supposed to rule as a king from the house of David;
- The Messiah was expected to rule the world; and
- The Messiah was expected to create world peace.

Of course, Jesus did none of these things and didn't even come close, as will be shown in the next chapter.

It must be asked: how did it happen that most authors of the Scriptures of the New Testament thought that Jesus was, in fact, the Messiah of Israel? The next chapter will deal with this topic.

CHAPTER 6
PROPHECIES REGARDING THE MESSIAH IN THE NEW TESTAMENT

VIEWS OF THE NEW TESTAMENT REGARDING THE PROPHETS

Most New Testament writings claim that the birth, ministry, death, and resurrection of Jesus of Nazareth was the fulfillment of various Old Testament prophecies. These claims must be scrutinized and an answer to the following question must be found: Did the authors of New Testament writings understand and interpret the books of the Old Testament correctly when they declared that the ancient prophecies predicted the coming of Jesus as the Messiah?

Something must be said about the title of "Messiah" as used in the New Testament. The name – or rather title – of "Christ" means "anointed" and is derived from the Greek Χριστός (*Christos*). It is the Greek equivalent of the Hebrew מָשִׁיחַ (*mashiyach*), which is rendered in English as "Messiah". The Hebrew word for "Messiah" is also transcribed into Greek as Μεσσίας (*Messias*) in John 1: 41 and 4: 25. In the letters of Paul, the title of "Christ" is often used as a proper name. The name "Jesus Christ" simply means "Jesus the Messiah".

It is necessary to quote two of the most important texts in the New Testament where it is stated that prophecies of the Old Testament point to Jesus of Nazareth as the Messiah of Israel:

"Philip found Nathanael, and said to him, 'We have found him, of whom Moses in the law, and the prophets, wrote: Jesus of Nazareth, the son of Joseph'" (John 1: 45).

"All the prophets testify about him [Christ], that through his name everyone who believes in him will receive remission of sins" (Acts 10: 43).

The same thought is also encountered in Rom 1: 1–3; Rom 3: 21–22; Luke 24: 25–27; Acts 3: 24–26; Acts 13: 27–29 &32; Acts 28: 23; and 1 Pet 1: 10–11.

There can be no doubt: various authors of books in the New Testament, who were Jews and grew up with the Old Testament, were convinced that the prophets of Israel predicted that Jesus of Nazareth would appear as the Messiah.

The Jews of Jesus' time had an intense need of a Messiah, a champion who would liberate them from the cruel pagan Roman overlords and the corrupt House of Herod that ruled over them with the approval of the Romans. The apocryphal Psalms of Solomon contained this prayer:

Ps Sol 17: 23–26[184]

23.	Behold, oh Lord, and raise up unto them their king, the son of David, at the time the which Thou seest, oh God, that he may reign over Israel Thy servant
24.	And gird him with strength, that he may shatter unrighteous rulers,
25.	And that he may purge Jerusalem from nations that trample (her) down to destruction. Wisely, righteously
26.	He shall thrust out sinners from (the) inheritance,

---

[184] As quoted by Gray, "The Psalms of Solomon", 631–52

> He shall destroy the pride of the sinner as a potter's vessel.
> With a rod of iron, he shall break in pieces all their substance,
> He shall destroy the godless nations with the word of his mouth.

Flavius Josephus, the Jewish historian, wrote about the reason why the Jews started the war against the Romans in AD 66:

> "But now what did the most elevate them in undertaking this war, was an ambiguous oracle, that was also found in their sacred writings; how 'About that time one, from their country, should become governor of the habitable earth.' The Jews took this prediction to belong to themselves in particular: and many of the wise men were thereby deceived in their determination. Now this oracle certainly denoted the government of *Vespasian*: who was appointed emperor in Judea."[185]

These words of Josephus tell of an expectation of the Jews on account of an oracle that a Messiah would help them in their war against Rome. It is possible that Josephus meant the following words of Ps 72: 8 and 11 about an unnamed Jewish king: "He shall have dominion also from sea to sea, from the River to the ends of the earth. (…) Yes, all kings shall fall down before him. All nations shall serve him."

This oracle, according to Josephus, actually foretold the victory by Emperor Vespasian who became the Roman emperor while leading the Roman army in Judea during the Jewish War of AD 66–70. A superficial reading of this oracle seems to confirm his explanation because Vespasian did rule over a vast empire.

Glenn Miller compiled a long list of quotations from docu-

---

[185] Josephus, *Wars*, VI/5/4.

ments dating from the last two centuries BC, as well as records from the first century AD, in which the Jewish expectation of a future Messiah was clearly expressed. In some texts, he is depicted as a human being, while other texts regard him as a heavenly figure, such as the "Son of Man" in the book of Daniel or the "Chosen One" of 2 Enoch. Miller quoted from faulty Greek translations of the Old Testament where certain passages were deliberately changed to point to a future Messiah. Miller also quoted from the Old Testament apocryphal books, Jewish Pseudepigrapha (such as 1 Enoch), documents from the Dead Sea Scrolls, and authors such as Philo of Alexandria and Josephus. These quotations demonstrate how the Jews of Jesus' time yearned for a Messiah, a king from the House of David, to liberate them.[186]

The findings of the previous chapter show that the belief that the Old Testament prophecies clearly foresaw the life, death, and resurrection of Jesus of Nazareth, have no foundation. One must ask: where did this conviction come from? The answer to this question is simple: Jesus operated under the delusion that he was the promised Messiah and he convinced his followers of this belief. That that was indeed the case, was already argued in Chapter 2, but it will become still more apparent during the rest of this chapter.

The Calling of Jesus as Messiah

Jesus must have been acutely aware of the Old Testament prophecies and the expectations of his people expectations and, therefore, he deliberately acted in such a manner that it amounted to a fulfillment of these prophecies.

It is highly probable and possible that Jesus saw events coinciding with his baptism by John the Baptizer as God's calling to

---

[186] Miller, "Messianic Expectations in 1st Century Judaism."

become the savior and king of Israel (Mark 1: 9–11; Matt 3: 13–17; Luke 3: 21–22). The total solar eclipse of 24 November AD 29[187] at about 10:40 local time over Galilee[188] very probably happened when Jesus was baptized and that he saw this as an indication that God called him to become *the* Messiah. The report of this event in *Mark 1: 9–11*, the oldest complete gospel, must be quoted in full:

> "It happened in those days, that Jesus came from Nazareth of Galilee, and was baptized by John in the Jordan. Immediately coming up from the water, he saw the heavens parting, and the Spirit descending on him like a dove. A voice came out of the sky, 'You are my beloved Son, in whom I am well pleased.'"

All three synoptic gospels report that the heavens were opened directly after Jesus' baptism – most probably the stars in the sky that became visible during the day when the light of the sun was blocked by the intervening moon during the eclipse.

It has to be remembered that the ancient Israelites thought that God's heaven was directly beyond the stars and that the stars were actually angels (Neh 9: 6; Job 22: 12–14; Job 38: 4–8; Ps 104:

---

[187] Gertoux, who compiled a credible chronology of Jesus' life, also places his baptism in AD 29, although he calculated that Jesus was baptized during August (Herod the Great and Jesus, 53.

[188] Although the Gospel of Matthew states that John was baptizing at the river Jordan in the "wilderness of Judea" (Matt 3: 1), John must actually have been in Galilee to the north of Judea at that time since Herod Antipas, the ruler of Galilee, had him arrested shortly after Jesus' baptism – and that could only have happened within Herod's area of jurisdiction (Matt 14: 3; Mark 1: 14; Mark 6: 17; Luke 3: 19–20; 3: 19–20). It also appears from the chronology in the Synoptic Gospels that Jesus concentrated his ministry initially to Galilee and only appeared in Judea later.

3; Ps 148: 2–3; Isa 40: 22).[189] In other words: when the stars unexpectedly became visible during day-time it seemed as if the heaven, the abode of God and the angels, was miraculously opened.

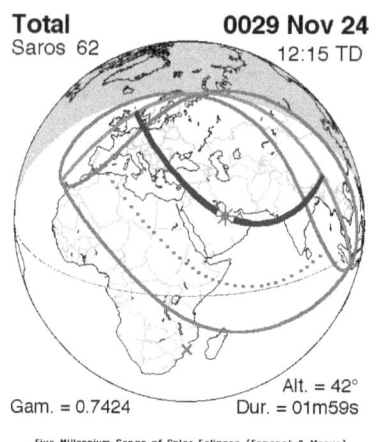

The path of the moon's shadow, where a total solar eclipse was visible, passed through the northern parts of Palestine on 24 November AD 29. The duration of totality was 2 minutes.[190]

During a solar eclipse "a pronounced fall in temperature" is experienced, due to the blocking of the rays of the sun. That causes a wind to blow from the warmer areas outside the path of the moon's shadow to the cooler areas where the heat of the sun is absent.[191]

A computerized reconstruction of the maximum extent of the almost total solar eclipse at 10: 40 local time on 24 November AD 29, as seen from Caesarea-Philippi, north of the Sea of Galilee, when almost 94% of the sun was blocked by the moon. A total eclipse would have been visible further north

---

[189] Scholtz, *The Prophecies of Revelation*, 30–41.
[190] NASA, Eclipse Website.
[191] Enc Brit, "Eclipse: sun".

That must also have been the case with the eclipse of 24 November AD 29 and people would also have noticed the sudden wind – apart from the appearance of the stars in the sky.

The Greek word for "wind", πνεῦμα (*pneuma*), is also the word used for "spirit", just as the Hebrew word for "wind" is also the word for "spirit" (רוּחַ – *ruach*). For the Jews, therefore, there was no real difference between a spirit and the wind or breath and, therefore, the gospels reported that the (Holy) Spirit "descended" upon Jesus at his baptism (Mark 1: 10; Matt 3: 16; Luke 3: 22) – while it was, in fact, only an unexpected but ordinary wind that blew.

Mark – the oldest gospel – merely reported that Jesus saw the Spirit (or the wind) descending on him *like* a dove or a pigeon (the Greek word may mean both species of birds) – not in the *form* of a dove. Luke 3: 22, though, added that "the Holy Spirit descended in a bodily form" on Jesus.

The Gospel of John (1: 32) states: "John testified, saying, 'I have seen the Spirit [πνεῦμα – *pneuma*] descending like a dove out of heaven, and it remained on him.'" This verse also compares the "Spirit" – or the "wind" – with a dove, without mentioning that a real dove was seen.

It is on account of Luke's description that illustrations of the event usually show a real dove coming down upon Jesus. But that is not what the reports in Mark and John said. They only compared the Spirit or the wind with the movement of air caused by the flapping of the bird's wings as it perches upon a person's shoulder or head. If this interpretation is correct, then Jesus would have perceived the unexpected solar eclipse and the blowing of the sudden wind as a direct message from God, declaring him to be God's "beloved Son" – in other words: the king of Israel.

It must be stressed that the only people ever called the "son of God" in the Old Testament were the kings of Israel (2 Sam 7: 14;

1 Chr 17: 13; 1 Chr 22: 10; 1 Chr 28: 6; Ps 2: 6–7, 12; Ps 89: 26–28) – except for the angels (Job 1: 6; 2: 1; 38: 8) and the people of Israel (Ex 4: 22; Deut 14: 1; Ps 82: 6; Jer 31: 9; Hos 11: 1). According to John 1: 49, the expressions "Son of God" and "king of Israel" are synonyms.

It must be stressed that the people in those days had no explanation for the occurrence of eclipses and they interpreted these as mysterious divine interventions.[192]

The Jewish newspaper Haaretz quoted Rabbi Blitz: "In Jewish tradition, a total solar eclipse is a warning to the Gentiles and a sign of judgment on the nations."[193]

That may also be how Jesus interpreted the event and he must have seen it as a confirmation of his calling to become *the* Messiah and liberator of the Jews.

We can speculate that Jesus and John planned this baptism specifically for that particular day because they, somehow or other, knew of the expected eclipse. Eshbal Ratzon of the University of Haifa has demonstrated that the so-called Astronomical Book of Enoch, part of the Dead Sea Scrolls, explained how to predict lunar and solar eclipses – something the ancient Sumerians, Babylonians, and Greeks could do.[194] It is, of course, impossible to determine whether Jesus and John knew of this book and its contents, or heard that this eclipse was predicted, but their ties with the Qumran community may have made this a possibility.

The constellations of stars that became visible around the darkened sun all proclaimed the same message to Jesus. Knowledge of the constellations was widespread in those days, as is evident from the fact that there are various allusions to Babylonian astrology

---

[192] Stephenson, "Eclipse".
[193] *Haaretz*, 19.03.2015.
[194] Ratzon, "The first Jewish Astronomers".

in the Old Testament and that most of the visions that John of Patmos had and which he described in the book of Revelation, were really descriptions of the night sky with its constellations and planets during AD 96.[195] This was also the case with many visions of Ezekiel and Daniel.

The eclipsed sun appeared just below the constellation of Ophiuchus or Serpentarius, the Snake Catcher. Ophiuchus is traditionally depicted as a man grasping a snake, the constellation of Serpens, the Serpent.

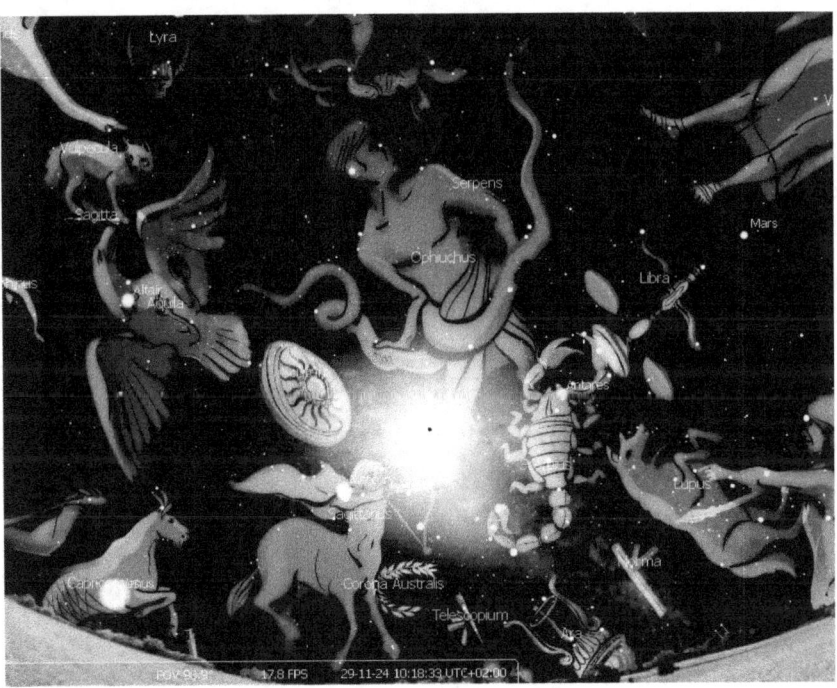

A computerized reconstruction of a part of the sky over Galilee during the solar eclipse of 24 November AD 29, showing the outlines of the stellar constellations.

According to Jewish stellar lore, the constellation of Serpens was a

---

[195] Scholtz, *The Prophecies of Revelation*, 27–41.

depiction of Satan, the Serpent that tempted Eve to eat from the forbidden fruit (Gen 3).[196]

In Job 26: 12–13 we also read:

> "He stirs up the sea with his power, and by his understanding he strikes through Rahab. By his Spirit the heavens are garnished. His hand has pierced the swift serpent."

The name "*Rahab*" (רַהַב) denotes a mythical sea monster. The Hebrew word for "serpent" is נָחָשׁ (*nachash*). It is clear that these two creatures are meant to be one and the same being that resided in "the heavens" – that is, between the stars.

Jesus would certainly have been conscious of these passages in the Hebrew Scriptures, as well as of the significance of the constellation of Serpens. He certainly would have connected that to his calling to become the savior of Israel who was destined to conquer the evil forces of Satan and paganism.

It is likely that Jesus alluded to this vision in Luke. 10: 18 –

> "He said to them, 'I saw Satan having fallen like lightning from heaven. Behold, I give you authority to tread on serpents and scorpions, and over all the power of the enemy. Nothing will in any way hurt you.'"

In the computerized reconstruction of the sky at the time of the solar eclipse, it is clear that the constellations of Serpens and Scorpius (the Scorpion) lie next to each other, just above the horizon. Both were regarded by the Jews as representations of Satan[197]. The constellations of Aquila (the Roman Eagle) and Scutum (the Roman

---

[196] Allen, *Star Names*, 375.

[197][197] Allen, *Star Names*, 362; Scholtz, *Revelation*, 189–91.

Shield) were also hovering on the horizon.[198]

From the perspective of Jesus, on the banks of the Jordan, it must have appeared as if these constellations were about to fall from heaven where they lay just above the horizon. The "lightning" that Jesus mentioned must have been the tiny sliver of the sun still visible behind the moon directly after totality had ended. It also appeared as if the Snake Catcher was trampling upon the Scorpion.

Another important constellation that became visible during the solar eclipse was Capricornus, the Goat. In Jewish stellar lore from the time of Jesus and subsequent centuries, this constellation was named גדיא (*Gadiya*, the kid goat)[199]. That reminds one of the exclamations of John the Baptist after he had baptized Jesus: "Behold, the Lamb of God, who takes away the sin of the world!" (John 1: 29). The planet Venus, the bright morning star, was at that time inside Capricornus, drawing the attention to this constellation. The Hebrew names of this planet was כוכבת (*Kokebet*, the she-star) and מַלְכַּת הַשָּׁמַיִם (*Meleket Hasshamayim*, the Queen of Heaven).

Libra, the Scales (Hebrew: מאזנים – *moznayim*), a symbol of justice[200], lay next to Serpens and Scorpius – conveying the idea that all satanic forces were to be judged by God.

Directly below the occluded sun the constellation of Corona Australis, the Southern Crown or Garland, a symbol of kingship or victory,[201] was visible. This garland was usually associated with the adjacent constellation of Sagittarius, the Archer, usually regarded as a conquering warrior[202] – another symbol of the Messiah.

All these celestial phenomena would have held a powerful

---

[198] Allen, *Star Names*, 57.
[199] Jacobus, "The Zodiac", 318, 323.
[200] Allen, *Star Names*, 273.
[201] Allen, *Star Names*, 172.
[202] Allen, *Star Names*, 352.

message: Jesus, who was baptized on that day, was destined and anointed by God to be the "beloved Son" of God, the Messiah and king of Israel, liberator of his people and conqueror of the Romans. It was, as it were, as if a voice from heaven proclaimed this message.

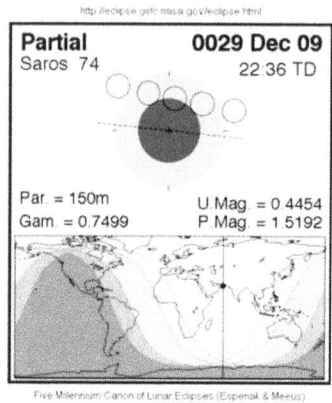

The white areas on this map show the parts of the world where the partial lunar eclipse of 9 December AD 29 was visible. The white circles in the top part of the illustration show how much of the moon was covered by the earth's shadow (the larger dark circle).[203]

It is noteworthy that a partial lunar eclipse occurred during the early evening of 9 December AD 29 – exactly a fortnight after the solar eclipse. Jesus must have been wandering through the desert at that time, struggling with demonic forces (Matt 4: 1–11). Jesus – and those who witnessed the solar eclipse at his baptism – must have seen this partial lunar eclipse as yet another confirmation that he was destined to become *the* Messiah and that delivery from the hated pagan Romans was due.

What is remarkable about this eclipse, is that the darkened moon lay within the constellation of Gemini and next to the planet Saturn. Gemini, The Twins, with its two bright stars, Castor and Pollux, reminded the Jews of Esau and Jacob, the twin sons of Isaac.[204] Another name for Jacob was Israel (Gen 32: 28).

Shlomo Sela points out, furthermore, that "a special link

---

[203] NASA, Eclipse Website.
[204] Orlov, *The Atoning Dyad*, 27.

[exists] between Saturn and Saturday, the holiest day of the week for the Jews". The Hebrew name for this planet is שבתאי (*Shabtai*) – a name connected to the word for "Shabath" – just as there is a link between Saturn and Saturday in the English language. Therefore, Saturn can be seen "as the planet in charge of the Jews."[205]

The eclipsed moon within Gemini and next to Saturn would have given Jesus the message that something special was due to happen to the Jews while they watched how their enemies would be darkened or vanquished with their special star protecting them.

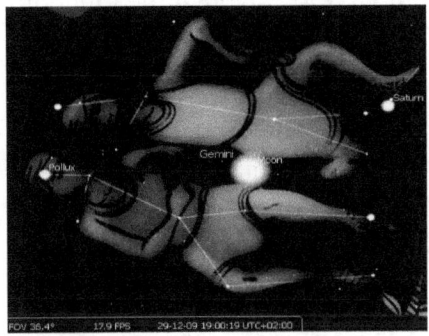

A computerized recreation of the eclipsed moon within the constellation of Gemini with its principal stars Castor and Pollux during the early evening of 9 December AD 29. Saturn is also part of the scene.

Jesus departed for the desert after his baptism and during this time he tried to make sense of the events surrounding his baptism. He reportedly experienced temptations by Satan, but afterwards was cared for by angels (Mark 1: 9–12; Matt 3: 13–4: 11; Luke 3: 21–22; 4: 1–13).

This period of forty days must be greatly exaggerated. Nobody can survive more than ten days without water, especially not in a desert environment in which Jesus experienced these temptations.[206] The period of forty days is rather a symbolic number,

---

[205] Sela, "Saturn and the Jews".
[206] Craighead and Nemeroff, *The Corsini Encyclopedia of Psychology and Behavioral Science*, 1587; Swaab, *Wij zijn ons Brein,* 247; Enc Brit, "Dehydration".

a reminder of the forty years the Israelites had spent in the desert after escaping from slavery in Egypt. It is also a reminder of Moses who reportedly stayed forty days on the mountain without eating and drinking, while receiving God's commandments (Ex 34: 28).

Anyway, if Jesus fasted for an extended period and consequently suffered from malnutrition and dehydration, it is very possible and highly probable that he would have experienced hallucinations with a religious content, in which he struggled with demonic forces, had encounters with angels and which he regarded as a confirmation of his calling from God to establish the kingdom of God in Israel.

The "angels" who cared for him after Satan had left were quite likely desert dwellers who found the disoriented, dehydrated, and undernourished Jesus somewhere in the desert and nursed him back to health.

These experiences must have been so real for Jesus that he afterwards told his friends and disciples about it – and the compilers of the gospels must have collected these stories from people who heard it from Jesus or from his friends or disciples.

It is now necessary to investigate what the various authors of the New Testament reported about what Jesus said about himself as the Israelite Messiah and how they interpreted certain passages from the Old Testament in support of the notion that the Hebrew Scriptures contained prophecies about specifically Jesus of Nazareth.

JOHN THE BAPTIST PREDICTED

The gospels more than once declared that the work of the prophet John the Baptist, as the forerunner of Jesus, was predicted in the Old Testament:

The Messiah would be Preceded by a Forerunner
John 1: 23

> He [John the Baptist] said, "I am the voice of one crying in the wilderness, 'Make straight the way of the Lord,' as Isaiah the prophet said."

Mark 1: 2–12 (Matt 3: 1–12; Luke 3: 1–18)

> 2. As it is written in the prophets, "Behold, I send my messenger before your face, Who will prepare your way before you.
> 3. The voice of one crying in the wilderness, 'Make ready the way of the Lord, Make his paths straight.'"
> 4. John came baptizing in the wilderness and preaching the baptism of repentance for forgiveness of sins.
> 5. There went out to him all the country of Judea, and all those of Jerusalem. They were baptized by him in the Jordan river, confessing their sins.
> 6. John was clothed with camel's hair and a leather belt around his loins. He ate locusts and wild honey.
> 7. He preached, saying, "After me comes he who is mightier than I, the thong of whose sandals I am not worthy to stoop down and loosen.
> 8. I baptized you in water, but he will baptize you in the Holy Spirit."

The prophecy quoted in these passages comes from Isa 40: 3–4 –

> "The voice of one who cries, prepare you in the wilderness the way of YHWH; make level in the desert a highway for our God. Every valley shall be exalted, and every mountain and

hill shall be made low; and the uneven shall be made level, and the rough places a plain."

Isaiah 40 is the first chapter of the second part of Isaiah, written during the Babylonian Exile. The people of Judah in exile were given the promise that their sins were forgiven, that Jerusalem would be rebuilt and that they must welcome YHWH in their midst.

This prophecy was meant to comfort the people of that time – not people who would live centuries later. Isaiah certainly did not have John the Baptist in mind when he wrote his prophecy, but both John and Mark erroneously interpreted it as pertaining to John as a herald for Jesus.

Christ's Forerunner would Come in the Spirit of Elijah
Matthew 11: 10–15

10.	For this is he, of whom it is written, 'Behold, I send my messenger before your face, who will prepare your way before you.'
11.	Most assuredly I tell you, among those who are born of women there has not arisen anyone greater than John the Baptizer; yet he who is least in the Kingdom of Heaven is greater than he.
12.	From the days of John the Baptizer until now, the Kingdom of Heaven suffers violence, and the violent take it by force.
13.	For all the prophets and the law prophesied until John.
14.	If you are willing to receive it, this is Elijah, who is to come.
15.	He who has ears to hear, let him hear.

Jesus referred to the last two verses of Malachi (ch 4: 5–6) –

"See, I will send the prophet Elijah to you before that great and dreadful day of the Lord comes. He will turn the hearts of the parents to their children, and the hearts of the children to their parents; or else I will come and strike the land with total destruction."

When Malachi referred to Elijah, whose name means "YHWH is my God", he meant himself as a successor of Elijah – not another wild prophet of centuries ahead. In Mal 3: 1 one reads that God called as prophet "my messenger" or "my angel", which is exactly the name of Malachi in Hebrew. In other words: Malachi saw himself as the successor of Elijah. Therefore, Jesus had it wrong when he declared that Malachi predicted the work of John the Baptist as a resurrected or reincarnated Elijah.

THE BIRTH OF JESUS OF NAZARETH

According to the gospels, events connected to the birth of Jesus of Nazareth were foreseen by the Old Testament.

The Massacre in Bethlehem
Matt 2: 16–23

16.	Then Herod, when he saw that he was mocked by the wise men, was exceedingly angry, and sent forth, and killed all the male children who were in Bethlehem, and in all the surrounding countryside, from two years old and under, according to the exact time which he had learned from the wise men.
17.	Then that which was spoken by Jeremiah the prophet was fulfilled, saying,
18.	"A voice was heard in Ramah, Lamentation, weeping and great mourning, Rachel weeping for her children; She wouldn't be comforted, because they are no more."

> 19. But when Herod was dead, behold, an angel of the Lord appeared in a dream to Joseph in Egypt, saying,
> 20. "Arise and take the young child and his mother, and go into the land of Israel, for those who sought the young child's life are dead."
> 21. He arose and took the young child and his mother, and came into the land of Israel.
> 22. But when he heard that Archelaus was reigning over Judea in the place of his father, Herod, he was afraid to go there. Being warned in a dream, he withdrew into the region of Galilee,
> 23. and came and lived in a city called Nazareth; that it might be fulfilled which was spoken through the prophets: "He will be called a Nazorean."

Matthew believed that Jer 31: 15 foretold that King Herod the Great would have all boys below two years of age in Bethlehem slaughtered. No independent record of this murderous campaign exists and it is certainly a piece of fiction, although Herod was notorious for his cruelty and paranoia. For instance, he murdered his wife and some of his children when he distrusted their loyalty.[207]

Nevertheless, in Jer 31: 15 we read the following (and it is quoted by Matthew as proof for his story):

> "A voice is heard in Ramah, lamentation, and bitter weeping, Rachel weeping for her children; she refuses to be comforted for her children, because they are no more."

When one reads the whole chapter in Jeremiah, it appears that he

---

[207] Enc Brit, "Herod".

referred to the laments of the Jews after the Babylonians had sacked Jerusalem in 586 BC. Jeremiah never intended his words to be applied to the time of Herod the Great, almost six centuries later.

It must be concluded that Matthew invented stories about Jesus to fit his interpretation of certain prophecies or statements from the Old Testament. He seems to have argued that since certain prophecies were to be found in the Scriptures, they simply must have been fulfilled during Jesus' life.

Matthew's statement that there was another prophecy that the Messiah would reside in Nazareth and be called a Nazorean, is unfounded. The fact that Jesus is called a Nazorean in this passage, simply means that his family belonged to the sect of the Nazoreans or Essenes – as has been pointed out in Chapter 2.

Jesus is often called a Nazorean in the gospels and Acts (Matt 2: 23; 26:71; Luke 18: 37, John 18: 5, 7; 19: 19; Acts 2: 22; 3: 6; 4: 10; 6: 14; 22: 8; and 26: 9). In other words: Jesus was a member of the sect of the Essenes.

The name "Nazorean" should not be confused with the name of "Nazarene" – as happened in most translations of the Bible. Saint Jerome, the translator of the Bible into Latin, the Vulgate, made this mistake and he used the word "Nazarenus" every time he encountered the Greek word Ναζωραῖος (*Nazoraios*) – except for Matt 2: 23. His example was followed by other translators.

However, the authoritative Greek–English dictionary of Arndt and Gingrich explains that Ναζωραῖος (*Nazoraios* – Nazorean) and Ναζαρηνός (*Nazarenos* – Nazarene) are two totally different and unrelated words and that there is no linguistic connection between them. The word "Nazarene" is used for people from the village of Nazareth where Jesus grew up. The name "Nazarene" was often used of Jesus and he was, accordingly, sometimes called "Jesus of Nazareth" or "Jesus the Nazarene"

(Mark 1: 24; Mark 10: 47; Mark 14: 67; Mark 16: 6; Luke 4: 34 and 24: 19).

The best proof that the names "Nazarene" and "Nazorean" are not synonyms or two versions of the same word, is found in Acts 24: 5 where Paul is called "a ringleader of the sect of the Nazarenes", according to most translations. This translation does not make sense. The sect in question certainly didn't consist of people from Nazareth only – they came from Jerusalem and other parts of Judea and Galilee. Paul can by no stretch of imagination be called a "Nazarene", a native of Nazareth. It makes much more sense to regard this sect to be the "Nazoreans" – in other words, Essenes – as stated explicitly in the Greek text and which is usually given a wrong translation by transforming "Nazoreans" into "Nazarenes".

The prophecies alluded to by Matthew in the passage quoted above had no bearing on Jesus of Nazareth whatsoever.

The Virgin Birth, and the Name of Immanuel
Matt 1: 22–23

22.	Now all this has happened, that it might be fulfilled which was spoken by the Lord through the prophet, saying,
23.	"Behold, the virgin shall be with child, and shall bring forth a son. They shall call his name Immanuel;" which is, being interpreted, "God with us."

Matthew, as well as Luke 1: 35, thought that Jesus would be born from a virgin on account of what they read in the Greek translation of Isaiah 7: 14 –

> "Therefore the Lord himself shall give you a sign; behold, a virgin shall conceive in the womb, and shall bring forth a son, and thou shalt call his name Emmanuel."

The Greek translation made a mistake, though, as has been demonstrated in the previous chapter. The original Hebrew did not mention a virgin (Greek: ἡ παρθένος – *he parthenos*), only "the young woman" or "the maiden" (Hebrew: הָעַלְמָה – *ha-almah*).

Matthew often thought that he had discovered prophecies about the Messiah in the Old Testament and decided that something like that must have happened in the life of Jesus because it had been predicted. Therefore, he invented episodes in the life of Jesus to fit those purported prophecies in the belief that they simply must have happened.[208] He used the erroneous Greek translation of Isa 7: 14 to convert Jesus' mother into a virgin. This passage in Isaiah can, therefore, not be seen as a prediction that Jesus would be born from a virgin.[209]

Joseph is often called Jesus' father (Matt 1: 17; 13: 55; Luke 3: 23; 4: 22; John 1: 45; 6: 42). According to Deut 22: 20–21, an unmarried pregnant girl had to be stoned to death – which did not happen to the supposedly pregnant unmarried Mary. If Jesus was really born out of wedlock, he would have been treated as an outcast in terms of Deut 23: 2, which stipulates that persons born out of wedlock may not be tolerated in the Israelite community. Jesus was, in fact, a very popular teacher whose parents must have been married in the normal way.

The Messiah in Egypt
Matt 2: 14–15

14.	He [Joseph] arose and took the young child and his mother by night, and departed into Egypt,

---

[208] Pretorius, *The Gospels,* 389, 401, 403.
[209] Pretorius, *The Gospels,* 391–395, 457–460.

> 15. and was there until the death of Herod; that it might be fulfilled which was spoken by the Lord through the prophet, saying, "Out of Egypt I called my son."

The purported prophecy that Jesus stayed in Egypt with his parents was taken from Hosea 11: 1 –

> "When Israel was a child, then I loved him, and called my son out of Egypt."

There can be not the slightest doubt that the words in Hosea had no connection whatsoever with the expected Messiah. It was the people of Israel, called the "son" of God, who were called out of Egypt where they were held as slaves, many centuries before the time of Jesus.

The Messiah Born in Bethlehem
Matt 2: 4–6

> 4. Gathering together all the chief priests and scribes of the people, he [Herod] asked them where the Christ would be born.
> 5. They said to him, "In Bethlehem of Judea, for thus it is written through the prophet,
> 6. 'You Bethlehem, land of Judah, are in no way least among the princes of Judah: For out of you shall come forth a governor, Who shall shepherd my people, Israel'".

The prophecy quoted above appears in Micah 5: 2 –

> "But you, Bethlehem Ephrathah, which are little to be among the thousands of Judah, out of you shall one come forth to

me that is to be ruler in Israel; whose goings forth are from of old, from everlasting."

These words may certainly be regarded as messianic in character. The messiah meant here was the king of the house of David, which had its ancestral home in Bethlehem. Micah wrote his book during the last half of the 8th century BC, during the reigns of Jotham, Ahaz, and Hezekiah, kings of Judah (Mic 1: 1) – two centuries after the time of David and two centuries before the Babylonian Exile. The international scene was uncertain in those days and Micah was confident that the kings of Judah would keep their country safe.[210]

In other words, the prophecy in Micah cannot be applied to the birthplace of Jesus. It is, in any case, doubtful whether Jeus was really born in Bethlehem. If there was indeed a census at the time of his birth (Luke 2: 1–3), his parents would have been counted at their usual place of residence, not at a legendary ancestral home town.[211]

THE MINISTRY OF JESUS

Jesus' Ministry would Begin in Galilee
Matt 4:12–17

12.	Now when Jesus heard that John was delivered up, he withdrew into Galilee.
13.	Leaving Nazareth, he came and lived in Capernaum, which is by the sea, in the region of Zebulun and Naphtali,
14.	that it might be fulfilled which was spoken through Isaiah the prophet, saying,
15.	"The land of Zebulun and the land of Naphtali, Toward the sea, beyond the Jordan, Galilee of the Gentiles,

---

[210] Enc Brit., "Nicah, Book of".
[211] Enc Brit., "Census".

> 16. The people who sat in darkness saw a great light, To those who sat in the region and shadow of death, to them did light spring up."

It does seem from the gospels that Jesus established his headquarters for his campaign to become the king of Israel in the Galilean town of Capernaum.[212] According to Matthew, this was the fulfilment of a prophecy in Isa 9: 1–2 –

> "But there shall be no gloom to her who was in anguish. In the former time he brought into contempt the land of Zebulun and the land of Naphtali; but in the latter time has he made it glorious, by the way of the sea, beyond the Jordan, Galilee of the nations. The people who walked in darkness have seen a great light: those who lived in the land of the shadow of death, on them has the light shined."

It seems as if this prophecy was written more or less at the time when the Assyrians conquered the northern Israelite kingdom in 721 BC, about twenty years after Isaiah started his career as a prophet. The "gloom", "anguish", "shadow of death" and the "darkness" in this passage seem to refer to these perilous times when the northern parts of the kingdom of Judah and Galilee were threatened by the Assyrian army.

Isaiah gave his people the assurance that Judah would not fall and that God would protect them.

This passage cannot be applied to the ministry of Jesus, many centuries afterwards. Matthew simply sought a passage in the Old Testament that he could twist to look like a prediction of Jesus' work in Galilee.

---

[212] Pretorius, *The Gospels*, 192.

Jesus Taught in Parables
Matt 13: 34–35

> 34. Jesus spoke all these things in parables to the multitudes; and without a parable, he didn't speak to them,
> 35. that it might be fulfilled which was spoken through the prophet, saying, "I will open my mouth in parables; I will utter things hidden from the foundation of the world."

The words quoted by Matthew were not spoken by a prophet but by the poet of Ps 78:1–2:

> "Hear my law, my people. Turn your ears to the words of my mouth. I will open my mouth in a parable. I will utter dark sayings of old."

Matthew did not quote the Psalm from the Hebrew, but from the Greek translation, which differs from the Hebrew. This Psalm is introduced as "A contemplation by Asaph." This poet merely wished to teach his audience some spiritual lessons in verse form by using parables. He never thought that the future Messiah would do the same. His quoted words, therefore, do not qualify as a prophecy.

Matthew apparently scoured the Old Testament to find "prophecies" that he could apply to the ministry of Jesus.

Christ's Parables Fell on Deaf Ears
Matt 13: 13–15

> 13. Therefore I speak to them in parables, because seeing they don't see, and hearing, they don't hear, neither do they understand.

> 14. In them the prophecy of Isaiah is fulfilled, which says, 'By hearing you will hear, and will in no way understand; Seeing you will see, and will in no way perceive:
> 15. For this people's heart has grown callous, their ears are dull of hearing, their eyes they have closed; or else perhaps they might perceive with their eyes, hear with their ears, understand with their heart, and should turn again; and I would heal them.'

This passage is quoted from Isaiah 6: 9–10 –

> "He [God] said, 'Go, and tell this people, hear you indeed, but don't understand; and see you indeed, but don't perceive. Make the heart of this people fat, and make their ears heavy, and shut their eyes; lest they see with their eyes, and hear with their ears, and understand with their heart, and turn again, and be healed."

Matthew's quoted Isaiah rather freely. The words in Isaiah are part of the scene where he saw God on his throne, who called him to become a prophet. There are certainly some parallels between the experiences of Isaiah and Jesus. Both encountered people who didn't understand their messages, but the words in Isaiah were certainly never meant to be a prophecy about the future Messiah.

Jesus Performed Miracles
Matt 11: 2–6

> 2. Now when John heard in the prison the works of Christ, he sent two of his disciples
> 3. and said to him, "Are you he who comes, or should we look for another?"

4.	Jesus answered them, "Go and tell John the things which you hear and see:
5.	the blind receive their sight, the lame walk, the lepers are cleansed, the deaf hear, the dead are raised up, and the poor have good news preached to them.
6.	Blessed is he, whoever finds no occasion for stumbling in me."

According to Matthew, Jesus quoted from Isaiah 35: 5–6 when he answered the disciples of John the Baptist, who wanted the assurance that Jesus was really the Messiah. Isaiah wrote:

> "Then the eyes of the blind shall be opened, and the ears of the deaf shall be unstopped. Then shall the lame man leap as a hart, and the tongue of the mute shall sing; for in the wilderness shall waters break out, and streams in the desert."

The words of Isaiah are indeed an apt description of the ministry of Jesus, as described in the gospels. However, Isaiah certainly did not predict how Jesus would go about a few centuries after his time. This whole chapter is a description of heavenly bliss, the conditions in the restored Paradise that the faithful would inherit.

Jesus the Redeemer of the Gentiles
Matt 12:15–21

15.	Jesus, perceiving that, withdrew from there. Great multitudes followed him; and he healed them all,
16.	and charged them that they should not make him known:
17.	that it might be fulfilled which was spoken through Isaiah the prophet, saying,

> 18. "Behold, my servant whom I have chosen; My beloved in whom my soul is well pleased: I will put my Spirit on him, He will declare judgment to the Gentiles.
> 19. He will not strive, nor shout; neither will anyone hear his voice in the streets.
> 20. He won't break a bruised reed, he won't quench a smoking flax, until he sends forth judgment to victory.
> 21. In his name, the Gentiles will hope."

As was his custom, Matthew found pronouncements in the Old Testament to apply to Jesus. In this case, he quoted extensively and freely from Isa 42: 1–4. Matthew thought that Jesus' ministry was a fulfilment of the following prophecy:

1. "Behold, my servant, whom I uphold; my chosen, in whom my soul delights: I have put my Spirit on him; he will bring forth justice to the Gentiles.
2. He will not cry, nor lift up his voice, nor cause it to be heard in the street.
3. A bruised reed will he not break, and a dimly burning wick will he not quench: he will bring forth justice in truth.
4. He will not fail nor be discouraged, until he have set justice in the earth; and the isles shall wait for his law."

The question is: who is this "servant" of the Lord? Is it the Messiah who was due to come centuries later?

It is clear from verses 19 and 22 of this chapter that the nation of Israel, the people of God, was the "servant" mentioned in the first verse – and not some or other future messianic figure.

The words from Isaiah quoted by Matthew, albeit with some alterations, seem to describe the ministry of Jesus accurately, but the words of Isaiah were only fulfilled in Jesus in a very indirect way.

Jesus Liberated the Captives
Luke 4: 16–21

16.	He came to Nazareth, where he had been brought up. He entered, as was his custom, into the synagogue on the Sabbath day, and stood up to read.
17.	The book of the prophet Isaiah was handed to him. He opened the book, and found the place where it was written,
18.	"The Spirit of the Lord is on me, Because he anointed me to preach good news to the poor. He has sent me to heal the brokenhearted, to proclaim release to the captives, recovering of sight to the blind, to deliver those who are crushed,
19.	And to proclaim the acceptable year of the Lord."
20.	He closed the book, gave it back to the attendant, and sat down. The eyes of all in the synagogue were fastened on him.
21.	He began to tell them, "Today, this Scripture has been fulfilled in your hearing."

The passage that Jesus read during his sermon in Nazareth came from Isaiah 61:1 –

> "The Spirit of the Lord YHWH is on me; because YHWH has anointed me to preach good news to the humble; he has sent me to bind up the broken-hearted, to proclaim liberty to the captives, and the opening [of the prison] to those who are bound; to proclaim the year of YHWH's favor, and the day of vengeance of our God; to comfort all who mourn."

This passage in Luke was adapted from Mark 6: 1–6 and expanded with material unique to Luke. In Mark this episode was placed at a later stage in Jesus' career, but Luke chose to describe it as the start of Jesus' ministry after his baptism and temptation in the desert, although he mentioned that Jesus had already healed sick people in Capernaum.

Christ Driving the Merchants from the Temple – Albrecht Dürer, 1511

According to Luke, Jesus held a sermon in the synagogue after having read a passage from Isaiah 61, which he applied to himself. This passage is, indeed, a fitting description of how Jesus saw his own career. It is, of course, impossible to determine whether Jesus really read this part of Isaiah or whether Luke made this story up as an introduction to his description of Jesus' ministry from that point on.

However, it must be remembered that this part of Isaiah was written after the end of the Babylonian Exile. The captives mentioned here are not – as Jesus meant – captives of sin or victims of oppression, but people who were held as prisoners of war or hostages by the Babylonians and who were released after Babylonia had been conquered by Persia.

The Foundation Stone
Mark 12: 10–11

10.	Haven't you even read this Scripture: 'The stone which the builders rejected, The same was made the head of the

> corner.
> 11. This was from the Lord, It is marvelous in our eyes'?"

Jesus quoted from Ps 118: 22 and applied it to himself, identifying himself as the corner stone of Israel. The words in this Psalm are as follows:

> "The stone which the builders rejected has become the head of the corner."

This foundation stone has nothing to do with a future Messiah. A careful reading of the whole Psalm reveals that God's everlasting love and kindness are compared with a solid and fixed corner stone.

The Question about the Messiah
Mark 12: 35–37 (Matt 22: 41–46; Luke 20: 41–44)

> 35. Jesus responded, as he taught in the temple, "How is it that the scribes say that the Christ is the son of David?
> 36. For David himself said in the Holy Spirit, 'The Lord said to my Lord, Sit at my right hand, Until I make your enemies the footstool of your feet.'
> 37. Therefore David himself calls him Lord, so how can he be his son?"

The Jewish teachers of the Law expected that the Messiah would be a descendant of King David, who was a mighty warrior. The Messiah was, therefore, supposed to be a warrior as well. Jesus tried to demonstrate, though, with a quotation from Ps 110: 1 that the Messiah would be more than David's son because David called him "Lord" or "Master", somebody who would conquer all evil forces. The relevant verse from Ps 110 is as follows:

"[A Psalm] of David. The Lord said to my lord, Be seated at my right hand, till I put all those who are against you under your feet."

Jesus saw it as his task not only to restore David's kingdom, but also to deliver his people from all evil forces, including evil spirits and false leaders.

The use by Jesus of Ps 110 is, though, questionable (if reported correctly). The "lord" mentioned in the first verse of this Psalm is none other than the Israelite king from the time of David, who received the promise that he would prevail over all of Israel's enemies. This king is also called "a priest forever in the order of Melchizedek" (verse 4) This Melchizedek was the king of Salem (Jerusalem) in the time of Abraham, as well as a priest of the High God of the Canaanites (Gen 14: 18–20). His name means "King of Righteousness". Melchizedek's priesthood had nothing to do with the Israelite priesthood of the temple in Jerusalem. David, therefore, saw himself in his capacity of the Israelite king as a successor of Melchizedek of earlier centuries and he certainly never had Jesus as Messiah in mind when composing this Psalm.

Jesus' words: "Therefore David himself calls him Lord, so how can he be his [own] son?", does not make sense because David didn't mention a descendant or the Messiah in Ps 110.

Jesus' Triumphant Entry into Jerusalem
John 12: 12–19

12.	On the next day a great multitude had come to the feast when they heard that Jesus was coming to Jerusalem,
13.	they took the branches of the palm trees, and went out to meet him, and cried out, "Hosanna! Blessed is he who comes in the name of the Lord, the King of Israel!"

14.	Jesus, having found a young donkey, sat on it. As it is written,
15.	"Don't be afraid, daughter of Zion. Behold, your King comes, sitting on a donkey's colt."
16.	His disciples didn't understand these things at first, but when Jesus was glorified, then they remembered that these things were written about him, and that they had done these things to him.
17.	The multitude therefore that was with him when he called Lazarus out of the tomb, and raised him from the dead, was testifying.
18.	For this cause also the multitude went and met him, because they heard that he had done this sign.
19.	The Pharisees therefore said among themselves, "See how you accomplish nothing. Behold, the world has gone after him."

Jesus thought that the time was ripe for him to claim the Jewish throne. To fulfil a prophecy of Zecheriah (ch 9: 9–10) that the Messiah would arrive on a donkey, Jesus deliberately pro-cured an ass to sit on, instead of entering the city on foot.

The crowd was jubilant, waved branches and yelled: "Hosanna! Blessed is he who comes in the name of the Lord, the King of Israel!" The religious authorities were understandably alarmed by this event.

No information was given on how the crowds knew that Jesus was to enter Jerusalem. The news of his imminent entry into the city must have been spread by his disciples and other supporters on his request. That was, of course before the time of TV announcements and communication through social media. Jesus' followers did a good job with the result that the crowds lined the road along which Jesus was expected to arrive from Bethany to the south-east of the city.

The Triumphant Entry int Jerusalem
Mark 11: 1–11 (Matt21: 1–11; Luke 19: 28–40)

1.	When they drew near to Jerusalem, to Bethsphage and Bethany, at the Mount of Olives, he sent two of his disciples,
2.	and said to them, "Go your way into the village that is opposite you. Immediately as you enter into it, you will find a colt tied, on which no one has sat. Untie him, and bring him.
3.	If anyone asks you, 'Why are you doing this?' say, 'The Lord needs him;' and immediately he will send him back here."
4.	They went away, and found a colt tied at the door outside in the open street, and they untied him.
5.	Some of those who stood there asked them, "What are you doing, untying the colt?"
6.	They said to them just as Jesus had said, and they let them go.
7.	They brought the colt to Jesus, and threw their garments on him, and Jesus sat on him.
8.	Many spread their garments on the way, and others were cutting down branches from the trees, and spreading them on the road.
9.	Those who went in front, and those who followed, cried, "Hosanna! Blessed is he who comes in the name of the Lord!

> 10. Blessed is the kingdom of our father David that is coming in the name of the Lord! Hosanna in the highest!"
> 11. Jesus entered into the temple in Jerusalem. When he had looked around at everything, it being now evening, he went out to Bethany with the twelve.

The story in the Synoptic Gospels agree essentially with John's report of the event. There can be no doubt: Jesus planned his triumphant entry into Jerusalem on the back of a donkey to demonstrate that he saw himself as the legitimate king of Israel. He made sure that a donkey would be waiting for him at a predetermined spot so that he could play the part of the Messiah, the king of Israel, as foretold by the prophet Zecheriah (ch 9: 9–10).

Jesus on the donkey – Fresco in the Theotokos Church, Bitola, Republic of North Macedonia

"Rejoice greatly, daughter of Zion; shout, daughter of Jerusalem: behold, your king comes to you; he is just, and having salvation; lowly, and riding on a donkey, even on a colt the foal of a donkey. I will cut off the chariot from Ephraim, and the horse from Jerusalem; and the battle bow shall be cut off; and he shall speak peace to the nations: and his dominion shall be from sea to sea, and from the River to the ends of the earth."

The crowd was waiting for him and greeted him as their king. They clearly understood his symbolic act of riding upon an ass. They followed him into Jerusalem, spreading their clothes on the road and waving branches broken from the trees. They cheered Jesus on as the son of David and the next king of Israel.

It has been shown in the previous chapter that the prophecy in Zecheriah cannot be applied to Jesus. The king on the back of an ass was none other than YHWH Himself who would appear as the judge on Judgement Day.

A Prophet like Moses
John 5: 45–47

45.	"Don't think that I will accuse you to the Father. There is one who accuses you, even Moses, on whom you have set your hope.
46.	For if you believed Moses, you would believe me; for he wrote about me.
47.	But if you don't believe his writings, how will you believe my words?"

Jesus provided no details of what Moses purportedly wrote about him. It is possible that he alluded to Deut 18: 15–16 –

> "YHWH your God will raise up to you a prophet from the midst of you, of your brothers, like me; to him you shall listen; according to all that you desired of YHWH your God in Horeb in the day of the assembly, saying, Let me not hear again the voice of YHWH my God, neither let me see this great fire any more, that I not die."

The book of Deuteronomy was only compiled during the last decades of the monarchy of Judea and finalized after the Babylonian

Exile.[213] At that time, the Judeans were rebuilding their temple and their lives and often felt bewildered. They needed spiritual leaders, including a prophetic messiah, somebody anointed by God. There were various prophets active during the time of the Israelite monarchies, as well as after the Exile. Anyone of them could have been meant in this passage from Deuteronomy and it is highly unlikely that the author(s) of Deuteronomy thought specifically of Jesus of Nazareth as a messianic prophet. They rather thought about somebody in their own time, a few centuries before Jesus' time.

The Messiah would be a Stone that Causes People to Stumble
1 Peter 2: 7–8

7.	For you therefore who believe is the honor, but for such as are disobedient, "The stone which the builders rejected, has become the chief cornerstone,"
8.	and, "A stone of stumbling, and a rock of offense." For they stumble at the word, being disobedient, whereunto also they were appointed.

Peter quotes freely from Isaiah 8: 14 –

> "He shall be for a sanctuary; but for a stone of stumbling and for a rock of offense to both the houses of Israel, for a gin and for a snare to the inhabitants of Jerusalem."

Isaiah certainly did not say anything about the future Messiah. The "stone of stumbling" would be YHWH Himself who would judge his people.

---

[213] Boshoff *et al.*, *Geskiedenis,* 138–40.

THE PASSION OF JESUS

Thirty Pieces of Silver
Matthew 27: 3–10

> 3, Then Judas, who betrayed him, when he saw that he was condemned, repented himself, and brought back the thirty pieces of silver to the chief priests and elders,
>
> 4. saying, "I have sinned in that I betrayed innocent blood." But they said, "What is that to us? You see to it."
>
> 5. He threw down the pieces of silver in the sanctuary, and departed. He went away and hanged himself.
>
> 6. The chief priests took the pieces of silver, and said, "It is not lawful to put them into the treasury, since it is the price of blood."
>
> 7. They took counsel, and bought with them the potter's field, to bury strangers in.
>
> 8. Therefore that field was called "The Field of Blood" to this day.
>
> 9. Then that which was spoken through Jeremiah the prophet was fulfilled, saying, "They took the thirty pieces of silver, the price of him who was priced, whom some of the children of Israel did price,
>
> 10. and they gave them for the potter's field, as the Lord commanded me."

According to Israeli Judge Chaim Cohn, an expert on ancient Jewish law, the story of how Judas betrayed Jesus and felt sorry about it afterwards, does not ring totally true. He was made into a scapegoat by the gospel authors to vilify the Jews as the killers of Jesus and to exonerate the Romans who were the real killers of Jesus.[214] If Judas was really this dishonest and treacherous villain, one would have expected Jesus to have gotten rid of him long before this time.

It seems likely that Matthew, as he often did, found a passage in the Old Testament, which looked like a prophecy regarding the Messiah and he applied it to Jesus by inventing an episode to fit the supposed prophecy. He found something in the book of Zechariah (ch 11: 12–13) that he could use to build a story (which differs substantially from the story of Judas' demise as told in Acts 1: 16–20).

> "I said to them, If you think good, give me my hire; and if not, forbear. So they weighed for my hire thirty [pieces] of silver. YHWH said to me, Cast it to the potter, the goodly price that I was prized at by them. I took the thirty [pieces] of silver, and cast them to the potter, in the house of YHWH."

The passage in Zech 11 tells how YWHW appointed the prophet as a shepherd who had to feed his flock, the people of Judah and Israel. The leaders of the people, however, dismissed him and paid him merely thirty shekels for his work. He threw it away in disgust because it was such a paltry sum – the money that had to compensate the owner of a slave who was injured by a bull or an ox (Ex 21: 32).

It must be concluded that Zechariah did not tell a real story – it was a parable to illustrate how he and his message were rejected by the leaders of his people and how he gave up his efforts in despair. This sad story of Zechariah had no bearing whatsoever on the purported money received by Judas for the betrayal of Jesus.

Judas' Treachery Foretold
John 13: 15–18

---

[214] Cohn, *The Trial and Death of Jesus,* 64–67.

> 15. For I have given you an example, that you also should do as I have done to you.
> 16. Most assuredly I tell you, a servant is not greater than his lord, neither one who is sent greater than he who sent him.
> 17. If you know these things, blessed are you if you do them.
> 18. I speak not of you all. I know whom I have chosen. But that the Scripture may be fulfilled, 'He who eats bread with me has lifted up his heel against me.'

Jesus told his disciples that they should serve each other, but he also warned that one of them, who was eating with him, would harm him. This treachery, by Judas, is presented as the fulfilment of a prophecy in Ps 41: 9 –

> "Yes, my own familiar friend, in whom I trusted, who ate bread with me, has lifted up his heel against me."

David, the poet, remarked in this Psalm how a friend aimed a kick at him, but that he would keep on trusting in God, despite this humiliation. Although this description may resemble the deed of Judas, the Psalm can certainly not be seen as a prophecy about his treachery. Throughout history, there were millions of cases where somebody was stabbed in the back by a friend.

A Replacement for Judas
Acts 1: 16–20

> 16. "Brothers, it was necessary that this Scripture should be fulfilled, which the Holy Spirit spoke before by the mouth of David concerning Judas, who was guide to those who took Jesus.

> 17. For he was numbered with us, and received his portion in this ministry.
> 18. Now this man obtained a field with the reward for his wickedness, and falling headlong, his body burst open, and all his intestines gushed out.
> 19. It became known to everyone who lived in Jerusalem that in their language that field was called 'Akeldama,' that is, 'The field of blood.'
> 20. For it is written in the book of Psalms, 'Let his habitation be made desolate, Let no one dwell therein,' and, 'Let another take his office.'"

This account of Judas' end, how he had an accident, after he was rewarded by obtaining a piece of real estate, differs in most respects from the story in Matthew. That means that at least one of the two versions cannot be trusted.

However, according to Peter, whose words are quoted above, the Psalms of David foretold the fate of Judas. The following words from the Psalms are meant: "Let their habitation be desolate. Let no one dwell in their tents" (Ps 69: 25) and "Let another take his office: (Ps 109: 8).

These phrases are certainly not prophecies aimed at Judas. They were rather only handy catch phrases used by the author to illustrate the plight of Judas.

Mrs Pontia Pilata's Dream
Matt 27: 19

> While he [Pontius Pilate] was sitting on the judgment seat, his wife sent to him, saying, "Have nothing to do with that righteous man, for I have suffered many things this day in a dream because of him."

This paragraph is part of Matthew's unique material, not copied from Mark or the Q-Document. He transformed this pagan woman, the wife of Pontius Pilate, into a prophetess by having a dream about Jesus.

One can only wonder how on earth Matthew got hold of this story since the trial of Jesus took place in camera and no Jews were present to witness this incident – if it happened at all.[215]

It is also a mystery how Mrs Pontia knew who the prisoner was who was being interrogated and tried by her husband. It is, anyway, highly unlikely that she would have dared to interfere with her husband's work as a judge. It is even possible that she stayed at home in Caesarea when Pilate travelled to Jerusalem to oversee security measures during the feast.

It is, therefore, most probably a piece of fantastic pious fiction, used to convince people that, at least, some Romans were sympathetic towards Jesus and that Christianity was an appropriate religion for Roman citizens.

Jesus' Thirst
John 19: 28

> After this, Jesus, seeing that all things were now finished, that the Scripture might be fulfilled, said, "I am thirsty."

It is very likely that Jesus called out that he was thirsty while hanging on the cross with a hot sun roasting him after he hadn't slept or ate or drank anything since the previous evening. John saw that remark as the fulfillment of a prophecy. He probably had the following words in mind:

"My strength is dried up like a potsherd. My tongue sticks to

---

[215] Cohn, *The Trial and Death of Jesus,* 147–49.

the roof of my mouth. You have brought me into the dust of death" (Ps 22: 15).

An unknown poet wrote these words to express his agony centuries before Jesus' time. He merely expressed his own suffering and never meant his words to be applied to the Messiah, many centuries later.

No Bones Broken and Body Pierced
John 19:32–37

32.	Therefore the soldiers came, and broke the legs of the first, and of the other who was crucified with him;
33.	but when they came to Jesus, and saw that he was already dead, they didn't break his legs.
34.	However one of the soldiers pierced his side with a spear, and immediately blood and water came out.
35.	He who has seen has testified, and his testimony is true. He knows that he tells the truth, that you also may believe.
36.	For these things happened, that the Scripture might be fulfilled, "A bone of him will not be broken."
37.	Again another Scripture says, "They will look on him whom they pierced."

According to the narrative in John's Gospel, the soldiers did not break the crucified Jesus' legs to hasten his death, because he was deemed to be dead already. Another soldier thrust his spear into Jesus' side to make sure that he had died. John regarded these developments as the fulfilment of the following Scriptures:

> Ps 34: 20 – "He protects all of his bones. Not one of them is broken."

Psalm 22:16 – "For dogs have surrounded me. A company of evil-doers have enclosed me. They pierced my hands and my feet."

The poet of these Psalms, David, merely described how he was tormented by his foes, although God preserved him so that his bones were not broken in the process. These descripttions were certainly applicable to Jesus while he was hanging on the cross, but they can certainly not be seen as predictions of how he was crucified.

Albrecht Dürer: Christ Crucified (1505)

Jesus' Clothes Divided
John 19:23–24

> 23. Then the soldiers, when they had crucified Jesus, took his garments and made four parts, to every soldier a part; and also the coat. Now the coat was without seam, woven from the top throughout.
> 24. Then they said to one another, "Let's not tear it, but cast lots for it, whose it will be," that the Scripture might be fulfilled, which says, "They parted my garments among them, For my cloak they cast lots." Therefore the soldiers did these things.

John's Gospel finds that it was the fulfillment of a Scripture when the four soldiers who crucified Jesus, divided his garments between themselves, but cast a lot to decide who would get his coat. The Scripture in question is Ps 22: 18 –

> "They divide my garments among them. They cast lots for my clothing."

David, the poet of this Psalm, merely told of the humiliation he suffered when he was robbed of his clothes by his enemies. He only reported his own experience and never meant to describe what Jesus would endure many centuries later, although his words may also be seen as a description of Jesus' fate.

THE RESURRECTED JESUS

The Walk to Emmaus
Luke 24: 13–35

13.	Behold, two of them were going that very day a village named Emmaus, which was sixty stadia from Jerusalem.
14.	They talked with each other about all of these things which had happened.
15.	It happened, while they talked and questioned together, that Jesus himself came near, and went with them.
16.	But their eyes were kept from recognizing him.
17.	He said to them, "What are you talking about as you walk, and are sad?"
18.	One of them, named Cleopas, answered him, "Are you the only one travelling in Jerusalem who doesn't know the things which have happened there in these days?"
19.	He said to them, "What things?" They said to him, "The

	things concerning Jesus, the Nazarene, who was a prophet mighty in deed and word before God and all the people;
20.	and how the chief priests and our rulers delivered him up to be condemned to death, and crucified him.
21.	But we hoped that it was he who would redeem Israel. Yes, and besides all this, it is now the third day since these things happened.
22.	Also, certain women of our company amazed us, having been early at the tomb;
23.	and when they didn't find his body, they came saying that they had also seen a vision of angels, who said that he was alive.
24.	Some of us went to the tomb, and found it just like the women had said, but they didn't see him."
25.	He said to them, "Foolish men, and slow of heart to believe in all that the prophets have spoken!
26.	Didn't the Christ have to suffer these things, and to enter into his glory?"
27.	Beginning from Moses and from all the prophets, he interpreted to them in all the Scriptures the things concerning himself.
28.	They drew near to the village, where they were going, and he acted like he would go further.
29.	They urged him, saying, "Stay with us, for it is almost evening, and the day is almost over." He went in to stay with them.
30.	It happened, when he had sat down at the table with them, he took the bread and gave thanks. Breaking it, he gave to them.

31.	Their eyes were opened, and they recognized him, and he vanished out of their sight.
32.	They said one to another, "Wasn't our heart burning within us, while he spoke to us along the way, and while he opened the Scriptures to us?"
33.	They rose up that very hour, and returned to Jerusalem, and found the eleven gathered together, and those who were with them,
34.	saying, "The Lord is risen indeed, and has appeared to Simon!"
35.	They related the things that happened along the way, and how he was recognized by them in the breaking of the bread.

This story, as it is written, seems to be improbable, especially due to the supernatural element of Jesus just disappearing into thin air – despite the next passage where Jesus told his disciples that he was not a spirit or a ghost but a man of flesh and blood (Luke 24: 39).

There may, nevertheless, be an element of truth in this story. It may be accepted that Jesus had indeed survived the crucifixion. He was given drugged vinegar to make him lose consciousness and to appear dead so that he could be removed from the cross (John 19: 29–30). His friends nursed him back to relative health with a huge amount of antiseptic herbs and plant extracts (John 19: 38–40).

It is, however, unlikely that somebody who was recovering from severe wounds, especially to his feet, would have been able to walk from Jerusalem to Emmaus, a distance of sixty stadia or about nine kilometers – unless this incident took place a long time after Jesus had survived the cross, months or years later.

The purpose of this story was obviously to demonstrate that

Jesus' crucifixion and resurrection was supposed to have been foretold by the Old Testament prophets – which is certainly not the case, as has been pointed out on different occasions in this book.

Jesus Appears to his Disciples
Luke 24: 36–49

36.	As they said these things, Jesus himself stood in the midst of them, and said to them, "Peace be to you."
37.	But they were terrified and filled with fear, and supposed that they saw a spirit.
38.	He said to them, "Why are you troubled? Why do questionings arise in your hearts?
39.	See my hands and my feet, that it is I myself. Touch me and see, for a spirit doesn't have flesh and bones, as you see that I have."
40.	When he had said this, he showed them his hands and feet.
41.	While they still didn't believe for joy, and wondered, he said to them, "Do you have anything here to eat?"
42.	They gave him a piece of a broiled fish and some honeycomb.
43.	He took it, and ate in front of them.
44.	He said to them, "This is what I told you, while I was still with you, that all things must be fulfilled, which are written in the law of Moses, the prophets, and the psalms, concerning me."
45.	Then he opened their minds, that they might understand the Scriptures.
46.	He said to them, "Thus it is written, and thus it was necessary for the Christ to suffer and to rise from the dead

> the third day,
>
> 47. and that repentance and remission of sins should be preached in his name to all the nations, beginning at Jerusalem.
> 48. You are witnesses of these things.
> 49. Behold, I send forth the promise of my Father on you. But wait in the city of Jerusalem until you are clothed with power from on high."

It may be accepted that Jesus did survive the crucifixion and that he did have meetings with his disciples afterwards. That Jesus was a man of flesh and bones – and not somebody with a spiritual or heavenly body as Paul argued in 1 Cor 15 – is borne out by the fact that he confirmed that he was not a spirit or a phantom, that he invited his disciples to inspect his limbs and that he begged for something to eat. They served him some fish – perhaps an indication that all this happened in Gallie, at the lake.

The object of this story was to emphasize, yet again, that the Old Testament was supposed to have contained prophecies regarding Jesus' crucifixion and resurrection. It has already been shown that the Old Testament nowhere predicted that the Messiah would be executed. If there are no prophecies in this regard, then his resurrecting would also not have been predicted.[216]

How Jesus managed to move around and visit his disciples is a mystery – unless this meeting took place a considerable time after the resurrection. This report may contain some legendary and mythological elements.

---

[216] Wright, *The Self-Revelation of God"*, 199.

Peter's Sermon
Acts 2: 14–42

14.	But Peter, standing up with the eleven, lifted up his voice, and spoke out to them, "You men of Judea, and all you who dwell at Jerusalem, let this be known to you, and listen to my words.
15.	For these aren't drunken, as you suppose, seeing it is only the third hour of the day.
16.	But this is what has been spoken through the prophet Joel:
17.	It will be in the last days, says God, I will pour forth of my Spirit on all flesh. Your sons and your daughters will prophesy. Your young men will see visions. Your old men will dream dreams.
18.	Yes, and on my servants and on my handmaidens in those days, I will pour out my Spirit, and they will prophesy.
19.	I will show wonders in the sky above, And signs on the earth beneath; blood, and fire, and billows of smoke.
20.	The sun will be turned into darkness, and the moon into blood, before the great and glorious day of the Lord comes.
21.	It will be, that whoever will call on the name of the Lord will be saved.
22.	"You men of Israel, hear these words. Jesus of Nazareth, a man approved by God to you by mighty works and wonders and signs which God did by him in the midst of you, even as you yourselves know,
23.	him, being delivered up by the determined counsel and foreknowledge of God, you have taken by the hand of lawless men, crucified and killed;

24. whom God raised up, having freed him from the agony of death, because it was not possible that he should be held by it.
25. For David says concerning him, I saw the Lord always before my face, For he is on my right hand, that I should not be moved.
26. Therefore my heart was glad, and my tongue rejoiced. Moreover my flesh also will dwell in hope;
27. Because you will not leave my soul in Hades, Neither will you allow your Holy One to see decay.
28. You made known to me the ways of life. You will make me full of gladness with your presence.
29. "Brothers, I may tell you freely of the patriarch David, that he both died and was buried, and his tomb is with us to this day.
30. Therefore, being a prophet, and knowing that God had sworn with an oath to him that of the fruit of his body, according to the flesh, he would raise up the Christ to sit on his throne,
31. he foreseeing this spoke about the resurrection of the Christ, that neither was his soul left in Hades, nor did his flesh see decay.
32. This Jesus God raised up, whereof we all are witnesses.
33. Being therefore exalted by the right hand of God, and having received from the Father the promise of the Holy Spirit, he has poured forth this, which you now see and hear.
34. For David didn't ascend into the heavens, but he says himself, The Lord said to my Lord, "Sit by my right hand,
35. Until I make your enemies the footstool of your feet."

> 36. "Let all the house of Israel therefore know assuredly that God has made him both Lord and Christ, this Jesus whom you crucified."
> 37. Now when they heard this, they were cut to the heart, and said to Peter and the rest of the apostles, "Brothers, what will we do?"
> 38. Peter said to them, "Repent, and be baptized, everyone of you, in the name of Jesus Christ for the forgiveness of sins, and you will receive the gift of the Holy Spirit.
> 39. For to you is the promise, and to your children, and to all who are far off, even as many as the Lord our God will call to himself."
> 40. With many other words he testified, and exhorted them, saying, "Save yourselves from this crooked generation!"
> 41. Then those who gladly received his word were baptized. There were added that day about three thousand souls.
> 42. They continued steadfastly in the apostles teaching and fellowship, in the breaking of bread, and prayer.

It is highly unlikely that Luke was able to repeat Peter's address accurately – that is, if Peter spoke at all to the people who assembled outside the building where the followers of Jesus were experiencing sparks of static electricity. Luke may simply have followed the example of ancient historians who invented speeches by famous people to fit certain occasions.

The impression is created that he addressed a large crowd because it was reported that 3 000 people were baptized on that day – an impossible figure if all of them had to be immersed in a pool or a bath somewhere in Jerusalem on the same day. Those who were baptized were most probably people who already believed in Jesus as the Messiah.

According to Luke, Peter quoted from Joel 2: 28–31 –

28. "It will happen afterward, that I will pour out my Spirit on all flesh; And your sons and your daughters will prophesy. Your old men will dream dreams. Your young men will see visions.
29. And also on the servants and on the handmaids in those days, I will pour out my Spirit.
30. I will show wonders in the heavens and in the earth: Blood, fire, and pillars of smoke.
31. The sun will be turned into darkness, And the moon into blood, Before the great and terrible day of YHWH comes."

This prophecy was never meant to describe events on that day of Pentecost, but it is, nevertheless, an appropriate description of certain aspects of that occasion. It mentions a darkened sun and a red moon – events that happened on the day when Jesus was crucified when a dust storm obscured the sun and a lunar eclipse occurred.[217]

Peter described Jesus' ascension as the fulfilment of a prophecy by David in Ps 16: 8–10 –

8. I have set YHWH always before me. Because he is at my right hand, I shall not be moved.
9. Therefore my heart is glad, and my tongue rejoices. My body shall also dwell in safety.

---

[217] Pretorius, *The Gospels*, 375.

10. For you will not leave my soul in Sheol, Neither will you allow your holy one to see corruption.

David merely described how God preserved him and he never had Jesus as the Messiah in mind with his words.

These words can certainly not be regarded as a prophecy that the Messiah would be resurrected. There is also a quotation from Ps 110: 1 to prove that Jesus was meant to ascend into heaven –

> "YHWH says to my Lord, 'Sit at my right hand, until I make your enemies your footstool for your feet.'"

However, this Psalm was never intended to be applied to the expected Messiah. The "lord" mentioned in the quoted verse is clearly the king from the house of David and he was given the promise in the rest of the Psalm that he would prevail over the enemies of his people.

Peter ended his address by telling the people that Jesus was declared the Christ or Messiah after his crucifixion and resurrection, which does not agree with the rest of the Gospels. Luke 1: 30–35, for instance, reported that the angel told the virgin Mary that her unborn son would be the Son of God and the king of Israel – many years before his crucifixion and resurrection.

It must be pointed out that Peter failed to mention in his address that Jesus' death on the cross was meant as a sacrifice to free sinners from eternal damnation in hell – as taught by Paul. He merely exhorted his audience to be baptized in the name of Jesus and confess their sins.

Christ Ascended to the Highest Heaven
Eph 4: 7–10

> 7. But to each one of us was the grace given according to the measure of the gift of Christ.
> 8. Therefore he says, "When he ascended on high, he led captivity captive, and gave gifts to men."
> 9. Now this, "He ascended," what is it but that he also first descended into the lower parts of the earth?
> 10. He who descended is the same also who ascended far above all the heavens, that he might fill all things.

Paul argued that Jesus Christ was taken up into heaven and to support his point of view he quoted from Ps 68: 18 –

> "You have ascended on high. You have led away captives. You have received gifts among men, yes, among the rebellious also, that the Lord God might dwell there."

The whole of Ps 68 deals with the might of God who protects his people and who is victorious over their enemies. The Hebrew text mentions in the quoted verse that He occupies a height, an elevated position, and that signifies his majesty. The future Messiah doesn't feature anywhere, much less the ascension of Jesus into heaven.

CLOSING THOUGHTS

The preceding paragraphs and arguments must make the following clear:

- The authors of the New Testament, but especially the author of the Gospel of Matthew, severely distorted the contents and intentions of numerous texts from the Old Testament to find "proof" for their contention that the prophets of the Old Testament foretold that Jesus of Nazareth would arrive as the

promised Messiah of Israel. They usually regarded a superficial resemblance of a certain text with their ideas as sufficient evidence and proof to settle the matter.
- There is not a single prophecy in the Hebrew Scriptures that points to Jesus of Nazareth as the ultimate Messiah of Israel.
- When Jesus proclaimed himself as *the* Messiah and the legitimate king of Israel after his baptism, he succeeded in convincing many people of his claim, especially when he intentionally acted in accordance with a prophecy by entering Jerusalem on the back of a donkey.
- Jesus was tragically deluded and his campaign to ascend the throne in Jerusalem fell apart when he was arrested and crucified.
- Jesus of Nazareth was not the founder of Christianity. The Christian religion was the invention of Paul of Tarsus who concluded on account of various visions and revelations that Jesus was more than an ordinary human, but the eternal divine Son of God. He interpreted the expression "son of God" as if Jesus was a mythological Greek hero, such as the many sons of Zeus and other deities in antiquity.
- Paul used Jesus' title of Messiah or Christ as a proper name for Jesus and coined the combination "Jesus Christ".
- The belief of various authors of the New Testament and Christians in general that the Old Testament contains numerous prophecies about the birth, life, ministry, death, resurrection, and ascension into heaven of Jesus of Nazareth proved to be wrong. No such prophecies could be identified when a thorough and rational search was undertaken.

CHAPTER 7
OLD TESTAMENT PROPHECIES REGARDING JUDGMENT DAY AND THE AFTERLIFE

The prophets of the Hebrew Scriptures often wrote about "the Day of YHWH" when God would judge his people, as well as other nations on account of their sins, crimes, and impiety. In some cases, this day would arrive soon, after which the people of God could live in peace and harmony. In other cases, this day was scheduled for the end of time, when God would judge the whole world and destroy all his enemies and all that is bad and detestable and evil.

In the discussions that follow, the words of the prophets regarding the "Day of YHWH" or Judgment Day will be discussed roughly in chronological order. The pronouncements of the prophets regarding the "Day of YHWH" that was due to happen soon, were already discussed in the chapter dealing with the prophecies of the Old Testament regarding current affairs.

The prophet who first wrote about Judgment Day and the afterlife was Isaiah and a selection of his prophecies in this regard will be discussed, after which other Hebrew prophets will be presented.

The ideas contained in the Hebrew Scriptures regarding death and the afterlife will also be dealt with in the last parts of this chapter.

JUDGMENT DAY IN PRE-EXILIC SCRIPTURES

Peace on Earth after Judgment Day
Isa 2: 3–5

3.	Many peoples shall go and say, Come you, and let us go up to the mountain of YHWH, to the house of the God of Jacob; and he will teach us of his ways, and we will walk in his paths: for out of Zion shall go forth the law, and the word of YHWH from Jerusalem.
4.	He will judge between the nations, and will decide concerning many peoples; and they shall beat their swords into plowshares, and their spears into pruning-hooks; nation shall not lift up sword against nation, neither shall they learn war any more.
5.	House of Jacob, come, and let us walk in the light of YHWH.

Isaiah evidently expected that peace, harmony, and prosperity would reign on earth after Judgment Day in the unknown future when God will judge all the peoples on earth. This happy time will usher in Jerusalem as center of the world because that is where YHWH will be worshipped.

Cosmic Events on Judgment Day
Isa 13: 6–13

6.	Wail you; for the day of YHWH is at hand; as destruction from the Almighty shall it come.
7.	Therefore shall all hands be feeble, and every heart of man shall melt:
8.	and they shall be dismayed; pangs and sorrows shall take hold [of them]; they shall be in pain as a woman in travail:

> they shall look in amazement one at another; their faces [shall be] faces of flame.
>
> 9. Behold, the day of YHWH comes, cruel, with wrath and fierce anger; to make the land a desolation, and to destroy the sinners of it out of it.
>
> 10. For the stars of the sky and the constellations of it shall not give their light; the sun shall be darkened in its going forth, and the moon shall not cause its light to shine.
>
> 11. I will punish the world for [their] evil, and the wicked for their iniquity: and I will cause the arrogance of the proud to cease, and will lay low the haughtiness of the terrible.
>
> 12. I will make a man more rare than fine gold, even a man than the pure gold of Ophir.
>
> 13. Therefore I will make the heavens to tremble, and the earth shall be shaken out of its place, in the wrath of YHWH of hosts, and in the day of his fierce anger.

This prophecy is directed at the whole of mankind. All sinners, evil-doers, and wicked people are warned that the Day of YHWH, Judgment Day, is at hand. On that day, God will destroy all his enemies. He will also create a new humanity, "more rare than fine gold", the people who will dwell with Him.

This prophecy retained a memory of the total solar eclipse of of 15 June762 BC, also mentioned by Isa 24: 23 and Amos 5: 8 and 8:9, as well as the terrible earthquake that Amos1: 1 recorded. Isaiah expected that these extreme cosmic events would also occur on Judgment Day.

Peace on Earth
Isa 19: 18–25

18.	In that day there shall be five cities in the land of Egypt that speak the language of Canaan, and swear to YHWH of hosts; one shall be called the city of destruction.
19.	In that day shall there be an altar to YHWH in the midst of the land of Egypt, and a pillar at the border of it to YHWH.
20.	It shall be for a sign and for a witness to YHWH of Hosts in the land of Egypt; for they shall cry to YHWH because of oppressors, and he will send them a savior, and a defender, and he will deliver them.
21.	YHWH shall be known to Egypt, and the Egyptians shall know YHWH in that day; yes, they shall worship with sacrifice and offering, and shall vow a vow to YHWH, and shall perform it.
22.	YHWH will strike Egypt, smiting and healing; and they shall return to YHWH, and he will be entreated of them, and will heal them.
23.	In that day shall there be a highway out of Egypt to Assyria, and the Assyrian shall come into Egypt, and the Egyptian into Assyria; and the Egyptians shall worship with the Assyrians.
24.	In that day shall Israel be the third with Egypt and with Assyria, a blessing in the midst of the earth;
25.	because YHWH of Hosts has blessed them, saying, Blessed be Egypt my people, and Assyria the work of my hands, and Israel my inheritance.

It is unknown how the people of Jerusalem reacted to this prophecy of Isaiah because he described a totally unthinkable and impossible situation. He predicted that the arch-enemies of Israel, the Assyrians, and the Egyptians, would become friends and worship the God of Israel in Jerusalem and elsewhere.

Something like this never happened, of course, but Isaiah didn't mean to predict something that would happen anytime soon. This condition of total peace on earth would only be possible on a renewed earth after Judgment Day when all evil, wickedness, crime, and cruelty have been removed from God's creation and the sinners have received their deserved punishment.

Part of the Isaiah Scroll from the Dead Sea Scrolls

Judgment Day
Isa 24: 21–23

21.	It shall happen in that day, that YHWH will punish the host of the high ones on high, and the kings of the earth on the earth.
22.	They shall be gathered together, as prisoners are gathered in the pit, and shall be shut up in the prison; and after many days shall they be visited.
23.	Then the moon shall be confounded, and the sun ashamed; for YHWH of Hosts will reign on Mount Zion, and in Jerusalem; and before his elders shall be glory.

On Judgement Day, not only the evil kings of the world will receive their deserved punishment – "the host of the high ones on high" will also become God's prisoners. This host consists of the sun, moon, and stars in the sky, which were worshipped by the pagans as their gods. They will be shut up in a prison called "the pit", which must be somewhere below the surface of the earth.

The Feast
Isa 25: 6–8

> 6. In this mountain will YHWH of Hosts make to all peoples a feast of fat things, a feast of wines on the lees, of fat things full of marrow, of wines on the lees well refined.
> 7. He will destroy in this mountain the surface of the covering that covers all peoples, and the veil that is spread over all nations.
> 8. He has swallowed up death forever; and the Lord YHWH will wipe away tears from off all faces; and the reproach of his people will he take away from off all the earth: for YHWH has spoken it.

According to Isaiah, a wonderful afterlife awaits the people of God. It will be a feast with copious amounts of top-quality wine and dishes of prime meat. There will be no place for tears of sorrow or sadness during this feast.

Death will disappear – presumably because everybody will share in God's eternity. This idea is repeated in 1 Cor 15: 26 – "The last enemy that will be abolished is death." Rev 7: 17 repeats the promise that God will dry up all the tears.

The Eternal City
Isa 26: 1–6

> 1. In that day shall this song be sung in the land of Judah: we have a strong city; salvation will he appoint for walls and bulwarks.
> 2. Open you the gates, that the righteous nation which keeps

	faith may enter in.
3.	You will keep [him] in perfect peace, [whose] mind [is] stayed [on you]; because he trusts in you.
4.	Trust in YHWH forever; for in Yah, YHWH, is an everlasting Rock.
5.	For he has brought down those who dwell on high, the lofty city: he lays it low, he lays it low even to the ground; he brings it even to the dust.
6.	The foot shall tread it down; even the feet of the poor, and the steps of the needy.

YHWH's abode, where the "righteous nation" will have "perfect peace" after Judgment Day, is described as a city with gates. The people of Judah will sing songs of joy about this wonderful promise.

That wonderful condition will be possible because the city of the godless has been destroyed totally.

The Leviathan
Isa 27: 1

In that day YHWH with his hard and great and strong sword will punish leviathan the swift serpent, and leviathan the crooked serpent; and he will kill the monster that is in the sea.

The Leviathan (Hebrew: לִוְיָתָן – *Livyathan*) was seen in the Old Testament as a mythological sea monster and was a symbol of all chaotic forces in creation. It is possible that this monster was linked to an astrological constellation, most probably Cetus, the sea monster or Scorpius, the Scorpion, regarded as a snake by the Jews.[218]

---

[218] Allen, *Star Names*, 162.

This passage contains the promise that all chaotic and evil forces will be demolished on the Day of YHWH.

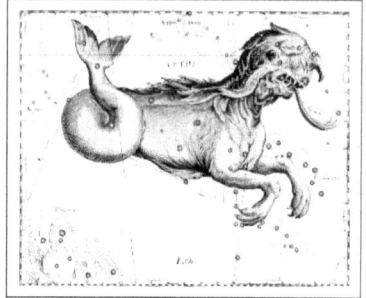 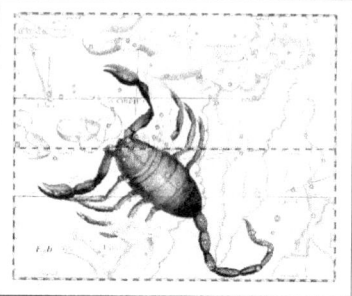

Cetus, the Sea Monster, and Scorpius, the Scorpion, drawn by Johannes Hevelius

Abundance

Isa 30: 19–26

19.	For the people shall dwell in Zion at Jerusalem; you shall weep no more; he will surely be gracious to you at the voice of your cry; when he shall hear, he will answer you.
20.	Though the Lord give you the bread of adversity and the water of affliction, yet shall not your teachers be hidden anymore, but your eyes shall see your teachers;
21.	and your ears shall hear a word behind you, saying, This is the way, walk you in it; when you turn to the right hand, and when you turn to the left.
22.	You shall defile the overlaying of your engraved images of silver, and the plating of your molten images of gold: you shall cast them away as an unclean thing; you shall tell it, Get you hence.
23.	He will give the rain for your seed, with which you shall sow the ground; and bread of the increase of the ground,

> 24. and it shall be fat and plenteous. In that day shall your cattle feed in large pastures;
> 24. the oxen likewise and the young donkeys that till the ground shall eat savory provender, which has been winnowed with the shovel and with the fork.
> 25. There shall be on every lofty mountain, and on every high hill, brooks [and] streams of waters, in the day of the great slaughter, when the towers fall.
> 26. Moreover the light of the moon shall be as the light of the sun, and the light of the sun shall be sevenfold, as the light of seven days, in the day that YHWH binds up the hurt of his people, and heals the stroke of their wound.

Isaiah draws a beautiful picture of conditions on a renewed country after Judgment Day, when the afterlife arrives. It will be a perfected version of the lifestyle the Israelites used to enjoy with abundant food supplies, enough water, fat animals, an absence of idolatry, and peace where everybody would be happy.

Isaiah thought in very concrete terms about the conditions after Judgment Day and the afterlife. He could not imagine an existence that differed in any fundamental way from that to which he was used – it would only be much better and even perfect.

Jerusalem the Center of the World
Mica 4: 1–6

> 1. But in the latter days it shall happen that the mountain of YHWH's house shall be established on the top of the mountains, and it shall be exalted above the hills; and peoples shall flow to it.
> 2. Many nations shall go and say, Come you, and let us go up

> to the mountain of YHWH, and to the house of the God of Jacob; and he will teach us of his ways, and we will walk in his paths. For out of Zion shall go forth the law, and the word of YHWH from Jerusalem;
>
> 3. and he will judge between many peoples, and will decide concerning strong nations afar off: and they shall beat their swords into plowshares, and their spears into pruning-hooks; nation shall not lift up sword against nation, neither shall they learn war any more.
>
> 4. But they shall sit every man under his vine and under his fig-tree; and none shall make them afraid: for the mouth of YHWH of Hosts has spoken it.
>
> 5. For all the peoples walk everyone in the name of his god; and we will walk in the name of YHWH our God forever and ever.
>
> 6. In that day, says YHWH, will I assemble that which is lame, and I will gather that which is driven away, and that which I have afflicted;
>
> 7. and I will make that which was lame a remnant, and that which was cast far off a strong nation: and YHWH will reign over them on Mount Zion from henceforth even forever.

Micah shared the view of Isa 26: 1–6 that Jerusalem will occupy a special place in God's plans for the last days when the earth will be cleansed of all evil and all people will worship the God of Israel. It will be a peaceful condition without warfare.

Judgment against all Nations

Jer 25: 30–38

30. Therefore prophesy you against them all these words, and tell them, YHWH will roar from on high, and utter his voice from his holy habitation; he will mightily roar against his fold; he will give a shout, as those who tread [the grapes], against all the inhabitants of the earth.

31. A noise shall come even to the end of the earth; for YHWH has a controversy with the nations; he will enter into judgment with all flesh: as for the wicked, he will give them to the sword, says YHWH.

32. Thus says YHWH of hosts, Behold, evil shall go forth from nation to nation, and a great tempest shall be raised up from the uttermost parts of the earth.

33. The slain of YHWH shall be at that day from one end of the earth even to the other end of the earth: they shall not be lamented, neither gathered, nor buried; they shall be dung on the surface of the ground.

34. Wail, you shepherds, and cry; and wallow [in ashes], you principal of the flock; for the days of your slaughter and of your dispersions are fully come, and you shall fall like a goodly vessel.

35. The shepherds shall have no way to flee, nor the principal of the flock to escape.

36. A voice of the cry of the shepherds, and the wailing of the principal of the flock! for YHWH lays waste their pasture.

37. The peaceable folds are brought to silence because of the fierce anger of YHWH.

38. He has left his covert, as the lion; for their land is become an astonishment because of the fierceness of the oppressing [sword], and because of his fierce anger.

The prophet Jeremiah, who was active during the last years of the kingdom of Judah and who experienced the conquest of Jerusalem by the Babylonians, wrote mostly about the political, religious, and moral conditions of his time, warning the king against an alliance with Egypt against the Babylonians. He often suffered from melancholy on account of the opposition he had encountered.

However, he also gave some indications about how he envisaged Judgment Day and the afterlife.

This prophecy is directed at the whole world, to all the nations on earth. The prophet portrays YHWH as an angry lion that roars as he catches his prey. All the nations of earth, although they fight each other, will not be able to flee from the judgment of God.

All the wicked people will be slain and their bodies will rot where they lie because nobody will be left to bury them.

The People of God
Jer 30: 22–24

22.	You shall be my people, and I will be your God.
23.	Behold, the tempest of YHWH, [even his] wrath, is gone forth, a sweeping tempest: it shall burst on the head of the wicked.
24.	The fierce anger of YHWH shall not return, until he has executed, and until he has performed the intents of his heart: in the latter days you shall understand it.

The anger of YHWH will be like a storm that sweeps away the godless and wicked people of the world. On the other hand, He will continue to be the God of his people.

YHWH will Gather the Nations
Zeph 3: 8–12

8.	"Therefore wait for me," says YHWH, "until the day that I rise up to the prey, for my determination is to gather the nations, that I may assemble the kingdoms, to pour on them my indignation, even all my fierce anger, for all the earth will be devoured with the fire of my jealousy.
9.	For then I will purify the lips of the peoples, that they may all call on the name of YHWH, to serve him shoulder to shoulder.
10.	From beyond the rivers of Cush, my worshipers, even the daughter of my dispersed people, will bring my offering.
11.	In that day you will not be put to shame for all your doings, in which you have transgressed against me; for then I will take away out of the midst of you your proudly exulting ones, and you will no more be haughty in my holy mountain.
12.	But I will leave in the midst of you an afflicted and poor people, and they will take refuge in the name of YHWH."

This prophecy, which dates from the last decades of the kingdom of Judah, is directed to all the nations on earth. The people of God are promised that people from other nations will come to worship God, even from far-away Kush in Africa. God also promised his people that the sinners will be removed from his people after the Day of YHWH, Judgment Day, in the future.

Gold and Silver will be Worthless
Ezek 7: 19–20

19.	They shall cast their silver in the streets, and their gold shall be as an unclean thing; their silver and their gold shall not be able to deliver them in the day of the wrath of YHWH:

> they shall not satisfy their souls, neither fill their bowels; because it has been the stumbling block of their iniquity.
>
> 20. As for the beauty of his ornament, he set it in majesty; but they made the images of their abominations [and] their detestable things therein: therefore have I made it to them as an unclean thing.

The focus of the book of Ezekiel was on the plight of the exiles in Babylonia before and after the destruction of Jerusalem. The idea of the Day of YHWH, Judgment Day, also received some attention. These two verses, which form a unit, are part of a chapter dealing with the Day of YHWH, the day in the near future when Jerusalem would be destroyed by the Babylonians. That would be God's punishment for the sins of the people of Judah.

However, the two verses quoted above are also applicable to the final judgment when all sinners will receive their just punishment. On that day, their riches, their gold, silver, and precious ornaments, will be worthless.

EXILIC AND POST-EXILIC TEXTS ABOUT JUDGMENT DAY

Ideal of the Second Isaiah.

Jacobs and Buttenwieser concluded: "According [to] the Deutero-Isaiah, who wrote his prophecies during the Babylonian Exile, God has called Israel for the realization of His purpose toward mankind in general. Israel, and not an individual, was 'the servant of God' (Isa 43, 44, and 53), with the regeneration of mankind and the spread of the true religion as purpose. The ideal Israel of the future was envisaged – not the people of the prophet's own time."[219]

---

[219] Jacobs & Buddenwieser, "Messiah".

These words must be kept in mind when dealing with the prophecies in Deutero-Isaiah and other prophets of his time:

The Nations will Come to Israel
Isa 60: 1–7

1.	Arise, shine; for your light is come, and the glory of YHWH is risen on you.
2.	For, behold, darkness shall cover the earth, and gross darkness the peoples; but YHWH will arise on you, and his glory shall be seen on you.
3.	Nations shall come to your light, and kings to the brightness of your rising.
4.	Lift up your eyes round about, and see: they all gather themselves together, they come to you; your sons shall come from far, and your daughters shall be carried in the arms.
5.	Then you shall see and be radiant, and your heart shall thrill and be enlarged; because the abundance of the sea shall be turned to you, the wealth of the nations shall come to you.
6.	The multitude of camels shall cover you, the dromedaries of Midian and Ephah; all they from Sheba shall come; they shall bring gold and frankincense, and shall proclaim the praises of YHWH.
7.	All the flocks of Kedar shall be gathered together to you, the rams of Nebaioth shall minister to you; they shall come up with acceptance on my altar; and I will glorify the house of my glory.

A wonderful future for the people of Israel is predicted. People from all over the world will flock to Israel with their treasures to worship the God of Israel. Peace and prosperity will reign on earth.

The Day of YHWH is Coming
Zech 14: 1–15

1.	Behold, a day of YHWH comes, when your spoil shall be divided in the midst of you.
2.	For I will gather all nations against Jerusalem to battle; and the city shall be taken, and the houses rifled, and the women ravished; and half of the city shall go forth into captivity, and the residue of the people shall not be cut off from the city.
3.	Then shall YHWH go forth, and fight against those nations, as when he fought in the day of battle.
4.	His feet shall stand in that day on the Mount of Olives, which is before Jerusalem on the east; and the Mount of Olives shall be cleft in the midst of it toward the east and toward the west, [and there shall be] a very great valley; and half of the mountain shall remove toward the north, and half of it toward the south.
5.	You shall flee by the valley of my mountains; for the valley of the mountains shall reach to Azel; yes, you shall flee, like as you fled from before the earthquake in the days of Uzziah king of Judah; and YHWH my God shall come, and all the holy ones with you.
6.	It shall happen in that day, that there shall not be light; the bright ones shall withdraw themselves:
7.	but it shall be one day which is known to YHWH; not day, and not night; but it shall come to pass, that at evening time there shall be light.

8. It shall happen in that day, that living waters shall go out from Jerusalem; half of them toward the eastern sea, and half of them toward the western sea: in summer and in winter shall it be.
9. YHWH shall be King over all the earth: in that day shall YHWH be one, and his name one.
10. All the land shall be made like the Arabah, from Geba to Rimmon south of Jerusalem; and she shall be lifted up, and shall dwell in her place, from Benjamin's gate to the place of the first gate, to the corner gate, and from the tower of Hananel to the king's wine-presses.
11. Men shall dwell therein, and there shall be no more curse; but Jerusalem shall dwell safely.
12. This shall be the plague with which YHWH will strike all the peoples who have warred against Jerusalem: their flesh shall consume away while they stand on their feet, and their eyes shall consume away in their sockets, and their tongue shall consume away in their mouth.
13. It shall happen in that day, that a great tumult from YHWH shall be among them; and they shall lay hold everyone on the hand of his neighbor, and his hand shall rise up against the hand of his neighbor.
14. Judah also shall fight at Jerusalem; and the wealth of all the nations round about shall be gathered together, gold, and silver, and clothing, in great abundance.
15. So shall be the plague of the horse, of the mule, of the camel, and of the donkey, and of all the animals that shall be in those camps, as that plague.

This rather jumbled and rambling prophecy of Zecheriah provides the reader with the prophet's vision of the end of times when all evil forces will be wiped out.

The city of Jerusalem is a symbol of the body of God's people who may expect attacks and even cruelty from those nations that do not recognize YHWH as the only God. But YHWH will intervene and strike his enemies with a plague so that their bodies simply rot away. The plague would strike their horses, mules, camels, donkeys, and other animals as well. To make matters worse, these enemies would fight amongst themselves.

That terrible day will be like the day when the sun disappeared and only reappeared during the late afternoon on 28 March 516 BC. God alone knows when that day will come. Zechariah also compared this day to the great earthquake in the time of Amos, when an earthquake will cause a cleft on the Mount of Olives to the east of the city.

He advised the people of Jerusalem who were to be attacked, to flee through the cleft in the Mount of Olives. YHWH will appear with his holy ones, the host of angels to achieve a victory over his foes. The tribe of Judah will also fight against the invaders from within the city.

After that, YHWH will dwell with his people and the heavenly Jerusalem will become a safe place. All the treasures of the godless attackers will become theirs. The city will be transformed into a fertile place with abundant water, flowing away to the Dead Sea and the Mediterranean Sea. This Jerusalem would be lifted up into the sky, together with her gates and other features, such as the king's wine press. YHWH would be recognized and worshipped as the only true God.

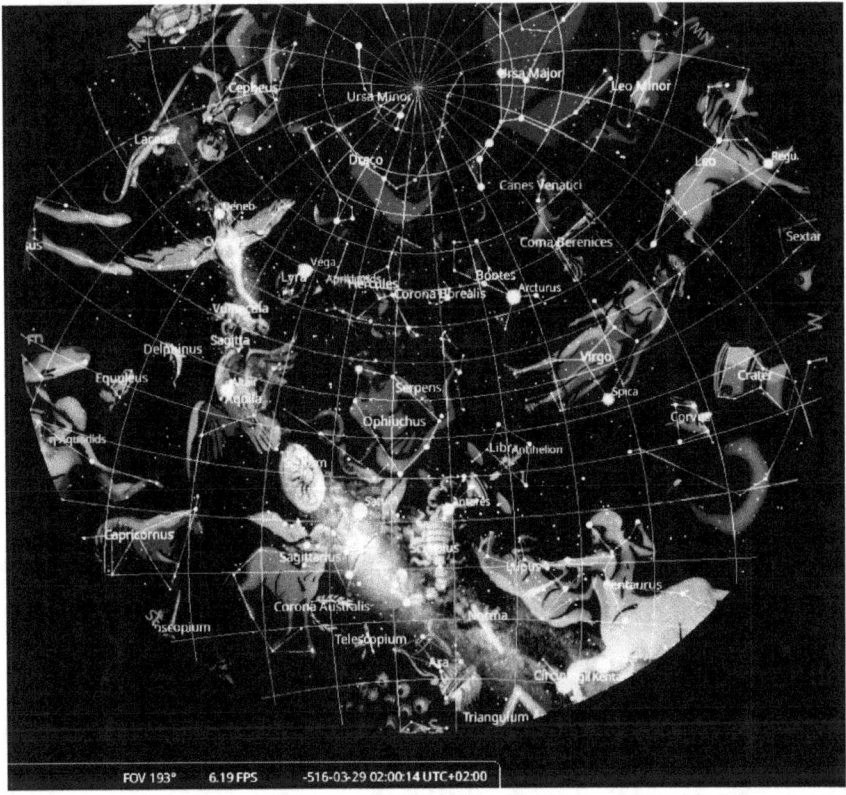

The night sky over Jerusalem, as described by Zechariah, sometime around 516 BC. The city of Jerusalem is to be found in Virgo. The enemies who attacked the city are the constellations of Scorpius, Hercules, Ophiuchus, and Boötes. Judah, who fought in Jerusalem, is Leo, the Lion. The Mount of Olives, that was torn in two, is clearly the Milky Way to the east of Virgo, with a blank stretch next to Aquila, the Eagle. The horse is Pegasus, the camel must be Centaurus, the mule is Sagittarius, and the donkey is Capricornus, the Goat. Leo Minor, the Small Lion, Lupus, the Wolf, and Ursa Major, the Great Bear, are the other animals. The water flowing to the east can be found in Aquarius, the Water Carrier, and the water flowing to the west is the celestial river, Eridanus, on the south-western horizon. The treasures of the nations are the faint stars of Coma Berenices, the Hair of Berenice, and Canes Venatici. Crater, the Chalice, is the wine press, the corner gate is Corvus, and the gate of Benjamin is Libra, the Scales, the sign of the tribe of Benjamin. God's throne is at the northern celestial pole.

It must be concluded that Zachariah thought of these happy conditions after the final battle against God's enemies would amount to a perfected sojourn in the country of Israel.

Zechariah based this scenario on his observation of the sky at night. The computerized reconstruction of the night sky over Jerusalem during Zachariah's time shows all the elements of this vision. After all, Zechariah explicitly said the God would be accompanied by his holy angels – in other words, the stars according to the ancient Hebrew cosmology.

Eternal Festivities
Zech 14: 16–21

16.	It shall happen, that everyone who is left of all the nations that came against Jerusalem shall go up from year to year to worship the King, YHWH of Hosts, and to keep the feast of tents.
17.	It shall be, that whoever of [all] the families of the earth doesn't go up to Jerusalem to worship the King, YHWH of Hosts, on them there shall be no rain.
18.	If the family of Egypt doesn't go up, and doesn't come, neither [shall it be] on them; there shall be the plague with which YHWH will strike the nations that don't go up to keep the feast of tents.
19.	This shall be the punishment of Egypt, and the punishment of all the nations that don't go up to keep the feast of tents.
20.	In that day shall there be on the bells of the horses, HOLY TO YHWH; and the pots in YHWH's house shall be like the bowls before the altar.
21.	Yes, every pot in Jerusalem and in Judah shall be holy to YHWH of Hosts; and all those who sacrifice shall come and

> take of them, and boil therein: and in that day there shall be no more a Canaanite in the house of YHWH of Hosts.

The fact that Zechariah repeatedly called God "YHWH of Hosts" in this continuation of the prophecy discussed in the previous section is a sure sign that he visualized God on his throne between the stars, the host of heavenly angels.

According to Zechariah, there will be a perpetual feast of tents and all God's people will take part while worshipping Him. The feast of tents was meant to commemorate the escape of the Israelites from slavery in Egypt. Should any Egyptian, Canaanite, or member of another nation refuse to take part, he can expect that YHWH will cause his country to dry up.

One reads of pots or cooking vessels in front of the altar, situated at God's throne. That must be sought in the stars in the tail of the constellation of Draco.

The Volcano
Joel 2: 1–11

1.	Blow you the trumpet in Zion, And sound an alarm in my holy mountain! Let all the inhabitants of the land tremble, For the day of YHWH comes, For it is close at hand:
2.	A day of darkness and gloominess, A day of clouds and thick darkness. As the dawn spreading on the mountains, A great and strong people; There has never been the like, Neither will there be any more after them, Even to the years of many generations.
3.	A fire devours before them, And behind them, a flame burns. The land is as the garden of Eden before them, And

> 4. behind them, a desolate wilderness. Yes, and no one has escaped them.
> 4. The appearance of them is as the appearance of horses, And as horsemen, so do they run.
> 5. Like the noise of chariots on the tops of the mountains do they leap, Like the noise of a flame of fire that devours the stubble, As a strong people set in battle array.
> 6. At their presence the peoples are in anguish. All faces have grown pale.
> 7. They run like mighty men. They climb the wall like warriors. They each march in his line, and they don't swerve off course.
> 8. Neither does one jostle another; They march everyone in his path, And they burst through the defenses, And don't break ranks.
> 9. They rush on the city. They run on the wall. They climb up into the houses. They enter in at the windows like thieves.
> 10. The earth quakes before them. The heavens tremble. The sun and the moon are darkened, And the stars withdraw their shining.
> 11. YHWH thunders his voice before his army; For his forces are very great; For he is strong who obeys his command; For the day of YHWH is great and very awesome, And who can endure it?

There can be no doubt: Joel described a volcanic outburst, together with an earthquake, just as Isaiah 4: 5–6 also mentioned one. It seems as if Joel personally witnessed the glowing rocks hurled into the air, the fires started by the red-hot rocks, and the creeping phalanx of lava that could not be stopped, just like an advancing army with horses and chariots.

Joel saw this event as a warning that the terrible Day of YHWH would occur soon.

Great Prosperity Awaits Israel
Joel 2: 20–32

20.	But I will remove the northern army far away from you, And will drive it into a barren and desolate land, Its front into the eastern sea, And its back into the western sea; And its stench will come up, And its bad smell will rise." Surely he has done great things.
21.	Land, don't be afraid. Be glad and rejoice, for YHWH has done great things.
22.	Don't be afraid, you animals of the field; For the pastures of the wilderness spring up, For the tree bears its fruit. The fig tree and the vine yield their strength.
23.	"Be glad then, you children of Zion, And rejoice in YHWH, your God; For he gives you the former rain in just measure, And he causes the rain to come down for you, The former rain and the latter rain, As before.
24.	The threshing floors will be full of wheat, And the vats will overflow with new wine and oil.
25.	I will restore to you the years that the swarming locust has eaten, The great locust, the grasshopper, and the caterpillar, My great army, which I sent among you.
26.	You will have plenty to eat, and be satisfied, And will praise the name of YHWH, your God, Who has dealt wondrously with you; And my people will never again be put to shame.

> 27. You will know that I am in the midst of Israel, And that I am YHWH, your God, and there is no one else; And my people will never again be put to shame.
> 28. "It will happen afterward, that I will pour out my Spirit on all flesh; And your sons and your daughters will prophesy. Your old men will dream dreams. Your young men will see visions.
> 29. And also on the servants and on the handmaids in those days, I will pour out my Spirit.
> 30. I will show wonders in the heavens and in the earth: Blood, fire, and pillars of smoke.
> 31. The sun will be turned into darkness, And the moon into blood, Before the great and terrible day of YHWH comes.
> 32. It will happen that whoever will call on the name of YHWH shall be saved; For in Mount Zion and in Jerusalem there will be those who escape, As YHWH has said, And among the remnant, those whom YHWH calls.

It is difficult to date the short book of the prophet Joel. He names a "northern army" in this passage and it may be applied to any invading or threatening army from the north during those times: the Assyrian Army, the Babylonian Army, the Persian Army, or even the Greek Army under Alexander the Great.

A likely time would be the middle of the fourth century BC. Joel alluded to a solar eclipse and a lunar eclipse in the passage quoted: "The sun will be turned into darkness, and the moon into blood." It is possible that he experienced the total solar eclipse on 29 February 356 BC and the total lunar eclipse a year later on 2 Feb 355 BC. The solar eclipse occurred at about midday, while the lunar eclipse was visible just before daybreak.

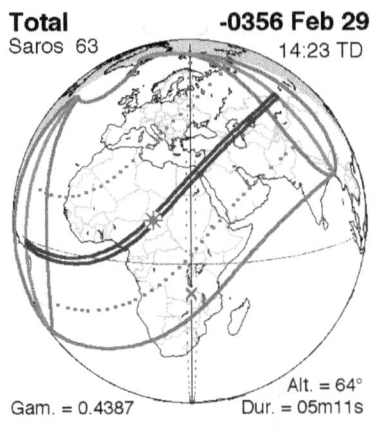
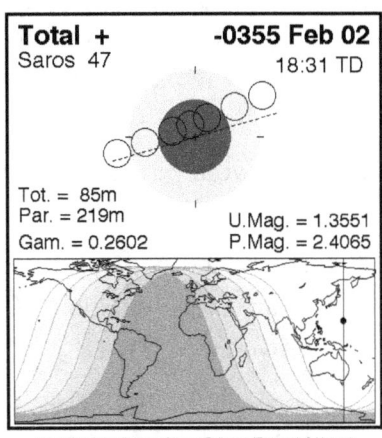

Five Millennium Canon of Solar Eclipses (Espenak & Meeus)

Five Millennium Canon of Lunar Eclipses (Espenak & Meeus)
NASA TP-2009-214172

Other possible combinations of total solar eclipses and lunar eclipses, visible from Palestine, were explored but the dates mentioned above seem to fit Joel's description best.

It seems that Joel also alluded to the volcano he mentioned earlier when he wrote about smoke and flames.

If the date of 356 BC is correct, the "northern army" would be the Persian Army, which defeated the Babylonian Army two centuries earlier. Judea was a heavily-taxed province of the Persian Empire at that time and the occupiers of their country caused them to yearn for better times.

Joel provided a promise from YHWH that the good times would arrive, but then only after "the great and terrible day of YHWH comes". These good times, which are almost too good to be true, would only be realized after Judgment Day. The good times are described in terrestrial terms, which the Jews of those times would have understood.

War, Disasters, and Prosperity
Joel 3: 9–18

9. Proclaim this among the nations: Prepare war. Stir up the mighty men. Let all the warriors draw near. Let them come up.
10. Beat your plowshares into swords, And your pruning hooks into spears. Let the weak say, "I am strong."
11. Hurry and come, all you surrounding nations, And gather yourselves together." Cause your mighty ones to come down there, YHWH.
12. "Let the nations arouse themselves, And come up to the valley of Jehoshaphat; For there will I sit to judge all the surrounding nations.
13. Put in the sickle; For the harvest is ripe. Come, tread, for the winepress is full, The vats overflow, for their wickedness is great."
14. Multitudes, multitudes in the valley of decision! For the day of YHWH is near, in the valley of decision.
15. The sun and the moon are darkened, And the stars withdraw their shining."
16. YHWH will roar from Zion, And thunder from Jerusalem; And the heavens and the earth will shake; But YHWH will be a refuge to his people, And a stronghold to the children of Israel.
17. "So you will know that I am YHWH, your God, Dwelling in Zion, my holy mountain. Then Jerusalem will be holy, And no strangers will pass through her any more.
18. It will happen in that day, That the mountains will drop down sweet wine, The hills will flow with milk, All the brooks of Judah will flow with waters; And a fountain will

> come forth from the house of YHWH, And will water the valley of Shittim."

According to Joel, Judgment Day or the Day of YHWH will arrive while war against the evil forces is being waged and natural disasters, such as a solar eclipse, a lunar eclipse, and an earthquake are experienced. This will be followed by a prosperous time with lots of wine, milk, and water.

The Sons of Levi to be Purified
Mal 3: 1–3

> 1. Behold, I send my messenger, and he shall prepare the way before me: and the Lord, whom you seek, will suddenly come to his temple; and the messenger of the covenant, whom you desire, behold, he comes, says YHWH of hosts.
> 2. But who can abide the day of his coming? and who shall stand when he appears? for he is like a refiner's fire, and like fuller's soap:
> 3. and he will sit as a refiner and purifier of silver, and he will purify the sons of Levi, and refine them as gold and silver; and they shall offer to YHWH offerings in righteousness.

Malachi announces that the day of Judgment will come when YHWH would cleanse and purify his people, especially the "sons of Levi", the priests at the temple.

The Successor of Elijah
Mal; 4: 1–6

> 1. For, behold, the day comes, it burns as a furnace; and all the proud, and all who work wickedness, shall be stubble; and

> the day that comes shall burn them up, says YHWH of Hosts, that it shall leave them neither root nor branch.
> 2. But to you who fear my name shall the sun of righteousness arise with healing in its wings; and you shall go forth, and gambol as calves of the stall.
> 3. You shall tread down the wicked; for they shall be ashes under the soles of your feet in the day that I make, says YHWH of Hosts.
> 4. Remember you the law of Moses my servant, which I commanded to him in Horeb for all Israel, even statutes and ordinances.
> 5. Behold, I will send you Elijah the prophet before the great and terrible day of YHWH come.
> 6. He shall turn the heart of the fathers to the children, and the heart of the children to their fathers; lest I come and strike the earth with a curse.

Malachi – whose name, מַלְאָכִי (*Mal'akiy*), means "My Messenger" or "my angel" (Mal 1: 1 and 3: 1) saw himself as the successor of Elijah, the great prophet of earlier centuries.

It was his task to pronounce God's judgment on all wicked people who refused to worship him. Their fate was to be burnt to ashes, to be annihilated. A great future awaited the faithful.

The Eternal Kingdom of God
Dan 2: 44–45

> 44. In the days of those kings shall the God of heaven set up a kingdom which shall never be destroyed, nor shall the sovereignty of it be left to another people; but it shall break

	in pieces and consume all these kingdoms, and it shall stand forever.
45.	Because you saw that a stone was cut out of the mountain without hands, and that it broke in pieces the iron, the brass, the clay, the silver, and the gold; the great God has made known to the king what shall happen hereafter: and the dream is certain, and the interpretation of it sure.

This prophecy of Daniel certainly has a messianic flavor, although it cannot be applied to the ministry of Jesus Christ while he was on earth. This prophecy rather deals with the eternal kingdom of God that is due to appear at Judgment Day.

The Fourth Animal
Dan 7: 18–28

18.	But the saints of the Most High shall receive the kingdom, and possess the kingdom forever, even forever and ever.
19.	Then I desired to know the truth concerning the fourth animal, which was diverse from all of them, exceedingly terrible, whose teeth were of iron, and its nails of brass; which devoured, broke in pieces, and stamped the residue with its feet;
20.	and concerning the ten horns that were on its head, and the other [horn] which came up, and before which three fell, even that horn that had eyes, and a mouth that spoke great things, whose look was more stout than its fellows.
21.	I saw, and the same horn made war with the saints, and prevailed against them;

22. until the ancient of days came, and judgment was given to the saints of the Most High, and the time came that the saints possessed the kingdom.
23. Thus he said, The fourth animal shall be a fourth kingdom on earth, which shall be diverse from all the kingdoms, and shall devour the whole earth, and shall tread it down, and break it in pieces.
24. As for the ten horns, out of this kingdom shall ten kings arise: and another shall arise after them; and he shall be diverse from the former, and he shall put down three kings.
25. He shall speak words against the Most High, and shall wear out the saints of the Most High; and he shall think to change the times and the law; and they shall be given into his hand until a time and times and half a time.
26. But the judgment shall be set, and they shall take away his dominion, to consume and to destroy it to the end.
27. The kingdom and the dominion, and the greatness of the kingdoms under the whole the sky, shall be given to the people of the saints of the Most High: his kingdom is an everlasting kingdom, and all dominions shall serve and obey him.
28 Here is the end of the matter. As for me, Daniel, my thoughts much troubled me, and my face was changed in me: but I kept the matter in my heart.

The first part of this chapter in Daniel was already discussed in Chapter 3 of this book. Daniel saw four animals in the sky, each one of them representing a kingdom – the Assyrian, Median, Persian, and Greek kingdoms.

This passage tells more about the fourth animal, which was identified as the constellation of Scorpius, the Scorpion, together with Libra, the Scales, directly in front of it, representing the ten kings who followed the fourth animal. These ten kings were the successors of Alexander the Great, the Greek conqueror who took possession of Palestine in 332 BC. The one horn that supplanted the others and caused trouble for the Jews, was certainly meant to be King Antiochus IV Epiphanes, who tried to introduce the cult of Zeus in the Jerusalem temple.

The Jews, under the leadership of the Maccabees, successfully revolted and managed to create an independent Jewish state. The overpowering of the occupying army of Antiochus is described by Daniel as a prelude to Judgment Day when all evil forces will be vanquished.

The saints, the faithful Jews, received the promise that they would reign with God into eternity.

1 ENOCH

The Judgment of Azazel
1 Enoch 55: 1–4

1.	And after that the Head of Days repented and said: 'In vain have I destroyed all who dwell on the earth.'
2.	And He swore by His great name: 'Henceforth I will not do so to all who dwell on the earth, and I will set a sign in the heaven: and this shall be a pledge of good faith between Me and them for ever, so long as heaven is above the earth. And this is in accordance with My command.
3.	When I have desired to take hold of them by the hand of the angels on the day of tribulation and pain because of this, I will cause My chastisement and My wrath to abide upon them, saith God, the Lord of Spirits.

> 4. Ye mighty kings who dwell on the earth, ye shall have to behold Mine Elect One, how he sits on the throne of glory and judges Azazel, and all his associates, and all his hosts in the name of the Lord of Spirits.'

According to Enoch, God was not satisfied with the outcome of the great flood in the time of Noah, because He failed to wipe out all evil from earth. His assistant, the "Elect One", was destined to act as judge on Judgment Day when Azazel, the chief of the devils, as well as all his associates, would be sentenced to eternal doom.

THE AFTERLIFE

It will appear from the discussion that follows that the Hebrew Scriptures contain conflicting and contradictory notions regarding the fate of man after death. Texts dealing with this subject date mostly from the post-exilic and Persian periods.

Resurrection of the Dead
Isa 26: 16–21

> 16. YHWH, in trouble have they visited you; they poured out a prayer [when] your chastening was on them.
> 17. Like as a woman with child, who draws near the time of her delivery, is in pain and cries out in her pangs; so we have been before you, YHWH.
> 18. We have been with child, we have been in pain, we have as it were brought forth wind; we have not worked any deliverance in the earth; neither have the inhabitants of the world fallen.
> 19. Your dead shall live; my dead bodies shall arise. Awake and sing, you who dwell in the dust; for your dew is [as] the dew

> of herbs, and the earth shall cast forth the dead.
>
> 20. Come, my people, enter you into your chambers, and shut your doors about you: hide yourself for a little moment, until the indignation be past.
>
> 21. For, behold, YHWH comes forth out of his place to punish the inhabitants of the earth for their iniquity: the earth also shall disclose her blood, and shall no more cover her slain.

The prophet Isaiah called upon his people to hide themselves in their homes to await the judgment of God when the godless will be punished and vanquished. Their painful stay on earth may be compared with the pain a woman feels when giving birth to a child – just as a new world is due to be born.

The deceased faithful may expect to be resurrected from their graves when YHWH comes forth for the judgment.

The Final Judgment
Isa 66: 10–24

> 10. Rejoice you with Jerusalem, and be glad for her, all you who love her: rejoice for joy with her, all you who mourn over her;
>
> 11. that you may suck and be satisfied with the breasts of her consolations; that you may milk out, and be delighted with the abundance of her glory
>
> 12. For thus says YHWH, Behold, I will extend peace to her like a river, and the glory of the nations like an overflowing stream: and you shall suck [of it]; you shall be borne on the side, and shall be dandled on the knees.
>
> 13. As one whom his mother comforts, so will I comfort you; and you shall be comforted in Jerusalem.

14. You shall see [it], and your heart shall rejoice, and your bones shall flourish like the tender grass: and the hand of YHWH shall be known toward his servants; and he will have indignation against his enemies.

15. For, behold, YHWH will come with fire, and his chariots shall be like the whirlwind; to render his anger with fierceness, and his rebuke with flames of fire.

16. For by fire will YHWH execute judgment, and by his sword, on all flesh; and the slain of YHWH shall be many.

17. Those who sanctify themselves and purify themselves [to go] to the gardens, behind one in the midst, eating pig's flesh, and the abomination, and the mouse, they shall come to an end together, says YHWH.

18. For I [know] their works and their thoughts: [the time] comes, that I will gather all nations and languages; and they shall come, and shall see my glory.

19. I will set a sign among them, and I will send such as escape of them to the nations, to Tarshish, Pul, and Lud, who draw the bow, to Tubal and Javan, to the isles afar off, who have not heard my fame, neither have seen my glory; and they shall declare my glory among the nations.

20. They shall bring all your brothers out of all the nations for an offering to YHWH, on horses, and in chariots, and in litters, and on mules, and on dromedaries, to my holy mountain Jerusalem, says YHWH, as the children of Israel bring their offering in a clean vessel into the house of YHWH.

21. Of them also will I take for priests [and] for Levites, says YHWH.

> 22. For as the new heavens and the new earth, which I will make, shall remain before me, says YHWH, so shall your seed and your name remain.
> 23. It shall happen, that from one new moon to another, and from one Sabbath to another, shall all flesh come to worship before me, says YHWH.
> 24. They shall go forth, and look on the dead bodies of the men who have transgressed against me: for their worm shall not die, neither shall their fire be quenched; and they shall be an abhorring to all flesh.

The author of this final prophecy in the book of Isaiah directed his words towards "all nations and languages" and "all flesh". That means that all people will be affected by the final judgment of YHWH, which will be brought about by the sword and fire.

Those who have defiled themselves with unclean food and who refused to worship YHWH will suffer eternal damnation because their corpses will not rot, the fire will continue to burn, and the worms consuming their flesh won't ever die. If the Old Testament ever had a graphic description of hell as the destination of the godless, then this prophecy contains just that.

On the other hand, there will also be a new heaven and a new earth, the eternal city of Jerusalem where YHWH has his residence and where his people will enjoy all conceivable blessings. All those residing in this Jerusalem will worship God.

The third part of Isaiah was written during the Persian period in the history of the Jews. The ideas contained in this prophecy regarding eternal punishment for sinners and eternal joy for God's people was certainly inspired by the Persian religion, Zoroastrianism, where similar ideas were to be found.

Resurrection of the Dead
Dan 12: 1–4

> 1. At that time shall Michael stand up, the great prince who stands for the children of your people; and there shall be a time of trouble, such as never was since there was a nation even to that same time: and at that time your people shall be delivered, everyone who shall be found written in the book.
> 2. Many of those who sleep in the dust of the earth shall awake, some to everlasting life, and some to shame and everlasting contempt.
> 3. Those who are wise shall shine as the brightness of the expanse; and those who turn many to righteousness as the stars forever and ever.
> 4. But you, Daniel, shut up the words, and seal the book, even to the time of the end: many shall run back and forth, and knowledge shall be increased.

According the revelation that Daniel received, there will be difficult times at the end, but Michael, the archangel and guardian of Israel, will secure the safety of God's people, those whose names were recorded in God's book.

At that time, the graves will be opened and the dead will be resurrected. The godless and foolish people will receive everlasting punishment, while the wise and pious people will receive glory and shine as stars in heaven.

Sheol

The concept of "Sheol", the realm of the dead, played an important role in the Hebrew Scriptures' thinking about the afterlife. To understand this concept, one has to be reminded of the ancient primitive world-view found in the Hebrew Scriptures – as has been explained in more detail in Chapter 1 of this book.

Exodus 20: 4 tells us that the Israelites thought that God's creation consisted of three layers on top of each other:

Layers of Creation
Ex 20: 4

> You shall not make for yourselves an idol, nor any image of anything that is in the heavens above, or that is in the earth beneath, or that is in the water under the earth.

The earth was regarded as a flat disk. The netherworld, consisting of the primal flood and the abode of the dead, was to be found beneath the earth's surface. Everything above its surface was regarded as part of the heavens.

Under the surface of the earth there was supposed to be a deep *abyss*, called תְהוֹם (*tehom* – Gen 1: 2). This word has many meanings: "deep, depths, deep places, abyss, the deep, deep of subterranean waters, primeval ocean, the grave." This abyss encompassed the whole of the underworld.

Just as the Mesopotamians, Persians, and Greeks, the ancient Israelites thought that the souls or spirits of dead people went to a place under the surface of the earth, called "Sheol" (Gen 42: 38 and 44: 31). The Hebrew word שְׁאוֹל (*Sheol*), is usually translated as "underworld, grave, hell, pit, the abode of the dead".

That this part of creation was indeed seen as being below the surface of the flat earth, is best illustrated by Num 16: 31–33 –

Falling into Sheol
Num 16: 31–33

> 31. It happened, as he [Moses] made an end of speaking all these words, that the ground split apart that was under them [a group of rebels];
> 32. and the earth opened its mouth, and swallowed them up, and their households, and all the men who appertained to Korah, and all their goods.
> 33. So they, and all that appertained to them, went down alive into Sheol: and the earth closed on them, and they perished from among the assembly.

This is, no doubt, a description of a sinkhole that suddenly caved in, consisting of a cave or hollow space under the earth's surface and of which the roof unexpectedly collapsed. This cavity was interpreted as part of Sheol.

Amos 9: 2 tells us that it was even possible to "dig into Sheol".

That this netherworld did not have its own reigning or managing deity, as the pagans thought, is displayed by Ps 139: 8 –

God in the Netherworld
Ps 139: 8

> If I ascend up into heaven, you [YHWH] are there. If I make my bed in Sheol, behold, you are there!

YHWH as creator of the world is ubiquitous and He is, therefore, also present in Sheol, just as He is present in heaven. It is impossible to hide from him in this place. It is clear that the poet of this Psalm thought of God in concrete physical terms.

Jacob Mourns Joseph
Gen 37: 34–35

OLD TESTAMENT PROPHECIES REGARDING JUDGEMENT DAY AND THE AFTERLIFE

34.	Jacob tore his clothes, and put sackcloth on his loins, and mourned for his son many days.
35.	All his sons and all his daughters rose up to comfort him; but he refused to be comforted. He said, "For I will go down to Sheol to my son mourning." His father wept for him.

When Jacob was told that his beloved son Joseph was killed, he expressed the hope to be reunited with him in Sheol.

The Depth of Sheol
Job 11: 7–8

7.	Can you fathom the mystery of God? Or can you probe the limits of the Almighty?
8.	They are high as heaven. What can you do? Deeper than Sheol: what can you know?

Nothing can be deeper below the surface of the earth than Sheol, the abode of the dead.

Sheol a Monster
Isa 5: 14

Therefore Sheol has enlarged its desire, and opened its mouth without measure; and their glory, and their multitude, and their pomp, and he who rejoices among them, descend [into it].

Sheol was thought of as a monster with a gaping mouth, devouring the dead.

The Dead Can't Praise God
Ps 88: 10

> Do you show wonders to the dead? Do the dead rise up and praise you?

The word used for *the dead* in the second part of this verse, is רְפָאִים *(repha'im)*, which means "shadows" or "ghosts". The souls of the dead in Sheol were thought to be mere shadows or silent ghosts.

Sheol is a Place of Silence:
Ps 115: 17

> The dead do not give praise to the Lord; or those who go down to the underworld.

The Hebrew word for *underworld* in this text, דּוּמָה *(dumah)*, actually means "silence". This silence results from the inability of the dead inside Sheol to speak because they are asleep with their fathers.

Ps 31: 18

> Let me not be shamed, oh Lord, for I have made my prayer to you; let the sinners be shamed, and let their mouths be shut in the underworld.

Dead people who have descended to the underworld are not able to speak anymore.

Isa 31: 18–19

> 18. For the underworld is not able to give you praise, death gives you no honor: for those who go down into the underworld there is no hope in your mercy.

> 19. The living, the living man, he will give you praise, as I do this day: the father will give the story of your mercy to his children.

There is also the idea that the spirit with its thoughts and memories disappears at death.

Spirits Vanish
Ps 146: 4

> His spirit departs, and he returns to the earth. In that very day, his thoughts perish.

The spirits or breaths of the dead turn to dust and lose their memories.

No Contact with the Dead
Lev 20: 6

> The soul that turns to those who have familiar spirits, and to the wizards, to play the prostitute after them, I will even set my face against that soul, and will cut him off from among his people.

It was forbidden, but also impossible, for the living to contact the dead. Leviticus 20: 6 clearly condemned any effort in this regard. The Hebrew word for *necromancers* or people with familiar spirits is הַיִּדְּעֹנִים (*hayidd'oniyim*) – strictly speaking, the persons who have (esoteric) knowledge, but also soothsayers or necromancers.

Isa 19: 3

> The spirit of Egypt shall fail in the midst of it; and I will destroy the counsel of it: and they shall seek to the idols, and to the charmers, and to those who have familiar spirits, and to the wizards.

Isaiah condemned the pagan Egyptian "spirit" of wizardry and communication with the dead. The Hebrew word for "those who have familiar spirits" in this passage is הָאֹבוֹת (*ha'obot*) – meaning "those who evoke the dead".

William Blake: The Ghost of Samuel Appearing to Saul (c 1800)

There is, though, a famous example of a prominent Israelite who did just that. We read in 1 Sam 28 that King Saul had a consultation or a séance at night with the witch of Endor and requested her to bring the spirit of the prophet Samual up because he wanted to know what the outcome of the looming battle against the Philistines would be. Samuel purportedly announced that he and his sons would join him in the netherworld the next day, which frightened Saul severely, and which could have prompted him to give up the fight and commit suicide.

One may wonder: was it really Samuel's spirit that spoke to Saul? Saul – and his two servants – did not see Samuel themselves and he asked the woman what she saw in the dark. She replied that she saw a man with a cloak coming from the earth. It is more than likely that the witch imitated Samuel's voice. The superstitious Saul and his servants erroneously believed that they indeed had contact with the late Samuel's spirit, who predicted Saul's imminent death.

No Afterlife

Although Trito-Isaiah and the book of Daniel taught the resurrection of the dead at the end of time, there are various texts in the Hebrew Scriptures that declare that there is no afterlife, that death is final. A selection of these texts is quoted below:

> By the sweat of your face will you eat bread until you return to the ground, for out of it you were taken. For you are dust, and to dust you shall return (Gen 3: 19).
>
> See now, I have taken it on myself to speak to the Lord, I who am but dust and ashes (Gen 18: 27).
>
> But man dies, and is laid low. Yes, man gives up the spirit [breath], and where is he? As the waters fail from the sea, and the river wastes and dries up, so man lies down and doesn't rise; until the heavens are no more, they shall not awake, nor be roused out of their sleep (Job 14: 10–12).
>
> But man, despite his riches, doesn't endure. He is like the animals that perish (Ps 49: 12).
>
> For all our days have passed away in your wrath. We bring our years to an end as a sigh. The days of our years are seventy, or even by reason of strength eighty years; yet their pride is but labor and sorrow, for it passes quickly, and we fly away (Ps 90: 9–10).
>
> Though the wicked spring up as the grass, and all the evil-doers flourish, they will be destroyed forever (Ps 92: 7).
>
> You take away their breath: they die, and return to the dust (Ps 104: 29).
>
> His spirit departs, and he returns to the earth. In that very day, his thoughts perish (Ps 146: 4).

> For that which happens to the sons of men happens to animals. Even one thing happens to them. As the one dies, so the other dies. Yes, they have all one breath; and man has no advantage over the animals: for all is vanity. All go to one place. All are from the dust, and all turn to dust again (Eccl 3: 19–20).
>
> For the living know that they will die, but the dead don't know anything, neither do they have any more a reward; for the memory of them is forgotten. Also their love, their hatred, and their envy has perished long ago; neither have they any more a portion forever in anything that is done under the sun (Eccl 9: 5–6).
>
> The Lord created human beings from the earth, and makes them return to earth again (Sir 17: 1).
>
> ... [A]ll mortals are dust and ashes (Sir 17: 32).

All these pronouncements have the same message: there is no afterlife. All that remains of man after his death is a small heap of dust. The fates of men and animals are the same, namely extinction, annihilation, a cessation of existence.

Destruction of Sinners
1 Enoch 55: 2–5

> 2. And the sinners devour all whom they lawlessly oppress: Yet the sinners shall be destroyed before the face of the Lord of Spirits, And they shall be banished from off the face of His earth, And they shall perish for ever and ever.
> 3. For I saw all the angels of punishment abiding (there) and preparing all the instruments of Satan.
> 4. And I asked the angel of peace who went with me: ' For whom are they preparing these Instruments?'
> 5. And he said unto me: "They prepare these for the kings and the mighty of this earth, that they may thereby be destroyed."

There can be doubt: this passage in Enoch teaches that the evil sinners will be destroyed on Judgment Day. Their destruction will be painful, but also total.

Punishment for the Allies of Satan
1 Enoch 54: 1–6

1.	And I looked and turned to another part of the earth, and saw there a deep valley with burning fire.
2.	And they brought the kings and the mighty, and began to cast them into this deep valley.
3.	And there mine eyes saw how they made these their instruments, iron chains of immeasurable weight.
4.	And I asked the angel of peace who went with me, saying: 'For whom are these chains being prepared?'
5.	And he said unto me: 'These are being prepared for the hosts of Azazel, so that they may take them and cast them into the abyss of complete condemnation, and they shall cover their jaws with rough stones as the Lord of Spirits commanded.
6.	And Michael, and Gabriel, and Raphael, and Phanuel shall take hold of them on that great day, and cast them on that day into the burning furnace, that the Lord of Spirits may take vengeance on them for their unrighteousness in becoming subject to Satan and leading astray those who dwell on the earth.'

The author of 1 Enoch visualized hell as a deep valley or abyss on earth where the ungodly sinners and allies of Satan were tortured by a hot furnace, while they were bound by heavy iron shackles.

Sinners Devoured in Sheol
1 Enoch 56: 8

In those days Sheol shall open its jaws,

> And they shall be swallowed up therein
> And their destruction shall be at an end;
> Sheol shall devour the sinners in the presence of the elect.

According to this passage in 1 Enoch, all sinners will be devoured by Sheol and they will be finally destroyed – presumably after having been tortured first.

TO WRAP UP

The following conclusions may be drawn at the end of this chapter:

- There are various prophecies in the Old Testament that the Day of YHWH would arrive – the day on which the godless and evil people would perish under God's wrath. That included those people of Israel who forgot YHWH as their God, who transgressed his laws, and worshipped pagan deities.
- The teaching of the Hebrew Scriptures regarding death and a possible existence beyond the grave is certainly not clear and without ambiguity or contradictions. Some texts foresee an existence after bodily death and the resurrection of the dead – either to glory or to humiliation. There is also the idea that the godless and evil people will be eradicated, while the righteous would inherit a happy existence with God, either in heaven or a renewed earth. Other texts deny that there is an existence after death, while others describe a shadowy existence in the realm of the dead in Sheol, somewhere below the surface of the earth.
- The afterlife for those who pass the examination on Judgment Day is often described in very concrete terms as a perfected earthly existence with abundant supplies of food, wine, and water, on the present earth that has been purified of all evil and wicked people. It would be heaven on earth.

These conflicting points of view are in contrast with the New Testament where an existence in an afterlife is taught as a certainty.

CHAPTER 8
NEW TESTAMENT PROPHECIES REGARDING JUDGMENT DAY AND THE AFTERLIFE

Although the New Testament is much shorter than the Old Testament, it contains many more descriptions of Judgment Day and the afterlife. The most important texts are scrutinized below:

JESUS OF NAZARETH

The Question about Rising from Death
Mark 12: 18–27 (Matt 22: 23–33; Luke 20: 27–40)

18.	There came to him Sadducees, who say that there is no resurrection. They asked him, saying,
19.	"Teacher, Moses wrote to us, 'If a man's brother dies, and leaves a wife behind him, and leaves no child, that his brother should take his wife, and raise up children to his brother.'
20.	There were seven brothers. The first took a wife, and dying left no children.
21.	The second took her, and died, leaving no children behind him. The third likewise;
22.	and the seven took her and left no children. Last of all the woman also died.

23.	In the resurrection, when they rise, whose wife will she be of them? For the seven had her as a wife."
24.	Jesus answered them, "Isn't this because you are mistaken, not knowing the Scriptures, nor the power of God?
25.	For when they will rise from the dead, they neither marry, nor are given in marriage, but are like angels in heaven.
26.	But about the dead, that they are raised; haven't you read in the book of Moses, at the Bush, how God spoke to him, saying, "I am the God of Abraham, the God of Isaac, and the God of Jacob?"
27.	He is not the God of the dead, but of the living. You are therefore badly mistaken."

The Sadducees, a liberal group of Jews, accepted only the Torah as divinely inspired. Since this collection of books doesn't mention the resurrection of the dead, they rejected such a notion.

They tried to trap Jesus with an absurd scenario of seven brothers who all married their eldest brother's widow in a row, without producing any heirs as provided for in Moses' laws. They wanted to know whose wife she would be in the resurrection.

Jesus firstly pointed out that gender differences disappear in the afterlife. He also reminded them by quoting from the Torah that God is not the God of dead people but of the still living ancestors who are in heaven with Him.

The Rich Man and Lazarus
Luke 16: 19–31

19.	Now there was a certain rich man, and he was clothed in purple and fine linen, living in luxury every day.

20. A certain beggar, named Lazarus, was laid at his gate, full of sores,
21. and desiring to be fed with the crumbs that fell from the rich man's table. Yes, even the dogs came and licked his sores.
22. It happened that the beggar died, and that he was carried away by the angels to Abraham's bosom. The rich man also died, and was buried.
23. In Hades, he lifted up his eyes, being in torment, and saw Abraham far off, and Lazarus at his bosom.
24. He cried and said, Father Abraham, have mercy on me, and send Lazarus, that he may dip the tip of his finger in water, and cool my tongue! For I am in anguish in this flame.
25. But Abraham said, Son, remember that you, in your lifetime, received your good things, and Lazarus, in like manner, bad things. But now here he is comforted and you are in anguish.
26. Besides all this, between us and you there is a great gulf fixed, that those who want to pass from here to you are not able, and that none may cross over from there to us.
27. He said, I ask you therefore, father, that you would send him to my father's house;
28. for I have five brothers, that he may testify to them, lest they also come into this place of torment.
29. But Abraham said to him, They have Moses and the prophets. Let them listen to them.
30. He said, No, father Abraham, but if one goes to them from the dead, they will repent.

> 31. He said to him, If they don't listen to Moses and the prophets, neither will they be persuaded if one rises from the dead.

The story of the rich man and Lazarus is another famous story that Jesus told to his listeners. As could be expected from an Essene, he depicted the rich man in the darkest colors possible. He was without generosity, lived in luxury, but ended up in Hades, in hell, after his death and a beautiful and expensive funeral.

On the other hand, Jesus' sympathy lay with the poor beggar, Lazarus, who lived in the greatest misery, but was taken by the angels after his death to Abraham's bosom in heaven.

Jesus taught that a wide unbridgeable canyon separates heaven and hell, which made it impossible to move from one side to the other. Jesus advised his listeners to pay attention to the commandments, warnings, and promises contained in the Scriptures to prevent eternal torture after death in Hades.

Jesus Speaks about the Destruction of the Temple
Luke 13: 1–2 (Matt 24: 1–2; Luke 21: 5–6)

> 1. As he went forth out of the temple, one of his disciples said to him, "Teacher, see what kind of stones and what kind of buildings!"
> 2. Jesus said to him, "Do you see these great buildings? There will not be left here one stone on another, which will not be thrown down."

According to Mark, Matthew, and Luke, Jesus predicted the destruction of the temple, which did occur during the Jewish War against Rome, AD 66–70.

It is highly improbable that Jesus would have spoken these

words since the restored kingdom of David, of which he was to become the sovereign, was meant to have Jerusalem as its capital with an intact temple. Jesus' words are often – erroneously – seen as a description of Judgment Day.

Troubles and Persecutions
Mark 13: 2–13 (Matt 24: 3–14; Luke 21: 7–19)

3.	As he sat on the Mount of Olives opposite the temple, Peter, James, John, and Andrew asked him privately,
4.	"Tell us, when will these things be? What is the sign that these things are all about to be accomplished?"
5.	Jesus, answering, began to tell them, "Be careful that no one leads you astray.
6.	For many will come in my name, saying, 'I am he!' and will lead many astray.
7.	When you hear of wars and rumors of wars, don't be troubled. For those must happen, but the end is not yet.
8.	For nation will rise against nation, and kingdom against kingdom. There will be earthquakes in various places. There will be famines and troubles. These things are the beginning of birth pains.
9.	But watch yourselves, for they will deliver you up to councils. You will be beaten in synagogues. Before governors and kings will you stand for my sake, for a testimony to them.
10.	The gospel must first be preached to all the nations.
11.	When they lead you away and deliver you up, don't be anxious beforehand, or premeditate what you will say, but say whatever will be given you in that hour. For it is not you who speak, but the Holy Spirit.

12.	Brother will deliver up brother to death, and the father his child. Children will rise up against parents, and cause them to be put to death.
13.	You will be hated by all men for my name's sake, but he who endures to the end, the same will be saved."

These purported predictions or prophecies of Jesus actually describe history, as seen from the time when Mark wrote his gospel during the seventies AD. There was a war when Jerusalem was razed, there were various false messiahs, the message of Jesus' teachings (the gospel) was proclaimed in other countries around the Mediterranean Sea where the Jesus people fled, and the followers of Jesus endured resistance and even persecution.

Matthew and Luke omitted that Jesus told only four of his disciples about the expected destruction of the temple. According to Luke, Jesus spoke to all his disciples while still in the temple – not on the Mount of Olives outside Jerusalem. These discrepancies undermine the credibility of this report.

The Awful Horror
Mark 13: 14–23 (Matt 24: 15–28; Luke 21: 20–24)

14.	But when you see the abomination of desolation, spoken of by Daniel the prophet, standing where it ought not (let the reader understand), then let those who are in Judea flee to the mountains,
15.	and let him who is on the housetop not go down, nor enter in, to take anything out of his house.
16.	Let him who is in the field not return back to take his cloak.
17.	But woe to those who are with child and to those who nurse babies in those days!

> 18. Pray that your flight won't be in the winter.
> 19. For in those days there will be oppression, such as there has not been the like from the beginning of the creation which God created until now, and never will be.
> 20. Unless the Lord had shortened the days, no flesh would have been saved; but for the elect's sake, whom he chose, he shortened the days.
> 21. Then if anyone tells you, 'Look, here is the Christ!' or, 'Look, there!' don't believe it.
> 22. For there will arise false christs and false prophets, and will show signs and wonders, that they may lead astray, if possible, also the elect.
> 23. But you watch. "Behold, I have told you all things beforehand."

That Mark described history is clear from verse 20 where he used the past tense, indicating that God had already shortened the days of hardship during the war. Matthew 24: 22 changed the past tense to future tense to preserve the pretense that Jesus predicted all these calamities at least four decades earlier.

According to Mark, Jesus purportedly warned his followers to flee and to hope that they would not have to get away with small children or during winter. It really happened that Jesus' followers, the Ebionites, fled from Galilee and Judea to Pella across the Jordan, Egypt, and Asia Minor when the Roman Army under Vespasian and Titus started to besiege the fortress of Jotapata in Galilee during December AD 67 – at the height of winter.[220]

Luke added that Jerusalem would be surrounded by a pagan

---

[220] History Today, "Jewish Roman Wars"; Goldberg, "A Chronology of the First Jewish Revolt".

army that would trample the city and that many men would be taken captive – which did happen on 30 August AD 70 when Jerusalem fell. Luke would certainly have known about it – as almost everybody else in the Roman Empire at that time.

Mark evidently thought that Jesus, a great prophet, must have foreseen the Jewish War and warned his followers to be ready for such an event and, therefore, he invented a prophecy by Jesus to insert into his narrative. Matthew and Luke expanded on it by adding details from known history.

The Coming of the Son of Man
Mark 13: 24–27 (Matt 24: 29–31; Luke21: 25–28)

24.	But in those days, after that oppression, the sun will be darkened, the moon will not give her light,
25.	the stars will be falling from the sky, and the powers that are in the heavens will be shaken.
26.	Then will they see the Son of Man coming in clouds with great power and glory.
27.	Then will he send forth his angels, and will gather together his elect from the four winds, from the ends of the earth to the ends of the sky.

Jesus often told his disciples that he expected to be crucified, but that he would survive and return. Mark changed this return date in the near future to Judgment Day and implied that the destruction of the temple would happen shortly before Judgment Day – which never happened that way because Judgment Day has not arrived yet, while Jerusalem fell centuries ago. Mark connected the astronomical phenomena during the time of the siege of Jerusalem and thereafter as signs of Jesus' return and Judgment Day.

Jesus expected twelve brigades of battle-ready angels to aid him in securing the throne in Jerusalem. Mark changed the appearance of these angels to Jesus' return on Judgment Day.

Matthew and Luke added some drama to Mark's description by adding trumpets – no doubt a memory of the Roman war trumpets that sounded during the war and the siege of Jerusalem – and the appearance of Jesus on the clouds.

The Lesson of the Fig Tree
Mark 13: 28–31 (Matt 24: 32–33; Luke 21: 29–33)

28.	Now from the fig tree, learn this parable. When the branch has now become tender, and puts forth its leaves, you know that the summer is near;
29.	even so you also, when you see these things coming to pass, know that it is near, at the doors.
30.	Most assuredly I say to you, this generation will not pass away until all these things are accomplished.
31.	Heaven and earth will pass away, but my words will not pass away.

Jesus told the parable of the fig tree that starts to produce small figs and new leaves when Spring arrives. He used this as an example to warn his followers that they would have to be ready for his return and victory with the aid of an army of angels.

Jesus also said that the present generation would experience his return. With that, he had his resurrection after his possible crucifixion and his victory over the enemies of his people in mind – not a far-way Judgment Day. This element is usually overlooked when Bible students think that Jesus meant Judgment Day.

No One Knows the Day or Hour
Mark 13: 32–37 (Matt 24: 36–44)

32.	But of that day or that hour no one knows, not even the angels in heaven, neither the Son, but only the Father.
33.	Watch, keep alert, and pray; for you don't know when the time is.
34.	"It is like a man, traveling to another country, having left his house, and given authority to his servants, and to each one his work, and also commanded the doorkeeper to keep watch.
35.	Watch therefore, for you don't know when the lord of the house is coming, whether at evening, or at midnight, or when the rooster crows, or in the morning;
36.	lest coming suddenly he might find you sleeping.
37.	What I tell you, I tell all: Watch."

Jesus warned his disciples to be ready at any moment for the coming of the kingdom of God. He illustrated that with the parable of the owner of the house who left everything in the hands of his servants who had to be ready for his return at any moment.

One often hears the argument that Jesus, as the Son of God and the Second Person in the Divine Trinity, must have been all-knowing, also during his stay on earth as a human being, and that is why he could make all these predictions about the future. In this passage, however, Jesus explicitly admitted that the Son didn't know when all these hardships, calamities, and his return would occur. Therefore, he could not have been all-knowing or omniscient.

The Judgment
Matt 25: 31–46

31. But when the Son of Man comes in his glory, and all the holy angels with him, then will he sit on the throne of his glory.
32. Before him all the nations will be gathered, and he will separate them one from another, as the shepherd separates the sheep from the goats.
33. He will set the sheep on his right hand, but the goats on the left.
34. Then the King will tell them on his right hand, 'Come, blessed of my Father, inherit the kingdom prepared for you from the foundation of the world;
35. for I was hungry, and you gave me food to eat; I was thirsty, and you gave me drink; I was a stranger, and you took me in;
36. naked, and you clothed me; I was sick, and you visited me; I was in prison, and you came to me.'
37. Then the righteous will answer him, saying, 'Lord, when did we see you hungry, and feed you; or thirsty, and give you a drink?
38. When did we see you as a stranger, and take you in; or naked, and clothe you?
39. When did we see you sick, or in prison, and come to you?'
40. The King will answer them, 'Most assuredly I tell you, inasmuch as you did it to one of the least of these my brothers, you did it to me.'
41. Then will he say also to them on the left hand, 'Depart from me, you cursed, into the eternal fire which is prepared for the devil and his angels;
42. for I was hungry, and you didn't give me food to eat; I was thirsty, and you gave me no drink;

> 43. I was a stranger, and you didn't take me in; naked, and you didn't clothe me; sick, and in prison, and you didn't visit me.'
> 44. Then will they also answer, saying, 'Lord, when did we see you hungry, or thirsty, or a stranger, or naked, or sick, or in prison, and did not help you?'
> 45. Then will he answer them, saying, 'Most assuredly I tell you, inasmuch as you didn't do it to one of these least, you didn't do it to me.'
> 46. These will go away into eternal punishment, but the righteous into eternal life.

This is another well-known parable, the parable of the sheep and the goats that would be separated into two separate herds. The conventional explanation is that it deals exclusively with the Final Judgment when Christ would return to judge the world. It does seem, though, that the original parable as Jesus told it, became jumbled and distorted during the decades before Matthew included it in his gospel.

Jesus expected to become the king of Israel with the help of a horde of holy angels. When he had gained the throne, he would make sure that his enemies and the godless would receive their deserved punishment. They would also be judged on how much generosity and charity they had practiced.

When no kingdom in Jerusalem was realized, those who retold the parable shifted the establishment of the kingdom to the far future, at the end of time, when Christ would come back to judge all the nations on earth. Their fates hinged on their conduct on earth.

Jesus' Ascension

Luke wrote two versions of Jesus' ascension into heaven. After his almost miraculous recovery after his ordeal on the cross, he must have been a broken man who went into hiding and only occasionally visited his disciples.

Albrecht Dürer: The Last Judgment (ca 1510)

Because of the visions he had and the revelations he had received, Paul was convinced that Jesus had ascended into heaven where he is seated at the right hand of his Father, after being brought back to life again after his crucifixion with a heavenly body (1 Cor 15; Rom 8: 34; Eph 1: 20; Col 3: 1). Paul also propagated the idea that Jesus would return to earth on Judgment Day (1 Cor 1: 7; 1 Cor 15: 23; 1 Thess 2: 1; 1 Thess 3: 13).

Luke, who wrote his gospel and the book of Acts during the eighties AD, adopted Paul's convictions and devised two versions of Jesus' ascension into heaven:

Luke 24: 49 – 53

49.	"Behold, I send forth the promise of my Father on you. But wait in the city of Jerusalem until you are clothed with power from on high."
50.	He led them out as far as to Bethany, and he lifted up his hands, and blessed them.
51.	It happened, while he blessed them, that he withdrew from them, and was carried up into heaven.
52.	They worshipped him, and returned to Jerusalem with great joy,
53.	and were continually in the temple, praising and blessing God.

Acts 1: 9–12

6.	Therefore, when they had come together, they asked him, "Lord, are you now restoring the kingdom to Israel?"
7.	He said to them, "It isn't for you to know times or seasons which the Father has set within His own authority.
8.	But you will receive power when the Holy Spirit has come on you. You will be witnesses to me in Jerusalem, in all Judea and Samaria, and to the uttermost parts of the earth."

> 9. When he had said these things, as they were looking, he was taken up, and a cloud received him out of their sight.
> 10. While they were looking steadfastly into the sky as he went, behold, two men stood by them in white clothing,
> 11. who also said, "You men of Galilee, why do you stand looking into the sky? This Jesus, who was received up from you into the sky will come back in the same way as you saw him going into the sky."
> 12. Then they returned to Jerusalem from the mountain called Olivet, which is near Jerusalem, a Sabbath day's journey away.

Luke expanded the second version of his story with extra details to make the disappearance of Jesus still more miraculous.

However, the two stories contain discrepancies, which diminish their credibility. From which point did Jesus ascend into heaven: Fram Bethany or the Mount of Olives, just outside Jerusalem? Why is the first version silent about Jesus' predicted return on the clouds?

It is also important to ask: Why doesn't any other gospel contain a similar report of an ostensibly very important event?

One may safely relegate these two stories to the realm of myths, devised by Luke to explain the disappearance of Jesus. One may also wonder: how much value can be placed on the prophecy about Jesus' return somewhere in the future?

PAUL THE APOSTLE

The Death, Resurrection, and Return of Jesus Christ
1 Thess 1: 10

> ... and to wait for his Son from heaven, whom he raised from the dead – Jesus, who delivers us from the wrath to come.

1 Thess 4: 13–18

> 13. But we don't want you to be ignorant, brothers, concerning those who have fallen asleep, so that you don't grieve like the rest, who have no hope.
> 30. For if we believe that Jesus died and rose again, even so those who have fallen asleep in Jesus will God bring with him.
> 31. For this we tell you by the word of the Lord, that we who are alive, who are left to the coming of the Lord, will in no way precede those who have fallen asleep.
> 32. For the Lord himself will descend from heaven with a shout, with the voice of the archangel, and with God's trumpet. The dead in Christ will rise first,
> 33. then we who are alive, who are left, will be caught up together with them in the clouds, to meet the Lord in the air. So we will be with the Lord forever.
> 34. Therefore comfort one another with these words.

1 Thess 2: 14–15

> 14. For you, brothers, became imitators of the assemblies of God which are in Judea in Christ Jesus; for you also suffered the same things from your own countrymen, even as they did from the Jews;
> 15. who killed the Lord Jesus and the prophets, and drove us out, and didn't please God, and are contrary to all men;

1 Thess 5: 1–3

6.	But concerning the times and the seasons, brothers, you have no need that anything be written to you.
7.	For you yourselves know well that the day of the Lord comes like a thief in the night.
8.	For when they are saying, "Peace and safety," then sudden destruction will come on them, like birth pains on a pregnant woman; and they will in no way escape .

If the first letter to the Thessalonians is Paul's earliest extant letter, then his references to the exalted Lord Jesus Christ, the divine Son of God, is the first we have in writing from him. Jesus is described as the Savior who brought deliverance from the horrors of Judgment Day to believers.

The only biographical details about Jesus in these passages are that the Jews killed him as they also killed the prophets, that he was resurrected, and he is expected to return on Judgment Day like a conquering general, when all the deceased faithful will be resurrected and those who are still alive, will be transformed and taken up into heaven.

Jesus' Resurrection and Appearances
1 Cor 15: 1–8

1.	Now I declare to you, brothers, the gospel which I preached to you, which also you received, in which you also stand,
2.	by which also you are saved, if you hold firmly the word which I preached to you – unless you believed in vain.
3.	For I delivered to you first of all that which also I received: that Christ died for our sins according to the Scriptures,

4.	that he was buried, that he was raised on the third day according to the Scriptures,
5.	and that he appeared to Cephas, then to the twelve.
6.	Then he appeared to over five hundred brothers at once, most of whom remain until now, but some have also fallen asleep.
7.	Then he appeared to James, then to all the apostles,
8.	and last of all, as to the child born at the wrong time, he appeared to me also.

Paul provided his readers with a list of people who purportedly had seen Jesus after his resurrection. It is noteworthy that he failed to mention the women who were the first to find the empty tomb, according to the gospels (Matt 28: 1–8; Luke 24: 1–10; John 20: 1–2).

This passage cannot be used as solid proof that Jesus really cheated death and was resurrected. Apart from Paul's subjective and uncorroborated visions and revelations, he mentions other people who purportedly saw Jesus after his resurrection – as told to him by unknown informants. Paul's information was, therefore, second-hand, or even third-hand.

There are no independent reports of any occasion when Jesus was supposed to have appeared to more than five hundred men, unless this is a skewed reference to the events on Pentecost when the Holy Spirit was poured out onto a group of apostles and other people (Acts 2).

Paul's declaration that "the Scriptures" foretold the death and resurrection of Christ is not correct. The only part of the Old Testament where something of the sort is seemingly written is Isa 52: 13–15 and 53: 1–13 where a description of the suffering "servant of YHWH" is given. This passage is often mentioned in the New Testament as a prophecy of the Messiah that was apparently fulfilled by

Jesus' crucifixion (Luke 22: 37; 24: 26–27; Acts 3: 18; 8: 26–40; 26: 22–23; Rom 15: 21; Phil 2: 7–11; Eph 5: 2; 1 Pet 2: 22–25; 3: 18).

However, it was shown in Chapter 5 of this book that the expression "servant of YHWH" was never used in the Old Testament for the expected Messiah. In Isa 52–53 it clearly pointed to the nation of Israel. It must be concluded that Paul's statement that "the Scriptures" – especially Isa 52–53 – contain prophecies regarding Christ's death and resurrection cannot be maintained.

The End
1 Cor 15: 24–28

24.	Then the end comes, when he will deliver up the kingdom to God, even the Father; when he will have abolished all rule and all authority and power.
26.	For he must reign until he has put all his enemies under his feet.
26.	The last enemy that will be abolished is death.
27.	For, "He put all things in subjection under his feet." But when he says, "All things are put in subjection," it is evident that he is excepted who subjected all things to him.
28.	When all things have been subjected to him, then the Son will also himself be subjected to him who subjected all things to him, that God may be all in all.

This text states that Christ will abdicate his position after Judgment Day when he will subject himself to God.

Similar thoughts are found elsewhere in 1 Corinthians. In chapter 3: 21–22 we are told: "All are yours, and you are Christ's, and Christ is God's." 1 Cor 11: 3 says: "But I would have you know, that the head of every man is Christ, and the head of the woman is the man, and the head of Christ is God."

These passages must be seen as a contradiction of the Christian doctrine of the trinitarian God – three divine, eternal persons in one Godhead. If Christ has God (the Father) as his head and he will subject himself to God (the Father) on Judgment Day, then he cannot be God as well. He will then, at most, be a lesser deity, such as the offspring of Zeus, father of the Greeks gods.

Paul's assertion "that God may be all in all" reminds one of the philosophy of pantheism, "the doctrine that the universe conceived of as a whole is God and, conversely, that there is no God but the combined substance, forces, and laws that are manifested in the existing universe."

A similar thought of Paul is also to be found in 1 Cor 12: 6 – "There are various kinds of workings, but the same God, who works all things in all" (see also Eph 1: 23 and Col 3: 11). That means that the whole of reality will be dissolved into God and that nothing outside of God will exist at the end. It seems as if Paul borrowed this pantheism from the ancient Greek philosophy of Stoicism that taught that the All and the Soul of the World are one and the same.[221]

One looks in vain for a clear doctrine of creation in Paul's letters and when he does speak of God as creator, it is in a pantheistic manner. For instance, in 1 Cor 1: 5–6 he wrote:

> "For though there are things that are called 'gods,' whether in the heavens or on earth; as there are many 'gods' and many 'lords;' yet to us there is one God, the Father, of whom are all things, and we to him; and one Lord, Jesus Christ, through whom are all things [exist], and we through him."

---

[221] Enc. Brit, "Pantheism".

In Col 1: 15–17, Christ is called the firstborn of creation, as well as the agent through which the whole of creation was brought about (*qv*). This boils down to the idea that Christ, as God, as it were, created himself when the universe had its origin – which is also a pantheistic notion.

With his pantheism, Paul's thoughts are at odds with the whole of the Old Testament where it is taken for granted that God, the creator, cannot be part of his creation, but is outside of it – in other words, He is transcendent, not imminent, and not to be confused with his creation.

The Resurrected Body
I Cor 15: 19–20. 35–58

19.	If we have only hoped in Christ in this life, we are of all men most pitiable.
20.	But now Christ has been raised from the dead. He became the first fruits of those who are asleep.
35.	But someone will say, "How are the dead raised?" and, "With what kind of body do they come?"
36.	You foolish one, that which you yourself sow is not made alive unless it dies.
37.	That which you sow, you don't sow the body that will be, but a bare grain, maybe of wheat, or of some other kind.
38.	But God gives it a body even as it pleased him, and to each seed a body of its own.
39.	All flesh is not the same flesh, but there is one flesh of men, another flesh of animals, another of fish, and another of birds.
40.	There are also celestial bodies, and terrestrial bodies; but the glory of the celestial differs from that of the terrestrial.

41. There is one glory of the sun, another glory of the moon, and another glory of the stars; for one star differs from another star in glory.
42. So also is the resurrection of the dead. It is sown in corruption; it is raised in incorruption.
43. It is sown in dishonor; it is raised in glory. It is sown in weakness; it is raised in power.
44. It is sown a natural body; it is raised a spiritual body. If there is a natural body, there is also a spiritual body.
45. So also it is written, "The first man, Adam, became a living soul." The last Adam became a life-giving spirit.
46. However that which is spiritual isn't first, but that which is natural, then that which is spiritual.
47. The first man is of the earth, made of dust. The second man is the Lord from heaven.
48. As is the one made of dust, such are those who are also made of dust; and as is the heavenly, such are they also that are heavenly.
49. As we have borne the image of those made of dust, let's also bear the image of the heavenly.
50. Now I say this, brothers, that flesh and blood can't inherit the kingdom of God; neither does corruption inherit incorruption.
51. Behold, I tell you a mystery. We will not all sleep, but we will all be changed,
52. in a moment, in the twinkling of an eye, at the last trumpet. For the trumpet will sound, and the dead will be raised incorruptible, and we will be changed.

> 53. For this corruptible must put on incorruption, and this mortal must put on immortality.
> 54. But when this corruptible will have put on incorruption, and this mortal will have put on immortality, then what is written will happen: "Death is swallowed up in victory."
> 55. "Death, where is your sting? Hades, where is your victory?"
> 56. The sting of death is sin, and the power of sin is the law.
> 57. But thanks be to God, who gives us the victory through our Lord Jesus Christ.
> 58. Therefore, my beloved brothers, be steadfast, immovable, always abounding in the Lord's work, because you know that your labor is not in vain in the Lord.

Paul wrote in this lengthy and rather jumbled passage that believers will be resurrected with a "heavenly body" or a "spiritual body". Since Christ is the "first fruit" of those who will be resurrected in glory, it goes without saying that he must also have left the grave with a "spiritual body". The same idea occurs in Phil 3: 20–21.

Likewise, 1 Pet 3: 18 declares that Christ was "put to death in the flesh, but made alive in the spirit" – in other words, he was resurrected only spiritually (whatever that means), and not bodily or physically.

It is probable and possible that Paul thought of this heavenly or spiritual body as composed of a fifth element, the so-called quintessence – apart from the four "ordinary" elements, namely fire, air, water, and earth – of which the celestial or astronomical bodies were supposed to be made, according to the Greek philosopher Aristotle.[222]

---

[222] Aristotle, *On the Heavens*, Book 1: 9.

One can only conclude that Paul thought of the resurrected "spiritual body" of Jesus as a heavenly or "celestial body" – composed of the same stuff as the sun, moon, and stars, which differs from the "dust" of our earth and with which he could ascend into heaven, between or beyond the stars (see also Eph 4: 10).

A similar thought is found in the philosophical sections of John's Gospel:

> "Very truly I tell you, whoever hears my word and believes him who sent me has eternal life and will not be judged but has crossed over from death to life. Very truly I tell you, a time is coming and has now come when the dead will hear the voice of the Son of God and those who hear will live. For as the Father has life in himself, so he has granted the Son also to have life in himself. And he has given him authority to judge because he is the Son of Man.
>
> "Do not be amazed at this, for a time is coming when all who are in their graves will hear his voice and come out—those who have done what is good will rise to live, and those who have done what is evil will rise to be condemned" (John 5:24–29).

The Resurrected Body
Phil 3: 20–21

20.	For our citizenship is in heaven, from where we also wait for a Savior, the Lord, Jesus Christ;
21.	who will change the body of our humiliation to be conformed to the body of his glory, according to the working whereby he is able even to subject all things to himself.

According to Paul, believers will receive bodies of glory on Judgment Day – the same type of body of glory with which Christ rose from the grave. No details of this type of body are given, but one may suppose that Paul thought of a "heavenly body" or a "spiritual body", which he mentioned in 1 Cor 15.

We also read in Acts 17: 31 –

> "For he has set a day when he will judge the world with justice by the man he has appointed. He has given proof of this to everyone by raising him from the dead."

JOHN OF PATMOS

The Key of David
Rev 3: 7

> To the angel of the assembly in Philadelphia write: "He who is holy, he who is true, he who has the key of David, he who opens and no one can shut, and that shuts and no one opens, says these things: …"

These words are the introduction to one of John's letters to the seven Christian communities in Asia Minor in which he informs the recipients of his letter that he is writing on behalf of Jesus Christ, "He who is holy, he who is true, he who has the key of David, he who opens and no one can shut, and that shuts and no one opens."

This means that Jesus Christ will be the judge on Judgment Day who will decide who will be admitted into heavenly glory and who will be excluded.

John found the expression "the key of David" in Isa 22: 22 – "The key of the house of David will I lay on his shoulder; and he shall open, and none shall shut; and he shall shut, and none shall open." These words are often interpreted as a prophecy about the Messiah, which was fulfilled in Rev 3: 7.

That was, however, never the intention of Isaiah. He wrote about a certain Elyakim, the royal steward of King Hezekiah. As steward he held the keys to the palace. A future Messiah was never meant.

When John used this phrase, "the key of David", he disregarded the original context and made something new of this expression, without providing the fulfilment of any prophecy.

The Rider on the White Horse
Rev 19: 11–21

11.	I saw the heaven opened, and behold, a white horse, and he who sat on it is called Faithful and True. In righteousness he judges and makes war.
12.	His eyes are a flame of fire, and on his head are many crowns. He has names written and a name written which no one knows but he himself.
13.	He is clothed in a garment sprinkled with blood. His name is called "The Word of God."
14.	The armies which are in heaven followed him on white horses, clothed in white, pure, fine linen.
15.	Out of his mouth proceeds a sharp, two-edged sword, that with it he should strike the nations. He will rule them with a rod of iron. He treads the winepress of the fierceness of the wrath of God, the Almighty.
16.	He has on his garment and on his thigh a name written, "KING OF KINGS, AND LORD OF LORDS."
17.	I saw an angel standing in the sun. He cried with a loud voice, saying to all the birds that fly in the sky, "Come! Be gathered together to the great supper of God,

> 18. that you may eat the flesh of kings, the flesh of captains, the flesh of mighty men, and the flesh of horses and of those who sit on them, and the flesh of all men, both free and slave, and small and great."
> 19. I saw the beast, and the kings of the earth, and their armies, gathered together to make war against him who sat on the horse, and against his army.
> 20. The beast was taken, and with him the false prophet who worked the signs in his sight, with which he deceived those who had received the mark of the beast and those who worshipped his image. They two were thrown alive into the lake of fire that burns with sulfur.
> 21. The rest were killed with the sword of him who sat on the horse, the sword which came forth out of his mouth. All the birds were filled with their flesh.

What John saw

John saw that the heaven was opened, as well as a white horse whose rider had a sword. He was followed by an army on horseback and clothed in white. John often incorporated war horses (Rev 6: 1–11; 9: 17–19; 18:13), and swords (Rev 2: 16; 6: 8; 13: 10; 19: 15) into his visions and it is likely that he witnessed Roman cavalry and foot soldiers in action during the Jewish War of AD 66–70 before he fled to Asia Minor.

This figure on the white horse symbolized Christ as a conqueror. He is, after all, called "the Word of God" (see John 1: 1-12) and his title, "KING OF KINGS, AND LORD OF LORDS", was also given to the Lamb (Christ) in Rev 17: 14. Moreover, he is characterized as a righteous judge (see Rev 20: 11–15). It was stated that his garment was spattered with blood – either the blood that flowed when He was crucified, or the blood of his vanquished foes.

The white horse was evidently the constellation of Sagittarius, the Archer, which was clearly visible in the south-eastern sky towards the end of August AD 96. John perceived the arrow in his bow to be a sword protruding from his mouth. The crown on his head must be sought in the constellation of Corona Australis, the Southern Crown, directly next to Sagittarius. This constellation also symbolized Jesus Christ in Rev 6:2 – the first horseman of the four horsemen sighted on that occasion.

Roman cavalry from a mosaic of the Villa Romana del Casale, Sicily, 4th century AD

The army with white clothing that followed the rider on the horse must be the angels in heaven, in other words: the starry clouds of the Milky Way, directly next to Sagittarius. We read in the Old Testament of more than one occasion when God or the angels assisted the Israelites in their battles against their enemies – for instance, with the fall of Jericho (Jos 6) or when Gideon and his band of 300 men vanquished the hordes of the Amalekites (Judg 7).

An ancient winepress found in Israel. The grapes were gathered in the pit with a diameter of 5m where they were crushed by the feet of the harvesters. The juice flowed into the hole in the bottom and from there through pipes into receptacles. John would have encountered a similar winepress on Patmos.

The "the winepress of the fierceness of the wrath of God" that was treaded (Rev 19: 15) may be sought in the constellation of Scutum, the Shield, directly next to Sagittarius. After all, both a shield and an ancient winepress had a round shape. The fact that John mentioned a winepress may be since the grape harvest on Patmos was still in progress during late summer, in August AD 96, and that he thought that it would be a fitting metaphor for God's judgment on a sinful world.

The angel standing on the sun that invited the birds in the sky to devour the flesh of God's enemies was the brightest object in the sky, the planet Venus on the western horizon. The last rays of the sun were still visible behind Venus. The birds in the sky were Aquila, the Eagle, and Cygnus, the Swan. Corvus, the Crow, had set earlier.

The beast that attacked the knight on the white horse, namely the Antichrist in the form of Cetus, the Sea Monster, was only to be seen the next morning. His ally, the False Prophet in the guise of Capricornus, the Goat, was visible directly behind the knight.

The following illustrations shows what John must have seen (with only the outlines of the various constellations drawn in the second and third illustrations):

A close-up view of Sagittarius (the Archer) on the southern horizon, together with Corona Australis (the Southern Crown), towards the end of August AD 96. Part of the Milky Way is to be seen in front of Sagittarius. Scutum (the Shield) is situated above the head of Sagittarius and represents a winepress

Early the next morning, John again saw the Antichrist, the beast from the sea (Cetus) and the beast from the earth (Capricornus) – whom he again calls the "False Prophet". They were allied to the kings of the earth and prepared for war against the rider on the white horse. The two beasts were thrown into the lake of fire that burns with sulphur, which happened when they disappeared behind the western horizon as dawn approached. There must, in addition, have been a sulphureous smell hanging around, blown over from the volcano in the south-east.

A similar fate for the sea monster is to be found in Isaiah: "In that day YHWH with his hard and great and strong sword will punish leviathan the swift serpent, and leviathan the crooked serpent; and he will kill the monster that is in the sea" (Isa 27: 1).

Isaiah (24: 21–22) also proclaims: "It shall happen in that day, that YHWH will punish the host of the high ones on high, and the kings of the earth on the earth. They shall be gathered together, as prisoners are gathered in the pit, and shall be shut up in the prison; and after many days shall they be visited."

The same fate awaited the dragon, Satan, some time later (Rev 20: 10).

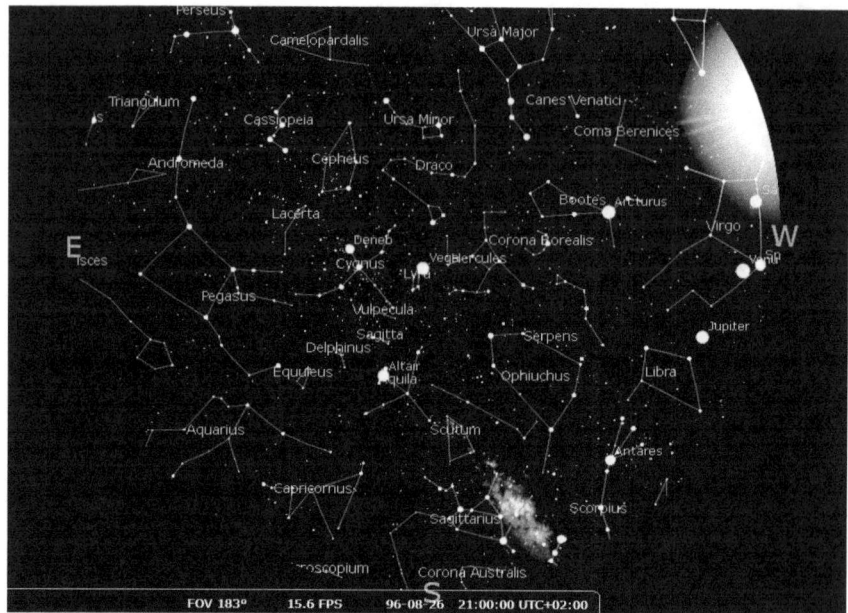

The outlines of Sagittarius (the Archer), Corona Australis (the Southern Crown), Capricornus (the Goat), and Scutum (the Shield), towards the end of August AD 96. Venus, the brightest object in the sky, lies on the western horizon within Virgo, while the last rays of the sun are still visible. Aquila (the Eagle) and Cygnus (the Swan), are gliding high in the middle of the sky.

The birds that were filled with the flesh of the kings, merchants and shipmasters were evidently the constellations of Aquila, the Eagle, and Cygnus, the Swan, situated directly to the north of Sagittarius. There were enough constellations around to represent the victims of these birds, including Hercules, Orion, Auriga, Perseus, and Gemini.

In the previous passage, in Rev 19: 7–9, John mentioned the marriage of the Lamb. The bride was identified as the moon. It must be pointed out that the moon (72% illuminated) was seen the next night next to the planet Mars, which was identified in Rev 16: 16 as the battle field of Armageddon. This scene must have been a confirmation to John of the threat posed by the two beasts to the bride of Christ, the faithful saints. That threat was removed, though, by the intervention of the knight on the white horse or Christ, and when dawn approached when the light of the sun – the pool of fire and sulphur – blotted the stars out.

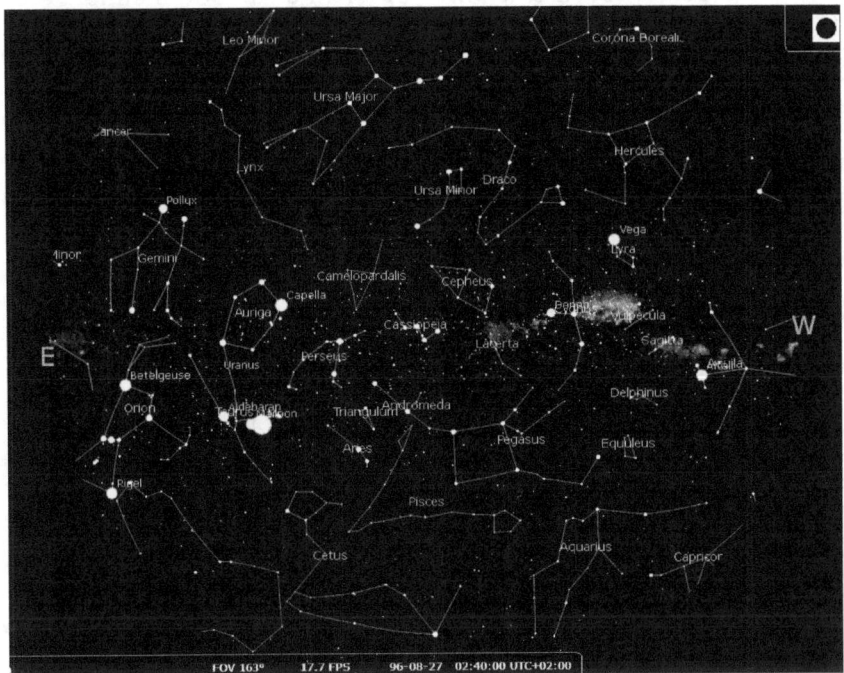

Cetus (the Sea Monster) and Capricornus (the Goat), visible late at night towards the end of August AD 96. Capricornus is on the point of disappearing behind the south-western horizon and Cetus followed a few hours later. Aquila (the Eagle) and Cygnus (the Swan) lie on the western part of the Milky Way. There is a near conjunction of the moon (72% illuminated) and the planet Mars next to the constellation of Aries (the Ram).

The message of John

These few verses describe Judgment Day when God's enemies, including the Antichrist and the False Prophet, will be vanquished by the return of Jesus Christ, together with his army of angels. The Antichrist or beast from the sea has been identified in Rev 13: 18 as Emperor Diocletian and the beast from the sea, the "False Prophet", has been identified as a representation or personification of all false religions and paganism. The final destination of God's enemies is the lake of fire and sulphur – in other words: eternal damnation in hell.

There are seven categories of enemies of God mentioned in this chapter: kings, captains, mighty men, those who sit on horses, free men, slaves, as well as small and great. In other words: God's enemies are to be found in all classes of people. Nobody will be able to rely on his or her social status when Judgment Day arrives. These people were also those who lamented the destruction of Babylon, the adulterous city of Jerusalem (Rev 18: 9–20). The symbolic number of seven describes God's complete action in eradicating any form of resistance against his authority.

The idea of a double-edged sword emanating from Christ's mouth is also to be found in Rev 1: 16. That means that Christ's words are incisive, that nobody is able to contradict him and that one is obliged to heed his words.

John repeats the image of Christ ruling over his enemies with a rod of iron. This idea also occurs in Rev 2: 27 and 12: 5. In the last-mentioned text Christ is the male child born from the woman who was attacked by the dragon, but who was taken up into heaven and was destined to rule all the nations with his rod of iron. The rod of iron conveys the message that nobody can withstand Christ's rule and judgment. The idea of an iron rod originally came from Ps 2: 9 – "You shall break them with a rod of iron. You shall dash them in pieces like a potter's vessel".

The image of the winepress, that occurred in Rev 14: 19–20, is repeated here. It serves to emphasize how thoroughly Christ's vengeance against his enemies will be – just as all the juice is completely pressed out of the grapes in a winepress, so He will vanquish his foes totally.

Another description of Judgment Day by John is given in a following chapter of his book. In this chapter, Judgment Day is described from a different perspective.

Satan is Bound
Rev 20: 1–3

1.	I saw an angel coming down out of heaven, having the key of the abyss and a great chain in his hand.
2.	He seized the dragon, the old serpent, which is the Devil and Satan, and bound him for one thousand years,
3.	and cast him into the abyss, and shut it, and sealed it over him, that he should deceive the nations no more, until the thousand years were finished. After this, he must be freed for a short time.

Introduction

Many Christian fundamentalists explain Revelation 20 in such a way that they expect a literal earthly kingdom of Christ of exactly a thousand years somewhere in the future – a position known as millennialism or chiliasm (from the Greek word for thousand: χίλιοι – *chilioi*). Those biblical students who adhere to this position usually regard the Jews as still being the beloved people of God and it is expected that they will accept Jesus Christ as their Messiah *en masse* and receive a special place of honor in the millennium.

The church father, St Irenaeus (ca AD 180), may be regarded as the first theologian to have espoused chiliasm in chapters 30–35 of Book V of his book Against Heresies. He argued that just as God created the world in six days and rested on the seventh day, the history of mankind will endure for 6 000 years and that a period of rest of 1 000 years is to follow during which the saints would inherit the earth after the second coming of Christ – those who "have part in the first resurrection".

It is necessary to examine this point of view thoroughly to demonstrate how these millennialists actually misread and distort the biblical text.

The main difficulty with the millennialist point of view is that it requires Christ to return to earth twice – at the start of the millennium and again after that when Satan must be overpowered for a second time. The Bible nowhere teaches that Christ will return repeatedly. There will only be a single second coming.

That millennialism is an artificial construct, which has little bearing on what John has actually written can be demonstrated by analyzing Revelation 20 in detail:

What John saw

After the two beasts from the sea and the earth had been banished (ch 19), it was the turn of the dragon, Satan, to be captured. He is also called "the old serpent" – a reference to Gen 3: 1 where Satan supposedly appeared in the form of a serpent to Eve, who lured her into eating from the forbidden fruit.

The dragon was also encountered in Chapter 12 where he threatened the pregnant woman and in Chapter 17 where he was allied to the prostitute. In these cases, the dragon was identified as the constellation of Scorpius, the Scorpion – a constellation regarded by the Jews as a snake or a dragon.[223]

John saw the constellation of Ophiuchus, the Serpent Catcher, standing upon Scorpius that was disappearing behind the south-western horizon where the abyss was located. This abyss was, according to John's perspective, the volcano that he saw earlier in April behind the horizon. It seemed as if the Snake Catcher was throwing the dragon/serpent into the abyss and binding him. It is easy to imagine the constellation of Serpens, the Serpent, on both sides of the Snake Catcher, to be a long chain held in his hands.

Verse 3 states that the Dragon had to be released for a short

---

[223] Allen, *Star Names,* 362.

time after being incarcerated. That simply means that he reappeared the next night in the sky before disappearing for a longer time later on as the seasons changed.

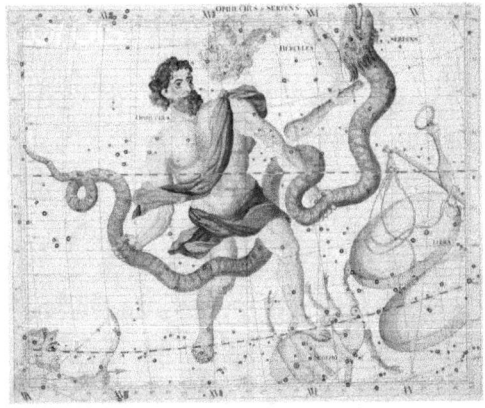

Ophiuchus, the Snake Catcher (aka Serpentarius), with Serpens, the Serpent, from an old star atlas. Scorpius, the Scorpion, is faintly visible under his feet.

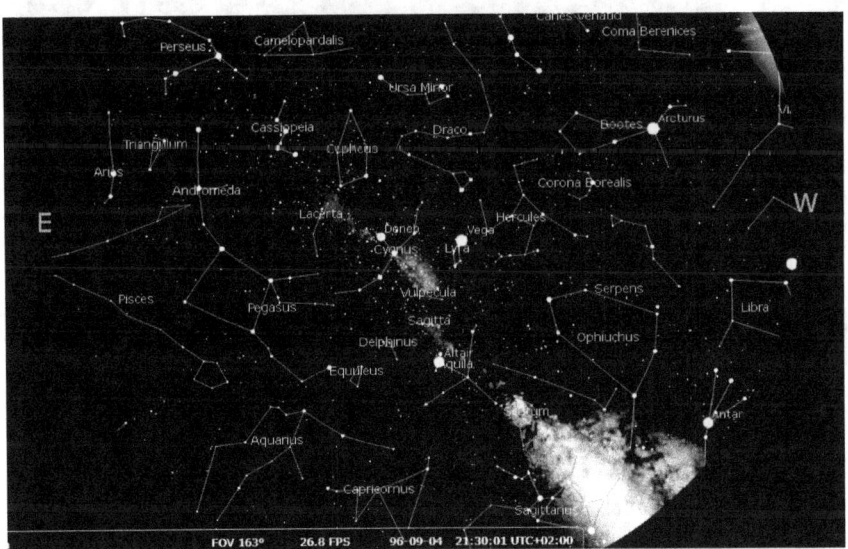

The outlines of Ophiuchus (the Serpent Catcher) and Scorpius (the Scorpion/Dragon) with its brightest star, Antares, on the south-western horizon towards the beginning of September AD 96. Scorpius is on the point of disappearing behind the horizon.

The Greek name, *Ophiuchus*, is derived from the Hebrew and Arabic name *Afeichus*, which means "the serpent held".[224] This name is also derived from the Greek word for a snake or serpent, namely *ophis* (Greek: ὄφις).

John's message

The first question that must be answered when analyzing this chapter is the question: what is meant by the "abyss"? The Greek word is ἄβυσσος *(abyssos)*, from which the English word "abyss" is derived. This word is also used in Rom 10: 7; Rev 9: 1, 2 & 11; 11: 7 and 17: 8. It is clear from these verses that the present abode or prison of Satan and his helpers is meant – and not hell. According to Rev 20: 10, Satan, together with the beast from the sea and the False Prophet, were only to be thrown into "the lake of fire and sulphur" on Judgment Day, sometime in the future.

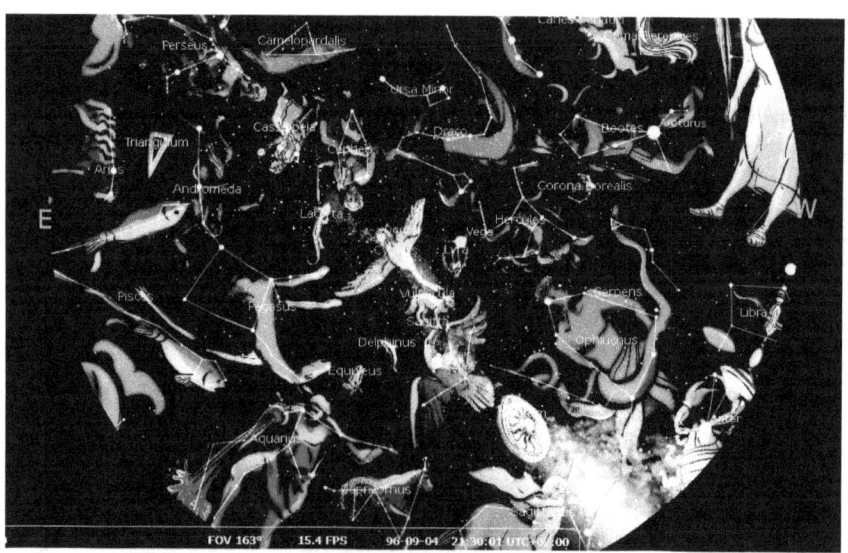

The same scene as in the previous illustration, but with the celestial figures of the various constellations added.

---

[224] Bullinger, "The Witness of the Stars".

John had in mind the ancient Greek idea of a place where the gods incarcerated their enemies. This place was called the "underworld" or Tartarus (Greek: Τάρταρος). In those days people thought of this abyss as being somewhere below the surface of the earth. Tartarus was sometimes called *Hades* (Greek: ᾅδης) – the abode of the dead. The word "Hades" was used in the Greek translation of the Old Testament for the Hebrew word "Sheol" (שְׁאוֹל) the place of the dead – and it is also used in this sense in the New Testament (Matt 16: 18). According to Rev 20: 13 & 14, Hades will give up all the dead on Judgment Day, after which Hades itself will be abolished by being thrown into the lake of fire and sulphur.

The only place where the name Tartarus is being used in the New Testament is 2 Pet 2: 4 – "For if God didn't spare angels when they sinned, but cast them down to Tartarus, and committed them to pits of darkness, to be reserved to judgment". In this text, Tartarus is the name of the place into which the rebellious angels – devils and demons – were imprisoned, while awaiting Judgment Day. The name Tartarus is, therefore, a synonym for the "Abyss".

It goes without saying that we cannot anymore accept the concept of a literal "abyss" where Satan is being kept prisoner. We know that there are no big hollow spaces inside the planet Earth. It has already been shown in Chapter 4 that a volcanic eruption to the south-east of Patmos during April AD 96 was interpreted by John as being a manifestation of this abyss.

John clearly wanted to communicate his conviction that Satan was only bound – and not annihilated. The idea that Jesus Christ overpowered Satan through his resurrection and ascension after his crucifixion is found in various texts of the New Testament (Matt 28: 18; Luk 10: 18; Joh 12: 31; Joh 16: 11; Col 2: 15; Heb 2: 14; 1 Joh 3: 8; 2 Pet 2: 4; Jud: 6). We also read in Rev 12: 7–12 that Satan and his evil angels or demons were thrown out of heaven.

In other words: the binding of Satan happened when Jesus Christ triumphed over him when he was resurrected and ascended into heaven according to the conventional Christian view. Therefore, the symbolic era of one thousand years in which Satan was bound started at the end of Jesus Christ's earthly work. It is, in other words, a mistake to place this period of a thousand years somewhere in the near or far future, as the fundamentalist millennialists believe.

In Col 2: 15 Paul explains the binding of Satan by using the simile of a Roman triumphal parade for a victorious general: Christ "stripped the principalities and the powers, he made a show of them openly, triumphing over them in it". During a Roman triumphal procession through the streets of the city of Rome, several important prisoners of war in chains were displayed and they were afterwards ritually executed.[225] John had a similar outcome for Satan in mind.

It is also clear that the number 1 000 has a symbolic meaning and that it cannot be taken literally. This number is made up of 10 X 10 X 10, alternatively: 10^3. The number of ten is symbolic of God's work and reign. A human being has, after all, ten fingers to perform his work and that is a pointer to God who is also working. According to the book of Exodus, God sent ten plagues onto Egypt and God proclaimed Ten Commandments to the Israelites. The fact that 1 000 is equal to 10^3 points to the triune God who is in control of everything during the symbolic millennium according to conventional Christianity.

The First Resurrection
Rev 20: 4–6

4.	I saw thrones, and they sat on them, and judgment was given to them. I saw the souls of those who had been

---

[225] Enc Brit, "Triumph".

> beheaded for the testimony of Jesus, and for the word of God, and such as didn't worship the beast nor his image, and didn't receive the mark on their forehead and on their hand. They lived, and reigned with Christ one thousand years.
>
> 5. The rest of the dead didn't live until the thousand years were finished. This is the first resurrection.
> 6. Blessed and holy is he who has part in the first resurrection. Over these, the second death has no power, but they will be priests of God and of Christ, and will reign with him one thousand years.

What John saw

During the early morning hours in early September AD 96, after the bright moon had disappeared, John saw the throne of God again at the northern celestial pole. It was surrounded by the thrones of departed saints who wielded power together with Christ. John got the image of thrones in heaven from Dan 7: 9–10 –

> "I saw until thrones were placed, and one who was ancient of days sat: his clothing was white as snow, and the hair of his head like pure wool; his throne was fiery flames, [and] the wheels of it burning fire. A fiery stream issued and came forth from before him: thousands of thousands ministered to him, and ten thousand times ten thousand stood before him: the judgment was set, and the books were opened."

The "fiery stream" in front of God's throne in this vision of Daniel must have been the Milky Way with its "thousands of thousands" of stars. Likewise, the saints that John saw must also be sought amongst the star clouds of the Milky Way.

John's message

The first three verses of Rev 20 give a terrestrial perspective. Verses 4–6, on the other hand, describe alternatively a heavenly and a terrestrial scene. The thrones on which deceased martyrs were sitting can only be in heaven and in God's eternity, where time does not exist as on earth (Ps 90: 4 and 2 Pet 3: 8). It is affirmed that these dead people will only be resurrected at the end of the 1 000 years.

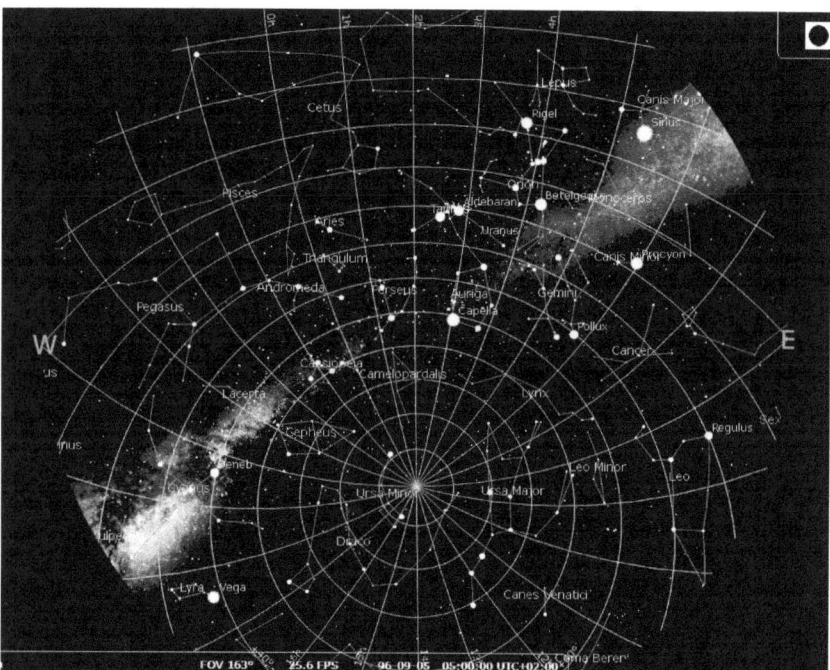

The sky during the early hours of 5 September AD 96, looking northwards. The throne of God is situated at the northern celestial pole and the Milky Way with its star clouds is clearly to be seen across the middle of the sky. The outlines of the constellation of Ursa Minor (the Little Bear) suggest a throne.

The idea of the millennialists that these deceased people will rule together with Christ *on earth* during the period of 1 000 years cannot be deduced from Rev 20: 4. We also cannot say that those who die are waiting somewhere until Judgment Day arrives and that they are then to be admitted into heaven. There are various biblical pronouncements that teach that those who die are immediately taken up into heaven with spiritual bodies (Luk 16: 22, 23; Luk 23: 34; 2 Cor 5: 1; 2 Tim 4: 18 & Heb 9: 27) – although we, who are still alive on earth and bound to the passage of time, still have to await Judgment Day, Resurrection Day, and the promised second coming of Christ, sometime in the unknown future (Matt 25: 31– 46; 1 Cor 15: 23–24 & 1 Pet 1: 5).

The deceased martyrs of Rev 20: 4 are, therefore, in heaven. From a terrestrial perspective, this is still in the unknown future. Those who have died and have left the restraints of time, however, arrive in heaven immediately after they have died. These martyrs do not sit on thrones on earth during the period of 1 000 years; they are already experiencing heavenly bliss, together with Christ, while those who are still living on earth are experiencing the symbolic millennium, the period between Jesus' ascension and his expected second coming.

Thrones on which the saints are to be seated are mentioned elsewhere in Revelation (Rev 3: 21; 4: 1–6; 4: 10–11; 5: 8–9). In all these cases, these thrones are in heaven and that must also be the case with the thrones mentioned in Rev 20: 4.

Where Rev 20: 5 says that the rest of the dead were not resurrected until the end of the 1 000 years one must realize that this is being said from a terrestrial point of view. When viewed from the dimension of time, Judgment Day and Resurrection Day are still somewhere in the unknown future. The rest of the dead are, therefore, the people who were still alive in John's day and awaiting Judgment Day.

This paradoxical state of affairs may be illustrated by the following diagram to illuminate John's mindset.

The state of affairs from the perspective of eternity is given above the thick line. Below the thick line time rolls on as we experience it on earth where one day is followed by another, while we are powerless to stop this flow. Points A, B, C, and D are the dates of death of four hypothetical or imaginary people – two of them in the past and two in the future. Seen from the dimension of time their dates of death are far apart, even centuries.

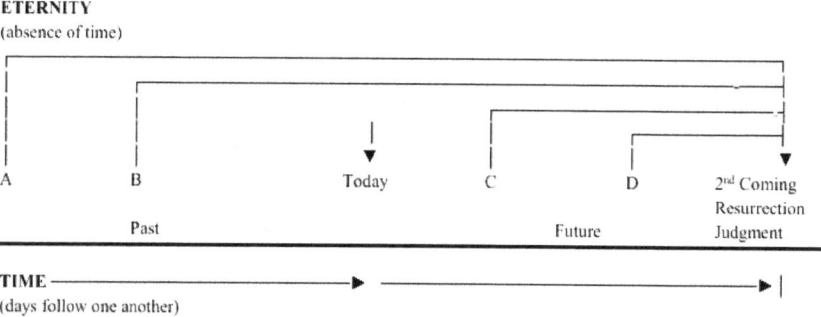

Viewed from the perspective of eternity it transpires that each one's date of death coincides with the resurrection and the final judgment. Time, to which we on earth are bound, simply disappeared for those who have died because they have left the time-bound existence on earth and entered God's eternity. The person who dies appears instantly before God's throne and receives either life everlasting or eternal damnation. For those who are still living on earth that is something still awaiting them in the unknown future.

We also read of a "first resurrection" and a "second death". It is important to note that a *second resurrection* and a *first death* are nowhere mentioned and one cannot read those into the text.

In Rev 20: 14–15 the "second death" is called the "lake of fire" (hell). The "second death" is, therefore, eternal punishment and death. According to Rev 20: 4–5 the "first resurrection" is the resurrection into heavenly glory.

We must understand that these two strange ideas are somehow connected. They are, after all, mentioned in the same breath. John, whose Greek was not quite up to standard, struggled to express himself and he tried to convey the idea that the resurrection of the blessed (the first resurrection) was far more desirable than eternal death (the second death). The (first) resurrection is, therefore, number one and (the second) death is placed on number two in order of preference or desirability.

Satan Destroyed
Rev 20: 7–10

7.	And after the thousand years, Satan will be freed out of his prison,
8.	and will come forth to deceive the nations which are in the four corners of the earth, Gog and Magog, to gather them together to the war; the number of whom is as the sand of the sea.
9.	They went up over the breadth of the earth, and surrounded the camp of the saints, and the beloved city. Fire came down out of heaven, and devoured them.
10.	The devil who deceived them was thrown into the lake of fire and sulfur, where are also the beast and the false prophet. They will be tormented day and night forever and ever.

What John saw

The symbolic period of thousand years was for John at most a few days long, since a thousand years and one day are the same for God (Ps 90: 4; 2 Pet 3: 8). The scene in the sky from 5 September to 8 September AD 96 would not have changed in any important respect. Satan (Scorpius) reappeared – as he did during previous nights – and he was at that stage, the early evening, almost below the western horizon where the last rays of the sun were still visible. For John, the sun was the symbol of the lake of fire and sulphur and that is where Satan was headed after his final annihilation. There he joined the Beast from the Sea (the Antichrist, *i e* Emperor Domitian) and the Beast from the Earth (the False Prophet, the personification of paganism and all false religions), represented by the constellations of Cetus and Capricornus.

It is noteworthy that the volcano on the island of Nisyros, southeast of Patmos, today still produces an overpowering "sulphurous smell"[226] and these fumes must have blown over to Patmos when the Sirocco, a southerly wind, blew over Patmos where John associated the fumes with "the lake of fire and sulphur".

Before his defeat, Satan misled large numbers of people – "the number of whom is as the sand of the sea". He even mobilized them to attack the "beloved city" – the celestial New Jerusalem, which are introduced in chapters 21 and 22. These multitudes must be sought in the star clouds of the Milky Way as they appeared during the evening at that time. The "beloved city" and "the camp of the saints" – symbols of the church and the faithful – must have been situated at the north celestial pole, where God's (invisible) throne was located.

The expression "God and Magog" needs an explanation. The name Magog appears in Gen 10: 2 as a son of Japheth, the son of

---

[226] Sattin & Franquet, *Exploring Greek Islands,* 160.

Noah. A certain Gog is mentioned in 1 Chr 5: 4 as the son of Joel. Both these names are also encountered in Ezek 38 and 39 as enemies of Israel where Gog is the prince of the land of Magog.

Malina and Pilch show – convincingly – that the name Gog in Revelation is derived from the Sumerian word for darkness and that this relates to the Sumerian concept of "dark planets". Since these ancient people had no inkling of the sphericity of the earth they had no real explanation for solar eclipses, lunar eclipses, and the phases of the moon. According to them, some mysterious dark object in the sky was responsible for these phenomena, obliterating parts of the moon or the sun. Similar ideas are to be found in the works of ancient authors and astrologers.[227]

That seems to explain John's reference to Gog and Magog as forces of darkness, allies of the dragon. The reconstruction of the sky over Patmos on 8 September AD 96 shows that there was a crescent moon, of which only 10% of the surface was illuminated, directly to the west of Scorpius (the dragon). It seems, therefore, likely that John regarded this darkened portion of the moon as a manifestation of Gog and Magog, allies of Satan.

The "fire [that] came down out of heaven" and devoured the Gog and Magog, together with their followers, could have been a near conjunction of the bright planets Jupiter and Venus in the western sky, directly next to the crescent moon within Libra, the Scales – forming a conspicuous single object. That this scene occurred specifically in Libra (the Scales) must have given John the additional message that the destruction of these evil forces was due to God's justice. After all, God's justice is compared with a pair of just or accurate balances in Ps 62: 9, Prov 11: 1, Prov 16: 11 and Is 40: 15.

---

[227] Malina & Pilch, *Revelation*, 234–37

The Jews of Qumran knew the constellation of Libra as מֹאזְנַיִם (*Moznayim*) and it was a sign of divine justice.[228] On the mosaic of the Zodiac in the Beth Alpha synagogue of the sixth century this constellation is depicted as a man holding a pair of scales in his right hand.

There is also a possibility that the fire from heaven was a series of meteor showers (shooting stars) during that night.

Detail of the antique zodiac mosaic floor at Hamat Tiberias Synagogue National Park, Tiberias, Galilee, Israel (4th century AD), showing Libra (the Scales), called מֹאזְנַיִם in Hebrew.

John's message

These verses make it clear that John was convinced that Satan, together with all antichristian forces and false religions, will come with a final assault on the church and the faithful before the end. They will, however, not be successful because they will be thrown into hell ("the lake of fire and sulphur") at Christ's expected second coming – just as important prisoners of war were ritually executed at the end of a triumphal parade in the city of Rome. John quotes 1 Enoch 10: 5 in this regard: "And on the day of the great judgment he [Azazel] shall be cast into the fire."

That Satan and his allies will be partially successful in luring people after them is in accordance with the general expectation in the Bible that circumstances on earth will deteriorate and that

---

[228] Jacobus, "The Zodiac", 321–22

wickedness, godlessness, and immorality will increase. Jesus warned his disciples: "Many false prophets will arise, and will lead many astray. Because iniquity will be multiplied, the love of many will grow cold" (Matt 24: 11–12).

The fire that descended from heaven (vs 9) is a reference to the fire that God sent onto the sacrifice of the prophet Elijah, through which he could triumph over the prophets of Baal (1 Kgs 18). The expression "fire and sulphur" comes from Ps 11: 6 – "On the wicked He will rain blazing coals; fire, sulphur, and scorching wind shall be the portion of their cup." It is also possible that sulphurous fumes were carried by the wind from the volcano in the southeast to Patmos and that John included these fumes in his narrative.

The Final Judgment
Rev 20: 11–20

11.	I saw a great white throne, and him who sat on it, from whose face the earth and the heaven fled away. There was found no place for them.
12.	I saw the dead, the great and the small, standing before the throne. Books were opened. Another book was opened, which is the book of life. The dead were judged out of the things which were written in the books, according to their works.
13.	The sea gave up the dead who were in it. Death and Hades gave up the dead who were in them. They were judged, each one according to his works.
14.	Death and Hades were thrown into the lake of fire. This is the second death, the lake of fire.
15.	If anyone was not found written in the book of life, he was cast into the lake of fire.

The book of life was opened – most probably the constellation of Ursa Minor, the Small Bear, next to the throne. All those whose names were not written in this book were thrown into the lake of fire – the sun behind the eastern horizon whose first rays were becoming visible as dawn approached.

Mosaic of Christ in his glory as heavenly judge, holding the book of life (Rev 3: 5; 20: 15), in the Hagia Sophia Cathedral in Istanbul (Constantinople) from the 13th century

Death and Hades were thrown in the lake of fire and sulphur. In other words: death was abolished and Hades was emptied of its inhabitants. Paul had the same idea: "The last enemy that will be abolished is death" (1 Cor 15: 26). In Rev 6: 8 John mentioned "a pale horse. He who sat on him, his name was Death. Hades followed with him." This pale horse was identified as the constellation of Equuleus, the foal of Pegasus. During the early morning of 9 September AD 96, Equuleus was situated on the western horizon, ready to disappear from sight – together with Pegasus, the Winged Horse. From John's perspective, Death and Hades were to be annihilated by the rays of the rising sun in the east.

It is possible that the volcano in the south-east had died down by this time and that John could also declare that Hades, the Abyss, was no more.

The Message of John

John's description of Judgment Day reminds one of the descriptions of the event found in Matt 25: 31–46 and 1 Thess 4: 13–17. These parts of Scripture teach that all people must appear before the divine throne where a review of each one's life will take place. Those who belong to Jesus Christ – those whose names are recorded in the book of life – will be granted life everlasting, while those who continued with a sinful and godless life will receive their due, which is eternal damnation in hell. The exalted Christ was the one who said in the opening scene: "I have the keys of Death and of Hades" (Rev 1: 18).

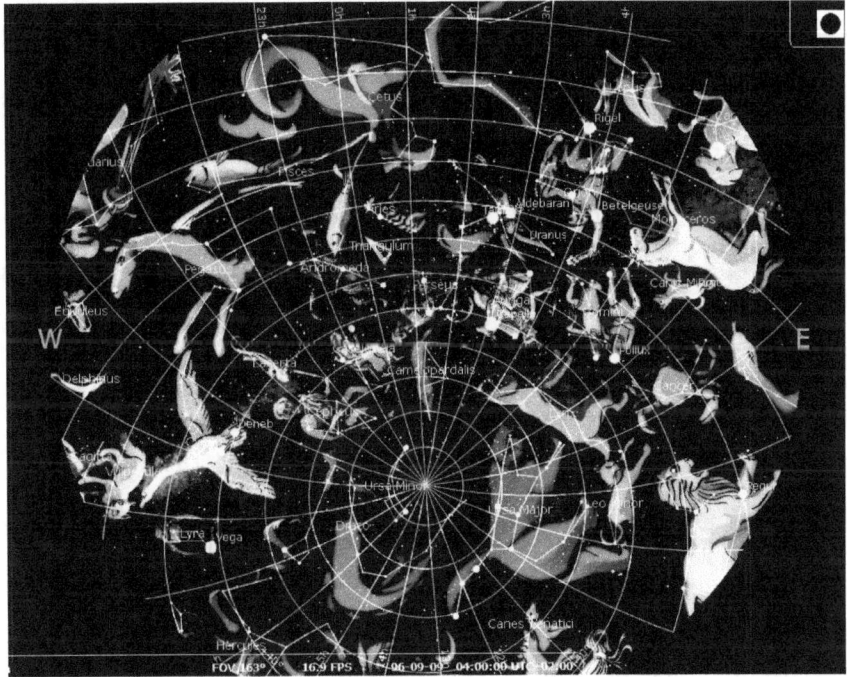

The north celestial pole with God's (invisible) throne, during early September AD 96, shortly before daybreak, looking northwards. The Milky Way is prominently visible and the seven stars in the body and tail of Draco – the seven lamps in front of God's throne – as well as Ursa Minor are also to be seen. Equuleus, the Foal of Pegasus, is about to disappear behind the western horizon.

The book of life was first mentioned in Rev 3: 5 – "He who overcomes will be arrayed like this in white garments, and I will in no way blot his name out of the book of life." We are assured that "only those who are written in the Lamb's book of life" will be permitted to reside in the New Jerusalem (Rev 21: 27). This book or scroll existed "from the foundation of the earth" (Rev 13: 8 & 17: 8). That means that believers may be sure that God knew already when He created the world who the people would be who would belong to Him.

A VERDICT

The contents of this chapter must be summarized as follows:

- Mark, Matthew, and Luke attributed to Jesus certain prophecies regarding the destruction of Jerusalem during the Jewish War of AD 66–70, prophecies which he certainly never pronounced, because they actually reported known history when they compiled their gospels only after the war. These passages are usually, but erroneously, interpreted as predictions of Judgment Day.
- Jesus often spoke about how it would happen that he resurrects the Israelite monarchy with the aid of a host of angels from heaven. When something like this never realized, the authors of the gospels transported Jesus' predictions to the far future, to Judgment Day – which was never his intention. When he told the parable of the sheep and the goats, it meant to describe what would happen after he had ascended the throne in Jerusalem, and not what would happen on Judgment Day.
- Paul incorporated ideas from Greek philosophy, including his pantheism, into his explanations of Judgment Day and the resurrected body with which believers would inherit eternal life,

when they would be dissolved into God. He thought of the resurrected body as composed of a different type of matter than that found on earth.

- Judgment Day is described in Revelation as a huge court scene with a heavenly judge who consults a book, containing the names of those who are to be admitted into heaven. Death and Hades, or hell, will be abolished.

It appears that the prophets of the New Testament had different and even conflicting views regarding Judgment Day and life after death.

CHAPTER 9
MUHAMMAD AND THE HOLY QUR'AN

Muslims, the adherents of the religion of Islam, believe that the founder of their faith, Muhammad, was the final messenger or prophet of God (called Allah in Arabic). They also recognize a long list of previous, lesser prophets mentioned in the Christian Bible, such as Moses, Solomon, and Jesus. According to Islam, their holy book, the Qur'an (meaning "Reading" or "Recitation"), was dictated word for word to Muhammad by the archangel Gabriel and even directly by God Himself.

This means that the Qur'an is deemed to be perfect and without error, and that every word in it must be true. Since it is God's message to Muhammad, the whole book must be regarded as the final and ultimate prophetic book.[229]

The aim of this chapter is to examine and explain some of the contents of the Qur'an to ascertain whether the claim of Muslims can be maintained by utilizing the test of rationality as explained in the first chapter. This test must be applied more vigorously and rigorously in the case of the Qur'an than with the Christian Bile, since the biblical books do not claim to have been dictated word for word by God or an archangel as in the case of the Qur'an.

Contemporary Christians have decided that the ancient and prescientific cosmology of the Bible may be disregarded as cultural

---

[229] Rahman, "Islam".

packaging, which leaves the core message of the Bible intact. In the case of the Qur'an, this cannot be done since every word in this book is thought to have been given by God.

Websites by WikiIslam, Stealth Team Megiddo, Dr. N.V.K. Ashraf, and others have compiled lists of unscientific, wrong, absurd, and irrational ideas in the Qur'an. This chapter will make use of some of these findings, together with an analysis done by the present author.

Muhammad receiving his first revelation from the angel Gabriel. From the manuscript Jami' al-Tawarikh by Rashid-al-Din Hamadani, 1307..

UNSCIENTIFIC NOTIONS

The Qur'an contains many statements about the earth, the sun, the moon, the stars, the heavens, and mankind that demonstrate Muhammad's prescientific and naïve views – views which cannot have been given to him by God because they are contradicted by established scientific insights. It may be countered that God could not have given Muhammad scientifically accurate messages because the people in seventh century Arabia would not have understood him. But if God really wanted to reveal Himself to Muhammad and to mankind in general, He could simply have given the prophet all his messages without these wrong and untrue statements. These absurdities and false notions could simply have been omitted, which did not happen.

Seven Heavens Created after the Earth
Surah 2: 30

> He it is Who created for you all that is in the earth; then He turned towards the heavens, and He perfected them as seven heavens; and He knows all things.

The Qur'an teaches erroneously hat the earth was created before the heavens were made. The earth is, in fact, much younger than the heavens, the rest of the universe. It is unclear where these seven heavens of the Qur'an are to be found. The idea that there are seven heavens is also found in Surahs 17: 44; 23: 86; 65: 12; 67: 3; and 71: 16–17.

Heaven and Earth Created Together
Surah 21: 31

> Do not the disbelievers see that the heavens and the earth were a closed-up mass, then We opened them out? And We made from water every living thing.

Although the Qur'an teaches elsewhere that the heavens were created after the earth, this text declares that they were created together when they were taken out of an unformed mass. This is a clear contradiction.

The idea that living beings were created from water is, of course, pure nonsense.

Creation in Six Days
Surah 50: 39

> And verily, We created the heavens and the earth and all that is between them in six periods/days, and no weariness touched Us.

This idea that the universe was created in six days was taken from Genesis 1 and Exodus 20. The same thought is also found in Surahs 7: 54; 10: 3; 11: 7; and 25: 29. There is, though, abundant evidence that the universe was created billions of years ago.

Earth Created in Two Days
Surah 41: 10–12

> 10. Say: 'Do you really disbelieve in Him Who created the earth in two days? And do you set up equals to Him?' That is the Lord of the worlds.
> 11. He placed therein firm mountains rising above its surface, and blessed it with abundance, and provided therein its foods in proper measure in four days – alike for all seekers.
> 12. Then He turned to the heaven while it was something like smoke, and said to it and to the earth: 'Come ye both of you, willingly or unwillingly. They said, 'We come willingly.'
> 13. So He completed them into seven heavens in two days, and He revealed to each heaven its function.

The world with its mountains and the rest of the universe as a whole were certainly not created in two plus two days – it was a process that took billions of years.

The Quran's arithmetic seems somewhat muddled because other passage say that the heavens and the earth were created in six days. In this passage, there is a total of eight days – two for the creation of earth, four for the provision of food for everybody, and two mor days for the creation of seven heavens.

Creation of the Stars and Planets
Surah 41: 12–13

12.	Then He turned to the heaven while it was something like smoke, and said to it and to the earth: 'Come ye both of you, willingly or unwillingly.' They said, 'We come willingly.'
13.	So He completed them into seven heavens in two days, and He revealed to each heaven its function. And We adorned the lowest heaven with lamps for light and for protection. That is the decree of the Mighty, the All-Knowing.

Surah 37: 7.

We have adorned the lowest heaven with an adornment-the planets;

Surah 67: 6

And verily, We have adorned the lowest heaven with lamps, and We have made them for driving away satans, and We have prepared for them the punishment of the blazing Fire.

Suddenly, the seven heavens were also made in two days – from smoke, of all things. The lowest heaven received lamps, the stars and planets. That means that the stars and planets are all close to the surface of the earth, hanging onto the lowest heaven – which is certainly not the case according to the science of astronomy.

It is a piece of folk-lore that the stars were made as protection and to scare away satans or evil spirits. An alternative translation states that these lamps were "missiles against the devils" – in other words, shooting stars or meteors targeted evil spirits.

Seven Heavens on Top of each Other
Surah 71: 16

> Have you not observed how Allah has created seven heavens tier upon tier?

The seven heavens form seven layers, on top of each other, from the lowest to the highest. There is, in fact, only a single universe.

God's Dwelling
Surah 2: 211

> Are they waiting for anything but that Allah should come to them in the coverings of the clouds with angels, and the matter be decided?

God's dwelling is believed to be between the clouds in the sky, where the angels also live. It is a well-known fact that the clouds are part of the earth's atmosphere, at most a few kilometers above the earth. There are certainly no angels living in the clouds.

Pillars of Heaven
Surah 13.3

> Allah is He Who raised up the heavens without any pillars that you can see. Then He settled Himself on the Throne. And He pressed the sun and the moon into service: each pursues its course until an appointed term. He regulates it all.

God's heaven, where his throne is, rests upon invisible pillars, which are presumably planted upon the earth.

Of course, such invisible pillars don't exist and God's throne is not part of such a heaven. The sun and the moon are supposed to orbit around the earth, although it is, in fact, the earth that circles around the sun.

The Sun's Orbit
Surah 13: 34

> And He it is Who created the night and the day, and the sun and the moon, each gliding along in its orbit.

Surah 31: 30.

> Hast thou not seen that Allah makes the night pass into the day, and makes the day pass into the night, and He has pressed the sun and the moon into service; each pursuing its course till an appointed term.

It is correct that the moon has an orbit around the earth, but the earth orbits around the sun – not otherwise.

Mountains
Surah 13: 32

> And We have made in the earth firm mountains lest it should quake with them.

According to this text, the function of mountains is to prevent earthquakes – which is plain rubbish.

Destruction of the Heaven and Stars
Surah 82: 2–3

> 2. When the heaven is cleft asunder,
> 3. And when the stars are scattered…

The heaven, with its stars, will disappear after Judgment Day, according to this surah. Nobody knows when or whether the universe with its trillions of stars will ever cease to exist. Such a danger does not seem to be a possibility during the coming few billions of years.

The Creation of Man
Surah 23: 12–14

12.	We created man from an extract of clay.
13.	Then We made him a seed, in a secure repository.
14.	Then We developed the seed into a clot of blood. Then We developed the clot into a lump. Then We developed the lump into bones. Then We clothed the bones with flesh. Then We produced it into another creature. Most Blessed is Allah, the Best of Creators.

Surh 96: 2 – 3

2. Convey thou in the name of thy Lord Who created,
3. Created man from a clot of blood.

The cave Hira in the mountain Jabal al-Nour where, according to Muslim belief, Muhammad received his first revelation

If these passages were meant to be a poetical or figurative rendering of how mankind was created, then one can accept them as such. It is, however, meant to be a factual descripttion, which cannot be seen as accurate in any way.

It is also stated in Surah 7: 13 that Adam, the first human being, was made from clay. There is, though, a huge chemical difference between lifeless clay from the earth and living human flesh. It is also not possible to extract a clot of blood from clay and transform that into the bones and flesh.

Sexes Created after Fertilization
Surah 75: 38–40

> 38. Was he not a drop of fluid, emitted forth?
> 39. Then he became a clot, then He shaped and perfected him.
> 40. Then He made of him a pair, the male and female.

The information about human reproduction of the Qur'an is totally wrong. It is stated that the fetus is formed from "a drop of fluid, emitted forth" – in other words, merely from a drop of semen. That is then formed by God into a clot, after which the sex of the fetus, male or female, is determined.

It is common knowledge that fertilization takes place when a male sperm cell combines with the female ovum and that the sex of the fetus is determined at that very moment.

Production of Semen
Surah 86: 6–8

> 6. So let man consider from what he is created.
> 7. He is created from a gushing fluid,
> 8. Which issues forth from between the loins and the breastbones.

The Qur'an has certainly confused ideas about human procreation. According to this passage, man is made from semen, which is produced somewhere in the belly. No consideration is given to the ovum of the female.

HISTORICAL ERRORS

There are various historical errors in the Qur'an. Examples are as follows:

Pharaoh Used Crucifixion
Surah 7: 124–25

124.	Pharaoh said, 'You have believed in him before I gave you leave. Surely, this is a plot that you have plotted in the city, that you may turn out therefrom its inhabitants, but you shall soon know the consequences.
125.	'Most surely will I cut off your hands and your feet on alternate sides. Then will I surely crucify you all together.'

Surah 20: 72

Pharaoh said, 'Do you believe in him before I give you leave? He must be your chief who has taught you magic. I will therefore surely cut off your hands and your feet alternately, and I will surely crucify you on the trunks of palm-trees; and you shall know which of us is severer and more abiding m punishment.'

Crucifixion was never a method of execution used by the ancient Egyptians. The Qur'an simply has it wrong in this regard.

Mary Confused with Miriam
Surah19: 28–31

28.	Then she brought him to her people, carrying him. They said, 'O Mary, thou hast brought forth a strange thing.
29.	'O sister of Aaron, thy father was not a wicked man nor was thy mother an unchaste woman!'
30.	Then she pointed to him. They said, 'How can we talk to one who is a child in the cradle?'
31.	He said, 'I am a servant of Allah. He has given me the Book, and made me a Prophet.'

These verses in the Qur'an tell the story of how Mary, the mother of Jesus, became pregnant while still being a virgin. She was confused with Miriam, the sister of Moses and Aaron.

It is also strange that the newly-born Jesus was able to speak Arabic – or whatever other language.

Mary is also confused with Miriam in Surah 3: 35–36.

Anybody familiar with the contents of the Christian Bible knows that Mary, Jesus' mother, lived many centuries after the time of Moses, Aaron, and Miriam.

A Barrier of Iron
Surah 18: 95–99

95.	They said, 'O Dhul Qamain, verily, Gog and Magog are creating disorder in the earth; shall we then pay thee tribute on condition that thou set up a barrier between us and them?'
96.	He replied, 'The power with which my Lord has endowed me about this is better, but you may help me with physical strength; I will set up between you and them a rampart.
97.	'Bring me blocks of iron.' They did so till, when he had levelled up the space between the two mountain sides, he said, 'Now blow with your bellows.' They blew till, when he had made it red as fire, he said, 'Bring me molten copper that I may pour it thereon.'
98.	So they (Gog and Magog) were not able to scale it, nor were they able to dig through it.
99.	Thereupon he said, 'This is a mercy from my Lord. But when the promise of my Lord shall come to pass, He will break it into pieces. And the promise of my Lord is certainly true.'

The Gog and Magog were evidently two troublesome and dangerous tribes or nations and they had to be kept in check. To achieve that, a giant barrier of Iron and copper was set up to prevent them from moving through the mountains.

No trace of such a barrier of iron and copper has ever been found and this story must be regarded as nothing but a legend, not history.

Moses and the Samaritans
Surah 20: 85–88

85.	He said, 'They are closely following in my footsteps and I have hastened to Thee, my Lord, that Thou mightest be pleased.'
86.	God said, 'We have tried thy people in thy absence, and the Samirī has led them astray.'
87.	So Moses returned to his people indignant and sad. He said, 'O my people, did not your Lord promise you a gracious promise? Did, then, the appointed time appear too long to you, or did you desire that wrath should descend upon you from your Lord, that you broke your promise to me?'
88.	They said, 'We have not broken our promise to thee of our own accord; but we were laden with loads of people's ornaments and we threw them away, and likewise did the Samirī cast.'

The "Samiri" mentioned twice in this passage are the Samaritans of whom we read in the Bible. They were the inhabitants of the region around Samaria, the old capital of the northern kingdom of Israel. After this kingdom was vanquished by the Assyrians in 722 BC, the elite of the kingdom were taken into exile, while those who stayed behind intermingled with pagan settlers. The Jews never accepted the Samaritans as fellow-Jews.[230]

---

[230] End Brit, "Samaritan".

According to this passage, these Samaritans lived in the time of Moses. That is a gross anachronism, because Moses lived many centuries before the Samaritans became part of history.

Mary Part of the Divine Trinity
Surah 5: 117

> And when Allah will say, "O Jesus, son of Mary, didst thou say to men, 'Take me and my mother for two gods beside Allah?'", he will answer, "Holy art Thou. I could never say that to which I had no right. If I had said it, Thou wouldst have surely known it. Thou knowest what is in my mind, and I know not what is in Thy mind. It is only Thou Who art the Knower of hidden things.

The Qur'an contains a very skewed version of the Christian doctrine of the divine Trinity. This doctrine states that the one single God is differentiated into three divine persons, namely the Father, the Son (Jesus Christ), and the Holy Spirit. According to the Qur'an, this Trinity purportedly consisted of Jesus, his mother Mary, and Allah. This amounts to a gross misrepresentation and a lack of knowledge.

CONTRADICTIONS AND ABSURDITIES

It is a fundamental rule in logics that two conflicting or contradictory statements cannot both be true. At least one of them must be untrue. There are certainly some conflicting statements in the Qur'an, just as there are in the Christian Bible. It is difficult to reconcile these contradictions with the notion that every word in the Qur'an came from God.

There are also some ridiculous absurdities in the Qur'an, which undermine the credibility of this book even further. It is unthinkable that an omniscient God could have revealed these crazy ideas to his own prophet-in-chief.

The very first verse in the Qur'an contains these words:

Surah 1: 1

> 1. In the name of Allah, the Gracious, the Merciful.

The Qur'an is supposed to be authored by God. We must ask: will God begin his own book by writing: "In the name of God...?" This sentence alone is proof that the book was written by some human being without logic and common sense.

God's Covenant with other Prophets

Surah 3: 81

> Allah received the covenant of the prophets, "Inasmuch as I have given you of Scripture and wisdom; should a messenger come to you verifying what you have, you shall believe in him, and support him." He said, "Do you affirm My covenant and take it upon yourselves?" They said, "We affirm it." He said, "Then bear witness, and I am with you among the witnesses."

A group calling itself "Stealth Team Megiddo" analyzed this Surah thoroughly and demonstrated the absurdity contained in it:

"A careful examination of Surah 3:81 reveals the following:

(1) Allah made a Covenant with the Prophets who lived before the time of Muhammad.

(2) These Prophets were called upon by Allah to pledge their support to a forthcoming Messenger who will to appear to them later.

(3) The Prophets agreed and Allah secured their pledge to help the forthcoming Messenger by establishing a Covenant with them.

(4) This upcoming Messenger will confirm the previous Scripture of Allah which is in the possession of the Prophets. Since the Prophets will be present at the time when this Messenger arrives, they will personally witness his confirmation of their sacred Book.

(5) Allah concludes the Covenant and bears witness with the Prophets to ensure the fulfillment of his Covenant.

As acknowledged by all Muslim scholars and clearly testified in Hilali-Khan's translation of the Qur'an, the Messenger in this Qur'anic verse refers to none other than Muhammad. This raises some very vital questions. Who were the Prophets who lived during the time of Muhammad's appearance as the Messenger of Allah? Who were the Prophets on hand to assist him? And who were the Prophets at hand to witness his confirmation of the previous Scripture? None!

Not a single Prophet lived during the time of Muhammad. And this is especially true regarding the Prophets with whom Allah concluded the Covenant. Yet, the Qur'an testifies that there would be prophets present during the time of this Messenger. In fact, Allah swore these Prophets into his service to assist this forthcoming Messenger. And Allah himself bore witness with the Prophets that he will be with them to ensure the accomplishment of this Covenant. But there were no Prophets present during the time of Muhammad. This leaves us with two options.

One: Allah was mistaken in his claim that there would be other Prophets during the appearance of this Messenger.

Two: The Messenger mentioned in Surah 3: 81 is referring to someone other than Muhammad. Either option spells disaster for Islam.

What is even more damaging for Islam is the fact that Muhammad excluded himself as the Messenger of Surah 3:81. Why do we say that? This is because Muhammad clearly ruled out the prospect for the co-existence of any other Prophets during his career as the Messenger of Allah. In other words, no other Prophets are supposed to exist anywhere on planet earth as a contemporary of Muhammad."[231]

This lengthy argument uncovers a serious absurdity in the Qur'an.

One must also ask: If God acknowledged the authority of these other prophets with whom He made a covenant, why are their Scriptures not read during prayer meetings in all mosques?

Body and Soul Reunited at the Resurrection
Surah 17: 98–99

98.	And he whom Allah guides, is the only one rightly guided; but as for those whom He allows to perish, thou wilt find for them no helpers beside Him. And on the Day of Resurrection We shall gather them together on their faces, blind, dumb and deaf. Their abode will be Hell; every time it abates, We shall increase for them the flame.
99.	That is their recompense, because they rejected Our Signs and said, "What! when we are reduced to bones and broken particles, shall we really be raised up as a new creation?"

---

[231] Stealth Team Megiddo, "Ten Reasons".

This passage teaches that body and soul will be reunited on the Day of Resurrection, Judgment Day, although the body has decayed in the grave. Similar ideas are to be found in Surahs 20: 55, 34: 7, and 75: 3–4.

However, something different is taught in the following passages:

Surah 31: 29

Your creation and your resurrection are only like the creation and resurrection of a single soul. Verily Allah is All Hearing, All-Seeing.

Surah 89: 28–31

28.	And thou, O soul at peace!
29.	Return to thy Lord well pleased with Him and He well pleased with thee.
30.	So enter thou among My chosen servants,
31.	And enter thou My Garden.

According to these passages, it is only the human soul that enters the garden of Paradise after death and Judgment Day. Which one of these two clashing ideas must be accepted?

The following passage contains a clear contradiction:

The Origin of Evil

Surah 4: 79–80

79.	Wheresoever you may be, death will overtake you, even if you be in strongly built towers. And if some good befalls them, they say, 'This is from Allah;' and if evil befalls them, they say, 'This is from thee.' Say, 'All is from Allah.' What has happened to these people that they come not near understanding anything?

> 80. Whatever of good comes to thee is from Allah; and whatever of evil befalls thee is from thyself. And We have sent thee as a Messenger to mankind.

We learn, on the one hand, that everything, blessings and evil, come from God. On the other hand, evil is something that man brings upon himself and for which he is responsible; it does not come from God. One must ask: is God responsible for bad things, or not? Both can't be true at the same time.

All are Submissive
Surah 30: 26

> To Him belongs everyone in the heavens and the earth. All are submissive to Him.

It is certainly absurd to think that all people on earth are submissive to God. The Qur'an itself frequently condemns the unbelievers, infidels, and pagans who refuse to submit themselves to God.

Jonah's Indefinite Stay in the Fish
Surah 37: 139–144

> 139. And Jonah was one of the messengers.
> 140. When he fled to the laden boat.
> 141. He gambled and lost.
> 142. Then the fish swallowed him, and he was to blame.
> 143. Had he not been one of those who praised,
> 144. He would have stayed in its belly until the Day they are raised.

This passage is certainly one of the most absurd tales in the Qur'an. It is stated as a realistic possibility that Jonah could have stayed until Judgment Day and Resurrection Day inside the belly of the fish that swallowed him, had he not started to praise God while inside the fish. That means that he would have died inside the fish at some time, but that the fish would have survived till the resurrection.

The Nature of Satan
Surah 7: 10–18

10.	And as for those whose scales are light, it is they who shall have ruined their souls because of their being unjust to Our Signs.
11.	And We have established you in the earth and provided for you therein the means of subsistence. How little thanks you give!
12.	And We did create you *and* then We gave you shape; then said We to the angels, 'Submit to Adam;' and they *all* submitted but Iblis *did not;* he would not be of those who submit.
13.	*God* said, 'What prevented thee from submitting when I commanded thee?' He said, 'I am better than he. Thou hast created me of fire while him hast Thou created of clay.'
14.	God said, 'Then go down hence; it is not for thee to be arrogant here. Get out; thou art certainly of those who are abased.'
15.	He said, 'Grant me respite till the day when they will be raised up.'
16.	*God* said, 'Thou shalt be of those who are given respite.'
17.	He said: 'Now, since Thou hast adjudged me as lost, I will assuredly lie in wait for them on Thy straight path.

18.	Then will I surely come upon them from before them and from behind them and from their right.'

Surah 18: 51–52

51.	*And remember the time* when We said to the angels, 'Submit to Adam,' and they *all* submitted except Iblis. He was one of the Jinn; and he disobeyed the command of his Lord. Will you then take him and his offspring for friends instead of Me while they are your enemies? Evil is the exchange for the wrongdoers.
52.	I did not make them witness the creation of the heavens and the earth, nor their own creation; nor could I take as helpers those who lead *people* astray.

Satan's initial name was Iblis and it is not quite clear what type of creature he was. In Surah 7: 10–18, where God addressed Adam, the first human being, Iblis was one of the angels in his entourage. The same story is to be found in Surah 17: 62–65 and Surah 38: 72–78.

However, in Surah 18: 51–52 Iblis is explicitly called "one of the jinn". According to the list of definitions given in the translation of the Qur'an used, the jinn are "evil spirits which inspire evil thoughts in the minds of men. They are the agents of Satan". Therefore, the angels and the jinn must not be confused with each other.

The confusion and even contradiction regarding the nature of Iblis led to much speculation and debate within Islamic scholarship. Angels are deemed to have been created of light and are incapable of sin, while jinn were created from fire and are able to commit sin. It is certainly no easy matter to solve this dilemma.[232]

When God created Adam, he ordered the angels to prostate themselves before this new creature. Iblis refused with the argument

---

[232] NW Enc, "Iblis"; End Brit, "Iblis".

that he was created from fire (the same as the jinn), while Adam was of a lower order in creation, having been created from clay.

The notions that there are creatures created from light, fire, or clay, must be deemed as unscientific hogwash.

Facing Mekka when Praying
Surah 2: 144

> We have seen the turning of thy face to heaven (for guidance, O Muhammad). And now verily We shall make thee turn (in prayer) toward a Qiblah which is dear to thee. So turn thy face toward the Inviolable Place of Worship, and ye (O Muslims), wheresoever ye may be, turn your faces (when ye pray) toward it.

Surah 2:50

> And from wheresoever you start forth for prayers, turn your face in the direction of Al-Masjid-al-Haram (at Makkah), and wheresoever you are, turn your faces towards, it when you pray.

Muslims are required to face Mecca, the holy city of Islam where Muhammad was born and lived, when they are praying. This is an impossible obligation because any Muslim who is praying at a mosque in Cape Town, Bali, Samarkand, or Birmingham and is looking straight ahead in the direction of where Mecca is supposed to be, he will, in reality, be staring into empty space. Mecca will be behind and below the horizon on account of the curvature of the earth as a globe – not at the point in space at which the praying person is looking.

This obligation leads to an impossible situation every time Muslims start their prayers.

The Jamia Mosque in Cape Town, the oldest mosque in South Africa (1850)

Solomon's Wisdom and Army
Surah 27: 16–18

16.	And Solomon succeeded David. He said, "O people, we were taught the language of birds, and we were given from everything. This is indeed a real blessing."
17.	To the service of Solomon were mobilized his troops of sprites, and men, and birds—all held in strict order.
18.	Until, when they came upon the Valley of Ants, an ant said, "O ants! Go into your nests, lest Solomon and his troops crush you without noticing."

According to this absurd tale in the Qur'an, King Solomon was able to converse with the birds and he even recruited some birds to serve in his army, together with human soldiers. It is not clear whether Solomon also understood the language of the ants.

QUESTIONABLE ETHICS

There are many ethical or moral prescriptions and practices in the Qur'an with which any civilized person can agree. There are, however, practices allowed or even encouraged with which no sane person can agree. Such practices and prescriptions must be compared with the Universal Declaration of Human Rights of the United Nations and ratified by the governments of most countries. This Declaration contains certain fundamental ethical principles that are accepted by most benevolent and rational people.

Some examples where unacceptable ethical practices are contained in the Qur'an are as follows:

Wife-beating
Surah 4: 35

> Men are guardians over women because Allah has made some of them excel others, and because they (men) spend of their wealth. So virtuous women are those who are obedient, and guard the secrets of their husbands with Allah's protection. And as for those on whose part you fear disobedience, admonish them and leave them alone in their beds, and chastise them. Then if they obey you, seek not a way against them. Surely, Allah is High, Great.

Islamic countries are well-known for the institutionalized discrimination against women who are treated as second-class citizens. This state of affairs is ordered in the Qur'an. The highest obligation of a woman is to obey her husband and should it become necessary, he is advised to chastise or beat her into subservience and submission.

Article 1 of the Universal Declaration states clearly: "All

human beings are born free and equal in dignity and rights." In Article 2 the following appears: "Everyone is entitled to all the rights and freedoms set forth in this Declaration, without distinction of any kind, such as race, color, sex, language, religion, political or other opinion, national or social origin, property, birth or other status." The following principle appears ion Article 5: "No one shall be subjected to torture or to cruel, inhuman or degrading treatment or punishment."

In other words: men and women are equals, discrimination against women is wrong, and corporal punishment must be regarded as unacceptable.

Unbelievers are the Worst Creatures
Surah 8: 55

> The worst of creatures in Allah's view are those who disbelieve. They have no faith.

According to the Qur'an, those who don't believe are the "worst creatures" on earth. Another translation calls them "the worst beasts". In other words, they are not fit to be called human beings and it is, therefore, permissible to treat them like dirt.

Articles 1 and 2 of the Declaration declares that all people are equal and that any form of discrimination is wrong.

Fighting Unbelievers
Surah 9: 5

> And when the forbidden months have passed, kill the idolaters wherever you find them and take them prisoners, and beleaguer them, and lie in wait for them at every place of ambush. But if they repent and observe Prayer and pay the Zakat, then leave their way free. Surely, Allah is Most Forgiving, Merciful.

Surah 9: 29

> Fight those from among the People of the Book who believe not in Allah, nor in the Last Day, nor hold as unlawful what Allah and His Messenger have declared to be unlawful, nor follow the true, religion, until they pay the tax with their own hand and acknowledge and, their subjection.

Surah 47: 5

> And when you meet in regular battle those who disbelieve, smite their necks; and, when you have overcome them, bind fast the fetters – then afterwards either release them as a favor or by taking ransom – until the war lays down its burdens. That is the ordinance. And if Allah had so pleased, He could have punished them Himself; but He has willed that some of you by others. And those who are killed in the way of Allah – He will never render their works vain.

It is a fact of history that Islam spread over large parts of the Middle East, Asia, and North Africa after Islamic armies had conquered those countries. Jews and Christians were initially tolerated as "People of the Book" and they could carry on with their religious practices, provided that they pay the Zakat, a tax imposed upon all non-Muslims.

This religious tax forced many Jews and Christians to convert to Islam to avoid this tax, which amounted to extortion.[233] Muslims also use these texts as a divine order to kill those Muslims who leave the faith to become Christians or whatever.

Muslims through the ages followed the example of Muhammad and obeyed the Qur'an, which called upon them to kill non-believers and to wage a holy war against infidels.

---

[233] Rahman, "Islam".

There are still today fanatic Muslim groups that resort to terrorism against those they regard as enemies of Islam. They are simply obeying Allah's orders and wishes in their holy book. Although a special status was accorded to "People of the Book", these people experienced hardship and harsh treatment through the ages in Muslim countries. This may explain the extreme reaction of the government of the country of Israel against Islamic terrorists in our time.

One sometimes hears the claim that Islam is a peaceful religion. These texts in the Qur'an prove the opposite. It is difficult to reconcile this belligerent attitude with the following verse:

The Prophet Muhammad and the Muslim Army at the Battle of Uhud, from the *Siyer-i Nebi*

Surah 2: 257

There should be no compulsion in religion.

A question was put to a Muslim cleric as to how people who had cut their ties with Islam have to be treated. The following reply was given: "The apostate is not to be put to death immediately after he falls into apostasy, especially if has doubts. Rather he should be asked to repent and be offered the opportunity to return to Islam and resolve his doubts, if any. If he persists in his apostasy after that, he is to be put to death."[234]

It is generally known that the Muslim author, Salman Rushdie, was sentenced to death in his absence in 1988 by die spiritual and political leader of Iran, Ruhollah Khomeini, for his alleged sacrilege in his novel The Satanic Verses. He survived several attempts on his life by Muslims, the latest in 2022, when he lost an eye and was severely wounded by 'n knife.

The quoted surahs are clearly contradicted by Article 3 of the Universal Declaration: "Everyone has the right to life, liberty and security of person." They also cannot be reconciled with Article 18: "Everyone has the right to freedom of thought, conscience and religion; this right includes freedom to change his religion or belief, and freedom, either alone or in community with others and in public or private, to manifest his religion or belief in teaching, practice, worship and observance."

The following is added in Article 30 of the Universal Declaration: "Nothing in this Declaration may be interpreted as implying for any State, group or person any right to engage in any activity or to perform any act aimed at the destruction of any of the rights and freedoms set forth herein." This article condemns, inter alia, the application of violence and the use of warfare to force people to convert to Islam.

Polygamy
Surah 4: 4

And if you fear that you will not be fair in dealing with the orphans, then marry of women as may be agreeable to you, two, or three, or

---

[234] Islam Q&A, 06/Rabi al-thani/1446, 09/October/2024.

> four; and if you fear you will not deal justly, then marry only one or what your right hands possess. That is the nearest way for you to avoid injustice.

Allah allowed Muslim men to marry up to four women who are regarded as their possessions. Women certainly had no say in what their husbands did, also when they decided to marry more women. In civilized societies, it is taken for granted that marriage consists of the union between one man and one woman.

Article 16 of the Universal Declaration says the following regarding marriage: "Men and women of full age, without any limitation due to race, nationality or religion, have the right to marry and to found a family. They are entitled to equal rights as to marriage, during marriage and at its dissolution.

"Marriage shall be entered into only with the free and full consent of the intending spouses."

This surah and this article can certainly not be reconciled.

Concubinage and Slavery
Surah 4: 26

> And whoso of you cannot afford to marry free, believing women, let him marry what your right hands possess, namely, your believing handmaids. And Allah knows your faith best; you are all one from another; so marry them with the leave of their masters and give them their dowries according to what is fair, they being chaste, secret paramours. And if, after they are married, they are guilty of lewdness, they shall have half the punishment prescribed for free women. This is for him among you who fears lest he should commit sin. And that you restrain yourselves is better for you; and Allah is Most Forgiving, Merciful.

Muslim men are allowed to marry slave girls who are also Muslims and with whom they had a romantic relationship on the sly. This type of relationship is not condemned, but it is declared that it would be better to get married.

Muhammad married many women, the youngest was Aisha when she was only 6–7 years old; the marriage was consummated later, when she was 9 years old and he was 53 years old. It may be argued that he made himself guilty of paedophilia.[235]

Muhammad to have any Woman he Wishes
Surah 33: 50

> O Prophet! We have permitted to you your wives to whom you have given their dowries, and those you already have, as granted to you by Allah, and the daughters of your paternal uncle, and the daughters of your paternal aunts, and the daughters of your maternal uncle, and the daughters of your maternal aunts who emigrated with you, and a believing woman who has offered herself to the Prophet, if the Prophet desires to marry her, exclusively for you, and not for the believers. We know what We have ordained for them regarding their wives and those their right hands possess. This is to spare you any difficulty. Allah is Forgiving and Merciful.

It seems that Muhammad, with his many wives and concubines, made sure that this practice was sanctioned by the Qur'an by inserting this surah into his collection of supposedly divine messages. He even recorded that there were women who offered themselves to him. He must have had his own heaven, with plenty of women, already on earth!

---

[235] Wikipedia, "Muhammad." (Wikipedia cites numerous sources for this marriage of Muhammad.

Heavenly Bliss for Believers
Surah 56: 27–38

> 27. And those on the Right—what of those on the Right?
> 28. In lush orchards.
> 29. And sweet-smelling plants.
> 30. And extended shade.
> 31. And outpouring water.
> 32. And abundant fruit.
> 33. Neither withheld, nor forbidden.
> 34. And uplifted mattresses.
> 35. We have created them of special creation.
> 36. And made them virgins.
> 37. Tender and un-aging.
> 38. For those on the Right.

Those "on the Right" are contrasted with those "on the Left", the unbelievers and infidels who will face everlasting fire in hell after death. The faithful men are promised a garden filled with delights after death, containing delicious fruit and beautiful and youthful virgins. It seems as if the Muslim heaven must resemble a brothel!

Heavenly Pleasures
Surah 78: 31–33

> 31. But for the righteous there is triumph.
> 32. Gardens and vineyards.
> 33. And splendid spouses, well matched.
> 34. And delicious drinks.

Another translation uses the expression "damsels with swelling breasts" instead of "splendid spouses". Muslim men received the promise that heaven would amount to a never-ending party or feast with enough to drink and crowds of voluptuous females.

Treatment of Slaves
Surah 2: 221

> Do not marry idolatresses, unless they have believed. A believing maid is better than an idolatress, even if you like her. And do not marry idolaters, unless they have believed. A believing slave is better than an idolater, even if you like him.

Surah 4: 36

> Worship Allah, and ascribe no partners to Him, and be good to theparents, and the relatives, and the orphans, and the poor, and the neighbor next door, and the distant neighbor, and the close associate, and the traveler, and your servants. Allah does not love the arrogant showoff.

Although Muslims are encouraged to treated their servants or slaves well, slavery as such is not condemned and regarded as a normal state of affairs.

This militates against Article 4 of the Universal Declaration: "No one shall be held in slavery or servitude; slavery and the slave trade shall be prohibited in all their forms."

OTHE PROPHETS IGNORED

It has already been mentioned that the Qur'an alludes to various biblical prophets. Below is a list of biblical prophets mentioned in the Qur'an:

1. Musa (Moses) mentioned 136 times
2. Ibrahim (Abraham) – 69 times
3. Nuh (Noah) – 43 times
4. Lut (Lot) – 27 times

5. Yusof (Joseph) – 27 times
6. Isa (Jesus) – 25 times
7. Adam – 25 times
8. Harun (Aaron) – 20 times
9. Sulayman (Solomon) – 17 times
10. Ishaq (isaac) – 17 times
11. Dawud (David) – 16 times
12. Yaqub (Jacob) – 16 times
13. Ismael (Ishmael) – 12 times
14. Shuayb – 11 times
15. Salih – 9 times
16. Zakaria – 7 times
17. Hud – 7 times
18. Yahya – 5 times
19. Muhammad – 4 times
20. Yunus (Jonah) – 4 times
21. Ayyub (Job) – 4 times
22. Idris (Enoch) – twice
23. Alyasa (Elisha) – twice
24. Elyas (Elijah) – twice
25. Thul Kifl (Ezekiel) – twice[236]

The following surah's are worth quoting in this regard:

Other Messengers
Surah 16: 36

To every community We sent a messenger: "Worship Allah, and avoid idolatry." Some of them Allah guided, while others deserved

---

[236] Project Quran, "What does the Quran say about Prophets?"

misguidance. So travel through the earth, and see what the fate of the deniers was.

Surah 3: 144

Muhammad is no more than a messenger. Messengers have passed on before him.

Muhammad and other Prophets
Surah: 46: 9

Say, "I am not different from the other messengers; and I do not know what will be done with me, or with you. I only follow what is in spired in me, and I am only a clear warner."

According to these passages, Muhammad was preceded by other messengers or prophets who were guided by Allah. Muhammad was even inspired to declare that he was no different from other messengers. That can only mean that the messages of the previous prophets to their communities must still be valid because they allegedly all gave the same message.

In other words: If the messages contained in the Hebrew and Christian Scriptures were guided by Allah, then all Muslims are obliged to accept those messages as well, alongside the messages of the Qur'an. That means that all editions of the Qur'an ought to contain the Hebrew and Christian Scriptures as well because all of them were inspired by God.

At this stage one must ask: Why do the Muslims never read from the Old Testament and the New Testament at their prayer meetings? Why do they ignore what David, Solomon, Ezekiel, Jesus, and the other prophets taught in these Scriptures? Are they perhaps afraid that it will transpire that the Qur'an grievously distorted the messages of these earlier prophets and that their messages contradict the Qur'an on certain points?

TO SUM UP

This analysis of some of the prophetic pronouncements in the Qur'an forces one to draw the following conclusions:

- There are so many scientific errors and unscientific notions in the Qur'an that this book could never have been dictated by an omniscient and truthful God.
- There are so many historical errors that the compiler of this book must have misunderstood many stories from the Bible and gave skewed and even absurd renderings of events in the past.
- Although the validity of the utterances of biblical prophets is acknowledged, these utterances are totally ignored.
- The Qur'an contains so many absurd utterances or contradictory statements that the veracity and credibility of the whole book must be questioned.
- Certain aspects of the ethics preached in the Qur'an are unacceptable.
- The Qur'an does not make the impression of a divinely dictated document. In most cases, God's words, plans, thoughts, and actions are presented in the third-person singular – in contrast with most of the Old Testament prophets who quoted the words of YHWH verbatim in the first-person singular. For the most part, the Qur'an consists of comments of a human author about what he deemed or even guessed to be God's thoughts, plans, and actions.
- All these flaws, errors, and mistakes compel one to conclude that Muhammad was personally responsible for the contents of the whole book. He may have lived under the impression that an archangel or God Himself gave him all sorts of messages, but all the words in the Qur'an are of a human origin.
- The Qur'an was only written down after Muhammad's death. He and his initial followers could not read and write and he

taught his messages to his adherents, who learnt them by heart. These memories were collected and written down at a later stage to form the Qur'an. There is no guarantee that the recollections of those who provided the material for the final book were accurate. After all, human memories are known to be fallible.

- There are no independent witnesses to corroborate Muhammad's visions and revelations. We have only his word that an archangel appeared to him or that he heard God's voice. It is a truism or an axiom that all claims, statements, and communications must be backed up by evidence to be accepted as true and reliable and acceptable. This requirement is lacking in the case of the Qur'an.
- It may be argued that Islam is meant only for the Arabs and not for the rest of humanity since the Qur'an is not supposed to be translated into other languages and the Qur'an is always recited in Arabic during prayer meetings. This is an absurd practice because God is supposed to understand all human languages.

CHAPTER 10
FINAL THOUGHTS

GENERAL OBSERVATIONS

Some general observations may be made after a careful analysis of the most important prophecies recorded in the Hebrew Scriptures, the Christian Scriptures, and the Muslim Scriptures:

- When Old Testament prophets commented on current affairs, the political and religious situations of their times, they usually gave a fair and acceptable description and evaluation, usually based on sound common sense.
- The comments and descriptions of Jesus of Nazareth, James the Just, Paul of Tarsus, and John of Patmos of the circumstances under which they lived, seem to have captured the mood and challenges of their times fairly accurately, although they were forced to refer to the Roman emperor and his oppressive pagan empire in hidden terms out of fear for reprisals, especially after the disastrous outcome of the Jewish War in AD 70.
- The Hebrew Scriptures contain many references to one or more messianic figures and more than one anointed person or entity was meant, namely YHWH (the God of Israel), the kings of Israel (especially King David and his descendants), the king of Persia, the nation of Israel as a whole, and unnamed champions and liberators of the people. None of these prophecies could be applied to Jesus of Nazareth and that must be the reason why most Jews never accepted Jesus as the promised Messiah.
- The authors of most books of the New Testament did their best

to portray Jesus as the promised Christ or Messiah of Israel. However, all their efforts were misplaced when they provided skewed and questionable quotations and interpretations of passages from the Old Testament.
- The authors of the gospels, especially the author of Matthew, believed certain statements in the Old Testament were prophecies regarding Jesus as Messiah and, therefore, they invented certain episodes in the life of Jesus in the belief that these events simply must have happened because they were foretold by the prophets.
- Jesus believed that he was chosen by God to be *the* Messiah and he convinced some Jews, mostly members of the Essene sect, of this claim. When he failed in his effort to become the successor of King David with the help of a host of heavenly angels, Paul transformed him into a celestial being, the divine Son of God, thereby constructing a new religion, Christianity. This new religion, with its trinitarian God was a merger or synthesis of the monotheism of Judaism and paganism with its polytheism.
- The prophets of the Old Testament had no clear ideas about the Day of YHWH or Judgment Day. Sometimes they thought of it as something of the near future, but otherwise they postponed it to the end of time. The afterlife received relatively little attention in the Hebrew Scriptures and there are some contradictory ideas.
- Paul's ideas regarding the afterlife differed fundamentally from those of Jesus. According to Jesus, one could attain eternal life simply by obeying God's commandments. Paul, on the other hand, taught that eternal life could only be reached through faith in Jesus Christ who died on the cross on behalf of repentant sinners, thereby suffering hell in their stead. These different opinions forces one to ask: was it really necessary for Jesus to be crucified to redeem or save sinners if people could reach

heaven in the afterlife by their own efforts as Jesus explained?
- There are more clear ideas in the New Testament regarding Judgment Day and the afterlife. There is one snag, though: it isn't clear when dead people have to appear before God's throne to be judged – was it directly after death, or was it only in the far future? John of Patmos seems to have solved this dilemma by implying that both possibilities must be accepted because they can be reconciled in God's eternity with its absence of time.
- The Qur'an contains a simplified Old Testament theology. Although it is presented by Muslims as the final and ultimate revelation of God, it contains many signs that it is the brain child of Muhammad himself. This book contains so many contradicttions, scientific misconceptions, unacceptable ethical prescriptions, and historical errors that it has forfeited all credibility.

Thomas Paine (Portrait by John Wesley Jarvis, c. 1806–1807)

The American rationalist of the eighteenth century, Thomas Paine (1737–1809), famously declared that "prophesying is lying professionally", since nobody was able to verify or confirm the revelations or visions of a prophet.[237]

This verdict by Paine is perhaps somewhat too harsh. When reading the Scriptures, one gets the impression that the various prophets were serious in their conviction that God spoke through them.

---

[237] Paine, *The Age of Reason*, 129.

It is, therefore, necessary to determine from a neuropsychological perspective how the mind of a prophet works.

NEUROSCIENTIFIC PERSPECTIVES

Dreams

Some prophets and other figures in the Bible claimed that God or an angel spoke to them during a dream. Examples are Jacob, Pharaoh, Joseph (the son of Jacob), King Nebuchadnezzar, Joseph (the father of Jesus), the wise men from the East, the wife of Pontius Pilate, and Paul of Tarsus.

Dreams can be described as "images, thoughts, or feelings that occur during sleep. Visual imagery is the most common."[238]

Dreams are, by their inherent characteristics, subjective and only the person who was dreaming can tell what the contents of the dreams were. There is, therefore, no way any dream can ever be confirmed or proved by an independent observer or witness and we only have the word of the dreamer about the dream.

It has been shown in previous chapters that especially the dreams connected to the nativity tales of Jesus were nothing but pious fiction. The reports in the gospels of Mathew and Luke of how Jesus was supposed to have been born, differ so much from each other that none of them can be deemed as describing real events.[239]

Dreams are produced by the brain during so-called "Rapid Eye Movement" (REM) Sleep, one of the phases of sleep that is repeated a few times each night. There are clear signs that even animals also dream while asleep.

Typical characteristics of dreaming include the following: It has a first-person perspective, it is involuntary, the content is often

---

[238] Suni, "Dreams".

[239] Pretorius, *The Gospels,* 393–403; 457–72.

illogical or even incoherent or bizarre, and the dream includes other people who interact with the dreamer and each other. Dreams often produce strong emotions and when these emotions amount to fear, anxiety, and panic the dream may be classified as a nightmare. People who suffer from post-traumatic stress disorder (PTSD) often experience nightmares.

Dreams are thought to have the following functions: They –
- Consolidate memories by transferring the contents of the short-term memory in the hippocampus to the long-term memory in the tempo-ral lobes;
- Erase irrelevant memories;
- Process emotions;
- May rework recent experiences; and
- Mmay produce solutions to problems.

This all means that the brain doesn't shut down during sleep, but stays active at a lower and slower level.[240]

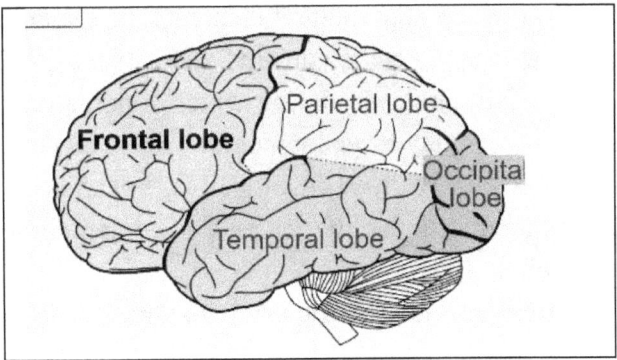

The lobes of the brain

The irrational and bizarre contents of dreams are attributed to the fact that the frontal lobe of the brain becomes inactive during sleep

---

[240] Suni, "Dreams"; Sinton and McCarley, "REM (Rapid Eye Movement) Sleep".

and dreaming. This large part of the brain was the last to develop during the process of evolution and it is much larger in humans than in higher animals, such as the primates.

Zillmer *et al.* describe the work of the frontal lobe as follows:

> "This area is akin to a conductor or executive of the brain – organizing, controlling and managing behavior, and making high-level decisions about socially appropriate behavior." [241]

The frontal lobe is also needed for planning ahead, the concentration of attention, comparing things, and understanding the feelings of others.[242]

This all means that dreamers are unable to think critically and rationally while dreaming since the frontal lobes of their brains has been switched off. Therefore, the dreaming person may have the most illogical, absurd, insane, and nonsensical dreams, which he or she may sometimes interpret as divine messages or revelations.

It must be stated: dreaming is a purely natural neurological process, without any supernatural elements. In ancient civilizations and unsophisticated societies dreams were seen as the wanderings of the spirit of the dreamer, during which supernatural entities and deceased relatives may be encountered. This view was also held by dreamers of whom we read in the Bible, but this idea cannot be entertained anymore in the light of contemporary scientific knowledge about the brain.

All this leads to the conclusion that there is no guarantee that God really communicated with certain biblical individuals through their dreams – that is, if they really had those dreams as reported.

---

[241] Zillmer *et al.*, *Principles of Neuropsychology*, 160.
[242] Villines, "What does the Frontal Lobe Do?"

Hypnotic Trances

Several investigations in the fields of psychology, sociology, and anthropology have demonstrated that shamans, seers, clairvoyants, oracles, diviners, mediums, and self-styled prophets usually receive their revelations or messages while experiencing a trance.[243]

Trances may be the result of either the ingestion of certain drugs or the induction of (self-)hypnosis, brought about by chanting, dancing, lack of sleep, or certain exercises and rituals.[244]

There are no direct examples of drugs used by scriptural prophets, although some scholars maintain that prophets such as Moses may have been "high" on some or other drug.[245] There is, however, no concrete evidence for these hypotheses and they must be seen as mere speculation. However, drugs such as cannabis and opium were known in antiquity and residues of burnt cannabis were found by archaeologists in an ancient shrine in Israel.[246] It is, therefore, not impossible that some biblical figures used drugs occasionally, but there is no compelling evidence.

Hypnosis may be described as follows:

> "Hypnosis is a form of dissociation in which a person's field of attention is narrowed to a single thought, feeling or idea. When experiencing this state of mind, normal distractions

---

[243] Ahlström, "Prophecy", Toriz, "Neuroanthropology of Shamanic Trance"; Flor-Henry, "Brain Changes during a Shamanic Trance"; Gosseries *et al.,* "Exploration of Trance States"; Helvenston, "Waking the Trance-Fixed"; Rowe, "Delegitimization of Trance-Possession"; Tuczay, "Trance Prophets and Diviners".

[244] Carter, *The Brain Book,* 186.

[245] Ehrman, "Was Moses High on Mt. Sinai?"

[246] Medical Brief, 18.02.2015; Enc Brit, "Drug Cult"; Fox, "Archaeologists Identify Traces of Burnt Cannabis".

and preoccupations may be kept out of mind."[247]

"Another special cognitive state sometimes confused with sleep is hypnosis. Hypnosis has been used clinically for hundreds of years and is primarily a phenomenon involving attentive receptive concentration. Clinicians practicing hypnosis suggest that when one is in a hypnotic state, attentional and perceptual changes may occur that would not have occurred had one been in a more usual state of awareness. In a responsive subject, hypnotic perceptual alteration is accompanied by reproducible changes in brain action."[248]

During hypnosis, a person's brain functions differently from ordinary wakeful states. The frontal lobe of the brain becomes more active, enabling the person to concentrate intensely on an idea, activity, or experience. When people are very busy with tasks that occupy their minds totally, they are in a light state of hypnosis.

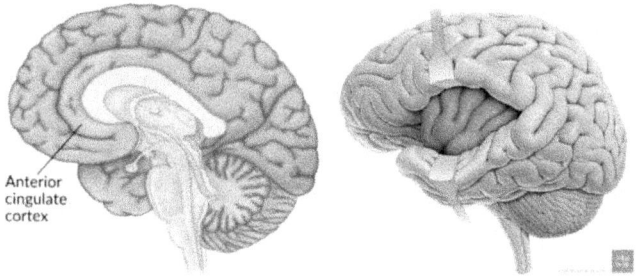

The anterior cingulate cortex and the insula inside the human brain

At the same time, the anterior cingulate cortex and the insula in the brain of the hypnotized person become inactive or switched off. Both these brain regions are involved in the registration of pain. The anterior cingulate cortex deals with assigning emotions to certain

---

[247] Carter, *The Brain Book,* 188.
[248] Fan *et al.,* "Attentional Mechanisms".

stimuli or events The insula makes the person aware of what is going on in his or her body and where all the body parts are in space.[249]

The fact that the frontal lobe becomes more active and the anterior cingulate cortex and the insula are switched off explains why a hypnotized person can concentrate strongly on a certain aspect of reality, getting totally absorbed in the process, while becoming oblivious of his or her surroundings, his or her own body, and even pain. Cases are known of people who acquired superhuman strength while in a trance, enabling them to perform extraordinary feats.

A manual on hypnosis states: "Hallucinating under hypnosis is appropriate and expected." The imagination of a deeply hypnotized person easily goes into overdrive and he or she can "see", "hear", "smell", and "feel" people and things that are not there. Psychologists who treat their patients with hypnotherapy use this ability to create a new "reality" in the minds of their patients. It is also possible to do so-called age regression where the person re-experiences incidents from his or her past as if he or she is really back at that stage.[250]

Prophetic Trances

The Bible contains several descriptions of prophets and other persons who fell into a trance and received messages from God or acquired remarkable abilities.[251]

Ahlström notes:

---

[249] Wolf *et al.,* "Functional Changes in Brain Activity Using Hypnosis"; Flint Rehab, "Anterior Cingulate Cortex"; Uddin, "Structure and Function of the Human Insula"; Dubuc, "Can States of Consciousness be Mapped in the Brain?"
[250] Temes, *The Complete Idiot's Guide to Hypnosis*, 35 & 49.
[251] Pilch, "Trance Experiences in the Bible"; Parker, "Possession Trance and Prophecy in Pre-Exilic Israel".

"That prophets employing ecstatic techniques have been called madmen is accounted for by descriptions of their loss of control over themselves when they are 'possessed' by the deity. Prophets in ecstatic trances often have experienced sensations of corporeal transmigration (such as the 6th-century-BC Old Testament prophet Ezekiel and the 6th–7th-century-AD founder of Islām, Muḥammad)."[252]

Some applicable biblical texts may be quoted in this regard:

Num 24: 2–3

2.	Balaam lifted up his eyes, and he saw Israel dwelling according to their tribes; and the Spirit of God came on him.
3.	He took up his parable, and said, Balaam the son of Beor says, The man whose eye was closed says ….

Judg 3: 9–10

9.	When the children of Israel cried to YHWH, YHWH raised up a savior to the children of Israel, who saved them, even Othniel the son of Kenaz, Caleb's younger brother.
10.	The Spirit of YHWH came on him, and he judged Israel; and he went out to war, and YHWH delivered Cushan-rishathaim king of Mesopotamia into his hand: and his hand prevailed against Cushan-rishathaim.

Judg 14: 6

The Spirit of YHWH came mightily on him [Samson], and he tore him as he would have torn a kid; and he had nothing in his hand: but he didn't tell his father or his mother what he had done.

---

[252] Ahlström, "Prophecy".

Judg 15: 14

> When he [Samson] came to Lehi, the Philistines shouted as they met him: and the Spirit of YHWH came mightily on him, and the ropes that were on his arms became as flax that was burnt with fire, and his bands dropped from off his hands.

1 Sam 19: 19–24

19.	It was told Saul, saying, Behold, David is at Naioth in Ramah.
20.	Saul sent messengers to take David: and when they saw the company of the prophets prophesying, and Samuel standing as head over them, the Spirit of God came on the messengers of Saul, and they also prophesied.
21.	When it was told Saul, he sent other messengers, and they also prophesied. Saul sent messengers again the third time, and they also prophesied.
22.	Then went he also to Ramah, and came to the great well that is in Secu: and he asked and said, Where are Samuel and David? One said, Behold, they are at Naioth in Ramah.
23.	He went there to Naioth in Ramah: and the Spirit of God came on him also, and he went on, and prophesied, until he came to Naioth in Ramah.
24.	He also stripped off his clothes, and he also prophesied before Samuel, and lay down naked all that day and all that night. Why they say, Is Saul also among the prophets?

1 Kgs 18: 45–46

45.	It happened in a little while, that the sky grew black with clouds and wind, and there was a great rain. Ahab rode, and went to Jezreel:

| 46. | and the hand of YHWH was on Elijah; and he girded up his loins, and ran before Ahab to the entrance of Jezreel. |

Ezek 8: 1–3

1.	It happened in the sixth year, in the sixth [month], in the fifth [day] of the month, as I sat in my house, and the elders of Judah sat before me, that the hand of the Lord YHWH fell there on me.
2.	Then I saw, and, behold, a likeness as the appearance of fire; from the appearance of his loins and downward, fire; and from his loins and upward, as the appearance of brightness, as it were glowing metal.
3.	He put forth the form of a hand, and took me by a lock of my head; and the Spirit lifted me up between earth and the sky, and brought me in the visions of God to Jerusalem, to the door of the gate of the inner [court] that looks toward the north; where was the seat of the image of jealousy, which provokes to jealousy.

The expression "spirit of YHWH" (Hebrew: רוּחַ יְהוָה – *ruach YHWH*) often occurs in these quoted texts. This expression has nothing to do with the New Testament notion of a separate divine person, the Holy Spirit. It simply means the power or the breath of YHWH, which enabled prophets and others to experience an altered state of consciousness and receive news or instructions from God.[253]

Acts 10: 9–11

| 9. | Now on the next day, as they were on their journey, and got close to the city, Peter went up on the housetop to pray, at |

---

[253] Encyclopaedia.com, "Spirit of God".

	about noon.
10.	He became hungry, and desired to eat, but while they were preparing, he fell into a trance.
11.	He saw heaven opened, and a certain container descending to him, like a great sheet, let down by four corners on the earth.

Acts 11:5

"I [Peter] was in the city of Joppa praying, and in a trance I saw a vision: a certain container descending, like it was a great sheet let down from heaven by four corners."

Acts 22:17–18

17.	It happened that, when I [Paul] had returned to Jerusalem, and while I prayed in the temple, I fell into a trance,
18.	and saw him saying to me, 'Hurry and get out of Jerusalem quickly, because they will not receive testimony concerning me from you.'

The Greek word for "trance" used in these texts is ἔκστασις – (*ekstasis*). The English word "ecstasy" is clearly derived from this Greek word. A dictionary explains its meaning as –

> "a throwing of the mind out of its normal state, alienation of mind, whether such as makes a lunatic or that of a man who by some sudden emotion is transported as it were out of himself, so that in this rapt condition, although he is awake, his mind is drawn off from all surrounding objects and wholly fixed on things divine that he sees nothing but the forms and images lying within, and thinks that he perceives with his bodily eyes and ears realities shown him by God."

This explanation is a good description of what happens when somebody experiences hypnosis.

Rev 1:10–11

10.	I was in the spirit on the Lord's Day, and I heard behind me a loud voice, as of a trumpet
11.	saying, "What you see, write in a book and send to the seven assemblies: to Ephesus, Smyrna, Pergamum, Thyatira, Sardis, Philadelphia, and to Laodicea."

Rev 4: 1–2

1.	After these things I looked and saw a door opened in heaven, and the first voice that I heard, like a trumpet speaking with me, was one saying, "Come up here, and I will show you the things which must happen after this."
2.	Immediately I was in the spirit. Behold, there was a throne set in heaven, and one sitting on the throne

Rev 17: 3

He [an angel] carried me away in the spirit into a wilderness.

Rev 21: 10

He [an angel] carried me away in the spirit to a great and high mountain, and showed me the holy city, Jerusalem, coming down out of heaven from God.

The Greek words used for "in the spirit" in these texts are ἐν πνεύματι (*en pneumati*). The word πνεῦμα (*pneuma*) has a wide range of meanings – "wind, breath, spirit, and life force". In this case, it is clearly used to describe a trance during which John heard voices and saw visions.

From the foregoing is must be clear that biblical prophets received their communications from God while in a trance or under hypnosis. It has been shown that a hypnotized person usually experiences hallucinations by seeing, hearing, smelling, tasting, and feeling things that are not there. All the texts quoted above show unambiguously that biblical prophets saw all sorts of visions and heard all sorts of pronouncements, which were the products of their brains or minds.

It cannot be guaranteed that God really used these trances to speak to various prophets. Their prophecies could just as well have been the result of the frontal lobes of their brains that became overactive and produced various voices and sights. It is impossible to ascertain whether these subjective experiences really came from God because we only have the unverified and unverifiable reports of the various prophets.

Epileptic Fits

The visions and revelations of two very influential religious figures may be attributed to the hallucinations caused by epileptic fits: Paul of Tarsus and Muhammad. Our known information about these two figures must be scrutinized.

The conventional view is that the visions of the **apostle Paul** of Christ must have been supernatural events. There is, however, also a realistic possibility that he experienced hallucinations. When one submits that so-called supernatural revelations and visions are by their very nature subjective and, therefore, impossible to be verified independently, then one must also accept that they cannot be anything but hallucinations or delusions.

The following passage provides important indications of Paul's physical and mental state:

Paul's Thorn in the Flesh
II Cor 12: 1–7

> 1. It is doubtless not profitable for me to boast. I will come to visions and revelations of the Lord.
> 2. I know a man in Christ, fourteen years ago (whether in the body, I don't know, or whether out of the body, I don't know; God knows), such a one caught up into the third heaven.
> 3. I know such a man (whether in the body, or apart from the body, I don't know; God knows),
> 4. how he was caught up into Paradise, and heard unspeakable words, which it is not lawful for a man to utter.
> 5. On behalf of such a one I will boast, but on my own behalf I will not boast, except in my weaknesses.
> 6. For if I would desire to boast, I will not be foolish; for I will speak the truth. But I forbear, so that no man may account of me above that which he sees in me, or hears from me.
> 7. By reason of the exceeding greatness of the revelations, that I should not be exalted excessively, there was given to me a thorn in the flesh, a messenger of Satan to buffet me, that I should not be exalted excessively.

The following relevant aspects regarding this passage must be pointed out:

- Although Paul employs the third-person singular, it is obvious that he refers to himself;
- He had experienced visions and revelations (plural) during which he heard voices uttering unspeakable words;

- He experienced Paradise and was caught up to the third heaven, the dwelling place of God and the angels above the heaven of clouds and the starry heaven; and
- He is not certain whether he had these experiences while in or out of his body.

The word used for "unspeakable" is ἄρρητος (*arretos*), which means "unsaid, unspoken, unspeakable, inexpressible, not to be spoken". It may mean Paul wanted to state that the words he heard were so profound that no human mind could comprehend them. It may, also, mean that he was unable to understand the words himself because they did not make sense. If the last possibility is the case, then this points to auditory hallucinations.

What exactly was this "thorn in the flesh"? Various possibilities may be given of which the most probable will be explored further on. The word for "thorn" that Paul uses, is σκόλοψ (*skolops*). It means "a pointed piece of wood, a pale, a sharp stake, splinter". It must, therefore, have been something very painful or uncomfortable.

The passage quoted above is not the only one in which he alluded to his visions and revelations. In numerous passages, such as Acts 16:9, 18:9 and 22: 17–21, 1 Cor 4: 1, 1 Cor 9: 1, 1 Cor 15: 3–8, 2 Cor 5: 16, 2 Cor 12: 12, Gal 1: 11–16, Eph 3: 2–3, and 1 Thess. 2: 4, we read of visions which Paul said he had had, mostly of the risen and glorified Christ, through which the "mysteries" of the gospel were revealed to him.

When reading these passages, one cannot but be reminded of the three accounts of Paul's conversion on the road to Damascus given in Acts 9: 3–19, 22: 6–16, and 26: 12–20. The following points may be made regarding these descriptions, while keeping in mind that the author of Acts wrote his history several decades after the event and that he could have become confused regarding certain details. After all, the accounts of Paul's conversion in Acts differ markedly from his own rendering of the event in Galatians 1.[254]

- Paul travelled to Damascus and suddenly saw a bright light, which his travelling companions couldn't see;
- He fell to the earth;
- He heard a voice; his companions reportedly also heard the voice but could not understand the words;
- The voice told him that it was Jesus, whose followers he had persecuted;
- He was blinded by the bright light and had to be led by the hand by his companions the rest of the way;
- He rarely moved for three days, not even eating and drinking;
- He recovered his eyesight after three days through the ministrations of Ananias, a local Christian, who also baptized him; and
- The whole experience must have been traumatic for Paul.

The DSM-5-TR of the American Psychiatric Association describes hallucinations as follows:

> "Hallucinations are perception-like experiences that occur without an external stimulus. They are vivid and clear, with the full force and impact of normal perceptions, and not under voluntary control. They may occur in any sensory modality, but auditory hallucinations are the most common in schizophrenia and related disorders. Auditory hallucinations are usually experienced as voices, whether familiar or unfamiliar, that are perceived as distinct from the indivi-

---

[254] Rylaarsdam *et al.*, "Biblical Literature".

dual's own thoughts."[255]

Investigators, such as the late neurologist Professor Oliver Sacks of the New York University Medical School, noted that hallucinations often have religious overtones for those who experience them. These people may be convinced that they experienced a profound spiritual awakening or an encounter with God, Jesus, another divine being, deceased loved ones, or other spiritual beings. Sacks points out that Joan of Arc, who had seizures, was convinced that God called her to become a religious and military leader in France in medieval times.[256]

Hallucinations may be caused by a variety of factors:

- Psychedelic drugs;
- A near-death-experience or out-of-the-body experience;
- Psychosis, such as schizophrenia;
- An attack of migraine;
- Epilepsy;
- Stroke;
- Delirium tremens;
- Sensory deprivation;
- Sensory defects;
- Loss of sleep;
- Hypnosis and trance states; or
- Traumatic brain injuries and brain tumors.[257]

The most important of these possibilities will be discussed below:

---

[255] APA, *DSM-5-TR*, 103.
[256] Sacks, *Hallucinations*; O'Callaghan, "Oliver Sacks Wants to Destigmatize Hallucinations".
[257] Wallis, "What do Hallucinations Tell"; West, "Hallucinations".

Temporal Lobe Epilepsy: Landsborough, a neurologist, presented a persuasive case that Paul's thorn in the flesh could have been left temporal lobe epilepsy.[258] In many cases, epilepsy is an inherited condition, but it may also be caused by trauma, infection, fever, tumors, or toxins. It is the result of an abnormal firing of neurons in one region of the brain, spreading to other parts. Many neurons lose their regular rhythm and switch to a rapid rhythm, due to the overproduction of Sestrin-3. The result is a seizure or a convulsion.[259]

Epilepsy may be due to abnormalities in the occipital lobe at the back of the head where the visual centers of the brain are located. This may result in visual hallucinations containing people and other aspects of reality. Partial blindness may accompany attacks.[260]

Abnormalities in the temporal lobes of the brain – just behind the eyes – are responsible for most cases of epilepsy.[261] If the abnormalities are centered in the speech centers within the left temporal lobe and the underlying limbic system, the attacks may be accompanied by auditory and/or visual hallucinations, which may be interpreted by the sufferer as having spiritual or religious significance.[262]

Paul's repeated visions, his temporary blindness, and his visual problems do seem to be the result of left temporal lobe epileptic seizures. Since this disease was known in antiquity as the "sacred disease", during which various gods – especially *Selene* (Σελήνη), the moon goddess – supposedly spoke to the sufferer, it

---

[258] Landsborough, "St Paul and Temporal Lobe Epilepsy".
[259] Kolb and Wishaw, *Fundamentals of Human Neuropsychology,* 757–58; University of Bonn, "Dragnet for Epilepsy Genes."
[260] NYU Langone Comprehensive Epilepsy Center, "Occipital Lobe Epilepsy".
[261] Landsborough, "St Paul and Temporal Lobe Epilepsy", 663.
[262] Hoffman et al. "Transcranial Magnetic Stimulation", 55; Elliot et al., "Delusions"; Korsness et al. "An fMRI Study", 610, 616.

may account for Paul's success with Gentile audiences who must have concluded that he was in direct contact with his God while experiencing a fit.

Mild Traumatic Brain Injury: A possibility not considered by any other investigator – as far as can be ascertained – is that Paul may have suffered from the after-effects of a concussion and a mild traumatic brain injury.

All three accounts of Paul's conversion in Acts mention that he fell to the ground when he saw a bright light. The severity of this fall is not mentioned.

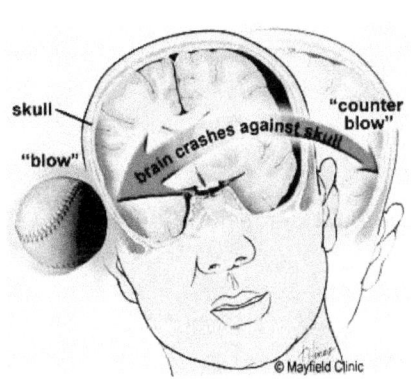

Should it have happened that he stumbled and fell he could have hit his head on the hard road surface or on a rock and suffered a concussion with a mild traumatic brain injury. Such a fall could have caused him to "see stars"[263], which may explain the bright light he saw. It is also possible that he was struck by lightning – the bright light that he saw – which must have caused a concussion.[264]

A concussion is usually called a closed brain injury since the skull was not penetrated. The traumatic brain injury (TBI) occurs when the brain is jolted within the skull due to a fall or a knock against the head. The bump against the head, whether from a heavy

---

[263] Zillmer, *Principles of Neuropsychol0gy,* 379; Spoor, "Concussion and your Vision".
[264] Lezak, *Neuropsychological Assessment,* 226–27.

object or the ground during a fall, causes the brain to move rapidly within the skull and bounce back.[265]

A mild TBI may not impair the victim's cognitive functioning in the long run, but some other conditions may result. These conditions may be due to the tearing of nerve fibers, bleeding in the brain (called hematomas), oedema (swelling in the brain), brain tumors that develop and meningiomas (benign tumors inside the meninges, the soft protective layer under the skull)[266]

Some of the consequences of a mild TBI are as follows:

- Epilepsy, especially left temporal lobe epilepsy, mostly due to scar tissue or tumors within the brain;[267]
- Headaches, including migraines;[268]
- Amnesia;[269]
- Temporary blindness;[270]
- Persistent problems with vision;[271]
- Personality changes, including mania, depression, increased

---

[265] Zillmer, *Principles of Neuropsychology,* 371, 375.
[266] Zillmer, *Principles of Neuropsychology,* 359; Kolb and Wishaw, *Fundamentals of Human Neuropsychology,* 759; Coetzer, "Auditory Hallucinations", 15.
[267] Zillmer, *Principles of Neuropsychology,* 379; Kolb and Wishaw, *Fundamentals of Human Neuropsychology* 757; Webb, "Auditory Hallucinations", 539; White, "Concussion"; Hishaw, "Concussion"; McAllister & Ferrell, 2002: 357; Lamar *et al.* 2014: 110–11.
[268] Webb, "Auditory Hallucinations", 539.
[269] Hishaw, "Concussion"; Fisher, "Seizures".
[270] Granacher, 2008: 285–87; Kaye & Herskowitz, "Transient Post-Traumatic Cortical Blindness", 206; Spoor, "Concussion" Metcalf and Bass, "Head Injuries".
[271] Kaye and Herskowitz, "Transient post-traumatic cortical blindness" 206; Hishaw, "Concussion"; Spoor, "Concussion".

aggression, and paranoia;[272]
- The development of Parkinson's Disease with its characteristic muscle tremors and rigidity;[273]
- Auditory and visionary hallucinations;[274] and
- Some patients develop "excessive verbal output, ... hypergraphia, altered sexuality (usually hyposexuality), and intensified mental life (obsessional cognitive and spiritual/religious ideation)."[275]

This condition is also known as the Geschwind Syndrome.[276]

It may be clear from the foregoing that Paul's "thorn in the flesh" may well have been caused by a mild TBI, contracted when he fell on the Damascus Road. This TBI may be an explanation for his temporary blindness, his shocked condition after the event (perhaps due to amnesia), his possible eye problems, his possible hallucinations during which he "saw" and "heard" the risen Christ, his possible epilepsy, and his personality profile. He needed a rest period of three years in Arabia and Damascus after his experience on the road to Damascus before he recuperated enough to start a career as a preacher, prophet, and travelling missionary (Acts 13: 1; Gal 1: 17–18).

---

[272] Kolb and Wishaw, *Fundamentals*: 756; Lezak, *Neuropsychological Assessment*: 247; Nicholl, "Neuropsychiatric Sequelae", 247.
[273] Zillmer, *Principles of Neuropsychology*, 424; Crane *et al.*, "Association of Traumatic Brain Injury'.
[274] Granacher, 2008: 172–73; Nicholl, 2009: 247; Webb, "Auditory Hallucinations", 539; Greenwald, "Hallucinations and Delusions"; McAllister and Ferrell, "Evaluation and Treatment of Psychosis", 357.
[275] Lezak, *Neuropsychological Assessment*, 246.
[276] Benson, "The Geschwind Syndrome", 411–21; Devinsky and Schachter: "Norman Geschwind's Contribution".

Paul's personality traits are congruous with a TBI, as well as with the Geschwind Syndrome. The symptoms of this syndrome are as follows:

- Hyperreligiosity – an extreme interest in religion and philosophy;
- Hypergraphia – a tendency to write compulsively;
- Atypical sexuality – usually a lack of interest in sexual activities;
- Circumstantiality – the tendency to repeat ideas; and
- Intensified mental life – much introspection and extreme emotional reactions[277]

Paul's interest and even obsession with religious matters cannot be denied. When reading his letters in one go one gets the impression of an author who could almost not stop his outpouring of ideas. He was very verbose and almost fanatical about the message he wanted to convey. He reacted aggressively and suspiciously towards those who did not agree with his ideas and called the curse of God upon them (Gal 1: 8–9; 2: 13; 1 Cor 16: 22). Although he was not against marriage, he was not married himself and seemingly had no interest in sex.[278] These traits are consistent with the symptoms of a mild TBI and the Geschwind Syndrome.

Because of all this, it won't be an exaggeration to state that Paul's visions and revelations were simply hallucinations, caused by a neurological condition – rather than supernatural com-munications from God.

These are some researchers who assert that the visions and revelations of **Muhammad** were the result of temporal lobe

---

[277] Benson: " The Geschwind Syndrome" 411–21" ; Devinsky and Schachter, "Norman Geschwind's Contribution".
[278] Sanders, "Paul, the Apostle, Saint".

epilepsy – just as could have been the case with Paul of Tarsus. Whether this was really the case cannot be determined with any degree of certainty today. However, he does seem to have displayed the typical symptoms of the Geschwind Syndrome, a variety of a temporal lobe epilepsy, including hyper-religiosity, hallucinations or visions, a quick temper, and verbosity.[279]

Visions Inspired by Astrology

Previous chapters of this book demonstrated how prophets such as Isaiah, Ezekiel, Zechariah, Daniel, and John of Patmos based their revelations on descriptions of astrological phenomena. We may accept that at least some of them were experiencing prophetic trances while they watched the skies to find messages from God. Apart from seeing biblical and mythological figures and beings in the astrological constellations, they also heard angels or even God's voice.

This aspect has been almost totally neglected by Bible students in the past – certainly due to their lack of knowledge of ancient astrology and the influence it had on ancient civilizations.

Extrasensory Perceptions, Visions, and Revelations?

There are many people in our enlightened age who still believe in various types of extrasensory perceptions, visions, and revelations. They are convinced that parapsychological phenomena, such as clairvoyance, precognition, and telepathy are abilities that certain people have acquired. They often base their belief on the biblical stories of people who supposedly have had remarkable supernatural mental powers and the numerous prophecies about the future.

Various scientific experiments have been performed since

---

[279] Aziz, "Did Prophet Mohammad (PBUH) have epilepsy?"; Freemon, "A Differential Diagnosis of the Inspirational Spells of Muhammad"; Veronelli et al., "Geschwind Syndrome".

the end of the nineteenth century to test these beliefs. No rigorous and conclusive evidence has yet been found to support the existence of these purported phenomena or abilities. In general, universities have been reluctant to recognize research into these fields as a valid scientific activity or discipline.[280]

Those who believe in the reality of all the forms of extrasensory perception argue that absence of evidence does not boil down to evidence of absence. Although the formal correctness of this argument must be granted, it must also be stated that those who are convinced of the reality of these phenomena must provide the evidence. It is, after all, a truism that he who alleges must prove his point with clear evidence. Proof for the existence of extrasensory perception, clairvoyance, telepathy, and precognition has – as yet – not been provided and it seems unlikely that such evidence will ever emerge in the light of all the investigations that have been done during more than a century.

Despite this, it does seem as if certain fortune tellers, clairvoyants and mind readers do achieve remarkable results by drawing secrets from their clients and providing them with sound advice about their futures. The successes of these charlatans depend upon their extraordinary ability to read body language and pick up almost-invisible clues in the behavior of people when confronted with intelligent guesses. People usually don't realize how much their unconscious mindsets and secret sins are revealed in their body language. These tricksters exploit the involuntary reactions of people when confronted with clever questioning.[281]

It has already been shown that many prophecies in the

---

[280] Enc Brit, "Extrasensory Perception"; "Telepathy", "Clairvoyance"; "Precognition"; "Parapsychological Phenomenon".
[281] Bonnafont, *Körpersprache;* Fast, *Body Language;* Nierenberg & Callero, *How to Read a Person like a Book.*

Scriptures may be dismissed as unconfirmed dreams or other neurological states such as hypnosis and epilepsy, with the accompanying hallucinations. The fact that there is no scientific evidence for the "gift of prophecy" as encountered in the Bible, (Num 11: 25–29; 1 Sam 10: 10–13; 19: 20–24; 2 Sam 23: 1,2; Joel 2: 28; John 16: 13; Acts 2: 17, 18, 29, 30; 11: 28; 21: 9, 10; Rom 12: 6; 1 Coe 12: 7–10;1 Thess 5: 20; 2 Peter 1: 20, 21), compels one to question or even dismiss the existence of this spiritual "gift".

A CREDULOUS AND RECEPTIVE PUBLIC

Prophets, seers, fortune-tellers, and clairvoyants have succeeded through the ages to deceive a credulous public. There were always those who believed even the most outrageous claims, predictions, and announcements. The success of these prophets depended upon their ability to exploit and satisfy some or other need, yearning, or wish of their followers.

People have the need to make sense of life, especially when they live in dangerous, uncertain, and difficult times. These prophets provided in that need by explaining catastrophic, calamitous, and cataclysmic events as the work of God.

A few examples must be briefly discussed:

Elijah
Elijah appealed to those Israelites who didn't like the religious innovations of King Ahab and his pagan queen, Jezebel. After having "proved" that YHWH is the only true God, he convinced his followers to help him to massacre the prophets of Baal.

John the Baptist
When John the Baptist started his career as a prophet in the Judean wilderness, the people flocked to him. He was critical of the haughty

and rich priestly class in Jerusalem, as well as the corrupt House of Herod, and the people loved his denouncements of these members of the elite. He paid with his life for being so outspoken.

Jesus of Nazareth
Jesus of Nazareth exploited the yearning of the Jews for political independent from the oppressive and pagan Roman Empire and many of them hailed him as their Messiah, the successor of King David. In addition, he was a charismatic preacher, a successful healer, and accomplished story-teller and people loved it. However, his belief that he was the Messiah of Israel led to his crucifixion and the tragic end of his dream. He was never the promised Messiah, although he convinced his credulous followers that he was just that.

Paul of Tarsus
Paul of Tarsus seems to have been an accomplished orator and an energetic wandering teacher and missionary. Because of the visions and revelations he had received, he transformed Jesus into a mythological being, the divine Son of God and savior of sinners. He appealed to Greek-speaking Jews and other Greek-speaking people in Syria, Asia Minor, and Greece.

In the process, he devised a new religion, Christianity, a mixture of Judaism and Greek ideas. The ancient world must have been ready for his ideas because Christianity eventually became the official religion of the Roman Empire. It is today the biggest religious group on earth, comprising one-third of all humans.

There were other prophets through history who managed to convince enough people of their wild and nonsensical ideas.

Joan of Arc
Joan of Arc (1412–1431) was a French peasant girl who was convinced that she had contact with some of the saints on account of

epileptic fits from which she sometimes suffered. She succeeded in rousing the French behind her in their struggle against English and Burgundian invaders of their country, even if she was only a teenager. Under her leadership, the English army was routed at Orleans and other places, against all odds. She was later captured by the English and tried in an ecclesiastical court, charged with blasphemy. She died on the stake, but was later rehabilitated by the Vatican when she was declared a saint.[282]

Nostradamus, *aka* Michel De Notredame, or Nostredame
Nostradamus (1503–1566), a French physician and astrologer, was the most well-known prophet during the Renaissance. He wrote enigmatic quatrains, rhymed verses, in a mixture of French, Latin, Spanish, and Hebrew in which he made predictions about the future. It is known that he often went into a trance and relied on dreams he had and those were the occasions when he produced predictions.

He published a collection of these predictions in 1555 in a book titled Centuries. His fame grew since it seemed as if some of his predictions were indeed fulfilled. His work was condemned by the Inquisition of the Roman Catholic Church in 1781.

It is difficult or even impossible to decide whether his predictions became true or not since they are very ambiguous and even unreadable with his jumbled language.[283]

Nongqawuse
A much more recent example of a tragic prophetess ought to be mentioned. Around 1857, a black Xhosa-speaking girl, Nongqawuse, convinced many of her people to believe her prophecies. At that time, there were repeated armed border clashes

---

[282] Lanhers & Vale, "Joan of Arc, Saint".
[283] Enc Brit, "Nostradamus"; Lemesurier, *The Unknown Nostradamus*.

between black people migrating from the north and white farmers who sought land to the east of the existing borders of the then British Cape Colony in South Africa. Her prophecies were welcomed by many of her people in those perilous times.

Nongqawuse, at that stage about 15 or 16 years old, purportedly met two men in a certain bush, whom she took for the spirits of her ancestors.

Nongqawuse (right) with fellow prophetess, Nonkosi

They told her that her people should kill all their cattle and destroy their crops. The result would be that dead people would rise from their graves and that new cattle and crops would miraculously appear.

Many people believed her prophecies and acted upon them. A great famine resulted and thousands died of starvation.

Religious Quacks

Hordes of religious quacks, preachers, gospel singers, and even certifiable people through the ages have predicted the date of the so-called rupture, the second coming of Christ, and Judgment Day. The world is still waiting for these events to occur. These self-appointed prophets conveniently forget what Jesus said: "But of that day or that hour no one knows, not even the angels in heaven, neither the Son, but only the Father" (Mark 13: 32).

LEGITIMIZING LAND CLAIMS

Perhaps the most important and far-reaching prophecy or promise in the Old Testament is to be found in Genesis 15 –

The Promised Land
Gen 15: 7–21

7.	He said to him, "I am YHWH who brought you out of Ur of the Chaldees, to give you this land to inherit it."
8.	He said, "Lord YHWH, whereby will I know that I will inherit it?"
9.	He said to him, "Take me a heifer three years old, a female goat three years old, a ram three years old, a turtle-dove, and a young pigeon."
10.	He took him all these, and divided them in the midst, and laid each half opposite the other; but he didn't divide the birds.
11.	The birds of prey came down on the carcasses, and Abram drove them away.
12.	When the sun was going down, a deep sleep fell on Abram. Now terror and great darkness fell on him.
13.	He said to Abram, "Know for sure that your seed will be sojourners in a land that is not theirs, and will serve them. They will afflict them four hundred years.
14.	I will also judge that nation, whom they will serve. Afterward they will come out with great substance.
15.	But you will go to your fathers in peace. You will be buried in a good old age.
16.	In the fourth generation they will come here again, for the iniquity of the Amorite is not yet full."
17.	It came to pass that, when the sun went down, and it was dark, behold, a smoking furnace, and a flaming torch passed between these pieces.

> 18. In that day YHWH made a covenant with Abram, saying, "To your seed have I given this land, from the river of Egypt to the great river, the river Euphrates:
> 19. the Kenites, the Kenizzites, the Kadmonites,
> 20. the Hittites, the Perizzites, the Rephaim,
> 21. the Amorites, the Canaanites, the Girgashites, and the Jebusites."

This passage is part of the J Document, which was compiled during the reign of King David, several centuries after the time of Abraham.

There were no independent witnesses who could affirm the accuracy of this alleged encounter between YHWH and Abraham. Abraham was reportedly also asleep during part of the time, when he may have dreamt, a very personal and subjective experience. In other words: there is no way this story can be confirmed and it is certainly a piece of fiction, concocted centuries after Abraham's time.

Although it is presented as a revelation from God, this story really contains a brief history of Israel – their enslavement in Egypt and the occupation of Canaan after the legendary Exodus.

The motive for this story is obvious: it had to serve as the legitimizing of the conquest of the Promised Land. It is also clear that Kind David had imperial aspirations and he dreamt of ruling over a wide stretch of earth: everything between the Nile in Egypt and the Euphrates in Babylonia. That meant that his empire would encompass all the nations living in these parts. To provide a firm base for this imperial dream, a story was devised in which God purportedly promised this whole stretch of earth to the seed of Abraham.

In the end, the Israelites never occupied the whole of the Middle East. They lived only in the region between the

Mediterranean and the Transjordanian territories. To this day, many Jews and Christians still base the Jewish claim to the country of Israel on this and similar promises and prophecies in the Torah. For them, the modern country of Israel is the fulfilment of these promises.[284]

LOOKING INTO THE FUTURE

Although it has been shown that prophets very often made monumental mistakes regarding their predictions, the present author wishes to make some necessary predictions. These predictions won't amount to guesswork or wishful thinking, but they depend on accurate statistics that indicate certain trends that are due to continue in the time to come. It is hereby submitted that the three monotheistic religions, Judaism, Christianity, and Islam, are due to lose more and more adherents during the coming decades.

Secular Judaism
Between 40% and 60% of the Jews in the country of Israel regard themselves as secular. They range from outright atheists, to agnostics, and Jews who just don't visit any synagogue anymore.[285]

Fifty percent of American Jews regard themselves as secular or not interested in religion, although they don't want to abandon their Jewish roots.[286]

This type of situation was unthinkable in previous centuries when it was taken for granted that every Jew would be a committed follower of Judaism.

---

[284] Maidrand, "Understanding the Promised Land of the Bible".
[285] Takle, "The Secular Jewish Renaissance Sweeping Israel".
[286] Goldstein, "Jewish Secularism".

When the Jewish-Dutch philosopher Benedict de Spinoza (1632–1677) published his rationalism and pantheistic ideas, the elders of the synagogue in Amsterdam banished him from the Jewish community in July 1656.

After this, he lived a lonely life in the village of Rijnsburg near Leyden and died in The Hague.[287] It is noteworthy that the book *The Institutes* by the Reformer, John Calvin, found a place in his library (as seen by the present author personally).

The reconstructed study of Spinoza in Rijnsburg, the Netherlands

Secularism in America

A similar tendency can be observed in America, which seems to be typical of the Western World, which was the stronghold of Christianity in previous centuries.

An investigation by the Pew Organization in 2025 found that 29% of Americans classify themselves as atheists, agnostics, or non-religious. A study done in 2021 has found, though, that the situation is more complex. Only 41% of Americans regard themselves as religious, whether they be Protestants, Catholics, Jews, or adherents of another religion. The group comprising non-religious and secular Americans amounts to 45% of all Americans, while 14% can be

---

[287] Enc Brit, "Spinoza".

classified as religious secularists – people who have links to a religious tradition, but whose word-view is secular.[288]

Secularism in Norway

Christianity is certainly on the decline in Norway, a typical affluent Nordic country in Europe. Christianity is certainly the largest religious group where there are also small numbers of adherents of other religions. Christians form, though, a rather small minority in this largely secularized country. In 2016, Christians comprised only 17,7% of the population, a drop of 20,8% since 2012.[289]

Secularism in Islam

The Islamic scholar, Mustafa Akyol, has found: "Across much of the Islamic world, many Muslims are disillusioned with the ugly things done in the name of their religion." This has resulted in many Muslims breaking away from their traditional religion.

He added: "In Iran, the Islamic Republic has ruled for 40 years now, but it has failed in its zeal to re-Islamize society. Instead, the opposite has happened." In Turkey, the power-hungry Islamist regime is often associated with injustice and corruption.

The numbers of Arabs who are cutting their ties with Islam are rising. Arabs who describe themselves as not religious were 8% of those polled in 2013. This trend rose to 13% in 2018.[290]

Iran

The government of the Islamic Republic of Iran claims that almost 100% of Iranians are Muslims. Independent investigations have,

---

[288] Campbell and Layman, "America the secular?".
[289] Statistisk Sentralbyrd, "Religious communities and life stance communities, 1 January 2016".
[290] Akyol, "A New Secularism Is Appearing in Islam".

though, drawn a different picture.

According to Poovan Tamim Arab, professor or religious studies at the Dutch University of Utrecht, and Ammar Maleki, assistant professor of public law and governance, Tilburg University, an independent survey found that only 40% of Iranians identify themselves as Muslims. About 9% of those polled called themselves atheists, while about 8% regarded themselves as followers of Zoroastrianism, the ancient religion of Persia.[291]

Mohammad Abolghassem Doulabi, a senior cleric for Iranian President Ebrahim Raisi, recently (2025) revealed that 50 000 of the 75 000 mosques in Iran have closed their doors, due to a lack of worshippers.[292]

Turkey

During 2019, Peter Kenyon wrote an article titled "Turks Examine their Muslim Devotion after Poll Says Faith Could be Waning". He cited statistics that show that the hold of Islam on the people of Turkey is weakening. For instance, only 65% of the Turks still fast during the holy month of Ramadan, as required by this faith.[293]

It seems as if young people are increasingly turning their backs on Islam. A report by the Central Asia-Caucasus Institute found in 2024:

> "Apparently, a not insignificant number of young people found the education in religious schools so unconvincing that they begun to doubt the precepts of Islam. While they did not go so far as to become atheists, they embraced a 'deist' approach instead, an individual spirituality decoupled

---

[291] Arab & Maleki, "Iran's secular shift".
[292] All Arab News Staff, "50,000 Mosques have Closed in Iran".
[293] Kenyon, "'Turks Examine Their Muslim Devotion'".

from Islamic principles."²⁹⁴

Selin Girit held interviews with several young Turks. They seem to embrace the philosophy is deism – the belief in a God who created all but who is no longer involved in his creation.

One young woman even told him: "But now I do not know whether there is a God or not, and I really do not care."²⁹⁵

Reaction of the West towards Islamic Fanaticism
The actions of extremist Islamic organizations such as Al-Kaida, Hamas, the Houthis, and Hezbollah are generally known.

Many Muslims seem to be ashamed of the deeds perpetrated by members of these organizations, but the alarm bells are also ringing in many European countries and America. People are increasingly worried about the immigration of people from Muslim countries – either as asylum-seekers, or economic migrants – to these countries and the establishing of mosques in many cities and towns. There is the fear that these mosques may be operating as recruiting centers for radical groups.

There is also the fear that Muslims may outbreed the indigenous people of many countries, eventually forcing Islamic laws and customs upon them. There are, though, signs that the Muslims who have settled in European countries could not escape from the increasing trend towards secularism and they are also severing their ties with their traditional religion.

CAN WE TRUST THE PROPHETS?

The scriptural prophets were sure that they spoke on behalf of God and that they received messages directly from God. A good example

---

[294] Central Asia-Caucasus Institute, "The Failure of Islamism in Turkey."
[295] Girit, "The Young Turks Rejecting Islam".

is Jeremiah who wrote in the first chapter of his book:

The Calling of Jeremiah
Jer 1: 4–7

4.	Now the word of YHWH came to me, saying,
5.	Before I formed you in the belly I knew you, and before you came forth out of the womb I sanctified you; I have appointed you a prophet to the nations.
6.	Then said I, Ah, Lord YHWH! behold, I don't know how to speak; for I am a child.
7.	But YHWH said to me, Don't say, I am a child; for to whoever I shall send you, you shall go, and whatever I shall command you, you shall speak.

Jeremiah claimed a special relation with YHWH who allegedly chose him to become a prophet, even before he was born. He initially protested when he became aware of the voice of God, but he was felt he given no choice in the matter.

The experiences of other prophets were similar. We must share the skepticism of Thomas Paine who pointed out that there is no independent corroborating evidence that God really spoke to any prophet. We only have their word that they were called by God and spoke on his behalf. The following biblical texts require that the truth of any matter must be established by comparing the testimonies from two or more independent witnesses: Num 35: 30, Deut 17: 6, 19: 15, Matt 18: 16, John 18: 17, and 2 Cor 13: 1. This requirement was not satisfied in the prophetic parts of the Sacred Scriptures

In addition, it has been demonstrated, time and again, that many prophecies amount to plain nonsense because they were never fulfilled as promised and they had their facts wrong.

It is one of the rules of natural justice, with the power of an ethical axiom, that promises and agreements must be honored. The Latin formulation is *pacta servanda sunt* and this is a corner stone of contract law.[296] All the prophets quoted in the chapters above made various promises on behalf of God, which proved in most cases to be empty promises. The moral principle of *pacta servanda sunt* was repeatedly violated.

It is an article of faith for most Protestants that the Bible with its prophecies must be accepted as the word of God. For instance, Articles 2 and 3 of the Belgic Confession, one of the doctrinal standards of Reformed Churches, contain the following statements:

Article 2
By What Means God is Made Known Unto Us
We know Him by two means: first, by the creation, preservation, and government of the universe; which is before our eyes as a most elegant book, wherein all creatures, great and small, are as so many characters leading us to contemplate the invisible things of God, namely, His eternal power and divinity, as the apostle Paul saith (Rom. 1:20). All which things are sufficient to convince men, and leave them without excuse. Secondly, He makes Himself more clearly and fully known to us by His holy and divine Word; that is to say, as far as is necessary for us to know in this life, to His glory and our salvation.

Article 3
The Written Word of God
We confess that this Word of God was not sent nor delivered by the will of man, but that holy men of God spake as they were moved by the Holy Ghost, as the apostle Peter saith. And that afterwards God, from a special care which He has

---

[296] Hendricks, "Pacta sunt Servanda".

for us and our salvation, commanded His servants, the prophets and apostles, to commit His revealed Word to writing; and He Himself wrote with His own finger the two tables of the law. Therefore we call such writings holy and divine Scriptures.

Article 3 mentions specifically the prophets as God's messengers. It has transpired, though, that much of what they did, said, and wrote cannot be accepted as truthful, reliable, acceptable, or trustworthy. That places a huge question mark over the reliability of the Hebrew and Christian Scriptures. It is no longer possible to affirm the view expressed in the Belgic Confession.

Likewise, there is every reason to doubt the reliability of the Qur'an. A careful analysis of this document demonstrated that it is tainted with numerous flaws, mistakes, contradictions, misunderstandings, and errors. It is just not possible to regard the Qur'an as the infallible word of God.

The following question needs an answer: how does the work of a biblical prophet differ from fortune-telling and the activities of pagan prophets, astrologers, sorcerers, diviners, and soothsayers? By this time, it must be evident that there is no fundamental difference. The only difference is that the biblical prophets thought that they stood in the service of the God of Israel, while the others served some or other pagan deity.

It must be stated: every scriptural prophecy must be approached with care because there is no guarantee that one can accept these pronouncements, predictions, and promises. The doctrine that the Sacred Scriptures were inspired by God or the Holy Spirit cannot be maintained any longer.

Another important conclusion at the end of this book is that a rational, responsible, honest, and scientific analysis of the actions of scriptural prophets and their prophecies have shown that many dogmas and other cherished beliefs of believers cannot be substantiated. Most Christian churches cherish the following beliefs:

- The mother of Jesus of Nazareth, Mary, was still a virgin when Jesus was born;
- Jesus was the ultimate Messiah of Israel and his appearance was promised in the Old Testament;
- Jesus had a dual nature, namely a divine nature and a human nature, combined in one person;
- Jesus, as Son of God, is the second person of the divine Trinity, together with God the Father and God the Holy Spirit;
- Jesus really died on the cross and was miraculously revived after two or three days in his tomb; and
- Jesus glided up into God's heaven on a cloud –

These beliefs can no longer be accepted or defended. It is a tenet of most Protestant churches that their doctrines, as formulated in various confessions and statements of faith, are faithful and accurate expressions of scriptural "truths", but this belief has been shown to be unfounded. The Scriptures, when studied and analyzed honestly, rationally, and thoroughly, often contradict the dogmas and articles of faith mentioned above.

Many former believers made the same conclusions – without a rigorous analysis and detailed investigations, such as was done in this work – and they have decided to happily carry on with their lives without any religious or spiritual convictions, connections, and ties, while upholding the universal ethical principles of honesty, integrity, responsibility, compassion, and tolerance.

A Personal Note
When the present author was admitted to the ministry after having completed the required theological training, he had to affirm with an oath and his signature that he regarded the doctrinal standards of Reformed Churches – the Begic Confession, the Heidelberg

Catechism, and the Canons of Dordt – as congruent with Holy Scripture. He also promised not to disseminate any teachings that could clash with these doctrinal standards.

By this time, it must be clear that the present author has broken his promises. This book is an indication that he no longer accepts certain Christian dogmas.

It was proved, though, that a thorough, scientific, responsible, critical, rational, and honest analysis of the Hebrew Scriptures and the Christian Scriptures contain numerous indications that these dogmas cannot be upheld any longer. These dogmas may only be defended with a superficial and uncritical reading of the Bible, but a more thorough investigation into what the various prophets did, said, and wrote, demonstrated unequivocally that these dogmas must be discarded if one wishes to uphold intellectual honesty and integrity.

Since the present author values intellectual truthfulness, accuracy, and sincerity, he cannot regard himself as bound by the oath of many years ago.

Much of the doctrinal standards of Christian churches of whatever variety just cannot be harmonized with what we do find in the Sacred Scriptures. It also transpired that much of the contents of the Scriptures do not make sense any longer and that is why so many people in the Western World, including Israel, have turned their backs on religion.

BIBLIOGRAPHY

Editions of the Bible
Passages from the Bible are quoted from the *World English Bible* as found on a CD with the title *The Bible Collection, Deluxe Edition*, and published by ValuSoft, a division of THQ Inc, Waconia MN, 2002.

The above-mentioned CD also contains the Hebrew text of the Old Testament and the Greek t************ext of the New Testament, as well as *Strong's Complete Greek & Hebrew Lexicon*. Other lexica utilized are mentioned under the heading of Literature.

In addition, the following editions of the biblical text in the original languages were consulted:

Elliger, K. and W. Rudolph, eds. *Biblia Hebraica Stuttgartensia.* Stuttgart: Deutsche Bibelgesellschaft, 1997.
Nestle, E. and E. Nestle, eds. *Novum Testamentum Graece.* Stuttgart: Deutsche Bibelstiftung, 1981.

The text of the Greek Translation of the Old Testament, the so-called Septuagint – also known as the LXX – was accessed from the following website: https://www.septuagint.bible/#

The text of the ancient Latin translation of the New Testament, the Vulgate, was found in the following publication:

Wordsworth, Iohannes et A.M. White, eds. *Novum Testamentum Latine: Secundum Editionem Sancti Hieronymi, ad Codicum Mauscriptorum Fidem Recensuerunt.* London: Oxford University Press, 1955.

Literature
Ahlström, Gösta W. "Prophecy." Chicago: Encyclopædia Britannica, 2010.

Akyol, Mustafa. "A New Secularism is Appearing in Islam". Cato Institute, 23 December 2019.
https://www.cato.org/publications/commentary/new-secularism-appearing-islam

All Arab News Staff, "50,000 mosques have closed in Iran – Are Iranians seeking truth outside of Islam?" All Arab, August 16, 2023.
https://allarab.news/50000-mosques-have-closed-in-iran-are-iranians-seek-truth-outside-of-islam/

American Psychiatric Association. *Diagnostic and Statistical Manual of Mental Disorders, Fifth Edition, Text Revision DSM-5-TR.* Washington DC: American Psychiatric Association Publishing, 2022.

Allen, R.H. *Star Names: Their Lore and Meaning.* New York: Dover, 1963.

Anonymous. "Muhammad and the Holy Monastery of Sinai".
http://www.sinaimonastery.com/en/index.php?lid=68

_____ "Study releases data of Mount Carmel's Geology in Israel." *Mining Technology,* 19 February, 1918.

Arab, Poovan Tamim, and Ammar Maleki. "Iran's secular shift: new survey reveals huge changes in religious beliefs". The Conversation, September 10, 2020.
https://theconversation.com/irans-secular-shift-new-survey-reveals-huge-changes-in-religious-beliefs-145253

Aristotle: *On The Heavens.* Translated by J. L. Stocks.
http://classics.mit.edu/Aristotle/heavens.html

Armstrong, Karen. *The Bible: The Biography.* London: Atlantic, 2007.

Armstrong, Karen. *Muhammad, a Biography of the Prophet.* London: Phoenix, 2001.

Aziz, Hasan. "Did Prophet Mohammad (PBUH) have epilepsy? A neurological analysis". *Epilepsy Behav.* 2020 Feb;103(Pt A):106654.
doi: 10.1016/j.yebeh.2019.106654. Epub 2019 Dec 9.
https://pubmed.ncbi.nlm.nih.gov/31822396/

Barclay, W. *The Revelation of John* (volume one). Edinburgh : The Saint Andrew Press, 1962
Barrett, Michael P.V. "Zecheriah, a Commentary".
https://www.thegospelcoalition.org/commentary/zechariah/
Belmont, M. "The Virgo Myth".
http://www.gods-and-monsters.com/virgo-myth.html
Ben-Daniel, John." The Parables of Enoch (1 Enoch 37–71): Provenance and Social Setting".
https://www.academia.edu/50310427/The_Parables_of_Enoch_1_Enoch_37_71_Provenance_and_Social_Setting
Ben-Menahem, Ari. "Cross-Dating of Biblical History via Singular Astronomical and Geophysical Events Over the Ancient Near East". *Quarterly Journal of the Royal Astronomical Society*, Vol. 33, p.175, September 1992.
https://ui.adsabs.harvard.edu/abs/1992QJRAS..33..175B/abstract
Benson, D.F. "The Geschwind Syndrome". *Advances in Neurology*. 1991; 55: 41,1–21.
Biblical Archaeological Society. "The Exodus: Fact or Fiction? Evidence of Israel's Exodus from Egypt". *Biblical Archaeology Society*, April 05, 2025.
https://www.biblicalarchaeology.org/daily/biblical-topics/exodus/exodus-fact-or-fiction/
Blank, Sheldon H. "Isaiah". Chicago: Encyclopaedia Britannica, 2010.
Bonnafort, Claude. *Die Botschaft der Körpersprache*. Genf: Ariston, 1979.
Boshoff, Willem *et al. Geskiedenis en Geskrifte: die Literatuur van ou Israel*. Pretoria: Protea, 2008.
Bright, Hilda. "Letter of Joy: An Easy English Bible Version and Commentary (2800 word vocabulary) on Paul's Letter to the Philippians".
https://www.easyenglish.bible/bible-commentary/philippians-lbw.htm

Bullinger, E.W. "The Witness of the Stars".
http://philologos.org/__eb-tws/chap13.htm

Burnett, Joel S. "Ammon, Moab and Edom: Gods and Kingdoms East of the Jordan". *Biblical Archaeological Society Library*, Nov/Dec 2019.
https://library.biblicalarchaeology.org/article/ammon-moab-and-edom-gods-and-kingdoms-east-of-the-jordan

Butler, H. "The Cult of Isis and Early Christianity". *A Journal of Academic Writing*, Vol.7 (2005): 72–77.

Campbell, David, and Godfrey Layman, "America the secular? What a changing religious landscape means for US politics". The Conversation, 1 April 2025.
https://theconversation.com/america-the-secular-what-a-changing-religious-landscape-means-for-us-politics-249892

Carter, Rita, *et al. The Brain Book*. London: Penguin Random House, 2019.

Cassella, Carly. "First Traces of Ancient Egyptian Hallucinogens Found in Old Jug". Yahoo News, Thu, November 28, 2024.
https://news.yahoo.com/first-traces-ancient-egyptian-hallucinogens-230554641.html

Central Asia-Caucasus Institute, "The Failure of Islamism in Turkey." 17 Dec 2024. —
https://www.silkroadstudies.org/resources/pdf/ATP_12.pdf

Chadwick, H. "John the Apostle, Saint." Chicago: Encyclopædia Britannica, 2010.

Cohn, H. *The Trial and Death of Jesus*. Old Saybrook, Ct: Konecky & Konecky, 1980.

Cornelius, F. *Geistesgeschichte der Frühzeit II/1*. Leiden: Brill, 1962.

Craighead, W.E. and C.B. Nemeroff, eds. *The Corsini Encyclopedia of Psychology and Behavioral Science, Volume 4*. Hoboken, NJ: John Wiley & Sons, 2002.

Decker, R.W. and Decker, B.B., "Volcano". Chicago: Encyclopaedia Britannica, 2010.

Deffner, Sebastian. "Static Electricity's Tiny Sparks" The Conversation, 6 January 2017.
Denova, Rebecca. "The Origin of Satan". World History Encyclopedia. https://www.worldhistory.org/article/1685/the-origin-of-satan/
Devinsky, J. and S. Schachter. "Norman Geschwind's Contribution to the Understanding of Behavioral Changes in Temporal Lobe Epilepsy: The February 1974 Lecture". *Epilepsy & Behavior*. **15** (4): 417–24.
Dubuc, Brono, Can States of Consciousness be Mapped in the Brain?" *The Brain from Top to Bottom* https://thebrain.mcgill.ca/flash/i/i_12/i_12_cr/i_12_cr_con/i_12_cr_con.html
Duling, Dennis. "The Jewish World of Jesus: A Historical Overview." James Tabor Blog, January 5, 2022. https://jamestabor.com/the-jewish-world-of-jesus-a-historical-overview/
Eames, Christopher. "Amos's Earthquake: A Mountain of Evidence". Armstrong Institute of Biblical Archaeology, February 25, 2021. https://armstronginstitute.org/319-amoss-earthquake-a-mountain-of-evidence
Ehrman, Bart. "Was Moses High on Mt. Sinai?" *The Bart Ehrman Blog*, January 27, 2023. https://ehrmanblog.org/was-moses-high-on-mt-sinai-part-1-platinum-post-by-douglas-wadeson-md/
_____ "Who was the Pharaoh of the Exodus?" Armstrong Institute of Biblical Archaeology, *Let the Stones Speak*, March-April, 2024. https://armstronginstitute.org/882
Encyclopaedia Brittanica. "Amelekites". Chicago: Encyclopædia Britannica, 2010.
_____ "Antipater". Chicago: Encyclopædia Britannica, 2010.
_____ "Assyria". Chicago: Encyclopædia Britannica, 2010.
_____ "Clairvoyance". Chicago: Encyclopædia Britannica, 2010.
_____ "Dehydration". Chicago: Encyclopædia Britannica, 2010.
_____ "Drug Cults". Chicago: Encyclopædia Britannica, 2010.

BIBLIOGRAPHY

_____ "Divination". Chicago: Encyclopædia Britannica, 2010.
_____ "Eclipse, Sun". Chicago: Encyclopædia Britannica, 2010.
_____ "Edom". Chicago: Encyclopædia Britannica, 2010.
_____ "Enoch". Chicago: Encyclopædia Britannica, 2010.
_____ "Ephraim". Chicago: Encyclopædia Britannica, 2010.
_____ "Essenes". Chicago: Encyclopædia Britannica, 2010.
_____ "Extrasensory Perception". Chicago: Encyclopædia Britannica, 2010.
_____ "Gladiator". Chicago: Encyclopædia Britannica, 2010.
_____ "Herod". Chicago: Encyclopædia Britannica, 2010.
_____ "Hour". Chicago: Encyclopædia Britannica, 2010.
_____ "Humanism". Chicago: Encyclopædia Britannica, 2010.
_____ "Iblis". Chicago: Encyclopædia Britannica, 2010.
_____ "Isaiah, Book of". Chicago: Encyclopædia Britannica, 2010.
_____ "James, the Letter of". Chicago: Encyclopædia Britannica, 2010.
_____ "Joseph". Chicago: Encyclopædia Britannica, 2010.
_____ "Magi". Chicago: Encyclopædia Britannica, 2010.
_____ "Melqart". Chicago: Encyclopædia Britannica, 2010.
_____ "Moses". Chicago: Encyclopædia Britannica, 2010.
_____ "Nostradamus". Chicago: Encyclopædia Britannica, 2010.
_____ "Oracle". Chicago: Encyclopædia Britannica, 2010.
_____ "Pantheism". Chicago: Encyclopædia Britannica, 2010.
_____ "Petra". Chicago: Encyclopædia Britannica, 2010.
_____ "Philo Judaeus". Chicago: Encyclopædia Britannica, 2010.
_____ "Parapsychological Phenomenon". Chicago: Encyclopædia Britannica, 2010.
_____ "Precognition". Chicago: Encyclopædia Britannica, 2010.
_____ "Rainbow". Chicago: Encyclopædia Britannica, 2010.
_____ "Samaritan". Chicago: Encyclopædia Britannica, 2010.
_____ "Samuel, Books of". Chicago: Encyclopædia Britannica, 2010.
_____ "Secularism". Chicago: Encyclopædia Britannica, 2010.
_____ "Spartacus". Chicago: Encyclopædia Britannica, 2010.
_____ "Static Electricity". Chicago: Encyclopædia Britannica, 2010.
_____ "Telepathy". Chicago: Encyclopædia Britannica, 2010.

_____ "Thera". Chicago: Encyclopædia Britannica, 2010.
_____ "Triumph". Chicago: Encyclopædia Britannica, 2010.
_____ "Tyre". Chicago: Encyclopædia Britannica, 2010.
_____ "Zechariah, Book of". Chicago: Encyclopædia Britannica, 2010.
Encyclopedia.com. "The Spirit of God".
  https://www.encyclopedia.com/religion/encyclopedias-almanacs-transcripts-and-maps/spirit-god
_____ "Samuel". May 23, 2018.
  https://www.encyclopedia.com/philosophy-and-religion/bible/old-testament/samuel
Encyclopedia of the Bible, "Elijah".
  https://www.biblegateway.com/resources/encyclopedia-of-the-bible/Elijah
Evelina G. "The Fascinating Story of the Jews in Egypt". *Judaica Webstore*, 19.05.2024.
  https://blog.judaicawebstore.com/the-history-of-jews-in-egypt/
Eusebius of Caesarea. *Historia Ecclesiastica, Liberi I & II*.
  http://www.documentacatholicaomnia.eu/03d/0265-0339,_eusebius_caesariensis,_church_history,_en.pdf
—— Ευσεβίου Καισαρείας, Εκκλησιαστική Ιστορία.
  http://www.documentacatholicaomnia.eu/03d/0265-0339,_Eusebius_Caesariensis,_Historia_Ecclesiastica,_GR.pdf
Eysenck, Hans. *Astrology: Science or Superstition?* New York, St Martin's, 1982.
Fast, Julius. *Body Language*. London: Pan, 1971.
Fam Jin et al. "Attentional Mechanisms". Encyclopedia of the Neurological Sciences Copyright 2003, Elsevier Science (USA).
Finkelstein, Israel, and Neil Asher Silberman. *The Bible Unearthed: Archaeology's New Vision of Ancient Israel and the Origin of its Sacred Texts*. New York: Touchstone, 2002.
Fisher, Martin. "Veleda and the Ancient German Seers."
  https://martinifisher.com/2024/03/07/veleda/

Flint Rehab, "Anterior Cingulate Cortex Damage: Understanding the Secondary Effects & Recovery Process." *Neurological Recovery Blog » Traumatic Brain Injury,* 14 November 2022. https://www.flintrehab.com/anterior-cingulate-cortex-damage/?srsltid=AfmBOoruDr0XWjODB3ooMCS5aY8QaOLl QZ6Qfhkl4Pz5und5_A3T9IbW

Flor-Henry, Pierre *et al.* "Brain Changes During a Shamanic Trance: Altered Modes of Consciousness, Hemispheric Laterality, and Systemic Psychobiology". *Cogent Psychology,* Volume 4, 2017 - Issue 1 https://www.tandfonline.com/doi/full/10.1080/23311908.2017.13 13522?scroll=top&needAccess=true#references-Section

Fox, Alex. "Archaeologists Identify Traces of Burnt Cannabis in Ancient Jewish Shrine." *Smithsonian Magazine,* June 4, 2020. https://www.smithsonianmag.com/smart-news/cannabis-found-altar-ancient-israeli-shrine-180975016/

Franz, G. "The king and I: the Apostle John and Emperor Domitian." *Bible and Spade, Spring 1999.* http://www.biblearchaeology.org/post/2010/02/11/The-King-and-I-Opening-The-Third-Seal-Part-3.aspx

Freemon, F.R. "A Differential Diagnosis of the Inspirational Spells of Muhammad". Epilepsia. 1976 Dec;17(4):423-7. doi: 10.1111/j.1528-1157.1976.tb04454.x. https://pubmed.ncbi.nlm.nih.gov/793843/

Freud, Sigmund. *Moses and Monotheism.* New York, Vintage, 1967.

Garsiel, Moshe. "The Book of Samuel: Its Composition, Structure and Significance as a Historiographical Source". *Journal of Hebrew Scriptures,* Volume 10, Article 5, 2010. http://www.jhsonline.org/

Gaum, Frits. *et al.*, eds. *Christelike Kernensiklopedie: CKE.* Wellington: Lux Verbi, 2008.

Gertoux, Gerard. "Herod the Great and Jesus: Chronological, Historical and Archaeological Evidence".

BIBLIOGRAPHY

file:///C:/Users/adelb/Downloads/Herod_the_Great_and_Jesus_C hronological%20(1).pdf

Girit, Selin. "The Young Turks Rejecting Islam".
BBC News, Istanbul, 10 May 2018.
https://www.bbc.com/news/world-europe-43981745

Goldberg, G.J. "A Chronology of the First Jewish Revolt against Rome according to Josephus".
https://www.josephus.org/warChronologyIntro.htm

Goldstein, Rebecca. "Jewish Secularism". My Jewish Learning.
https://www.myjewishlearning.com/article/jewish-secularism/

Gordon, Cyrus H.; Rendsburg, Gary A. (1997) [1953], *The Bible and the Ancient Near East*, New York City, New York and London, England: W. W. Norton & Company,

Gosseries, Olivia, *et al.*, "Exploration of Trance States: Phenomenology, Brain Correlates, and Clinical Applications". *Current Opinion in Behavioral Sciences*. Volume 58, August 2024.

Gottheil, Richard, and Enno Litmann. "Enoch, Books of (Ethiopic and Slavonic). *Jewish Encyclopedia*.
https://www.jewishencyclopedia.com/articles/5773-enoch-books-of-ethiopic-and-slavonic

Granacher, R.P. *Traumatic Brain Injury: Methods for Clinical and Forensic Neuropsychiatric Assessment*. Boca Raton Fl: CRC, 2008.

Gray, G.B. (transl). "The Psalms of Solomon, translated from Greek and Syriac Manuscripts" (*in:* Charles, R.H. ed. *The apocrypha and pseudepigrapha of the Old Testament in English*. Oxford: Clarendon, 1913.
http://wesley.nnu.edu/sermons-essays-books/noncanonical-literature/noncanonical-literature-ot-pseudepigrapha/the-psalms-of-solomon/

Greeka, "Volcanoes in Greece & the Islands".
https://www.greeka.com/about/nature/volcanoes/

Greenwald, B.D. "Hallucinations and Delusions after a Brain Injury". *Brainline.Org.*, 2015.

http://brainline.org.content/2010/12/hallucinations-and-delusions-after-a-brain-injury.html

Hachlili, R. *The Zodiac in Ancient Jewish Synagogal Art: A Review.* Jewish Studies Quarterly, Volume 9, pp. 219—258, 2002.

Hagedorn, Anselm C. "Taking the Pentateuch to the Twenty-First Century". *The Expository Times* 2007; 119; 53–58. http://ext.sagepub.com/cgi/content/abstract/119/2/53

Hammond, M. "Trajan". Chicago: Encyclopædia Britannica, 2010.

Hawking, Stephen, and Leonard Mlodinow. *The Grand Design.* London: Bantam, 2010.

Helvenston, Patricia A., and Paul G. Bahn "Waking the Trance-Fixed". *Cambridge Archaeological Journal*, October 2013, 13(02): 213–24

Hendricks, Ross. "Pacta Sunt Servanda: A Cornerstone Of Contractual Certainty In South African Law." https://schoemanlaw.co.za/pacta-sunt-servanda-and-contractual-certainty/

Heyns, Johan Adam & Jonker, Willem D. *Op Weg met die Teologie.* Pretoria: NG Kerkboekhandel, 1974.

Hirsch, Emil G. "Servant of God". Jewish Encyclopedia, 1906. https://www.jewishencyclopedia.com/articles/13444-servant-of-god

Hirsch, Emil G. "Urim and Thumim". Jewish Encyclopedia, 1906. https://jewishencyclopedia.com/articles/14609-urim-and-thummim#:~:text=In%20Israel%20the%20Urim%20and,and%20Thummim%2C%20even%20kings%20bowed.

Hishaw, G.A. "Concussion and Epilepsy: What is the Link?" *Practical Neurology.* May/June 2012. http://practicalneurology.com/2012/06/concussion-and-epilepsy-what-is-the-link

History Today, "Jewish Roman Wars". https://www.heritage-istory.com/index.php?c=resources&s=war-dir&f=wars_romanjewish

Hoffman, R.E. *et al.* "Transcranial Magnetic Stimulation of Left Temporal Cortex and Medication-Resistant Auditory

Hallucinations". *Arch Gen Psychiatry,* vol 60, January 2003: 49–56.
http://www.neuro.hk/img/tmshallucinationsschizophrenia.pdf

Holladay, William. *A Concise Hebrew and Aramaic Lexicon of the Old Testament.* Grand Rapids: William B. Eerdmans, 1988.

Hood, M. Sinclair & Emily D. Townsend Vermeule. "Aegean Civilizations". Chicago, Encyclopedia Brittanica, 2010.

Hyatt, J. Philip. "Jeremiah". Chicago: Encyclopaedia Britannica, 2010.

Ice, Thomas D. "Is Modern Israel Fulfilling Prophecy?" Liberty University, Article Archive, May 2009.
https://digitalcommons.liberty.edu/cgi/viewcontent.cgi?article=1023&context=pretrib_arch

Institute for Biblical & Scientific Studies. "Biblical Archaeology: Mt Sinai".
https://www.bibleandscience.com/archaeology/mtsinai.htm

Islam Q&A, 06/Rabi al-thani/1446 , 09/October/2024.
https://islamqa.info/en/answers/14231/punishment-for-apostasy-in-islam

Jacobs, J. & Eisenstein, J.D.: "Zodiac".. *Jewish Encyclopaedia, 1906.*
http://www.jewishencyclopedia.com/articles/15277-zodiac

Jacobs, Joseph & Fishberg, Maurice. "Epilepsy". Jewish Encyclopedia, 1906.
https://www.jewishencyclopedia.com/articles/5818-epilepsy

Jacobs, Joseph, and Moses Buttenwieser. "Messiah". *Jewish Encyclopedia, 1906.*
https://www.jewishencyclopedia.com/articles/10729-messiah

Jacobus, H.R. "The Zodiac Sign Names in the Dead Sea Scrolls (4q318): Features and Questions". *Aram,* 24 (2012) 311–31.
file:///c:/users/user/downloads/the_zodiac_sign_names_in_the_dead_sea_sc.pdf

Jones, Alan. *The Koran: Foreword and Introduction.* London: Phoenix, 1994.

Jones, S. *In the Blood: God, Genes and Destiny.* London: Flamingo, 1997.

Josephus, Flavius, *Antiquities of the Jews, Book II, Containing the interval of 220 Years, from the Death of Isaac to the Exodus out of Egypt.*
   https://penelope.uchicago.edu/josephus/ant-2.html
———   *Antiquities of the Jews, Book XVII, Containing the interval of 14 Years, From the death of Alexander and Aristobulus, to the banishment of Archelaus.*
   https://penelope.uchicago.edu/josephus/ant-17.html
———   *The wars of the Jews, or history of the destruction of Jerusalem* (tr W Whiston). Project Gutenberg E-Book, 2009
   https://www.gutenberg.org/files/2850/2850-h/2850-h.htm#link6noteref-20
Joubert, Gideon. *Die Groot Gedagte: Abstrakte Weefsel van die Kosmos.* Kaapstad, Tafelberg, 1997.
Kaye, E.M. and J. Herskowitz. "Transient Post-Traumatic Cortical Blindness: Brief v Prolonged Syndromes in Childhood. *Journal Of Child Neurology*, 1986 Jul: 1(3): 206–10.
   http://www.ncbi.nlm.nih.gov/pubmed/3598126 Kenyon, Peter. "Turks Examine Their Muslim Devotion after Poll Says Faith Could be Waning". NPR, February 11, 2019.
   https://www.npr.org/2019/02/11/692025584/turks-examine-their-muslim-devotion-after-poll-says-faith-could-be-waning
Kinvig, H.S. *et al.*: "Analysis of Volcanic Threat from Nisyros Island, Greece, with implications for aviation and population exposure." *Nat.Hazards Earth Syst. Sci.*, 10, 1101–1113, 2010
   www.nat-hazards-earth-syst-sci.net/10/1101/2010/
   doi:10.5194/nhess-10-1101-2010
Kinzig, Wolfram, "The Nazoreans". In: Oskar Skarsaune and Reidar Hvalvik, Eds., *Jewish Believers in Jesus*, Peabody, MS, Hendrickson, 2007, 463–87.
Knight, George Angus Fulton. "Maccabees". Chicago: Encyclopaedia Brittanica.
Kolb, B. & Wishaw, I.Q. *Fundamentals of Human Neuropsychology.* New York: Worth, 2012.

König, Franz Cardinal. "Zoroaster". Chicago: Encyclopedia Britannica, 2010.

König, Adrio. "Teologie" (*In:* I.H.Eybers, A. König & J.A. Stoop : *Inleiding in die Teologie.* Pretoria : NG Kerkboekhandel, 1978: 1–36).

Landsborough, D. St Paul and temporal lobe epilepsy. *Journal of Neurology, Neurosurgery and Psychiatry* 1987: 50: 659–64. http://www.ncbi.nlm.nih.gov/pmc/articles/PMC1032067/pdf/jnnpsy00553-0001.pdf

Korsness *et al*. 2010. An fMRI study of auditory hallucinations in patients with epilepsy. *Epilepsia*, 51(4), 2010, 610–17. http://onlinelibrary.wiley.com/doi/10.1111/j.1528-1167.2009.02338.x/pdf

Lanhers, Yvonne &Malcolm G.A. Vale, "Joan of Arc, Saint." Chicago: Encyclopaedia Britannica, 2010.

Lemesurier, Peter. *The Unknown Nostradamus: the Essential Biography for his 500th Birthday*. John Hunt, 2003.

Lezak, Muriel D. *et al*. Neuropsychological Assessment. New York: Oxford University Press, 2012.

Loubser, Michael. *Dating Adam: An Analysis of Biblical Chronology*. Scotburgh: M Loubser, 2017.

MacArthur, John. *Bible Introductions – Colossians.* Blue Letter Bible. https://www.blueletterbible.org/Comm/macarthur_john/bible-introductions/colossians-intro.cfm#:~:text=Author%20and%20Date.-,Background%20and%20Setting,Jewish%20legalism%20and%20pagan%20mysticism.

MacCarter, Kyle. "Edomite in 12 Easy Lessons". *Biblical Archaeology Asoociation Library*, Nov/Dec 1996.

Magiorkinis, E. *et al*. "Hallmarks in the History of Epilepsy: From Antiquity till the Twentieth". *Ancient History Encyclopaedia*, 2012. http://www.ancient.eu/article/394/#

Maidrand, "Understanding the Promised Land of the Bible". Christian Social Action, 18 August 2021.

https://christiansforsocialaction.org/resource/understanding-the-promised-land-of-the-bible/

Malina, B.J & Pilch, J.J. *Social-Science Commentary on the Book of Revelation*. Minneapolis: Fortress Press, 2000.

Manuel, Frank Edward. "Deism". Chicago: Encyclopædia Britannica, 2010.

Mark, Joshua J. "Moses". *World History Encyclopedia*, 28.09.2016.
https://www.worldhistory.org/Moses/
https://library.biblicalarchaeology.org/sidebar/edomite-in-12-easy-lessons/

Mcallister, T.W. and R.B. Ferrell. "Evaluation and Treatment of Psychosis after Traumatic Brain Injury." *Neurorehabilitation*. 17 (2002) 357–368.
http://iospress.metapress,com/content/j7kx3b4tqq7dapqe/

McGrath, "He Shall Be Called a Nazorean."
jfmcgrat@butler.edu

McKenzie, John L. "Samuel". Chicago: Encyclopaedia Britannica, 2010.

Merriam Webster Dictionary, "Haruspex".
https://www.merriam-webster.com/dictionary/haruspex

Metcalf, E. and P.F. Bass, P.F. "Head Injuries can Lead to Serious Vision Problems". *Everyday Health Media, 2009.*
http://www.everydayhealth.com/vision-center/head-injuries.aspx

Miller, Glen. "Messianic Expectations in 1st Century Judaism – Documentation from Non-Christian Sources".
https://www.christian-thinktank.com/messiah.html

NASA, "Five Millennium Catalog of Solar Eclipses". NASA Website.

Nasr, Sayyed Hossein. *Muhammad, Man of God*. Chicago: ABC International Group, 1995.

New World Encyclopedia. "Iblis".
https://www.newworldencyclopedia.org/entry/Iblis#:~:text=Iblis%20was%20a%20Jinni%2C%20a,)%20to%20Jahannam%2C%20or%20Hell.

Nicholl, J. "Neuropsychiatric Sequelae of Traumatic Brain Injury". *Semin Neurol* 2009; 29(3): 247–55.
http://medscape.com/viewarticle/706300_1

Nierenberg, Grard, and Henry Calica. *How to Read a Person like a Book*. London: Thorsons, 1973.

NYU Langone Comprehensive Epilepsy Center, "Occipital Lobe Epilepsy".
http://epilepsy.med.nyu.edu/epilepsy/types-epilepsy/occipital-lobe-epilepsy#sthash.h3SfUMzV.dpbs

Oakes, Leona and Lucia Gahlin. *Ancient Egypt*. London: Hermes House, 2004.

O'Callaghan, Tiffany. Oliver Sacks wants to Destigmatize Hallucinations. *New Scientist, Nov 11 2012*. Nicholl, 2009.

Oden, T.C. *Pastoral Theology : Essentials of Ministry*. San Francisco: Harper & Row, 1982.

Onfrey, M. *In Defence of Atheism: The Case Against Christianity, Judaism and Islam*. Translated by Jeremy Leggatt. London: Profile, 2007.

Orlov, A. *The Atoning Dyad: The Two Goats of Yom Kippur in the Apocalypse of Abraham*. Studia Judaeoslavica, 8; Leiden: Brill, 2016.

Paine, Thomas. *The Age of Reason*. Reprint, London: Freethought, 1880.
http://www.gutenberg.org/files/3743/3743-h/3743-h.htm

Pape, W. Handwörterbuch der Griechischen Sprache, Zweiter Band. Braunschweig: Friedrich Ludwig und Sohn, 1849.

Parker, Simon B. "Possession Trance and Prophecy in Pre-Exilic Israel". *Vetus Testamentum*, Vol. 28, Fasc. 3 (Jul., 1978), pp. 271–85.
https://doi.org/10.2307/1517036•https://www.jstor.org/stable/1517036

Perowne, Stewart Henry *et al*. "Jerusalem" . Encyclopaedia Brittanica

Pixner, Bargil. "Jerusalem's Essene Gateway: Where the Community Lived in Jesus' Time". *Biblical Archaeological Review* May/June 1997.
http://www.centuryone.org/essene.html

Pocock, Helen. *Christ has Everything that you Need: An Easy English Commentary (2800 word vocabulary) on Paul's Letter to the Colossians.*
https://www.easyenglish.bible/bible-commentary/col-lbw.htm

Pretorius, Albertus. *Heaven and Hell, Life After Death as Viewed from Scripture and Neuropsychology.* Eugene, OR: Wipf & Stock, 2024.

──── *Jesus of Nazareth: a Deluded Messiah.* Eugene, OR: Wipf & Stock, 2022.

──── *The Gospels Explained: A Novel and Rational Guide to the Gospel Narratives.* Eugene, OR: Wipf & Stock, 2024/

──── *To Hell with the Devil, an Analysis of the Scriptures; Teachings about Satan.* Eugene, OR: Resource, 2024.

──── *Who, Where, and What Is God?* Eugene, OR: Wipf & Stock, 2022.

Project Quran. "What does the Quran say about Prophets?"
https://www.projectquran.com.au/single-post/prophets?srsltid=AfmBOop99rLCpm9tYfv5DvM9Bjzm4L211Krl0lanhx4LvfNdf24mQbCc

Rabbat, Nasser O. "Damascus". Chicago: Encyclopaedia Britannica, 2010.

Rahman, Fazlur. "Islam". Chicago: Encyclopaedia Britannica, 2010.

Ratzon, Eshbal. "The First Jewish Astronomers: Lunar Theory and Reconstruction of a Dead Sea Scroll". *Science in Context* 30(2), 113–139 (2017).
file:///C:/Users/User/Downloads/first_jewish_astronomers_lunar_theory_and_reconstruction_of_a_dead_sea_scroll%20(1).pdf

Riggs A.J. & Riggs, J.E. "Epilepsy's Role in the Historical Differentiation of Religion, Magic and Science. *Epilepsia,* March 2005, vol 46(3): 452–53 (abstract).
http://onlinelibrary.wiley.com/doi/10.1111/j.0013-9580.2005.55405.x/full

Rowe, Miranda. "Delegitimization of Trance-Possession". Delegitimization of Trance-Possession

Interdisciplinary SeminarResearch religion yoruba
https://confluence.gallatin.nyu.edu/context/interdisciplinary-seminar/delegitimization-of-trance-possession

Rydelnik, Michael. "Is the Modern State of Israel the Fulfillment of Prophecy?" Chosen People Ministries.
https://chosenpeople.com/is-the-modern-state-of-israel-2/

Rylaarsdam, J. Coert (ed.). "Biblical Literature". Chicago: Encyclopaedia Britannica, 2010.

Sacks, Oliver. *Hallucinations*. New York: Picador, 2012.

SA History Online, 2025. "Nongqawuse".
https://www.sahistory.org.za/people/nongqawuse

Sanders, E.P. "Paul, the Apostle, Saint." Chicago: Encyclopaedia Britannica, 2010.

Sattin, A. & Franquet, S. *Explorer Greek Islands*. Basingstoke: AA Publishing, 2000.

Schimmel, Annemarie. "Islam". Chicago: Encyclopædia Britannica, 2010.

Scholtz, Adelbert. *The Prophecies of Revelation, a Reconstruction of the Visions of John of Patmos*. Mauritius: Lambert Academic, 2017.

Schulze, L.F. "Inleiding in die Grondslag van die Gereformeerde Teologie." *In die Skriflig*, 29(1 & 2), 1995" 5-28

Sinensky, Rav Tzvi. "Ezra Chapter 3: An Imperfect Inauguration".
https://etzion.org.il/en/tanakh/ketuvim/sefer-ezra/ezra-chapter-3-imperfect-inauguration

Sela, Shlomo, "Saturn and the Jews". In *Blog of the Katz Center for Advanced Judaic Studies, University of Pennsylvania*, November 10, 2017.
https://katz.sas.upenn.edu/resources/blog/saturn-and-jews

Sinton, Christopher M., and Robert W. McCarley. "REM (Rapid Eye Movement) Sleep". In: *Encyclopedia of the Neurological Sciences*, Elsevier Science (USA), 2003.

Smyth, Kenneth. "Elijah". Chicago: Encyclopaedia Britannica, 2010.

Spoor, T. "Concussion and Your Vision". *Sarasota Retina Institute*, 3 March 2013.

http://www.sarasotaretinainstitute.com/2013/03/concussion-and-your-vision-part-1/

Stanford Encyclopedia of Philosophy. Aristotle's Logics."
https://plato.stanford.edu/entries/aristotle-logic/

Statista, "Countries with the largest Jewish population 2022".
https://www.statista.com/statistics/1351079/jewish-pop-by-country/?srsltid=AfmBOopW56eXjnEaRp_I5xCcgqaF-jPtqn6e5eYfnYzHxO85J4MT_R7h

Statistisk Sentralbyrd, "Religious communities and life stance communities, 1 January 2016".
https://www.ssb.no/en/kultur-og-fritid/statistikker/trosamf/aar/2016-11-25

Stealth Team Megiddo. "Ten Reason why Muslims Should Become Christians."
https://aslamsheriqbal.wordpress.com/category/10-reasons-why-muslims-should-become-christians

Stephenson, F.R. "Eclipse". Chicago: Encyclopaedia Britannica, 2010.

Steinmeyer, Nathan. "A Jewish Curse Text from Elephantine". *Biblical Archaeology Society,* 27 October 2023.
https://www.biblicalarchaeology.org/daily/ancient-cultures/ancient-egypt/a-jewish-curse-text-from-elephantine/

Stieglitz, R." The Hebrew Names of the Seven Planets". *Journal of Near Eastern Studies*: April 1981, 40 (2): 135,

Strugnell, John. "John the Baptist, Saint." Chicago: Encyclopaedia Britannica, 2010.

Suni, Eric. "Dreams: Why They Happen & What They Mean". Sleep Foundation, May 2, 2024.
https://www.sleepfoundation.org/dreams

Swaab, J. *Wij zijn ons Brein: Van Baarmoeder tot Alzheimer.* Amsterdam: Uitgeverij Contact. 2010.

Takle, Lee. "The secular Jewish renaissance sweeping Israel". South African Jewish Report, 29 August 2024.
https://www.sajr.co.za/the-secular-jewish-renaissance-sweeping-israel/

BIBLIOGRAPHY

Temes, Roberta. *The Complete Idiot's Guide to Hypnosis.* Indianapolis: Alpha Books, 2000.

Tisdall, William St. Clair Towers. *The original sources of the Qur'an.* London: Society for Promoting Christian Knowledge, 1911.

Toriz, "Neuroanthropology of Shamanic Trance: a Case Study with a Ritual Specialist from Mexico". *Frontiers in Psychology,* 2024 Mar 5;15:1325188. doi: 10.3389/fpsyg.2024.1325188 https://pmc.ncbi.nlm.nih.gov/articles/PMC10948424/

Tuczay, Crista. "Trance Prophets and Diviners in the Middle Ages". Research Gate, *January 2005.* https://www.researchgate.net/publication/285379349_Trance_pr ophets_and_diviners_in_the_middle_ages

Uddin, Lucina, *et al.* "Structure and Function of the Human Insula". *Journal of Clinical Neurophysiology* 34(4): p 300–06, July 2017. https://journals.lww.com/clinicalneurophys/abstract/2017/07000/ structure_and_function_of_the_human_insula.2.aspx

United Nations. "Universal Declaration of Human Rights." https://www.un.org/en/about-us/universal-declaration-of-human-rights

Veronelli, Laura *et al.* "Geschwind Syndrome in frontotemporal lobar degeneration: Neuroanatomical and neuropsychological features over 9 years". Cortex. 2017 Sep:94:27–38. doi: 10.1016/j.cortex.2017.06.003. Epub 2017 Jun 27. https://pubmed.ncbi.nlm.nih.gov/28711815/

Villines, Zawn. "What does the Frontal Lobe Do?" *Medical News Today,* 30 November 2023. https://www.medicalnewstoday.com/articles/318139

Visser, A.J. *De Openbaring aan Johannes.* Nijkerk: Callenbach, 1962.

Volcano Café, "Ancient Foundations: the Earth of the Bible: Part II: Volcanics in the Fertile Crescent". *Volcano Café,* 01.05.2018. https://www.volcanocafe.org/ancient-foundations-the-earth-of-the-bible-part-ii-volcanics-in-the-fertile-crescent/

Volcano Discovery, "Volcanoes of Turkey".
https://www.volcanodiscovery.com/turkey.html
Volcano World. Nisyros, Greece.
http://volcano.oregonstate.edu/vwdocs/volc_images/europe_west_asia/nisyros.html
Wallis, G. "What do Hallucinations Tell is about the Brain?" *Brain Metrics, June 27 2013.*
http://www.nature.com/scitable/blog/brain-metrics/what_do_hallucinations_tell_us

Ward, Keith. *Is Religion Irrational?* **Oxford: Lin Hudson, 2011.**

Weather Spark, "Climate and Average Weather Year Round in Jerusalem Israel".
https://weatherspark.com/y/98866/Average-Weather-in-Jerusalem-Israel-Year-Round
Webb, J. et al. "Auditory Hallucinations Associated with Headaches Following Traumatic Brain Injury". *Cns Spectr.* 2010: 15(8): 539–40.
http://www.cnsspectrums.com/aspx/articledetail.aspx?articleid=2789
White, J. "Concussion, Traumatic Brain Injury and Seizures."
http://mnepilepsy.org/news/concussion-traumatic-brain-injury-and-seizures/
Wikipedia, "List of the Dead Sea Scrolls".
https://en.wikipedia.org/wiki/List_of_the_Dead_Sea_Scrolls
Wolf, Thomas Gerhard *et al.* "Functional Changes in Brain Activity Using Hypnosis: A Systematic Review". *National Library of Medicine,* Brain Sci.2022 Jan 13;12(1):108.
doi: 10.3390/brainsci12010108
https://pmc.ncbi.nlm.nih.gov/articles/PMC8773773/
Wright, N.T. "The Self-Revelation of God in Human History: A Dialogue on Jesus with N.T. Wright". In Antony Flew. *There is a God: How the World's most Notorious Atheist Changed his Mind.* New York: Harper Collins, 2007.

Young, T. Coyler. "Iran, Ancient". Chicago: Encyclopædia Britannica, 2010.

Zillmer, Eric A, *et al*. *Principles of Neuropsychology*. Belmont CA: Wadsworth, 2008.

Zucker, Shay. "Hebrew Names of the Planets". *Proceeding of the International Astronomical Union, 2011*.
https://www.cambridge.org/core/services/aop-cambridge-core/content/view/ADDA9D0415FA615717B64E709DA7706F/S1743921311002432a.pdf/hebrew_names_of_the_planets.pdf

LIST OF ILLUSTRATIONS

Simulations of the Night Sky
All views of the constellations on the night sky were generated by a free program that can be downloaded from https://stellarium-web.org/

Maps of Solar Eclipses and Lunar Eclipses
All the maps of the world showing solar and lunar eclipses were downloaded and copied from the NASA website containing eclipses

Frontispiece
Mosaic of Moses at the Burning Bush, from St. Catherine's Monastery, Sinai (eighth century)
        https://library.biblicalarchaeology.org/department/parsing-the-divine-name/mosaic-of-moses-at-burning-bush_2b01ktw/
        https://fortnightlyreview.co.uk/2014/07/mango-sinai-mosaic/

Chapter 1
Aristotle
        Enc Brit."Aristotle".
Outside Cover of the DSM-5-TR
        https://www.psychiatry.org/psychiatrists/practice/dsm
The entrance to the Oracle of the Dead (Tartarus) at Baia near Naples.
        http://www.societe-perillos.com/per_navel_2.html
Simplified biblical world-view
        https://www.semanticscholar.org/paper/Biblical-Cosmology%3A-The-Implications-for-Bible-Roberts/63e1b44d3474477155cf534b3ee4c4f331f3e5f6

Chapter 2
Fresco from a synagogue in Dura Europos, depicting the discovery of

LIST OF ILLUSTRATIONS

baby Moses by the Egyptian princess Thermouthis. Ca. 244–355 CE.
https://anetoday.org/westwood-moses-antiquities/
Moses with the Ten Commandments on Stone Tablets by Rembrandt, 1659.
https://en.wikipedia.org/wiki/Moses_Breaking_the_Tablets_of_the_Law
Babylonian panels of Marduk (center) and other winged creatures
https://en.wikipedia.org/wiki/Marduk
https://www.metmuseum.org/art/collection/search/322595?sortBy=Relevance&ft=assyrian&offset=80&rpp=20&pos=86
King Hammurabi of Babylon standing before the winged god Marduk on his throne
https://en.wikipedia.org/wiki/Hammurabi
The three Magi from the East
https://commons.wikimedia.org/wiki/File:Three_Wise_Men_from_the_East._Part_of_the_mosaic_on_the_left_wall_of_the_Basilica_of_Sant%27Apollinare-Nuovo._Ravenna,_Italy.jpg
Christ on the Cross, 1632 by Diego Velázquez
https://www.diego-velazquez.org/christ-on-the-cross.jsp
The Apostle Paul
https://en.wikipedia.org/wiki/File:Paul_head_mosaic.jpeg
The Tomb of John of Patmos
https://kimshistorytravel.com/where-was-john-buried/

Chapter 3
Pharaoh on his Throne
https://za.pinterest.com/pin/346847608779701569/
Moses by Michelangelo
https://en.wikipedia.org/wiki/Moses_%28Michelangelo%29
Elijah Taken Up in a Chariot of Fire by Giuseppe Angeli, c. 1740/1755
https://www.nga.gov/artworks/41685-elijah-taken-chariot-fire
A Voilcano at Night

LIST OF ILLUSTRATIONS

    https://www.dailysabah.com/gallery/spectacular-eruptions-from-mount-etna-light-up-night-sky/images?gallery_image=35763

Map showing the country of Edom
    https://en.wikipedia.org/wiki/Edom

The entrance to the ancient city of Petra
    https://www.historyhit.com/locations/petra/

Pegasus as drawn by Johannes Hevelius. Equuleus is faintly visible next to Pegasus.
    https://itoldya420.getarchive.net/amp/media/johannes-hevelius-pegasus-091c51

Sagittarius and Centaurus, drawn by Johannes Hevelius
    https://en.wikipedia.org/wiki/File:Sagittarius_Hevelius.jpg
    https://en.wikipedia.org/wiki/Centaurus_%28Greek_mythology

The relief stone of Darius the Great in the Behistun Inscription
    https://en.wikipedia.org/wiki/Darius_the_Great

Taurus, the Bull, and Aries, the Ram, as illustrated by Johannes Hevelius
    https://en.m.wikipedia.org/wiki/File:Taurus_by_Johannes_Hevelius.JPG
    https://en.wikipedia.org/wiki/Aries_%28constellation%29

Orion, the Hunter, and Gemini, the Twins, as drawn by Hevelius
    https://commons.wikimedia.org/wiki/File:Johannes_Hevelius_-_Orion.jpg
    https://commons.wikimedia.org/wiki/File:Gemini_Hevelius.jpg

Perseus, the Hero, with the head of Medussa, as illustrated by Hevelius
    https://commons.wikimedia.org/wiki/File:Johannes_Hevelius_-_Perseus.jpg

The constellations of Ophiuchus with Serpens and Virgo, as drawn by Hevelius
    https://en.wikipedia.org/wiki/Ophiuchus
    https://en.wikipedia.org/wiki/Virgo_%28constellation%29

The constellations of Boötes and Hercules, as drawn by Hevelius
    https://commons.wikimedia.org/wiki/File:Bootes.jpg
    https://gl.wikipedia.org/wiki/Ficheiro:Hercules_Hevelius.jpg

LIST OF ILLUSTRATIONS

A chariot with two horses and two warriors on an ancient Greek drinking vessel, dating from ca 510 BC
    https://en.wikipedia.org/wiki/Chariot
Drawing of the constellations of Leo and Ursa Major by Hevelius
    https://commons.wikimedia.org/wiki/File:Leo_Hevelius.jpg
    https://commons.wikimedia.org/wiki/File:Ursa_Major_Hevelius.jpg
The constellations of Lupus and Scorpius, as drawn by Hevelius
    https://commons.wikimedia.org/wiki/File:Johannes_Hevelius_-_Lupus.jpg
    https://en.wikipedia.org/wiki/File:Scorpio_Hevelius.jpg
The constellations of Aries and Capricornus, by Hevelius
    https://commons.wikimedia.org/wiki/File:Johannes_Hevelius_-_Prodromus_Astronomia_-_Volume_III_%22Firmamentum_Sobiescianum,_sive_uranographia%22_-_Tavola_BB_-_Aries.jpg
    https://commons.wikimedia.org/wiki/File:Capricorn_Hevelius.jpg
The Zodiac on the mosaic floor of the Beth Alpha
    https://en.wikipedia.org/wiki/Zodiac_mosaics_in_ancient_synagogues

Chapter 4

Salome with the head of John the Baptist, by Caravaggio, c 1607–10.
    https://en.wikipedia.org/wiki/Beheading_of_John_the_Baptist
Albrecht Dürer: Christ Carrying his Cross (1512)
    https://www.metmuseum.org/art/collection/search/391187The
Albrecht Dürer: Outpouring of the Holy Spirit
    https://www.myartprints.co.uk/a/albrecht-duerer/outpouringoftheholyghostd.html
Conversion of St Paul by Caravaggio
    https://en.wikipedia.org/wiki/Conversion_on_the_Way_to_Damascus
The Four Horsemen

LIST OF ILLUSTRATIONS

> https://www.metmuseum.org/art/collection/search/336215

A silver denarius coin minted during the reign of Emperor Domitian.
> https://www.royalmint.com/shop/ancient/EmperoDomitian-silver-Denarius/

A map of the Aegean Sea,
> https://www.in2greece.com/mappages/nisiaegeou/dodekanisa/aalldodekanisa.htm

An aerial photo of the Greek island of Nisyros
> https://wemarriedadventure.com/2017/08/04/greek-adventure-riding-the-volcano-in-nisyros/

An aerial photo of the Greek island of Nisyros with its volcanic crater.

A volcanic eruption at night: Stromboli
> https://www.dreamstime.com/photos-images/night-stromboli-island.html

Detail of the antique zodiac mosaic floor at Hamat Tiberias Synagogue National Park
> https://biblelandpictures.com/product/1264-1-tiberias-synagogue/

A photo of the constellation of Scorpius
> http://www.abc.net.au/science/starhunt/tour/virtual/scorpius/

Ophiuchus/Serpentarius (the Serpent Catcher), Serpens (the Serpent – the only constellation consisting of two separate parts) and Scorpius (the Scorpion/Dragon).
> https://en.wikipedia.org/wiki/Ophiuchus

A statue of Mary, the mother of Jesus, and her child, with a crown with 12 stars on her head and a crescent moon at her feet, by the medieval sculptor Tilman Riemenschneider (*ca* 1490).
> https://www.pinterest.com/yangzhijian100/religion-statue

Chapter 5

An old drawing of the constellation Leo by Hevelius
> https://creazilla.com/media/traditional-art/6955851/johannes-hevelius---leo

King David playing the harp

LIST OF ILLUSTRATIONS

https://en.wikipedia.org/wiki/David
The four-winged guardian figure of Cyrus, bas-relief on a doorway pillar
https://en.wikipedia.org/wiki/Cyrus_the_Great
Isaiah 53 in the Great Isaiah Scroll
https://commons.wikimedia.org/wiki/File:Great_Isaiah_Scroll_Ch53.jpg
The Good Shepherd
https://www.ncregister.com/blog/a-good-shepherd-lays-down-his-life
A reconstruction of the Menorah of the Temple in Jerusalem manufactured by the Temple Institute.
https://en.wikipedia.org/wiki/Temple_menorah7 lamps:

Chapter 6

Christ Driving the Merchants from the Temple – Albrecht Dürer, 1511
https://uploads7.wikiart.org/images/albrecht-durer/christ-driving-the-merchants-from-the-temple-1511.jpg
Jesus on the donkey
https://en.wikipedia.org/wiki/Palm_Sunday
Albrecht Dürer: Christ Crucified (1505)
https://www.wikiart.org/en/albrecht-durer/christ-on-the-cross

Chapter 7

Part of the Isaiah Scroll from the Dead Sea Scrolls
https://en.wikipedia.org/wiki/Isaiah_Scroll
Cetus, the Sea Monster, and Scorpius, the Scorpion, drawn by Johannes Hevelius
https://commons.wikimedia.org/wiki/File:Johannes_Hevelius_-_Cetus.jpg
https://commons.wikimedia.org/wiki/File:Johannes_Hevelius_-_Scorpius.jpg
The Ghost of Samuel Appearing to Saul, by William Blake
https://www.nga.gov/artworks/11498-ghost-samuel-appearing-saul

LIST OF ILLUSTRATIONS

Chapter 8
Albrect Dürer: The Last Judgment (ca 1510)
> https://www.metmuseum.org/art/collection/search/388072

Roman cavalry from a mosaic of the Villa Romana del Casale, Sicily, 4th century AD
> https://en.wikipedia.org/wiki/Roman_cavalry#/media/File:Roman_cavalry_-_Big_Game_Hunt_mosaic_-_Villa_Romana_del_Casale_-_Italy_2015.JPG

An ancient winepress found in Israel.
> http://www.ancient-origins.net/news-history-archaeology/innocent-boys-meticulously

Ophiuchus, the Snake Catcher (also called Serpentarius), with Serpens, the Serpent, from an old star atlas. Scorpius, the Scorpion, is faintly visible under his feet.
> http://themindunleashed.com/2013/08/the-13th-zodiac-sign-ophiuchus.html

Detail of the antique zodiac mosaic floor at Hamat Tiberias Synagogue National Park, Tiberias, Galilee, Israel (4th century AD), showing Libra
> http://www.theearthchild.co.za/from-venus-to-jupiter-here-is-an-ancient-roman-astrology-reading-for-each-individual

Mosaic of Christ in his glory as heavenly judge
> http://www.approachguides.com/blog/hidden-gem-in-istanbul-the-deesis-in-hagia-sophia/

Chapter 9
Muhammad receiving his first revelation from the angel Gabriel. From the manuscript Jami' al-Tawarikh by Rashid-al-Din Hamadani, 1307.
> https://en.wikipedia.org/wiki/Islam

The cave Hira in the mountain Jabal al-Nour where, according to Muslim belief, Muhammad received his first revelation.
> https://humanjourney.us/ideas/muhammad-origins-of-islam/history-of-mohammad/

LIST OF ILLUSTRATIONS

Mosque in Cape Town, oldest mosque in South Africa
    https://en.wikipedia.org/wiki/Queen_Victoria_Mosque
Muhammad and the Muslim Army
    https://en.wikipedia.org/wiki/Muhammad

Chapter 10
Thomas Paine (Portrait by John Wesley Jarvis, c. 1806–1807)
    https://en.wikipedia.org/wiki/Thomas_Paine
Frointal Lobe
    https://en.wikipedia.org/wiki/Frontal_lobe
The anterior cingulate cortex and the insula inside the human brain
    https://www.flintrehab.com/anterior-cingulate-cortex-damage/?srsltid=AfmBOoo3Ibj0cp9EAgvvhKCm27ELbbLHpJGGbk_j0IdO35DWHHeHqpt0
    https://www.kenhub.com/en/library/anatomy/insula-en
Brain oncussion
    https://www.sportsconcussion.co.za/about-concussion/overview-of-concussion/
Nongqawuse
    https://en.wikipedia.org/wiki/Nongqawuse
The reconstructed study of Spinoza in Rijnsburg, the Netherlands
    https://commons.wikimedia.org/wiki/File:Spinoza%27s_room_in_the_Spinozahuis_Rijnsburg_1.JPG
Map of the Promised Land
    https://www.biblestudy.org/maps/division-of-promised-land-to-twelve-tribes-israel.html

INDEX OF SCRIPTURAL TEXTS

OLD TESTAMENT

Genesis
Book of –	26, 128
Ch 1	230
Ch 3	287
Ch 37–50	31
1: 2	437
1: 7	246
1: 26–31	281
2: 17	88
3: 1	481
3: 14–16	286
3: 14–19	88
3: 15	280
3: 19	443
3: 24	319
5: 21–22	61
6: 1–4	62, 189
7: 11	246
10: 2	491
14: 18–20	376
15: 7–21	564
17: 19–20	287
18: 27	443
25: 1–4	34
32: 5	330
32: 28	354
37: 3–10	90
37: 34–35	439
41: 14 – 37	91
44: 31	437
49: 9–10	288

Exodus
Book of –	26
Ch 3 & 4	36
Ch 20	38
Ch 41	14
1: 11	35
3: 1	34
4: 20	330
4: 22	350
17: 8–15	95
18: 8–12	34
19: 4	275
19: 16–18	37, 245
20: 4	13, 437
20: 13	98
20: 18	37
21: 32	383
22: 18	20
24: 17	37
24: 18	34
28: 6–16	82
34: 28	356
39: 2–9	82
42: 26	330

Leviticus
Book of –	32, 94, 127
16: 8	82
19: 15	6
19: 26	20

20: 6	441	**Joshua**	
27: 29	97	Book of –	28
		3: 10	97
Numbers		5: 14 – 15	291
Book of –	127	6: 17	97
Ch 1	38	8: 24–26	97
Ch 6	69	10: 10–14	97
Ch 22	330	18: 10	82
11: 25–29	557		
12: 3	97	**Judges**	
16: 31–33	437	Book of –	28
21: 1–3	97	3: 9–10	540
21: 6–9	289	5: 20	25
22: 7–41	20	14: 6	540
24: 2–3	540	15: 14	540
24: 17	289		
32: 40	105	**1 Samuel**	
35: 30–34	98, 566	Book of –	28
		Ch 3 & 4	99
Deuternomy		Ch 9	21
Book of –	22, 28, 32, 49, 127, 128, 380–81	Ch 28	442
		3: 19–20	99
		7: 8–16	101
Ch 5	38	9: 3–14	330
1: 17	6	9: 15–17	100
3: 13	105	10: 10–13	557
4: 19	20, 47	14: 41	82
14: 1	332, 350	15: 10 & 11	100
17: 6	566	15: 23	20
18: 10–12	20	16: 1–13	101
18: 15–18	290, 380	19: 19–24	541
19: 15	566	19: 20–24	557
21: 23	235	25: 20–23	330
22: 20–21	365	28: 3, 7, 9	20
23: 2	365		
30: 1–5	96		
32: 2	65		

2 Samuel			22: 10	350
Book of –	28		28: 6	350
7: 14	72, 350			
7: 8–16	101, 292, 307		**2 Chronicles**	
			Book of –	29
1 Kings			23: 1	78
Book of –	28		24: 20–22	212
Ch 7 & 8	17		30: 16	211
Ch 18	103, 494		33:6	20
Ch 21	104		36: 22–23	309
2: 4	102			
3: 9	40		**Ezra**	
3: 10–14	40		Book of –	29
8: 25	102		2: 53	122
18: 45–46	541		2: 1–2, 64	164
22: 19	46		3: 8	164
			3: 12	177
			5: 2	164
2 Kings				
Book of –	28		**Nehemiah**	
Ch 1	104		Book of –	29, 148
Ch 2	104		Ch 4	117
7: 2	246		7: 55	122
12: 17–18	105		9: 6	47
16: 9	105		12: 1–16	58
23: 28–30	307, 332		12: 22 & 23	78
1 Chronicles			**Job**	
Book of –	29		Ch 1 & 2	163
Ch 6	30		1: 6	350
Ch 17	292		2: 1	350
Ch 24	248		9: 9	46
4: 42	965: 4		11: 6	494
5: 4	492		11: 7–8	439
10: 13	20		14: 10–12	443
17: 13	350		22: 12–14	347
21: 1–2	163			

INDEX OF SCRIPTURAL TEXTS

26: 12–13	352	89: 26–28	72, 350
37: 22	46	89: 36	307
38: 31	46	89: 4, 36–77	102
38: 4–8	347	89: 34–37	294
38: 8	350	90: 4	487, 491
		90: 9–10	443
Psalms		92: 7	443
2: 6–7, 12	72, 350	103: 20–21	47
2: 9	277, 479	104: 3	347
5: 2	331	104: 29	443
16: 8–10	397	109: 8	385
19: 1–2	252	110: 1	375, 398
22: 15	387	115: 16	440
22: 16	388	118: 17–24	295
22: 18	389	118: 22	375
24: 10	331	132: 10–16	295
28: 8	305	139: 8	438
31: 18	440	146: 4	441
34: 20	387	148: 2–3	47, 347
41: 9	384		
44: 4	331	**Proverbs**	
45: 6–8	293	Ch 8–9	212
48: 2–3	48	8: 23	296
49: 12	443	11: 1	492
62: 9	492	16: 11	492
68: 18	399	16: 33	82
69: 25	385	18: 5	6
72	330		
72: 8 & 11	345	**Ecclesiastes**	
74: 12	331	3: 19–20	444
78:1–2	369	9: 5–6	444
82: 6	332, 350		
84: 9	443305	**Isaiah**	
88: 10	440	Book of –	17, 23, 27, 43,

607

	44, 49, 115, 117, 144, 146, 297	24: 21–23	405, 476
1: 1	44	24: 23	403
2: 2	48	25: 6–8	406
2: 3–5	402	26: 1–6	406
2: 19–22	115	26: 16–21	432
4: 2	164	27: 1	407, 476
4: 2	329	30: 19–26	408
4: 5–6	116, 423	31: 18–19	440
5: 14	439	34: 5–15	120
6: 1	115	35: 5–6	371
6: 1–8	44, 247	40: 3–4	357
6: 5	331	40: 22	347
6: 9–10	370	41: 8–9	312
7: 10–17	297	42: 1–4 307,	372
7: 14	298, 364	44: 1	313
8: 14	381	45: 1–7	308
8: 19, 20	20	47: 13–14	20
8: 21	331	49: 1–7 144,	308
9: 1–2	368	52: 13–53: 12	310, 312, 313, 464
9: 5–7	102, 299, 307	53: 2	164, 329
10: 20–23	117	54: 5–8	160
11:1	164, 329, 361	59: 16–21	314
11: 1–10	300	60: 1–12	146, 415
11: 5	273	61: 1–7	148, 373
11: 9	48	62: 21	362
11: 11–16	118, 192	63: 1–6	149
13: 6–13	402	65: 25	48
13: 10	27, 46	66: 8–11	193
15: 16	17	66: 10 – 24	433
17: 1–4 119			
19: 3	441	**Jeremiah**	
19: 18–25	403	Book of –	27, 49, 126
22: 6	105	1: 2	19
22: 22–23	301, 471	1: 4–7	571

3: 6–8	160	16: 48–58	139
10: 7	331	17: 22–24	164, 316
14: 11–18	128	20: 40	48
16: 14–16	194	28: 12–19	317
22: 30	127	29: 6–14	141
23: 5	164, 329	30: 1–5	1 42
23: 5–8	302	30: 8	28
25: 11,12	336	34: 23–25	321
25: 30–38	411	34: 29	164
29: 10	336	36: 24–26	195, 312
30: 8–10	315	37: 24–28	322
30: 18–24	129		
31: 9	332, 350	**Daniel**	
31: 10–14	135	Book of –	23, 29, 178
31: 15	360	2: 31–45	178
33: 12–18	303	2: 44–45	428
33: 15	164, 329	7: 1–10	181
33: 17	102	7: 9–10	486
42: 7–16	131	7: 13–14	332
42: 8	78	7: 16–18	333
44: 11 – 18	133	7: 18–28	429
50: 29–32	136	7: 25	281
51: 51–57	136	8: 3 – 12	185
		9: 20–27	334
Ezekiel		10: 21	275
Book of –	28, 50, 137	11: 7	361, 362
Ch 38 & 39	492	12:1	275
1:1 – 2: 5	50	12: 1–4	436
1: 3	19		
1: 22	247	**Hosea**	
7: 19–20	414	11: 1	366
8: 1–3	545		
13: 1–5	137	**Joel**	
16: 1–3	138	1: 1	19
16: 8–21	160	2: 1–11	421

2: 20–32	423	5: 2	366
2: 28–31	396, 557	**Nahum**	
2: 30–31	29	Book of –	28, 122
3: 9–18	426	1: 7–11	123

Amos
Book of –	27, 42, 104
1: 1–2	43
1: 3–5	104
2: 6–16	105
3: 1–2	160
5: 4–9	107
5: 8	27
5: 21–27	109
8: 1–3; 7–10	110
8: 9	27
9: 1–10	111
9: 2	438
9: 12–13	113

Habakkuk
Book of –	27, 304
3: 12–13	304

Zephaniah
Book of –	27, 123
1: 7–18	123
3: 1–7	125
3: 8–12	413

Haggai
Book of –	28
2: 6–9	*176*
2: 10–19	*177*
2: 20–23	*323*

Obadiah
Book of –	28, 150
1: 1–4	*150*

Jonah
1: 1	19
1: 7	834: 1–6

Micah
Book of –	114, 305
1: 1	367
4: 1	48
4: 1–6	409
5: 10 –15	114
5: 1–8	305

Zechariah
Book of –	28, 58, 151
1: 1	19
1: 7 – 15	152, 256
1: 18–21	156
2: 1 – 8	159
3: 1–10	162
3: 8	329
4: 1–14	325
5: 1 – 11	166
6: 1–8	169, 256
6: 9–15	328
6: 11 & 12	164
7: 1–14	171

INDEX OF SCRIPTURAL TEXTS

9: 9–10	273, 329, 331, 377	**Malachi**	
		Book of –	19
10: 1–12	174	1: 1	17
12: 10–14	331	3: 1	324
13: 7	216	*3: 1–3*	*427*
14: 1–15	416	3: 10	246
14: 6–7	29, 59	*4: 1–6*	*428*
14: 16–21	420	*4: 5–6*	*324, 358*

APOCRYPHAL BOOKS

Enoch		24: 6	275
Book of –	29, 59, 187	*48: 1–10*	*337*
1: 9	60	*52: 1–9*	*340*
5: 1–9	*189*	*54: 1–5*	*445*
7: 1	*190*	*55: 1–5*	*431, 444*
8: 1–4	*191*	56: 8	444
9: 6–9	*191*		
10: 5	493	**Jubilees**	
14: 18	46	Book of –	23

NEW TESTAMENT

Matthew		3: 13–4: 11	355
Gospel of –	23, 29	3: 16	349
1: 1–17	72	4: 1–11	354
1: 17	64, 365	4:12–17	367
1: 22–25	63, 364	5: 18	19
2: 1	67	5: 18–19	76, 215
2: 1–12	66	5: 38–4 7	98
2: 3–6	306, 366	6: 9	72
2: 13–15	65, 365	6: 10	72
2: 16–23	359	6: 22–23	209
2: 23	71, 361–63	9: 37–38	207
3: 1	347	10: 7–16	207
3: 7–12	199, 357	10: 24–25	206
3: 13–17	347	10: 32–33	217

11: 2–6	370	23: 37–39	217
11: 10–15	358	24: 1–2	450
11: 13–14	68, 325	24: 3–14	451
11: 21–24	208	24: 11–12	494
11: 27	72	24: 15–28	452
12:15–21	371	24: 22	453
12: 18–23	308	24: 26–28, 37, 39–41	
12: 23	65		219
13: 13–15	369	24: 29–31	454
13: 34–35	368	24: 32–33	455
13: 55	64, 365	24: 34	72
14: 1–12	201	24: 35	19
14: 3	247	24: 36–44	456
15: 14	206	24: 38	220
15: 22	65	25: 31	72
16: 18	484	25: 31–46	301, 456, 488
16: 27–28	72	25: 31–46	496
17: 12–13	68	25: 41	275
17: 15	553	26: 29, 64	72
18: 16	569	26: 31–35	215
19: 16–30	212	26: 53–56	19
19: 17	76	26:71	71, 361
19: 28	73	27: 3–10	382
20: 21	73	27: 11	73
21: 1–11	378	27: 19	385
21: 9	65, 72	27:35	19
21: 11	70	27: 37	74
22: 23–33	447	27: 54	72
22: 36–40	76	28: 1–8	464
22: 41–46	375	28: 18	484
22: 42–45	65	28: 20	76
23: 4	210		
23: 9	72	**Mark**	
23: 13	212	Gospel of –	23, 24, 30
23: 23	209	1: 2	324
23: 25–27	209	1: 2–12	357
23: 29–32	211	1: 9–12	347, 355
23: 34–36	211	1: 10	349

1: 24	363	3: 16–17	199
16: 6	373	3: 19–20	347
6: 14–29	201	3: 21–22	347, 349, 355
8: 38	217	3: 23	64, 65, 365
9: 1	72	3: 23 – 38	72
10: 17–31	212	4: 1–13	355
10: 32–33	216	4: 16–21	372
10: 47	65, 363	4: 22	64, 365
11: 1–11	73, 378	6: 39–40	206
11: 4–11	331	7: 16	70
11:10	65	9: 7–9	201
12: 10–11	374	9: 19	70
12: 18–27	447	9: 26	217
12: 35–37	375	9: 27	72
13: 2–13	451	10: 2–12	207
13: 14–23	452	10: 13–16	208
13: 20	72	10: 18	352
13: 24	30	10: 25–28	76, 214
13: 24–27	454	11: 34–36	209
13: 28–31	455	11: 39–41	209
14: 27–31	215	11: 42	209
13: 32	560	11: 43	210
13: 32–37	456	11: 44	210
14: 62	217	11: 46	210
14: 67	363	11: 47–48	211
15: 2	73	11: 49–51	211
15: 26	74	11: 52	212
16: 6	363	12: 8–9	216
		12: 15	83
Luke		13: 1–2	450
Gospel of –	23, 30	16: 17	215
1: 26–38	63	16: 19–31	448
1: 30–35	398	16: 29	22
1: 35	364	17: 20	73
1: 67–80	197	17:22–37	219
2: 1–3	367	18: 18–30	212
3: 1–18	357	18: 37	71, 361
3: 7–9	199	18: 38	65

19: 11	73	1: 49–51	72, 217, 350
19: 28–40	378	1: 6, 19–27	204
19: 29–44	73	2: 12–25	204
19: 41–44	217	3: 35	72
20: 27–40	447	4: 9	117
20: 41–44	375	4: 19	70
21: 20–24	452	4: 25	343
21: 29–33	455	5: 21	72
21: 32	72	5:24–29	470
21: 5–6	450	5: 45–47	380
21: 7–19	451	6: 15	73
21: 25–28	454	6: 42	64, 365
21: 34–38	218	6: 46	72
22: 31–34	215, 218	7: 6 & 30	204
22: 37	312, 465	7: 40	70
22: 69	217	7: 42	306
23: 3	73	8: 18	72
23: 27–31	220	8: 20	204
23: 38	74	8: 42	72
24: 1–10	464	9: 17	70
24: 13–35	389	10: 14	321, 323
24: 19	70	10: 35	19
24: 25–27	312, 344	12: 12–19	331, 376
24: 26–27	465	12: 38, 39	19
24: 36–49	392	12:23	204
24: 39	391	13:1	204
24: 49 – 53	460	13: 15–18	383
		13: 36–38	215
John		16: 13	560
Gospel of –	24, 30	18: 5, 7	71, 361
1: 1–3	230	18: 17	569
1: 6, 19–27	200	18: 33	73
1: 21	325	19: 19	71, 74, 361
1: 23	357	19:23–24	388
1: 29	353	19: 28, 36, 37	19, 386
1: 32	349	19:32–37	387
1: 41	343	19: 38–40	71, 240, 391
1: 45	64, 344, 365	19: 38–42	293

INDEX OF SCRIPTURAL TEXTS

20: 1–2	464	18: 19–21	81
		18: 37	361
Acts		19: 11–29	81
Book of –	74, 75, 547	19: 19	20
Ch 2	464	20: 17	81
Ch 15	76, 234, 238	21: 9, 10	557
1: 6	73	21: 18	240
1: 9 – 12	460	21: 19–30	76
1: 16–20	383, 384	21: 27 – 24: 27	238
1: 26	82	22: 3	75
2: 1–13	221	22: 8	71, 361
2: 14–42	393	22:17–18	543
2: 17, 18, 29, 30	557	22: 17–21	547
2: 22	71, 361	24: 5	362
3: 6	361	24: 19	363
3: 6	71	26: 9	71, 361
3: 22	70, 349	26: 22–23	312, 465
3: 18	312, 465	28: 23	344
3: 24–26	344		
4: 10	71, 361	**Romans**	
4: 34	363	The letter to –	75
6: 14	71	1: 3	65, 144
7. 37	70	1: 20	566
8: 26–40	312, 465	3: 19–26	235
9: 26	77	3: 21–22	344
10: 9–11	542	8: 34	460
11: 5	543	10: 7	483
11: 28	557	12: 6	19
12: 17	249	15: 18	19
13: 1	19, 553	15: 21	312, 465
13: 27–29 &32	344		
13: 34–35	217	**1 Corinthians**	
15: 2	77	Letter to –	75
15: 13–21	240	Ch 15	393, 471
16:9	547	1: 5–6	466
16: 26	264	1: 7	4 60
17: 31	471	1: 10–17	237
18:9	547	2:10	19, 77

4: 1	547	1: 13–20	229
9: 1	547	2: 8–12	231
11: 3	465	2: 15	484, 485
12: 6	466	3: 1	460
15: 1–8	463	3: 11	460
15: 3–8	547		
15: 23	460	**1 Thessalonians**	
15: 23–24	488	Letter to –	75
15: 24–28	465	1: 10	461
15: 26	406, 495	2: 1	460
16: 22	554	2: 4	550
		2: 14–15	462
2 Corinthians		3: 13	460
Letter to –	75	4: 13–18	462, 496
1: 5	77	5: 1–3	463
1: 23	466	5:20	560
3: 2–3	547		
4: 10	470	**2 Thessalonians**	
5: 1	488	Letter to –	75
5: 16	547		
12: 12	547	**1 Timothy**	
13: 1	11, 36, 566	Letter to –	75
		1: 3	81
Ephesians			
Letter to –	75	**2 Timothy**	
1: 20	460	Letter to –	75
2: 19–21	295	4: 18	488
3: 3	19, 77		
3: 3–5	227	**Titus**	
3: 8–12	227	Letter to –	75
4: 7–10	398	1: 12	74
5: 1	312		
5: 2	465	**Hebrews**	
		2: 14	484
Colossians		9: 27	488
Letter to –	75	13: 5	83
1: 15–17	467		
1: 26–27	19, 77		

James
1: 1	239
1: 10	240
2: 1–7	240
2: 2	239
5: 1–6	240–41

1 Peter
1: 5	488
1: 10–12	19
1: 10–11	344
2: 6	295
2: 7–8	381
2: 22–25	312
3: 18	312, 469
4: 11	18

2 Peter
1: 19–21	19
1: 20, 21	557
2: 4	277, 484, 487
2: 22–25	465
3: 8	491
3: 15–16	77
3: 18	465

Jude
Letter of –	63
1: 6	275
1: 14–15	60

Revelation
Book of –	24, 30, 63, 77, 242
1: 1, 4 & 9	77, 243
1: 3	80, 243
1: 9	81
1: 10	80
1:10–11	547
1: 16	479
1: 18	496
1: 19	80, 243
2: 1	80
2: 16	473
2: 27	479
3: 5	495, 497
3: 7	471
3: 21	488
4: 1–2	547
4: 1–6	488
4: 1–11	243
4: 2	80
4: 6	252
4: 8	252
4: 10–11	488
5: 8–9	252, 488
5: 14	252
5: 5	248, 288
5: 6	252
5: 8	249
5: 14	249
6:1 & 7	252
6: 1–11	252, 473
6:2	474
6: 8	473, 495
6:12	264
6: 12–17	262
7: 11	249, 252
7: 14	249
7: 17	406
8:5	264
8: 16	249
9: 1, 2 & 11	485
9: 17–19	254, 473
10: 6	243
11: 2–3	281

11: 7	485	19: 4	249, 252
11:13 & 19	264	19: 7–9	477
12: 1–17	269	19: 9	80
12: 5	479	19:10	80
12: 7–12	484	19: 11–21	472
12: 9	89, 274	19: 15	473, 474
12: 16	276	20: 1–3	480
13: 5	281	20: 4–6	485
13: 8	497	20: 10	476
13: 10	473	20: 11–15	273, 301, 473
13: 18	478	20: 13 & 14	484
14: 3	249, 252	20: 14–15	490, 495
14: 13	80	21: 5	80
14: 19–20	479	21: 10	80
15: 7	252	20: 7–10	490
16: 16	477	20: 11–20	494
16:18	264	21: 10	547
17: 3	80, 547	21: 27	497
17: 8	485, 497	22: 7, 10 & 18–19	
17: 14	473		80
18: 9–20	479	22: 6–12	243
18:13	254, 473	22: 8	77
19: 11, 14 & 21	254	22: 9	80

THE QUR'AN

Book of –	84–86, 499	4: 26	526
1: 1	512	4: 35	521
2: 211	504	4: 36	528
2: 30	501	4: 79–80	515
2:50	519	5: 117	511
2: 144	519	7: 10–18	517
2: 221	528	7: 13	506
2: 257	524	7: 124–25	508
3: 35–36	86	8: 55	522
3: 81	512	9: 5	522
3: 144	530	9: 29	523
4: 4	525	13: 3	504

13: 32	505	34: 7	515
13: 34	504	37: 7	503
16: 36	530	37: 139–44	516
17: 44	501	41: 10–12	502
17: 98–99	514	41: 12–13	503
18: 51–52	518	46: 9	530
18: 95–99	509	47: 5	523
19: 28	86	**50: 39**	**502**
19: 28–31	508	**56: 27–38**	**527**
20: 72	508	**65: 12**	**501**
20: 55	515	67: 3	501
20: 85–88	510	67: 6	503
21: 31	501	71: 16–17	501, 503
23: 12–14	506	75: 3–4	515
23: 86	501	**75: 38–40**	**507**
27: 16–18	520	**78: 31–33**	**528**
30: 26	516	**82: 2–3**	**505**
31: 29	515	**86: 6–8**	**507**
31: 30	505	**89: 28–31**	**515**
33: 50	526		

www.ingramcontent.com/pod-product-compliance
Lightning Source LLC
Chambersburg PA
CBHW052108010526
44111CB00036B/1572